Mary Mc Williams Marsh

1930

ABRAHAM LINCOLN
His Path to the Presidency

ABRAHAM LINCOLN

His Path to the Presidency

By

ALBERT SHAW

*Profusely Illustrated
with Contemporary Cartoons
Portraits and Scenes*

NEW YORK
THE REVIEW OF REVIEWS CORPORATION
1929

PREFACE

ABRAHAM LINCOLN attained the Presidency through two processes. The second of these was the sequel of the first, with a totally different time scale. The first was slow like the growth of a tree that has survived the buffeting of storms and the heat and cold of changing seasons. The second was swift like a horse-race or a football game. Through the first process Lincoln had become what is known as "presidential timber." There are those who like to think of him as a mystical character, a superman without the usual background of recognized growth, suddenly lifted from obscurity to the highest place, by unseen powers guarding the fate of America. But hero-worshippers who prefer a Lincoln thus enshrouded are not careful students of available information. Our Presidents and other foremost leaders in Cabinets, in Congress, and on the Bench, have as a rule made their way through years of gradual advancement. Abraham Lincoln was no exception; and he became a presidential possibility by virtue of a thirty-year period of testing and maturing, through experiences that lifted him to the rank of a well-seasoned statesman, as he turned his fiftieth year.

The second process, as I have remarked, was a rapid and exciting one. Among the many millions of American fellow-citizens in a given election year, there are a few men, perhaps twenty, perchance a round hundred, who are no longer on the slow upward path to recognition, but who are already inside the ring fence of what we may call the "presidential field." Some of these belong to one party, some to another. Some are so prominent that they and their friends have high expectations. Any one of the others, all being admittedly competent, might under given circumstances be chosen as a party's nominee. The field is large enough, and its envied occupants are numerous enough to include—generally speaking—all those recipient though less conspicuous aspirants termed in political parlance "dark horses." Lincoln, having climbed the long ascent to this field of presidential candidates, must go through the further process, with all its hazards and complications, that finally leaves all rivals behind, bringing him to the White House in a time of great emergency.

I am defining these two processes as explaining the purpose and method of the present volume and of the one which accompanies it as its companion and sequel. The first volume relates to the process of Lincoln's preparation, and I have chosen to call it "His Path to the Presidency." The second volume deals with the affairs of politics and government in "The Year of His Election." For the purposes of this second volume, the year in question begins in March, with Lincoln's return from his speaking adventure in New York and his tour of New England. It ends on the fourth day of the following March, thus including the occurrences of the four months during which Buchanan was rounding out his term, while Lincoln was waiting in the capacity of President-elect. In these trying months he was planning for his administration, selecting his Cabinet, settling in his own mind the main points of his policy, noting the efforts of President Buchanan to keep the peace, and watching with eager attention the progress of the Secession movement in the South, as it culminated in the forming of the Confederate government under the Presidency of Jefferson Davis.

Lincoln's earlier career was well worth while in each successive step on its own account. He had chosen in youth to take the risks and chances of public life. He became a competent lawyer; but the rewards of that profession were not at any time the measure of his ambition. He was an enthusiast for canals, railroads and all forms of Western development. He was thinking, however, in terms of State policy, and in no sense was he aspiring to be a promoter of enterprises that might perchance make him a capitalist or a president of railroads. He was not impecunious; but the seeking of wealth seems never to have had a place in his day-dreams. His mind, to sum it up, was political; and his ambition was to represent his fellow-citizens in public office.

In view of such ambitions, Lincoln's circumstances had their advantages. A new State was the best conceivable laboratory in which an earnest and eager student of institutions, and of democratic government, might acquire the mental habits of a political philosopher along with thorough training in our complicated mechanism. This first volume, therefore, attempts to survey the influences and to recount the experiences that had shaped the career of Lincoln until, in the year 1860, he had become one of the men regarded even beyond the confines of Illinois as fit for the presidency.

It is hardly needful to explain, after the foregoing remarks, that my own chapters are rather in the sphere of presidential politics than in that of detached biography. I am referring frequently, however, to the writings of Lincoln biographers. All future students of the character and career of the great President will be indebted to Messrs. Nicolay and Hay, to William H. Herndon and others of the Illinois group of Lincoln's associates, to contemporary authors like Horace Greeley and Henry Wilson, and particularly to later investigators among whom must be mentioned with grateful appreciation such biographers as Joseph H. Barrett, Ida Tarbell, William E. Barton, Louis A. Warren, Carl Sandburg and, among the foremost, my friend of long years the late Senator Beveridge.

While acknowledging the value of the work of Lincoln's biographers, I must hasten to remark that for my purposes the lives of many other public men have been almost as essential. One understands better the firm and lifelong convictions that made Lincoln a consistent Nationalist, when he has studied also the lives of John Marshall, John Quincy Adams, Daniel Webster, Henry Clay, and several others who, like these four, were among Lincoln's mentors and teachers. It is well to remember that he served in Congress with Adams, was present when the "Old Man Eloquent" was stricken on the floor of the House, and was one of the Congressional committee that attended the funeral in Massachusetts. As a devoted follower of Henry Clay, Lincoln had visited the Whig idol in his Kentucky home. He knew Webster, Calhoun, Hayne and other Northern and Southern statesmen of the period culminating in 1850.

In his rise to leadership in Illinois, Lincoln's contacts were such that, for a full understanding, one must read the biographies of Stephen A. Douglas, Lyman Trumbull, the Washburnes, and other Western contemporaries, including Ohio and Indiana leaders as well as those of Kentucky, Iowa, and other States of the Mississippi Valley. To read books about Lincoln while ignoring those relating to the lives of James Buchanan, William H. Seward, Salmon P. Chase, Charles Sumner, Jefferson Davis, Alexander H. Stephens, and less remembered men like Crittenden of Kentucky and

Wilmot of Pennsylvania, is to come short of a rounded understanding. Besides the biographies, there are the balanced judgments of such approved historians as Rhodes, Schouler, Channing and McMaster, not to mention many other writers who have dealt with shorter periods or particular situations.

Thus far I have made no reference to the use of the one especial form of original material that the reader will immediately find to be most distinctive of these volumes. Political caricature is a kind of current record that has some of the qualities of a partisan public diary. It is nowadays a recognized feature of many newspapers, and of periodicals of weekly or monthly issue. It uses pictorial exaggeration to express or to affect public opinion. In due time it falls into the perspectives of historical material. In its very nature, however, it has a tendency to be destroyed, as of merely passing interest. We are slowly learning that much ephemeral material has high value for the historian of social life and manners, as also for the historian of politics.

In the case of cartoons relating to public men and controversial situations, there could be no serious dispute as to the interest and value that they acquire. The lapse of time converts them from the status of waste paper to that of prized material for the study of the history of certain forms of illustrative art. But most of all it makes them valuable for their vivid and pungent comments upon the personages and issues of politics and social life. For several decades political cartooning in the United States made use of lithography as its principal method of reproduction. The posters were prepared to meet the exigencies of one party situation or another, and were widely sold (perhaps more usually at ten cents apiece) and were doubtless distributed in many instances by political campaign managers. Within recent years it has been discovered that, when not destroyed, they had become increasingly rare, while some were unobtainable at any price. For the most part, even the cartoons that found place in the pages of newspapers and periodicals have not been available at immediate notice for the students who might like to see them. Complete files of the earlier periodicals are seldom to be discovered in any library, or in the hands of any known collector.

The assembling of cartoons relating to the life and times of Lincoln has not been the task of a moment. A slight brochure of this character that I prepared many years ago attracted attention, and led to the plan of the relatively extensive project that is in part realized in the two present volumes. While these are complete in themselves, it is well to anticipate certain inquiries by stating that volumes dealing with Lincoln's career as President, and with the domestic and foreign situations that confronted him in the Civil War period, are far advanced in preparation.

So much information pertaining to these cartoons is presented in explanatory captions that to go into further detail in this preface would be to waste space. The reader will find that the cartoons in the first volume relate mainly to situations in which Lincoln was actively concerned, as a Whig politician and later as a Republican. They were familiar to him, and served for his entertainment and instruction, precisely as political cartoons today may amuse or edify party leaders in their home States or at Washington. In the second volume, on the other hand, most of the cartoons are those that were issued after Lincoln had himself become a figure in the arena of presidential politics. He now appears, therefore, as the familiar "Rail-Splitter," or as a champion of the

Northern cause. I have hoped that the use of these illustrations would not only awaken interest and afford entertainment, but that they would also help to give reality to the study of American history and politics, thus serving an educational purpose.

For many posters otherwise almost impossible to find, I have been indebted to the helpful co-operation of the Library of Congress, the New York Public Library, and the New York Historical Society. I have received special assistance from the Illinois State Historical Society. But for the aid of the Chicago Historical Society, I should not have been able to find copies of that fugitive publication of 1860 known as the *Rail-Splitter*. Acknowledgment also should be made to the Abraham Lincoln Association of Springfield, Illinois. Many years ago I obtained generous assistance from a Philadelphia collector, the late John C. Browne. Discriminating readers will be especially attracted by several etchings of the late Adalbert John Volck of Baltimore. During his life-time some of his unpublished plates made in the early War period, intensely anti-Lincoln in their character, came into my possession through direct dealing with him. A number of these will appear in the later volumes.

The reader will find numerous portraits of Lincoln, reproduced from photographs, and also those of public men who were Lincoln's contemporaries. The majority of these have been engraved from my collection of original photographs by the famous Matthew Brady, or from various other engravings and pictures also in my own possession. For certain photographs representing the work of Leonard Volk the sculptor, and his son Douglas Volk the painter, I make grateful acknowledgements to my friend Douglas Volk. A similar expression is due to several other sculptors, including George Grey Barnard and Lorado Taft. My thanks are due to Harry MacNeil Bland of the Robert Fridenberg Galleries, New York, for some Lincoln cartoons, and to several other friends for similar aid. Convention scenes and other pictorial embellishments are from diverse sources, including files of almost forgotten periodicals, now scarce enough to be inaccessible to the general reader.

Howard Florance, who has for many years been associated with me in editorial work, has rendered invaluable aid in collecting from many sources—East and West, North and South, and from foreign countries—the cartoons and other pictorial material for these two volumes and for those that are in preparation. The explanatory captions of some of the earlier poster cartoons have required unusual knowledge of political history; and to these details Mr. Florance has given unsparing attention. I have also had the benefit of the timely assistance of other members of an editorial staff that is familiar with American politics, with bibliography, and with such worthy crafts as those of proof-reading and indexing. Among these I should mention especially my friend William Bristol Shaw. Throughout all the processes of illustration and make-up of pages, Mr. Florance has been of indispensable assistance.

ALBERT SHAW.

CONTENTS

CONTENTS—*Continued*

CONTENTS—*Concluded*

ABRAHAM LINCOLN

From a photograph made at Springfield, Illinois, in June, 1860

ABRAHAM LINCOLN

CHAPTER I

Lincoln's Place in History

The influence of time upon our estimates of historical events—Some American statesmen whose achievements survive—Representative European tributes to Lincoln

WRITTEN RECORDS have continued to be the main reliance of historians and biographers. With such facts as they can find, and with inferences derived from their own logical processes, they send forth their volumes to supply beaten trails for succeeding authors—who may, after all, try to blaze fresh paths for themselves. By one means or another, new facts come to light. Often the prejudices that have blinded men—due to partisanship, the surviving uncharitableness of religious sects, false pride of race, or the instinctive dislike of the unfamiliar in speech and manners—are cast aside in the later accounts, even as time softens the landscape of a war-devastated area.

Thus it is a mistake to speak too confidently of the verdicts of history. Such verdicts are constantly undergoing modification, and sometimes they are quite sharply reversed. Research in the fields of politics, of government, and of the biography of men whose names have survived as having been actual leaders in civil or military affairs, has been benefited by the methods of modern science. The new scholarship in these subjects is more anxious to find the truth than to perpetuate a prejudice or to bolster up a party position.

"ALL SEEMS WELL WITH US"

The four-year struggle between the North and the South was ended; and Lincoln when this cartoon was drawn was more widely accepted than at any other moment in his own lifetime. Even while the periodical containing it was being printed the world was shocked by the news of the President's death from an assassin's bullet.

In some cases we are justified in feeling that we are probably arriving at something like well-balanced and final estimates of historical events. Particularly, we attain a measure of satisfied agreement about individuals who have played eminent parts on the stage of affairs in their own periods. This remark is applicable as regards some—though not all—of the long line of men who have served in that most powerful of modern positions, the Presidency of the United States. And the same thing could be said of a series of statesmen, jurists, military leaders, who rank with Presidents in the foreground of the shifting scenes of our national drama.

For example, the whole world seems to have arrived at settled opinions as regards the high qualities of human nature, of dignity, and of responsible leadership that were displayed throughout the career of George Washington. There is by no means a finality of agreement as to the personal qualities and public services of Thomas Jefferson or Alexander Hamilton. Benjamin Franklin attained an amazing fame in his day in all countries, and he still holds his place as an admired personage of the brilliant and mentally-aroused world of the last half of the Eighteenth Century.

I

But perhaps the final word will not be said about Franklin for another half-century.

The late Senator Beveridge has so reconstructed for us the personality of John Marshall and, above all, has so recounted the public services of that pre-eminent jurist, that it will be a long time before anyone ventures to write further about him, unless to add certain sidelights to be derived from the study of Marshall's contemporaries.

But it is not my purpose here to check off the long list of the names of Americans of high distinction, in order to deal with their individual progress toward some accepted estimate in later times. Webster, Clay and Calhoun will eventually be subjected to new tests from many standpoints, by future investigators and competent scholars.

Thanks to the researches that find a center in the recent work of archivists at Jackson,

MATT MORGAN'S LINCOLN—AN ENGLISH VIEW
Virtually unknown to authorities on political caricature, and to collectors of Lincolniana, are the American Civil War cartoons of Matthew Somerville Morgan, published in a London periodical called *Fun*. They were not complimentary to President Lincoln, nor ever favorable to the Northern cause.

Mississippi, Dr. and Mrs. Dunbar Rowland, we have new material for arriving at a better understanding of the services of Andrew Jackson and Jefferson Davis. It becomes evident that Jackson has been to some extent the victim of mistaken emphasis, on the part of the eulogists of contemporaries whom Jackson opposed. His greatest fame is to come with a new appreciation of the importance of his earlier achievements as a creative nationalist. Judge Winston's recent biography of Andrew Johnson is a contribution toward a just estimate of a President who is evidently destined to fare better in the pages of all future historians than in those of many who have written hitherto under the spell of partisanship.

It is plain that General Robert E. Lee's assured position as a character of singular nobility will, by common consent, increasingly serve to adorn our revised American annals, and will suffer no decline in the judgments of critics at home and abroad. About General Grant there was once much controversy due to the military rivalries of the Civil War, and still more surviving from the political storms and strivings of his presidential period. Later biographers will, it may be said, so winnow the facts and so interpret them as to allay many of the prejudices that have lingered, particularly by reason of the attacks of the political reformers in the difficult decade following Grant's inauguration as President in 1869.

Towering above all the other successors of George Washington there stands in the appreciation of mankind the figure of Abraham Lincoln. Looking back from the days when these chapters make their addition to the many volumes that have been written on the life and times of Lincoln, we find him in office at a midway point. The country through its growth in territory and in population had attained its continental grandeur, an enviable place in the family of nations, and the leadership of the western hemisphere. But it had to adjust its constitutional theories to the new historical and physical facts. The written Constitution was one thing, while the Nation, after the Louisiana Purchase and the Mexican War, was a profoundly altered reality.

Chief Justice Marshall was trying to stretch

the Constitution to meet the sweeping changes produced by the settlement of a million pioneer families in what was recently Indian country, and by the admission of many new States. Lincoln was a product of this newer America, west of the Alleghenies, that was no part of the coalition of thirteen British colonies, founded in the Seventeenth Century. This was actually national domain, in the same sense that later acquisitions like Alaska were national, and wholly subject to the nation's mandate, rather than to the strict compacts of the Constitution of 1787.

One hundred and forty-four years will have elapsed between the election of Washington in 1788 and the presidential election of 1932. Seventy-two years, or eighteen quadrennial periods, are covered between the election of 1788 and that of 1860, when Lincoln swept the field. Between the election of 1860 and that which occurs in 1932, there extends another like term of seventy-two years, or eighteen quadrennial periods. The achievements of Washington and the policies of Jefferson shaped the country's history and development all the way to the presidency of James Buchanan, whom Lincoln succeeded.

The historic transactions with which the name of Lincoln is identified have essentially controlled the national and international policies of the United States throughout the generations that have followed. The two parties evolved in Lincoln's maturity were so well devised and compacted as organizations that each has continued until the present day, without real loss of identity, and with less modification of principles or change of constituencies than could well have been expected.

The principal change lies in the fact that party cleavages are no longer deep enough to endanger the welfare of the country. The areas of harmony and agreement are vastly greater than those of difference. There is no virtue whatever in treating party rivalry as a mild form of civil warfare. Two well-balanced parties, with equal patriotism, afford the country needed opportunity to debate pending measures and to test out the qualities of public men. The possibility of a change of party control at Washington brings freshness and virility

LINCOLN OF THE LONDON "PUNCH"

This is typical of cartoons drawn during the Civil War by John Tenniel. It is *Punch's* first portrait of Lincoln— May 11, 1861—and the only one showing him without a beard. In the smoke from the White House fireplace before which Lincoln meditates are what the caption refers to as "Blacks." "What a nice White House this would be, if it were not for the Blacks."

into situations that might otherwise tend to become stale and undesirable, with power too firmly grasped in the hands of certain men and groups, as was the case in Mexico, for example, in the days of President Diaz.

The point toward which I am making approach relates to the public character and influence of Lincoln. His birthday, like that of George Washington, has become a national holiday. The Republicans, naturally, are most disposed to use his name as a political asset. But the Democrats also appeal to him and his record, and hold him up as a reproach to Republicans of lesser fame or more doubtful virtue, both past and present. The North has accepted General Lee with warm admiration, while less inclined to admit final evidence of the long and distinguished record of Jefferson Davis. The South, with steadily increasing desire to know and to understand, has begun to see Abraham Lincoln in a true light, as the

LEONARD VOLK'S BUST OF LINCOLN
Made from life in April, 1860, in the sculptor's studio at Chicago, with the aid of the mask reproduced below. Volk's wife was a cousin of Stephen A. Douglas, and he had met Lincoln during the famous debates of 1858. Lincoln sat for this bust every day for a week and afterward praised it highly. Volk later made statues of both Douglas and Lincoln for the Illinois State Capitol at Springfield.

chose to proceed, with indefatigable industry and with unsurpassed training and ability, to gain and weigh fresh knowledge, and to interpret the facts as a whole in order to arrive at estimates that might remain unshaken. Our accepted views of Lincoln's qualities are strongly confirmed by these latest researches, just as certain new facts of an ancestral and biographical character, brought to light by Dr. William E. Barton, Mr. Louis A. Warren, and others, have helped us to understand Lincoln's backgrounds with higher appreciation.

Doubtless we know enough about Lincoln, as matters stand, to feel confident in the favorable opinion we hold. We shall always regret, however, that we have no record of hundreds of speeches made by him in the Legislature of Illinois. We know something of his manner of reasoning before judges and juries, but we are the poorer in that we shall never possess

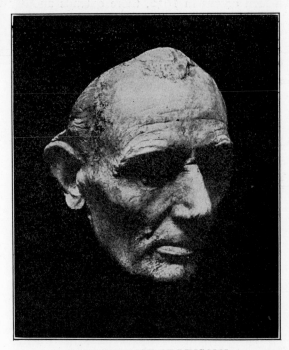

THE LIFE MASK OF LINCOLN
Made by Leonard W. Volk at his studio in Chicago, in April, 1860, the month before Lincoln's nomination. This plaster cast is the standard upon which all accurate portraiture of the younger, beardless Lincoln is based. The sculptor's reminiscences tell us that the whole process for making the mould consumed about an hour's time. "Being all in one piece, with both ears perfectly taken, it clung pretty hard, as the cheekbones were higher than the jaws at the lobe of the ear." But Lincoln worked it off without break or injury, though it hurt as it pulled a few hairs out with the plaster.

man whose devotion was never sectional. Everywhere it is conceded that it was Lincoln's steadfast aim to keep the country together for the sake alike of all its parts and sections, and because he foresaw long vistas of future greatness for a united America.

Unquestionably the world is in agreement in its belief that Abraham Lincoln's place is a worthy and permanent one, not only in our American Hall of Fame, but in the Pantheon of democratic leaders who have helped to change the world since the collapse of the old régime, and to make life worth living for the common man. The lamented Mr. Beveridge, whose posthumous volumes on Lincoln appeared in the autumn of 1928, has presented the man himself in his formative period, in a more thorough way than any previous writer. This was a difficult work, because the author

THE BEARDLESS LINCOLN OF GEORGE GREY
BARNARD

This is the sculptor's model, which he used in the creation of the bronze statue erected at Cincinnati in 1917, with a replica at Manchester, England. Barnard tells us that he saw "the mighty man who grew from out the soil and the hardships of the earth. . . . a man made like the oak trees and the granite rocks." He relied largely upon the life mask, for he believed an imaginary Lincoln to be an insult to the American people.

©Douglas Volk, 1908.

LINCOLN THE PRESIDENT—A PORTRAIT BY
DOUGLAS VOLK

The artist is a distinguished portrait painter whose interest in Lincoln dates back to his own childhood, when Lincoln came to his father's studio in Chicago, early in 1860, to sit for the bust reproduced on the preceding page. He has made careful studies from the bust and life mask. Douglas Volk's conception may well be accepted as the standard bearded Lincoln of the presidential period, as later generations have come to portray him.

the volumes that could have been compiled if court stenographers had taken down his lucid arguments.

His record in the Legislature was subjected to a searching investigation by Mr. Beveridge, who found in the surviving journals ample evidence of Lincoln's constant activity in the debating of questions both local and general. To have read full reports of a hundred of Lincoln's best speeches in the Legislature would have made it easier to understand the political and oratorical maturity disclosed by Lincoln in the debates with Douglas in 1858. Also, the Cooper Union speech would not have seemed so amazing if its hearers could have realized the extent of Lincoln's preparation as a political student, and the long training as a public speaker to which he had subjected himself. As I

have remarked, it is a loss not to have those earlier speeches preserved, except for a few casual fragments. But the various samples of Lincoln's early writing and speaking that we actually possess are enough to convince us that we should not have been disappointed with the countless efforts that were never set down on paper. We know that Lincoln arrived at his later position of unquestioned pre-eminence through continuous application, over a long period, to the study of English diction and to mastery of the art of logical presentation.

Certain young Englishmen of ardent spirit had conceived a high opinion of Lincoln even before the tragedy of his death had softened the hearts of the greater number who had spoken of him with contempt and ridicule. But in England, as elsewhere in the world, the historical position of Lincoln is no longer in

ENGLAND ACCEPTS THE WASHINGTON IDEAL
In the caption of this cartoon from *Punch* of January, 1863, George III asks George Washington—both being in spirit land—what he thinks of his fine republic now, Washington replying "Umph!" The Father of His Country, creator of a nation out of thirteen former British colonies, would not have approved of civil strife and disunion, in the opinion of this English journal.

dispute. A volume might be made of mere quotations from later British tributes. There appeared in 1916 a worthy British biography of Lincoln by Lord Charnwood. It is a frank and discriminating study, the eulogistic tone of which is in full accord with the sentiment of the world at large. Mr. Basil Williams, in his preface to that work, characterizes Lincoln as "one of the few supreme statesmen of the last three centuries." Continuing, Mr. Williams says: "He was misunderstood and under-rated in his lifetime and even yet has hardly come to his own, for his place is among the great men of the earth. To them he belongs by right of his immense power of hard work, his unfaltering pursuit of what seemed to him right, and above all by that childlike directness and simplicity of vision which none but the greatest carry beyond their earliest years."

Lord Charnwood, referring to Lincoln's

speeches in the debates with Douglas, comments as follows upon their qualities of thought and language: "Passages abound in these speeches which to almost any literate taste are arresting for the simple beauty of their English, a beauty characteristic of one who had learned to reason with Euclid and learned to feel and to speak with the authors of the Bible. And in their own kind they were a classic and probably unsurpassed achievement. Though Lincoln had to deal with a single issue demanding no great width of knowledge, it must be evident that the passions aroused by it and the confused and shifting state of public sentiment made his problem very subtle, and it was a rare profundity and sincerity of thought which solved it in his own mind. In expressing the result of thought so far deeper than that of most men, he achieved a clearness of expression which very few writers, and those among the greatest, have excelled."

From a much more extended comment upon Lincoln's methods in statement and argument, we may quote the following sentences from Lord Charnwood: "Grave difficulties are

AN ENVELOPE DESIGN OF 1861
It carried a letter addressed to "His Exc., Abraham Lincoln, President of the United States," and was one of many millions of such envelopes—with various kinds of emblems, caricatures, and slogans—which were in general use at the time. This particular envelope has been chosen here to show how Washington was held up as an inspiration and example in the period of national crisis, even in the personal mail of President Lincoln.

WHEN WASHINGTON WAS THE SOLE STANDARD
BY WHICH PRESIDENTS WERE JUDGED

In Lincoln's time the embodiment of all that was right and good in Presidents was Washington. Now Lincoln himself shares that honor. Here the bust of Washington, on the
pedestal that bears the names of Adams and Jefferson, looks on while Lincoln (with one
knee on the ground) battles with Douglas, and Breckinridge strives with Bell, in the four-
cornered rivalry for the Presidency in 1860. It was a Fourth of July cartoon, published
in the New York weekly periodical *Vanity Fair* and drawn by Louis S. Stephens, many of
whose cartoons appear in subsequent chapters.

handled in a style which could arouse all the interest of a boy, and penetrate the understanding of a case-hardened party man. But if in comparison with the acknowledged masterpieces of our prose we rank many passages in these speeches very high—and in fact the men who have appreciated them most highly have been fastidious scholars—we shall not yet have measured Lincoln's effort and performance. For these are not the compositions of a cloistered man of letters, they are the outpourings of an agitator upon the stump. The men who think hard are few; few of them can clothe their thought in apt and simple words; very, very few are those who in doing this could hold the attention of a miscellaneous and large crowd. Lincoln's wisdom had to utter itself in a voice which would reach the outskirts of a large and sometimes excited crowd in the open air. It was uttered in strenuous conflict with a man whose reputation quite overshadowed his; a person whose extraordinary and good-humoured vitality armed him with an external charm even for people who, like Mrs. Beecher Stowe, detested his principles."

This English scholar had studied Lincoln's utterances, had read the standard American biographies, and had mastered the essential facts of Lincoln's dominance of the diplomatic, political, military and administrative policies and decisions of his years as President. Lord Charnwood understood the peculiar nature of the Presidential office, which in war times rises in its authority to a virtual dictatorship. He had, also, the benefit of the large collection of fresh estimates and reminiscences called forth by the celebration in 1909 of the centenary of Lincoln's birth. Tributes in speeches, articles and books assignable to the date of February, 1909, show clearly that

LED BY LINCOLN'S PRINCIPLES
Homer Davenport, cartoonist of the New York *Evening Mail* during the campaign of 1904, saw the spirit of Lincoln guiding Theodore Roosevelt during his Presidency.

Southern statesmen, and leaders of opinion in all professions, had reached mature conclusions favorable to the permanence and nonsectional character of Lincoln's reputation.

It is hardly less worth while to discover some contemporary opinions of Lincoln as a man and a statesman that have come to life more recently. One finds not a few such opinions in the correspondence of European publicists and men of letters. To recall a casual instance, I have in mind a speech made by the eminent English philosopher, Frederic Harrison. He was a guest at a banquet in Chicago on Washington's birthday in 1901. Expressing the sympathy and good will of his own nation for the citizens of the American republic, he was desirous, as he declared, "above all to tell them of the admiration and the profound homage with which the founder of the American republic is looked upon by all rational people of Great Britain today." He felt that the spirit of Washington had been exhibited "in later years by his successors in that great office." Turning to a portrait of Lincoln in the Union League Club where he was speaking, he referred to tributes paid in London at a meeting held just after Lincoln's death. He said that Abraham Lincoln had been to him in his youth "the type of the republican chief," and he looked upon him "as indeed a worthy successor of the founder of the Republic himself."

Mr. Harrison reminded his hearers that he had himself published in England a small volume at the end of the Civil War, from which he proceeded to quote a brilliant tribute he had paid at that time to the American Republic and to its leader. Speaking of the Americans of the Civil War period, he had said in that contemporary volume: "They displayed the most splendid examples of energy and fortitude which the modern world has seen, with which the defense of Greece against Asia and of France against Europe alone can be compared in the whole annals of mankind. They developed almost ideal civic virtues and gifts; generosity, faith, firmness; sympathy the most affecting, resources the most exhaustless, ingenuity the most magical."

Following these sentences came a tribute to

WHAT WOULD LINCOLN DO?

With that question as the title of its cartoon, *Puck* in 1904 invoked the memory of Lincoln as a comment on the activities of President Roosevelt.

Lincoln that seems to me remarkable in the prophetic character of its appreciative words, when one considers that it was penned in England in 1865 by a young professor of Jurisprudence and International Law who was already a competent critic of politicians and rulers. "They brought forth the most beautiful and heroic character who in recent times has ever led a nation, the only blameless type of the statesman since the days of Washington. Under him they created the purest model of government which has yet been seen on the earth—a whole nation throbbing into one great heart and brain, one great heart and brain giving unity and life to a whole nation. The hour of their success came; unchequered in the completeness of its triumph, unsullied by any act of vengeance, hallowed by a great martyrdom." As one who knew Frederic Harrison in his later years, and who remembers well his visit to the United States in 1901, I have pleasure in quoting his reference in that year

to what he had said thirty-six years earlier.

In the convention that nominated Lincoln in 1860, a young German named Carl Schurz was chairman of the Wisconsin delegation and an eager supporter of Seward. Acquiescing in the Lincoln nomination, this young man, who had been in America only a few years, proved himself the most eloquent and effective of campaign speakers, using English fluently but speaking also to German audiences in their native tongue. His career was long and distinguished, and I also knew him well in his later years. On March 2, 1929, there occurred the centenary of Schurz's birth and this gave incentive to the publication of a volume of his intimate letters early in that year, by the State Historical Society of Wisconsin. These letters are remarkable for the light they throw upon contemporary affairs.

Some of the letters written to friends in Germany are intended to convey a true picture of conditions in this country. The affairs of the government were not quite encouraging in 1864 when Lincoln was a candidate for re-election. The tendency to disparage the northern cause, and to belittle its leader who was a candidate for a second term, was general not only in England and France but in Germany and elsewhere abroad. Endeavoring to correct the views of one of his German friends, Schurz wrote of Lincoln: "He is a man of profound feeling, just and firm principles, and incorruptible integrity. One can always rely upon his motives, and the characteristic gift of this people, a sound common sense, is developed in him to a marvelous degree. If you should sometime find opportunity to read his official papers and his political letters, you will find this demonstrated in a manner which would surprise you. I know the man from personal observation as well as anyone and better than most. I am quite familiar with the motives of his policy. I have seen him fight his way heroically through many a terrible battle, and work his way with true-hearted strength through many a desperate situation. I have often criticized him severely and subsequently have not infrequently found that he was right."

Then there occurs, as this letter to the friend in Germany proceeds, the following words, surprising, as written by a recently naturalized German-American in October, 1864, in the sweep of their now justified predictions:

"Lincoln's personality has in this crisis a quite peculiar significance. Free from the aspirations of genius, he will never become dangerous to a free commonwealth. He is the people personified; that is the secret of his popularity. His government is the most representative that has ever existed in world history. I will make a prophecy which may perhaps sound strange at this moment. In fifty years, perhaps much sooner, Lincoln's name will stand written upon the honor roll of the American Republic next to that of Washington, and there it will remain for all time. The children of those who now disparage him will bless him."

After the completion of their ten-volume biography of Lincoln, his war-time secretaries, John G. Nicolay and John Hay, prepared two volumes of "Abraham Lincoln's Complete Works, Comprising His Speeches, Letters, State Papers and Miscellaneous Writings." While this collection is invaluable, it seems scanty, indeed, as we see what the editors were able to discover of documentary material for the period from 1832 until we reach the Lincoln-Douglas debates of 1858. Only a little more original writing has been found since 1894, when these standard volumes were published. Many biographical details, indeed, have been unearthed since Messrs. Nicolay and Hay wrote their indispensable history of Lincoln and his times, most of their volumes dealing with the Presidental years, about which they were intimately informed, as Lincoln's daily associates and confidential helpers.

Such personal contact affords a kind of knowledge that can never be replaced by research, however scientific. So true is this statement that the men and women who delve in archives would promptly reply that one of the chief objects of their research is to bring to light the correspondence and papers of various people who had themselves enjoyed personal contact with a leader like Lincoln, and had set down facts and impressions in private letters or diaries. Thus we are obtaining many new sidelights on Lincoln, as the biographers of literally hundreds of other people discover family papers that are contemporary rather than reminiscent.

We learn much of ancient times from the pages of classical historians; but even more that is illuminating, and that is giving us fresh knowledge of early civilizations, we gain from the discoveries of archaeologists. On the walls of tombs are found pictorial records of extraordinary value to the student. Even those prehistoric men who lived for protection in caverns made sketches—and in some cases elaborate and well-authenticated drawings—on their rocky walls, that give us new ideas about our remote ancestors. Written words are, indeed, a main resources in studying more recent centuries. But we rely also upon works of art and architecture, and upon objects excavated, as in the buried cities of Pompeii and Herculaneum, in Greece, Egypt, and Mesopotamia, that throw light upon public as well as private affairs.

It may be said, too, that portraiture, caricature, and illustrative art have given us much knowledge of the personages of more recent history, while also revealing gusts of feeling and trends of opinion. From the very beginning of the art of printing, the illustrators took an appreciable part in the new methods of spreading knowledge, affording entertainment, propagating doctrines, and defaming or glorifying individuals.

The chief purpose of the present work is to bring before the reader the issues in the sphere of American politics about which Abraham Lincoln was concerned, and to make use —with great profusion, if not exhaustively—of the cartoons and caricatures with which Lincoln himself was familiar in his younger days. As we proceed, however, we find the cartoonists making Lincoln a central figure when at length, in 1860, he was cast for the leading part in the drama of American politics and government.

Lincoln's face and form are not infrequently reappearing in the cartoons of later times, as representing in some sense the accepted standard by which to test the political actors of today. It is to be noted that the Lincoln drawn by cartoonists of the present time is always beneficent and dignified, making an appeal to our feelings of regard and veneration. Nothing could be in greater contrast than the cartoons of his own lifetime, which afforded him so much amusement, though at times doubtless, causing him passing annoyance Caricatures that belittled him or grossly misrepresented him were likely to create impressions unfavorably affecting public opinion, and thus to make his tasks the more difficult to perform.

A great school of caricaturists had arisen in England; and this form of political satire had become well-known and much practised in France, Germany, and other European countries. It had been taken up in the United States

DOWNFALL OF THE IDOL OF '76

A cartoon by Matt Morgan, published in *Fun* (London), November, 1863. An effigy of George Washington is being burned by President Lincoln, who mocks the Father of his Country—in the original caption—with the following words: "I'll warm yer! Your old Constitution won't do for U. S.!" The fire is being fed by decrees which are stigmatized as destroying principles of American liberty.

at an early period, but was of slow development. Washington seems to have been exempt from the attacks of the caricaturists, but this was due to the lack of artists and wood engravers, rather than to respect for the man or the office. The lithographers were more successful than the wood engravers, and rapidly throughout the United States the political draughtsmen learned to put their pictures on the smooth stones of the lithographic press. Perhaps the reproduction of a number of the earlier lithographed political posters may help us to understand one of the sources from which Lincoln himself, through seven or eight presidential elections prior to his own, derived amusement as he pursued his continuing studies in current politics and in the personalities of public men.

A SOUTHERN CARICATURE OF LINCOLN IN THE WAR PERIOD

This is one of the Confederate caricatures of Adalbert J. Volck, here published for the first time. They were engraved on copper plates, in Baltimore, and buried to prevent seizure. The President and his players "come to play a pleasant comedy, a kind of history." Chase, Secretary of the Treasury, is at the window. Cameron, Secretary of War, is the puppet whose wire runs through the highest hole. Welles, Secretary of the Navy, rows the boat, and back of him is General Butler. The three other generals, in the foreground, are Frémont, Scott, and McClellan.

THE FATE OF THE RAIL SPLITTER—ABE LINCOLN

Northern boasts of hanging Jeff Davis to a sour apple tree were matched by Southern resentment toward Lincoln as the embodiment of opposition to the course that the Southern States had chosen to pursue. This wood engraving was printed in Richmond in 1861.

CHAPTER II

The Presidential Office

Powers and responsibilities of the chief executive—A target for criticism—Lincoln's place in history in contrast with that of Buchanan, his predecessor

THAT WHICH, for short, we may call "America's success" affords the basis upon which some great political reputations are built. To move with the tides and winds of manifest destiny is to reach the quiet havens of secure fame. The combined efforts of millions of people confronting hardships and difficulties—but for the most part seizing opportunities in a buoyant spirit under conditions of unprecedented freedom — have brought about our national aggrandizement. This thrilling epic of a people's rise to greatness has reached universal recognition since the display of its resources and power at the climax of the World War.

Conquest of forest stretches and trackless plains; growth in population, industry and social well-being; rapid attainment of economic and political power—all this unrivalled story of progress within the compass of a century or two is an ever-fascinating study. Not only have these millions of people in a few successive generations made the country what it is by their labors, in courageous pursuit of their ideals, but it is they who have, generally speaking, made the decisions which constitute the turning points in our history. Leadership has not been superimposed: the country itself has trained the leaders, appointed them, and used them for its resistless purposes.

We may sympathize fully with the idealization of a national heroine like Joan of Arc, or with the romance that associates the Ferdinands and Isabellas with the discovery of America and the creation of European empires. We may be indulgent rather than critical when we read the fervent pages that glorify Queen Elizabeth, the heaven-ordained destruction of the Spanish Armada, and the world-wide dominion that resulted from Britain's conquest of the oceans. But Washington's leadership was not that of a superman or a miracle-worker. Neither was Lincoln's that of the humble and obscure child of the frontier cabin who had heard mysterious voices calling him to rise, receive endowments of transcendent wisdom, and save his country for the glory of God, through the freeing of the slaves and the elevation of mankind at large. Washington was simply the best representative of the combined wisdom and energy of the American colonies. Lincoln was a tried and tested character, trained for the exigencies of his time, and chosen by hosts of determined and competent people to take the lead in a crisis.

Public opinion has been the dictator more truly in the United States than elsewhere. Yet we have so devised our institutions that prevailing sentiment must express itself through representatives and chosen agents. The Presidents have been from the first, as they remain today, the people's Agents-in-Chief. History and biography, following traditions to some extent but also deferring to an instinct which demands that mass move-

ments shall be typified or personified in the names of leaders, have usually concurred in the easy and convenient practice of setting our political agents on pinnacles.

The framers of the Constitution of 1787 were deeply conscious of all that the country had suffered during and after the Revolution from the lack of a strong central government. They created the office of the Presidency, having in mind first of all George Washington, and then a succession of men of character, capacity, and training who should have stood the tests of experience, and grown in the estimation of their fellows into fitness for the chief executive office. They devised the electoral college, as a means by which a small body of representative men from all the States could from time to time choose a President with their superior knowledge of individual candidates, of public wishes, and of permanent considerations as distinguished from momentary controversies. The machinery has not been operated in the precise manner that was in the minds of those who built it. But it has always been available, and the Electoral College might conceivably function again at some future time in accordance with its original theory,

The important thing was the creation of the Presidential office itself. Its range of authority clothed it with as much dignity as lay in human nature to assume. The President was made wholly responsible for the executive business of civil government. He became, ex-officio, for his term of office, the commander-in-chief of both army and navy. Executive

LONG ABE A LITTLE LONGER

A drawing by Frank Bellew, published in *Harper's Weekly* in 1864, after President Lincoln's re-election.

"IN HEIGHT SIX FEET, FOUR INCHES, NEARLY; LEAN IN FLESH"

Such was Lincoln's own description of a figure that lent itself to the imagination and skill of the caricaturist. Douglas was as short and stocky as Lincoln was tall and thin. Leonard Volk, who measured both of them for statues in 1860, told Lincoln that he was just one foot taller than Douglas. The opportunity was irresistible to the cartoonist who favored Lincoln. In 1860 there were four candidates for the Presidency. Lincoln and Douglas are in the lead in this race to the White House, with Breckinridge third and Bell in the rear.

departments were created, and provision was made for appointive heads of these departments. But there was no suggestion of a Cabinet in the British or European sense of the word. The President was not to depute or share his authority.

In England, there was the King, with his privy council; the Parliament, with the House of Commons gradually winning prestige over the House of Lords as modern democracy made its slow gains. But the American Presidency did not imitate a king possessing inherent prerogatives; nor did it set up a prime minister, who, under the British system, is merely the chairman and chief personage of a ministry that carries on the government through majority influence in the Houses of Parliament. There are, of course, certain constitutional and legal analogies; but the dif-

ferences of structure are quite fundamental. The American convention of 1787 was deliberately working out a plan of union for thirteen States, which were destined to become far more numerous. It had to distinguish, both legally and practically, between the so-called sovereign authority of the States and the sovereignty of the nation in the exercise of its delegated authority. In recent years many students of the history and the science of government have criticised our constitution-makers for their attempt to establish the legislative, executive, and judicial functions as separate and co-ordinate branches of government. There are some who would have the legislative power over-ride the opinions and decisions of the higher courts of law. And there are many others who would subordinate the executive to the legislative branch.

There are others, approaching from an opposite standpoint, who would seek to increase the practical power and efficiency of the executive by giving the President and his department heads more influence in legislative programs. They would favor a more pervasive leadership, and would provide seats for our so-called Cabinet in the Senate and House of Representatives. Nevertheless, the framework of American government, as erected in the Eighteenth Century by a convention made up of men remarkable for ability and foresight, has now survived well into the Twentieth Century, and it bids fair to resist assaults, so far as its essential features are concerned, for a long time to come.

At the very apex of the system there continues to stand the office of the President.

THE IDEALIZED LINCOLN OF FRANCE

This title page of a French periodical dated November 23, 1873, shows Lincoln so much greater than Uncle Sam that a magnifying glass is used by the one to see the other.

While its essential nature is fairly expressed in the Constitution itself, its real character had to be worked out in experience. The feeble kind of central government that we were carrying on during and immediately after the Revolution made very slight appeal to the ambition of those who sought distinction. It was not viewed with favor by men whose motive it was to render the highest public service. Such men preferred to hold office in their respective States. It was no small mark of wisdom on the part of the Constitution-makers of 1787 that they should have established in the Presidency a position of such high prestige, and such wide range of authority and discretion, that it should have continued from the first to stand alone and quite unrivalled in the whole world of politics and government. It was also remarkable that this untried office should first have been filled by a man of such qualifications as George Washington.

Men in politics who attain lofty position, whether they seek it or not, are quite certain to find themselves praised at one moment and blamed at another, often losing the support and confidence of friends in times of emergency, and always exposed to the attacks of partisan or personal enemies. Those who reach the high places have usually come up by process of survival. They have fought political battles and camped on the fields of strife. They have learned to receive hard blows, while by long experience they have acquired the arts of attack and defense. Few of them, it is true, are indifferent to disparagement or criticism, but they do not quail or retreat under fire.

The Presidency carries with it such a burden of responsibility that those who attain the post have almost invariably tried to rise above narrow views, to see ahead, and to pursue courses that would commend themselves when the petty strifes and controversies of the day had been forgotten. But the very fact that the Presidency is so conspicuous a place makes it a shining mark. No President has ever escaped the harsh and unjust attacks of opponents, the libels of poisoned pens, and the innuendo or malice of whispered slander.

Each President of the United States has had to do his work exposed to storms that could

"YOU HAVE SWOLLEN THE EARTH WITH THE BLOOD OF MY CHILDREN"

A London periodical called *Fun* printed weekly caricatures during our Civil War, by Matt Morgan and other artists, which ranked well with those of *Punch* not only in draughtsmanship and virility but also in their disparagement of Lincoln and the Northern cause.

This cartoon, published in December, 1864, is *Fun's* comment on the result of the presidential election. Columbia is speaking: "Lincoln, you have brought me to this, yet I have not flinched to perform my part of the contract. I still cling to you that you may fulfill yours. You have swollen the earth with the blood of my children. Show me what I am to gain by this, or look for my dire vengeance in the future."

Almost to the very end *Fun* portrayed Lincoln as the leader of a lost cause. But when the news of assassination reached London "the veil was torn from all eyes," and *Fun* paid graceful tribute.

not always be anticipated. He might well expect to be buffetted by winds from every quarter, rather than to enjoy smooth sailing for a single season. He could hope to be vindicated by posterity, but it was hard to believe that the abuse of his enemies might not permanently blacken his reputation, remembering that a great analyst of human nature in an unhappy moment had declared that "the evil that men do lives after them; the good is oft interred with their bones." However, it was not for the President to be too self-conscious, or to pose for the place he fancied he would like to occupy in the pages of biographers and historians not yet born.

Thus the personality of our Presidents enters importantly into the subject matter of American political history. A President can not answer attacks because of the position he holds. For that very reason he is likely to be more sensitive than he had been when, in some other political capacity, he had been contending upon an equal plane with his fellows. The very loftiness of the position gives to the President at times a sense of painful isolation. He alone must bear the burden of momentous decisions.

It is fitting therefore that our students of politics and history should concern themselves with the manners and characteristics of Presidents, as well as with their official acts and utterances. As the position of our country becomes more significant in relation to world affairs, there is an increasing interest in the study of our foreign policies and relationships. And since the making of treaties and the conduct of negotiations is a strictly presidential function, our historical students are studying the careers of former Presidents with increasing care, especially in view of occasions afforded by many new opportunities to inspect secret archives, collections of letters, and various papers and documents that had formerly been inaccessible.

When one has considered our history from this Presidential standpoint, he is likely to use addition rather than subtraction in revising his estimate of the character and ability of most of the men who have filled the office in lengthening succession. At least it may be said that no other country—whether in modern times or in any historic period—can present in unbroken series a similarly long list of men holding positions of authority who could for a moment be compared with the American Presidents.

Undoubtedly some Presidents have far exceeded others in ability and in wisdom. That a revision of estimates should be going on from time to time is quite inevitable. The intense prejudices of contemporary partisanship are sure to survive in some quarters. As I intimated in the preceding chapter, the very name of Jefferson has, until lately, been odious to dwindling numbers who have inherited the prejudices and dislikes of the Hamilton-Jefferson feud. New England's view of President Polk had been so firmly established by reason of opposition to the Mexican War that even yet the more impartial verdicts of history are not accepted. Although George Washington was much reviled at times, he was too far above partisan or sectional controversy, and too obviously a disinterested public servant, to suffer any damage in historical reputation from the calumnies that so infuriated him while President. It has been easy to set him on a pedestal, from which he will never be dethroned. Personal and partisan controversies, as I have shown, long raged about the name and memory of Andrew Jackson. But through the perspectives of history Jackson's fame grows brighter, because he was inseparably associated with transactions that have had momentous consequences.

In Buchanan's time, impelling forces that President Buchanan had done little or nothing to evoke, and which he did little or nothing to guide or control, were shaping the immediate movements of history. He was greatly blamed by the South for his pro-Northern attitude, and at the same time he was execrated by the North for his lack of the Jacksonian qualities of impetuous boldness, as the Secession cause was gaining momentum. It makes a great difference in the reputation of a man in political authority whether or not in his own period the course of affairs reaches a favorable turn. Thus Lincoln was even more execrated than Buchanan, and for much the same reasons. But the war that Buchanan was trying to avert

"MR. LINCOLN, WE HAVE FAILED UTTERLY"

Disparagement and ridicule of Lincoln in England lasted throughout the war. This is a cartoon from the London *Punch,* by the famous John Tenniel, published in September, 1864, just before the presidential election. Mrs. North is talking to her attorney: "You see, Mr. Lincoln, we have failed utterly in our course of action; I want peace, and so, if you cannot effect an amicable arrangement, I must put the case into other hands."

by temporizing methods, and that Lincoln was blamed for precipitating, came to its successful conclusion a few days before Lincoln's assassination.

And thus the name of the martyred President was destined to be forever identified with the dramatic climax of a struggle that he had led on to a successful termination. Buchanan's name became historically associated with failure, and Lincoln's with success. Mr. Buchanan spent several years, following his retirement from the White House, in study and reflection. He wrote a volume of self-justification. Undoubtedly he had reached a firm theory as to the course that history would have pursued

if he himself had been elected for a second term in 1860.

Lincoln, slowly developing, had attained national prominence in the sharp controversies of the Buchanan period. Senator Douglas of Illinois was the leader of the Democratic Senate; and, in the test of local experience, Lincoln had come forward as the one man in Illinois who could successfully cope with Douglas in the platform discussion of great issues. The East then seized upon certain personal characteristics, and never quite understood the later Lincoln. The South did not discriminate much, but regarded Lincoln as essentially opposed to the spread of slavery, at a time when slavery must either extend its domain or accept defeat and face its decline and fall. Foreign countries, notably England, had various reasons for seeing Lincoln through the eyes of prejudice and bitter dislike.

Nevertheless, within the years of the Twentieth Century there has been witnessed the remarkable growth in world-wide appreciation of Lincoln as a lofty character and a great statesman to which I have already alluded. The prejudice of the South has slowly but surely abated. The New England attitude has grown less apologetic of Lincoln as untutored and uncouth. A school of English admirers finds in Lincoln one of the great historic leaders of an expanded Anglo-Saxondom.

This new appreciation of Lincoln which has at last made its way South of the Mason and Dixon Line, and which is increasingly expressed in eulogies on Lincoln's birthday, is deeply gratifying, not only because it honors the memory of an American embodying the nation's best traits, but also because it testifies to the essential right-mindedness of our generation. We honor ourselves in paying tribute to those who have shown unflinching courage while bearing heavy burdens, often in sorrow and in pain, with the result of great and permanent good to the republic.

Few people of the present day, however, are even faintly aware of the added embarrassments that Lincoln suffered, through attack and misinterpretation. The prestige of a public man counts not a little in times when anxious business is on hand. Ridicule and disparagement of Lincoln in England rendered it far more difficult than it should have been to deal with a number of serious controversies that required delicate diplomatic handling.

John Bright, writing to the American historian Motley after the assassination of Lincoln, remarked: "The shock produced in this country was very great. All your friends were plunged into sorrow, and all your enemies into shame, and from that time there has been a rapid change of opinion and of feeling here on all American questions." Mr. Bright added that having followed Lincoln's career with growing interest he had "seen in all his speeches, and in all his public papers and ad-

dresses, something different from, and something higher than, anything that has ever before proceeded from the tongue of president or potentate."

That the President should have been hated and ridiculed in the South after his election, and especially after the outbreak of the War, could not have been otherwise in view of the intensity of Southern resentment and alarm. Thus President Lincoln was treated in the Confederate States precisely as President Jefferson Davis was treated in the North.

But it was the constant criticism and nagging of Northern politicians and newspapers that served chiefly to hurt the President's prestige and to embarrass his leadership. There were many dissensions in his own Cabinet, which were reflected in the press. He had to deal on the one hand with Congress, and on the other with military leaders who had political views. Then there were the politicians who kept thrusting themselves with selfish aims into the military situation.

How Lincoln dealt with all these difficulties and pursued his way through the stormiest of political weather can only be appreciated as one turns back to the period itself. It is evident that it would be quite impossible to understand the character and career of Theodore Roosevelt without a study at short range of the bitter controversies through which he passed, the modes of attack used by his enemies, and his sturdy championship of causes and principles. How the clouds of detraction disappeared, and how Roosevelt was duly revealed as the typical American of his own period, representing the country's highest standards, and waging an ever-courageous fight for what seemed to him the best courses to pursue, affords an inspiring object-lesson for young citizens. In like manner, we can best understand Lincoln by studying his career in its contacts with current public opinion, and in the drastic ordeals of the most crucial of all presidential administrations. The subjects at issue, and the personalities of the Lincolnian period, are susceptible of a vivid kind of presentation in the cartoons of that epoch. It is well to perceive, meanwhile, that Lincoln's fame is due to his use of opportunities afforded by the unique presidential office.

CHAPTER III

The Education of a Future President

A wealth of substitutes for schooling—Lincoln's autobiography of his early years—A surveyor, postmaster, and merchant who liked to read books—His resemblance to Marshall

IT WAS ALWAYS assumed, until a good while after his death, that Lincoln was inferior in education when compared with all his predecessors—with the possible exception of Andrew Jackson. Lincoln himself had done much to give currency to this impression. Like many other successful men who have risen by their own efforts, he had always estimated too highly the advantages to be derived from long years spent in school and college. Those who differ about the nature and processes of education do not, as a rule, analyze closely their definitions. To those who regard education as the exclusive concern of schools, and religion as non-existent apart from the observances and the authority of churches, Abraham Lincoln was sadly lacking in education and in religion. But judging him by results rather than by methods and processes, Lincoln was a man whose mental power was highly developed in relation to the subject matter with which an American public man of his day had to deal.

He was unusually well educated, just as he was deeply religious. As a boy he had the intellectual eagerness that would, indeed, have led him much farther along paths of general or special scholarship if his opportunities had been those of Thomas Jefferson or John Quincy Adams. But men who attain leadership have grown strong through a conquest of obstacles. They have converted their seeming disadvantages into positive assets. The test of real education lies in the equipment that has been gained at a given age—let us say twenty-one or thirty-five—through the use of available opportunities. The man himself is so much greater than the varying accidents of his environment that the question of his standing in the community, when he has reached the years of mature manhood, depends as a rule almost wholly upon his aims and ideals, and the courage and energy he shows in the pursuit of his

chosen objects. Among leaders in any field of activity, the great questions that ultimately arise have to do with attainments in wisdom, in power, and in responsible character.

Thus the distinction between the man trained in schools, and the man who has found his own means—apart from the exactions and routine of schoolmasters—for keeping alive the process of intellectual growth, tends to disappear in later life.

In the case of a boy on the frontier, like young Abraham Lincoln, everything depended upon his actual use of time, upon his ability to concentrate, upon his memory as an aid to the

A NEW BABY DOWN AT TOM LINCOLN'S

Lincoln's birthday, in each year, sees the publication of cartoons that reflect some phase of the President's career and carry some lesson for the current generation. This cartoon is by H. T. Webster, drawn for the New York *World.*

21

accumulation of knowledge, and upon his attitude toward the neighborhood, as determining whether or not he was fitted by nature to lead rather than to follow.

The hardships of frontier life in Lincoln's time were great, but they were for the most part borne easily because poverty was not of the hopeless, stagnant kind that was so prevalent in Europe. As Lincoln was fully aware, we had been engaged for two hundred years in the creation of a great nationality upon wholly new principles. We had our own differences as regards the relative value of National authority and local or State self-direction. But these differences of view were hardly distinguishable when in both theory and practice our democratic institutions were compared with the social and political institutions of Europe. Everybody believed in equality, so far as opportunity could make men equal. This feeling of equality gave hope, zest, buoyancy, to pioneer life. Schooled or unschooled himself, every public man was helping to lay foundations for a universal school system to make our future democracy safe in its sense of fitness for its privileges.

It was inconceivable that a lad in an English farm laborer's squalid hut a century ago should have remarked to his neighbors that he expected some day to be Prime Minister of England or Lord Chief Justice. In all of England not a single boy so circumstanced could have broken through the social, political, and legal barriers. Yet there is testimony to the fact that Lincoln as a lad was wont to remark that he would some day be President. And there were boys in each of more than two thousand counties who could reasonably hope for honorable advancement in public life. Lincoln merely meant that he had read the life of George Washington and the speeches of Henry Clay; had studied the Constitution of the United States and the Constitution and statutes of the State where he lived; and that he knew enough about the facts and the personalities of American politics to see that there was nothing like miraculous intervention required to level the obstacles along the pathway between the western log cabin and the White House.

How men rise to the task of community-building and nation-making is marvelous evidence of certain high qualities inherent in human nature. When they are consciously engaged in organizing the institutions of a commonwealth that is to grow stable, populous and cultured and to hold an enviable place in the esteem of mankind, the task has its notable reactions upon their own development of dignity. The youthful Lincoln came in contact with men who were substituting the forms of law and order for the rough and lawless ways of the backwoodsmen of the new Northwestern States. He was impelled to express himself, and to play his part. He listened to itinerant preachers, and himself began to practice the art of oratory. He walked many miles to hear lawyers argue cases at the court house; and thus, hearing one of the Breckin-

THE LOG CABIN IN WHICH LINCOLN WAS BORN

Now preserved inside the memorial building shown on the opposite page. Thomas Lincoln and Nancy Hanks were married in 1806, living at Elizabethtown, Kentucky, and then moving to a farm previously bought in what was then Hardin (now LaRue) County in the same State. Abraham, their second child and first son, was born in this one-room log cabin, or one similar to it, on February 12, 1809, and it was his home for eight years.

©Canfield and Shook, Louisville
THE MEMORIAL AT LINCOLN'S BIRTHPLACE, HODGENVILLE, KENTUCKY
Erected by popular subscription to mark the birthplace and to shelter the log cabin. The cornerstone
was laid by President Roosevelt on February 12, 1909, the centenary of Abraham Lincoln's birth.

ridges, he came to the definite conclusion that he would be a lawyer and a public personage. But he had also learned much else that was valuable throughout his entire life, before he took up in a definite way the study and practice of law.

We are concerned in these pages with Abraham Lincoln in relation to American politics, and to those larger issues of statesmanship with which he was occupied in his last years, as he had climbed the ladder of political success until he had attained the place of chief magistrate and supreme executive authority. With various matters belonging strictly to his private life we are not here occupying ourselves, except as they have a bearing upon his preparation for the public career.

There are, however, many details of interest that have justified the explorations of recent biographers. As we have already intimated, we are now much better acquainted with Lincoln's genealogy than he was himself. Thousands of American families, pushing westward in the restless, irresistible movement that drove back the Indians, and overcame almost incredible hardships in establishing settlements,

lost the threads of ancestral connection. Lincoln's own case was marvelously like that of an immense number of people who were building up the States west of the Alleghenies. He knew that his grandfather, Abraham Lincoln, was a settler in Kentucky, who, like so many others, had directly migrated from Virginia. This earlier Abraham Lincoln was stealthily murdered by an Indian, while his son Thomas was a small boy.

Thomas's father, grandfather, and great-grandfather had partaken of the average opportunities for education and prosperity that had become the common lot in Massachusetts, in Pennsylvania, and in Virginia, the Lincoln forebears having lived in these three original States of the Union. But Thomas Lincoln was too young at his father's death to have acquired accurate knowledge of the family history. One must know a good deal about actual conditions of life in Kentucky, Ohio, Indiana, and Illinois during the period between the Revolution and the Mexican War to pass judgment upon Thomas Lincoln. His lot was a hard one, and his life—like that of the great majority of his neighbors—was humble and obscure. He had inherited enough of acceptable personality, however, to have secured Nancy Hanks for his wife, and thus to have endowed the future President with a loving, sympathetic and capable mother. After her death when the lad was nine years of age, Thomas Lincoln gave another evidence of his worth as a man, and his wisdom in a matter of crucial importance, by providing Lincoln with a step-mother of rare native intelligence and consistent Christian character, and with the maternal qualities that enabled her to supply some of the most desirable things in home life, regardless of mere poverty.

Such conditions within the circle of family existence far outweigh the trivial facts about discomfort in log cabins with no electric lights but rather with tallow candles and the glow of wood fires on broad open hearths. Since almost everyone in the United States, except those descended from recent immigrants, belongs to families that have lately or more remotely lived in log cabins, there is nothing strange or significant in the outward circumstances of Lincoln's youth.

WHERE LINCOLN LIVED BEFORE HE WENT TO THE WHITE HOUSE

In his eighth year the family moved from Hodgenville in Kentucky to Gentryville in Indiana. There Lincoln grew up. When he was twenty-one the family moved again, and he helped his father to settle in Illinois, near Decatur. In the following year, 1831, Lincoln began his own career, at New Salem. He was elected to the Legislature in 1834, and in 1837 moved to the New State capital at Springfield, as an advantageous location for a young lawyer and politician.

It was not, then, these supposed privations of the frontier that should cause us surprise as we contemplate the rise of Lincoln to his firm place among the immortals of history. Rather it is worth while to note the opportunities that such a life afforded. To counterbalance the lack of the discipline of schools, he had the discipline of labor and the freedom to seek directly the things that his soul craved.

In a somewhat casual statement that Lincoln wrote for a fellow politician in Illinois, when he had attained national prominence, are the following brief notes. Few autobiographies of public personages are so lacking in egotism:

I was born February 12, 1809, in Hardin County, Kentucky. My parents were both born in Virginia, of undistinguishable families—second families, perhaps I should say. My mother, who died in my tenth year, was of a family of the name of Hanks, some of whom now reside in Adams, and others in Macon Counties, Illinois. My paternal grandfather, Abraham Lincoln, emigrated from Rockingham County, Virginia, to Kentucky, about 1781 or '2, where, a year or two later, he was killed by Indians, not in battle but by stealth, when he was laboring to open a farm in the forest. His ancestors, who were Quakers, went to Virginia from Berks County, Pennsylvania. An effort to identify them with the New England family of the same name, ended in nothing more than a similarity of Christian names in both families, such as Enoch, Levi, Mordecai, Solomon, Abraham, and the like.

My father, at the death of his father, was but six years of age, and he grew up literally without education. He removed from Kentucky to what is now Spencer County, Indiana, in my eighth year. We reached our new home about the time the State came into the Union. It was a wild region, with many bears and other wild animals still in the woods. There I grew up. There were some schools, so called, but no qualification was ever required of a teacher beyond 'readin', 'writin' and 'cipherin' to the Rule of Three. If a straggler, supposed to understand Latin, happened to sojourn in the neighborhood, he was looked upon as a wizard. There was absolutely nothing to excite ambition for education. Of course when I came of age I did not know much. Still, somehow, I could read, write, and cipher to the Rule of Three, but that was all. I have not been to school since. The little advance I now have upon this store of education, I

IN ILLINOIS, WHEN LINCOLN WAS A MEMBER OF THE LEGISLATURE

Illinois became a State in 1818, but its early development was slow. This drawing, published in 1844 as the frontispiece of Wilkey's "Western Emigration," sets forth the experience of one Illinois settler in the Lincoln period who gave up and came out of the state with "a broken-winded horse, a broken-hearted wife, a broken-legged dog, and the broken constitutions of three fever-and-ague sons." Fourteen years earlier than the date of this cartoon, Abraham Lincoln, then just turned twenty-one, had gone into Illinois with his father, leaving the older State of Indiana.

have picked up from time to time under the pressure of necessity.

I was raised to farm work, which I continued till I was twenty-two. At twenty-one I came to Illinois, and passed the first year in Macon County. Then I got to New Salem, at that time in Sangamon, now in Menard County, where I remained a year as a sort of clerk in a store. Then came the Black Hawk war, and I was elected Captain of Volunteers—a success which gave me more pleasure than any I have had since. I went through the campaign, was elated, ran for the Legislature the same year (1832), and was beaten—the only time I have ever been beaten by the people. The next, and three succeeding biennial elections, I was elected to the Legislature. I was not a candidate afterwards. During this legislative period I had studied law, and removed to Springfield to practise it. In 1846 I was once elected to the Lower House of Congress, but was not a candidate for re-election. From 1849 to 1854, both inclusive, practised law more assiduously than ever before. Always a Whig in politics, and generally on the Whig electoral tickets, making active canvasses. I was losing interest in politics, when the repeal of the Missouri Compromise aroused me again. What I have done since then is pretty well known.

If any personal description of me is thought desirable, it may be said, I am in height, six feet, four inches, nearly; lean in flesh, weighing on an average, one hundred and eighty pounds; dark complexion, with coarse black hair, and gray eyes. No other marks or brands recollected.

Yours very truly,

A. Lincoln.

If Lincoln's vanity had been greater, he would have been at more pains to talk about himself and to place on record the story of his early experiences. His fragmentary schooling, a little of it in Kentucky, and more in Indiana, was undoubtedly of some value. That he had learned to read and write unusually well as a mere lad is beyond doubt. Under whatever inspiration at the beginning, he persistently cultivated the practice of writing down quotations from books or fugitive poems from newspapers, and he committed many things to memory. He became remarkably well versed in the Bible and in due time he found opportunity to read Shakespeare. It was typical that he should have read and memorized Aesop's

Fables. He was devoted to the poetry of Robert Burns; and while he was not even a second-rate poet himself, it was to his credit that he should have written a great many third-rate verses in his attempt to acquire a flexible use of the English language. We have ample testimony that he was regarded as the most indefatigable reader of his neighborhood, so that older people were lending him books, and his reputation as an earnest seeker for knowledge admitted him to homes a good many miles apart, where he was a welcome visitor.

His physical prowess was a matter of fame throughout the region. It never afterwards occurred to his mind that his youthful experiences as farmer and forester, occupying fully ten years, would be counted by our present-day authorities as educational, in the full sense of the word. His brief career as a postmaster and a merchant had also their value since they utilized in practical ways some of his acquisitions, in reading, writing, and arithmetic. In addition, they gave him more time for reading than farm work allowed, and they helped him to discover in himself certain capacities for dealing with the people about him. He was thus daily cultivating his accomplishments as a public character, a raconteur and entertainer, and a leader in tasks of social reform. He was a faddist in a creditable sense. For instance, he advanced the wholly new idea that boys should not be cruel to animals. He was setting a sturdy example of what the followers of Thomas Hughes in England would have called "muscular Christianity" and what the disciples of Theodore Roosevelt cultivated.

It was no small part of Lincoln's education that he should have known so much about public lands. There was the question of Indian titles. Public and private land surveying, and the administration of the Government's land offices, the laying out of roads, all these were matters of familiar knowledge. The whole process of an organized rural community within a given area, such as a surveyed township of public land, with a certain number of settlers, who had come with government land warrants to locate claims and make homes, was as clear as daylight to young Lincoln.

In these new counties and townships certain forms assumed fresh life that had come down through the centuries from early periods of English local government. The settlers of southern Indiana and southern Illinois had brought the Virginia system of County government with them, while the settlers of northern Illinois, coming from New England and New York often by way of northern Ohio or southern Michigan, had brought their more highly developed institutions of the parish, or the township as they called it. When leaders from the north and south of this longitudinally extensive territory of Illinois met to form a State constitution in 1818, they found it necessary to work out a compromise between the New England town system and the Virginia county system. The early territorial and State legislatures of Indiana and Illinois were borrowing civil and penal codes from the older States, with such modifications as they found desirable. They were establishing local and higher courts of justice, and adopting codes of procedure.

It would be hard to invent, for young lawyers and aspiring publicists, better schools of training in the principles of constitutional government, of legislation, of jurisprudence, and of parliamentary law than were afforded by the process of setting up the major and minor institutions of a new State. Merely to have observed these constitutional beginnings in any such state was virtually a course of instruction in politics and government. Better still, to have had a part in working them out and putting them into effect, was more than an ordinary professional education. As a member of the Legislature and as a young practising lawyer, Lincoln had these unexcelled educational opportunities for growth in the sphere of public life and service.

W. H. Herndon, who was Lincoln's law partner for twenty-five years, referring to Lincoln as a reader and a student, made the following remarks in a private letter, afterwards published:

Mr. Lincoln was not a great general reader, but was a special one. When he wished to know anything he hunted it up and dug it out to the small, fibrous end of the very taproot. I say that Mr. Lincoln was a practical man, and hence he was a special man; that is, he worked for a practical and paying end. He did not much care to know anything that he would have no use for. Politics was his constant study and newspapers his ever present library.

Mr. Herndon's reflections are less important than his testimony. What he had observed and what he remembered—for this letter was written in Mr. Herndon's old age—was the patient industry with which Lincoln devoted himself to practical law cases and to actual issues of politics and government. But more significant than anything else, is the testimony that Lincoln made the "newspapers his ever-present library." Fortunately, we know what newspapers were available and what they contained. Precisely what the late James Ford Rhodes studied as the "research" material for much of his valuable political history of the United States, Mr. Lincoln had studied day by day forty or fifty years earlier. It happened that Lincoln read newspapers for the serious, practical purposes he had in mind, and they made him a man of broad, current intelligence regarding public affairs.

The late Dr. Talcott Williams, himself a prodigious reader, with an almost unequalled knowledge of American biography and political history, in 1920 wrote at my request an article entitled "Lincoln, the Reader," which is perhaps the best statement both for facts and for interpretation that has ever been made. Dr. Williams regarded Lincoln's education as a continuing process, through a devotion to reading that became more marked and more fruitful in results from his early beginnings to his election in 1860.

"Lincoln," says Dr. Williams, "to an amazing degree *is* the books he read. . . . Reading was his education. In these college days of required reading, taken up with about the enthusiasm and spontaneity of a tax assessment, the average student is haltered and fed at a manger, stall-fed. He knows little of the free pasture of letters and nothing of the joy of discovery 'when a new planet swims into his ken.' Lincoln's was all of this last sort; every book a discovery; every author ruled over a realm of gold. He was unschooled; his reading was his education." Dr. Williams finds

JOHN MARSHALL, CHIEF JUSTICE OF THE UNITED STATES

Lincoln was twenty-six years old when Marshall died. During that entire period, and even before Lincoln was born, Marshall had been presiding over the Supreme Court and writing its important decisions. It was a time when the precise meaning of the Constitution was often in doubt. The decisions of Marshall were read and discussed not alone by lawyers but by all those who were politically minded. They formed a part of Lincoln's training.

Lincoln "reading when the plow halted at the end of the furrow, on the way to the mill, on the fence watching cattle, wherever and whenever the book came, after a walk of from ten to twenty miles to the house that was reputed to have the precious treasure of a new book."

The influence of Lincoln's later reading upon his mature style is admirably shown by Dr. Williams in characterizing the stately utterances of the Presidential period. But it is particularly pertinent for us to note the importance attached by Dr. Williams to the study by Lincoln of our great political documents such as the Declaration of Independence, the "Ordinance for the Government of the Territory Northwest of the Ohio," the Federal Constitution, and the fundamental and statute laws of his own State. "Lincoln faced here," says Dr.

GENERAL LAFAYETTE'S ARRIVAL AT INDEPENDENCE HALL,
PHILADELPHIA, SEPTEMBER 28, 1824
Lafayette was only twenty years old when he came to America to aid the Colonies in the struggle
for independence in 1777. He returned in 1824, remaining more than a year and making an extensive
tour. The scene reproduced above is from a silk handkerchief printed in Germantown. Pennsylvania, to commemorate the visit of Lafayette to Philadelphia.

Williams, "the priceless advantage of our American system of written constitutions for the man whose youth was without the advantages of education or property. In England a lifetime, one might almost say two or three lifetimes from father to son, are needed before the English unwritten constitution can be understood in all its network of precedents and traditional practice. Any man with an alert mind who reads the Federal Constitution can understand the framework of our federal empire, its dual sovereignty, and the constant limitations on the powers of its consonant parts."

Lincoln's own idea of educational development through adult years was expressed in his eulogy on Henry Clay, delivered in the State House at Springfield, July 16, 1852. Referring to the fact that little was known of Henry Clay's ancestry, and even of his father who had died when Clay was a small boy, Lincoln continued: "Mr. Clay's education to the end of his life was comparatively limited. I say 'to the end of his life,' because I have understood that from time to time he added something to his education during the greater part of his whole life. Mr. Clay's lack of a more perfect early education, however it may be regretted generally, teaches at least one profitable lesson: it teaches that in this country one can scarcely be so poor but that, if he will, he can acquire sufficient education to get through the world respectably."

In the Library at William and Mary College, Virginia, is preserved the dingy and discolored volume of Blackstone's Commentaries that was owned and diligently used by John Marshall. He was patiently laying the foundations, in his father's log house in the uplands of northern Virginia, for his subsequent career as the great Chief Justice, whose masterly interpretations made the Constitution a working reality. Marshall was still on the bench when Lincoln was reading his own similar copy of Blackstone, and was beginning his local career as lawyer and member of the Legislature. Marshall's law studies had been benefited by a few weeks or months of study at William and Mary College while on furlough as a soldier in the later period of the Revolution. But he was not, like Jefferson and Madison, a man of scholastic training who had studied the classics and had enjoyed such advantages as William and Mary had given in the case of Jefferson or the influences and opportunities of Princeton as in Madison's case. Washington's was the greatness of sheer mastery, in a period that inevitably brought the best men to the front, regardless of schools. He also was a man of intellectual attainments, who grew in stature with every opportunity, and whose contacts and advantages were varied and important.

Of all the early statesmen it seems most satisfactory to select Marshall as the prototype of Lincoln. It should be remembered also that Marshall's decisions were a part of the subject matter of current political discussion during Lincoln's first twenty-six years (till Marshall's death in 1835) and ever afterwards. The newspapers of Lincoln's young manhood dealt principally with affairs of politics and government. Lincoln, at first hand or at second, could not escape being a student of Marshall's decisions; and it is impossible to avoid the conclusion that Lincoln's constitutional views were largely shaped by Marshall's reasoning. Thus Lincoln attached himself in very early life to the school of thought that was best expressed by Marshall, and from which Jefferson, Madison, and Monroe were ever more strongly tending to dissent.

It happens that in the late Mr. Beveridge's monumental life of John Marshall there occurs a passage comparing Lincoln with Marshall

LAFAYETTE AT THE TOMB OF WASHINGTON

From a colored lithograph widely circulated in 1857, upon the one-hundreth anniversary of the birth of Lafayette. It depicts an incident during the visit of Lafayette to America in 1824, when the distinguished Frenchman went to Mount Vernon to visit the grave of the leader under whom he had served in the Revolutionary War.

LAFAYETTE, A TERROR TO DESPOTISM

Reproduced from an old French engraving colored by hand. The French nation assisted by M. de Lafayette attacks the vipers representing despotism and surviving abuses of the feudal system, which had been terrorizing the people. After his services in the struggle for American independence Lafayette played a prominent part in the French revolutions of 1789 and 1830.

that is so felicitious, and so true to the facts, that I shall not fail to gratify my readers if I quote it at some length:

Indeed, the resemblance of Marshall to Lincoln is striking. Between no two men in American history is there such a likeness. Physically, intellectually, and in characteristics, Marshall and Lincoln were of the same type. Both were very tall men, slender, loose-jointed, and awkward, but powerful and athletic; and both fond of sport. So alike were they, and so identical in their negligence of dress and their total unconsciousness of, or indifference to, convention, that the two men, walking side by side, might well have been taken for brothers.

Both Marshall and Lincoln loved companionship with the same heartiness, and both had the same social qualities. They enjoyed fun, jokes, laughter, in equal measure, and had the same keen appreciation of wit and humor. Their mental qualities were the same. Each man had the gift of going directly to the heart of any subject, while the same lucidity of statement marked each of them. Their style, the simplicity of their language, the peculiar clearness of their logic, were almost identical. Notwithstanding their straightforwardness and amplitude of mind, both had a curious subtlety. Some of Marshall's opinions and Lincoln's state papers might have been written by the same man. The 'Freeholder' questions and answers in Marshall's congressional campaign, and those of Lincoln's debate with Douglas, are strikingly similar in method and expression.

Each had a genius for managing men; and Marshall showed the precise traits in dealing with the members of the Supreme Court that Lincoln displayed in the Cabinet.

Both were born in the South, each on the eve of a great epoch in American history when a new spirit was awakening in the hearts of the people. Although Southern-born, both Marshall and Lincoln sympathized with and believed in the North; and yet their manners and instinct were always those of the South. Marshall was given advantages that Lincoln never had; but both were men of the people, were brought up among them, and knew them thoroughly. Lincoln's outlook upon life, however, was that of the humblest citizen, Marshall's that of the well-placed and prosperous. Neither was well educated, but each acquired, in

different ways, a command of excellent English and broad, plain conceptions of government and of life. Neither was a learned man, but both created the materials for learning.

Of Lincoln's first twenty-one years of life, the initial seven years made him a Kentuckian, and the next fourteen years spent in Indiana, not far from the Ohio River, made him a Hoosier. Dismissing from our minds the false impressions produced by writers unacquainted with the life of that period, we would do well to adopt the less morbid and more sensible view of Lincoln as a fortunate and promising young man, whose opportunities had been upon the whole quite as advantageous as those of the majority of individual Americans who rose to eminence in the Nineteenth Century. A good mother had given him a proper start in life, had taught him to read, and had left him when she died with the companionship of a congenial sister. A stepmother with children of her own soon followed to preside admirably over the enlarged family circle. Practical work was no hardship to a lad who was growing tall and strong, and acquiring the physical prowess of a young Hercules.

Living near the Ohio River, Lincoln as a boy had seen hundreds of steamboats carrying passengers of cosmopolitan variety, besides all sorts of merchandise, domestic and foreign. He heard preachers and lawyers, and developed an early taste for public speaking. To know something of what the river activities of the Ohio and Mississippi signified in that period, and yet to fail in understanding the adventurous and instructive nature of Lincoln's first trip down these rivers to New Orleans, is merely to prove one's own lack of imagination. These experiences of Lincoln's were as mentally transforming and as important as George Washington's trip to the Ohio for Governor Dinwiddie, or the youthful visit he made to the West Indies. They might be compared with John Quincy Adams's early experiences in visiting Europe.

Lincoln was sixteen in the year 1825, when General Lafayette was spending memorable months as the guest of our nation, touring various parts of the country, and occupying space

THE OLD FRENCH CHURCH AT VINCENNES

Lincoln was twenty-one when he helped his father move from Indiana to Illinois. They passed through Vincennes, the old French trading post on the Wabash founded in 1731, and afterward capital of the Indiana Territory.

in the newspapers every day. Lafayette was in a steamboat wreck on the Ohio, near Troy, Indiana, no great distance from Lincoln's home. So far as I am aware, we have no evidence that Lincoln actually saw Lafayette in that situation. But so overwhelming was the enthusiasm that attended the movements of the gallant Frenchman who had fought through our Revolution, and had made a later record of leadership in his own country, that nobody neglected any possible opportunity to set eyes upon him in the years 1824 and 1825.

A brochure entitled "Lincoln the Hoosier," published at Indianapolis in 1927, gives us what is undoubtedly the normal and true picture of our young American in these years of growth to manhood. It contains admirable paragraphs on the migration of the Lincoln family to Illinois:

Lincoln had almost grown to manhood. He was, as he says, almost six feet four inches in height. In trials of strength with those of his age and older, he had proved himself a superior man.

His father had relinquished to the Government part of his farm and now held but eighty acres. Brilliant reports were coming to them of the fertility of land in Illinois. Thomas Lincoln probably did not know that for four generations the Lincolns had been born in one State, married in another, and died in a third. Thomas Lincoln was only preparing for the fulfillment of the destiny of his race.

So a contract of sale was drawn up and the Gentrys later came into possession of what is historically known as the Lincoln Farm, the farm which for fourteen years was the home of the sixteenth President, the home where the various influences that make character were steadily at work. The family prepared to leave the familiar scenes, and the little knoll to the south of the cabin, where sleeps Nancy Hanks Lincoln, and her neighbors, victims of that peculiar malady.

A team of oxen and an ox-cart sufficed for the family on its pilgrimage. The neighbors gathered round and said a sad farewell. The Lincolns had become genuinely liked.

Slowly they took their way westward and northward. At Vincennes they stopped for the last time in Indiana. There Lincoln could not have failed to see the new cathedral, its tall, thin spire standing out high above all the other buildings of that time. Here also he must have visited the home of General William Henry Harrison, a building of such magnificence and beauty as he could never have seen with the possible exception of the days he

WHERE LINCOLN EMBARKED FOR NEW ORLEANS

This is the ferry-landing at Rockport, Indiana, where Lincoln set out on his first flatboat voyage down the Ohio and Mississippi, in 1828. He was working for Mr. Gentry, of Gentryville, Indiana, and was hired to help take a load of produce to New Orleans. Three years later, after he had moved to Illinois, Lincoln made a second flatboat voyage to New Orleans. This sketch and the one on the facing page are by Constance Forsyth, made on the spot for a booklet entitled "Lincoln the Hoosier."

spent in New Orleans. Here, certainly, he saw a printing press for the first time in his life.

Vincennes also was the oldest town in Indiana that Lincoln had ever visited. He could hardly have known the romantic history of that city except in a general way. But it is such a place and such a history as must have kindled his imagination and left with him a fine and permanent picture of Indiana as he passed out of it in 1830.

In Indiana he was leaving behind the burial spot of his mother. He was leaving the scene of his first efforts at labor and at scholarship. Here he had hewn great timbers and split rails. Here he had delivered his first addresses; here he had written his first articles; here become imbued with his first ambitions of service and achievement. Here he had known his first great sorrow. Here he had first thrilled to the touch of a woman's hand. Here he had caught his first glimpses of the greater world as it went by on the bosom of the great Ohio. Here he had learned to labor and to wait, to earn his bread by the sweat of his brow, to look the world in the face and, unashamed, to ask of it a just recognition.

A RAFT ON THE MISSISSIPPI IN LINCOLN'S YOUTH
While living at Gentryville, Indiana, Lincoln's employer sent him down the Ohio and Mississippi rivers to New Orleans with a raft-load of produce. With him was his employer's young son, Allen Gentry. Three years later, while living in Illinois, Lincoln and his half-brother, John D. Johnston, and a second cousin, John Hanks, hired themselves out to take a flatboat to New Orleans.

CHAPTER IV

A Frontier Youth Encounters Slavery

Lincoln's flat-boat voyages to New Orleans—The family moves from Indiana to Illinois—A period of national expansion—Henry Clay and the turbulent campaign of 1824

To THE MAKING of the character and capacity of any man who achieves worthy success in after life, every early experience, remembered or not, will have contributed in its measure. Diaries were not often kept in log cabins, as indeed they are too seldom kept anywhere. Marvelous things happen, and are wholly lost because never written down, and because deaths, migrations, or other circumstances so frequently break the thread of transmission by word of mouth. The patient biographer is likely to learn, even in cases where the written materials are most abundant, that what we can find out is only fragmentary after all. It is always much less than the sum total of a rounded and full record. Washington left extensive diaries, but for the most part the entries tantalize us by their meagerness. They had no other purpose than to serve as memoranda for Washington himself. He had no thought of helping posterity to know details about the life of a great man.

It happens, however, that Washington was involved in large affairs from his very youth, and he was obliged to make written reports and to carry on extensive correspondence about things of a public nature. If Lincoln had been in Washington's place, he would have been entirely capable of making the famous journey and writing the significant report of 1753. The French were then building forts in the Ohio Valley. Washington was a young surveyor, not yet twenty-two years old. Governor Dinwiddie of Virginia, on behalf of the British

Government, sent Washington as a messenger to warn the French at Fort Duquesne, now Pittsburgh, and to find out what they were doing, what they claimed, and what they intended. Washington did his errand, made a careful and well-informed report, and this was published as a small volume in London.

I am not writing the story of Washington, but I am making allusions that have some bearing upon the circumstances that affect the career of Lincoln, and that help us the better to comprehend it. Washington's report was followed by activities—including the Braddock expedition—that led to the momentous French and Indian War, and to the ultimate acquisition by the United States of the Ohio Valley, where Lincoln was born, and in which he spent his lifetime until he journeyed to Washington to take the presidential oath of office on March 4, 1861. Far greater resemblances than differences appear if we dwell upon essential things and disregard some matters of external circumstance, when we compare the early lives of Washington and Lincoln.

As for the records that disclose matters of a more personal and private kind, in both cases the investigators have been at work, with their labors still uncompleted. Thus genealogists have been studying the Washington family, even as they have been studying that of Lincoln; and it is likely to appear that as regards the dignity and standing of the two families at the time of their early migration from England to the United States—the Lincoln family to Massachusetts and the Washington family to Virginia—there would be little to choose.

For the most part, families have always taken their own affairs for granted, and have been exceedingly careless about preserving accurate records for the enlightenment of their descendants. Through the efforts of a number of later collectors of data, including Miss Tarbell, Dr. Barton, the late Senator Beveridge, Mr. Warren, and Mr. Sandburg, we have been bringing to light things about the life and times of Lincoln that were indeed well known to his associates but that had been lost because the familiar things are so seldom set down on paper at the very time, by those who could do it best.

Without apology for repetition, it should be emphasized that Lincoln was the product of great movements in an amazing period of modern history. He was identified with American nationalism at its most expansive stage, during the first half of the third century of the settlement of English-speaking people on this continent. Thomas Jefferson was still President, during the three weeks that followed Lincoln's birth, and he survived as the illustrious Revolutionary patriot who had written the Declaration of Independence. Then as now his fame

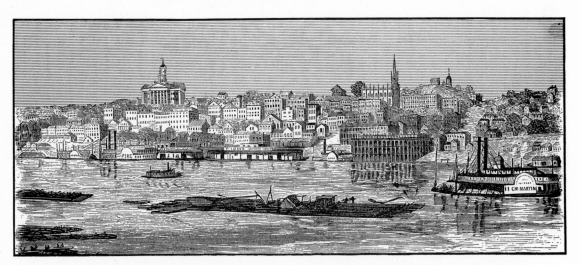

VICKSBURG, THEN THE LARGEST CITY IN MISSISSIPPI, WHICH LINCOLN SAW ON HIS WAY TO NEW ORLEANS

From an early print. Note the flatboats, and the steamers that were already appearing on the river.

was that of a personage of unfading world renown. And his busy and influential life at Monticello continued until Lincoln was in his eighteenth year.

To have memorized the Declaration while its author was still living was to render the more real and vivid the political doctrines as well as the events of the period—fifty years to a day—from July 4, 1776, to Jefferson's death on July 4, 1826. No one could forget that it was Jefferson who had in 1803 seized the opportunity afforded by certain exigencies in the great game of European imperialism to buy from Napoleon the country west of the Mississippi. It was with the problems arising from the settlement and political adjustment of all this vast Louisiana territory, as followed by later acquisitions, that Lincoln had to deal through his public career.

While still living in Indiana, at the age of nineteen, Lincoln had joined in building a flatboat, and with another adventurous youth, whose father was his employer, he had floated down the Ohio and the Mississippi to New Orleans. Thousands of young men had thus embarked upon our western rivers for long journeys. There was nothing uncommon in the adventure; but because Lincoln was himself uncommon his impressions and observations were an important element in his education and in the forming of his opinions. He came into some contact with people of three races and colors, but particularly he encountered the institution of Slavery as a social and economic fact in the settlements and on the plantations which his flatboat passed, and at the many landing places where he and his comrade briefly paused.

New Orleans was a comparatively small city, but highly cosmopolitan with its population of French and Spanish Creoles, its slave market, its shipping under various flags, and its experience of just twenty-five years of American rule. Steamboats for a number of years had been plying the western rivers, and Lincoln's return (1828) was made as a steamboat passenger.

The removal of Lincoln's father and family by ox-teams from Indiana to Illinois had occurred when the youth was twenty-one, and his own master. To be exact, the move began on March 1, 1830, less than a month after his twenty-first birthday. Having assisted his father in building a log house, clearing land and settling the family, the vigorous and adaptable young man found some local employment through the winter, and—as a part of a local tradesman's business enterprise—he was engaged in the early spring to help build another flatboat and to carry a cargo of agricultural products down the Mississippi.

It was in the early summer of 1831, soon after his twenty-second birthday, that Lincoln made his second voyage as a flatboat navigator to New Orleans. He had been learning and thinking, in these three years; and he was the better prepared, as a responsible citizen rather than an adventurous boy, to observe conditions and to form opinions. He found himself strongly out of sympathy with slavery. Again, he found himself drawn toward the policy of internal and coastwise improvements—roads, canals, waterways, harbor construction, and shipping encouragement—that the Whigs were advocating. We had a vast country to occupy and develop, and Lincoln followed Clay in believing in the constructive American policies that the Whigs (and afterwards the Republicans) proclaimed, as against the Democratic view that these things were no part of the business of the federal government under strict interpretation of the Constitution.

The year 1832 marks a turning point in American politics. The Federalists, in spite of the ability and eminence of their leaders, had over-reached themselves in the bitterness of their antagonism to the Jeffersonian policies that had culminated under Jefferson's successor, James Madison, in the War of 1812. The Federalists were relatively conservative and pro-British. They were concerned with the shipping and commercial interests of the eastern seaboard, and regarded Jefferson's embargo policies as more fatal to their ships and ocean trade than the high-handed and piratical policies of the European governments which, in rivalry with one another, had attempted to control the movements of neutral merchantmen. Late in Madison's second term the Federalist leaders had held a convention behind

THE SLAVE MARKET AT NEW ORLEANS

In 1828 and again in 1831 Lincoln made the river voyage to New Orleans. On the second trip he
spent a month there, and it is known that he visited the slave market. He was twenty-two years
old, and what he saw impressed itself deeply. The illustration is from an old English engraving.

closed doors at Hartford, in opposition to the
war and the Administration. They had lost
all hold upon the sympathies not only of the
South and West, but of great masses of plain
citizens in the East.

The Federalism of Presidents Washington
and John Adams, supported by the financial and
constructive genius of Alexander Hamilton
and the statesmanship of John Jay and many
others, stands well upon its own merits and
needs no defense, although it made some mistakes and was not tactful enough in appealing
to the new spirit of democracy. Once in
power, President Jefferson and President
Madison had adopted federalistic methods for
all practical purposes, by such bold measures
as the acquisition of Louisiana and the policies
that were involved in the War of 1812.

The Hartford Convention had the misfortune to have been held as the war was ending,
and just before General Andrew Jackson's
thrilling victory at New Orleans over an army
of British regulars, led by the Duke of Wellington's brother-in-law, General Pakenham,
The Hartford Convention was not, in fact,
wholly secessionist, its fire-eaters having been
brought under control of wiser and more
patient men. It was not so objectionable as has
usually been assumed. But certain of its members, who were sent to Washington to present
its views, arrived just as the news of Jackson's
victory, relayed from New Orleans, had
crossed the Potomac to the national capital.
The whole country was emotionally wild over
the great victory of January 8, 1815, and it was
especially welcome at Washington because in

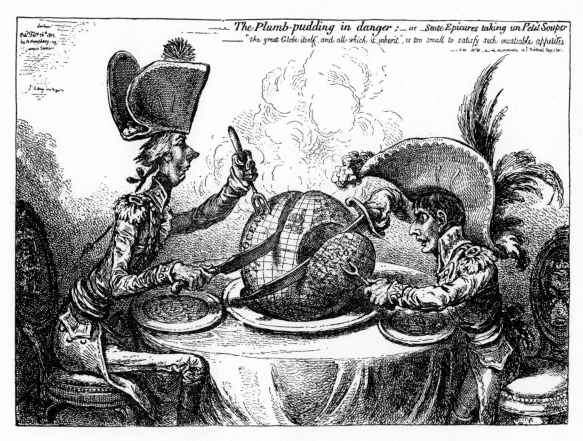

The Plumb-pudding in danger : — or _State Epicures taking un Petit Souper_
— "the great Globe itself, and all which it inherit", is too small to satisfy such insatiable appetites

THE PERIOD IN WHICH LINCOLN GREW UP—A CARTOON BY GILLRAY

Lincoln was twelve years old when Napoleon died. French victories over Austrians and Russians at Austerlitz, over Prussians at Jena; British defeats of Napoleon by Nelson at Trafalgar and by Wellington at Waterloo—these events, still fresh in memory, shaped the destinies of Europe and of America while Lincoln was young. When he went to New Orleans in 1828 it was but twenty-five years after the great Louisiana territory had been purchased from France. This drawing, was made by James Gillray, the leading English caricaturist of that period. Pitt, Prime Minister of England, and Napoleon are dividing the world between them. It is reproduced here as throwing a sidelight upon the time in which Lincoln grew up, and also as indicating the influence of European caricaturists upon their fellow-craftsmen in America.

August, less than five months earlier, several British regiments under General Ross had occupied the federal city and burned the Capitol and the White House, with other public buildings, thus deeply humiliating our officialdom.

James Monroe, who had filled many public positions since his service as a young officer in the Revolution, and who was Secretary of State in Madison's Cabinet, was the unrivalled heir-apparent of what was then called the "Virginia dynasty." The fact that our commissioners had signed a peace treaty in Ghent on Christmas Eve, some two weeks before the Battle of New Orleans, without any express references to the causes of the combat, or the questions at

issue, might have furnished the Federalists with some ground for criticizing so costly and destructive a war against the British Empire. But in politics military victories count for more than diplomatic documents. Jackson's victory had simply wiped out the Federalist party as a nation-wide influence, and it had given the Democrats an ascendency that lasted (with the brief interruption of Harrison's single month in 1841 and the Taylor-Fillmore quadrennium, 1849-53) until the election of Abraham Lincoln himself in 1860.

In those days the dominant party called itself "Republican," or "Democratic-Republican"; but these designations were soon dropped in

A POSTER CARICATURE OF THE CAMPAIGN OF 1824

The reader will note an extraordinary improvement in the drawing of campaign posters as he advances from this chapter through the next half-dozen. This is a very early example. The four candidates for the Presidency in 1824 are pictured as engaged in a foot race: John Quincy Adams, Andrew Jackson, William H. Crawford, and Henry Clay. Their admirers make various comments— puns being a favorite form of humor—"Hurrah for our *son Jack!* "You needn't be so *Cla*-morous! "He'll even get the better of the *Quincy*," etc. Clay, toward the right has not yet started to run. Jackson wears his military uniform.

favor of the useful name "Democratic," which has always since held its place. The nomination of Mr. Monroe was brought about by a caucus of Republican members of Congress. It is worth remembering that Henry Clay was then in Congress from Kentucky, and that he was present at this meeting of members that made Monroe the party candidate. With Ohio and Indiana admitted as States (having followed Kentucky, Vermont, Tennessee, and Louisiana, as additions to the original thirteen) there were now nineteen States in the Union. Mr. Monroe received the electoral votes of all except Massachusetts, Connecticut, and Delaware. Those three States supported Rufus King of New York as Federalist candidate. But the party that had passed the Alien and Sedition Laws, and had been responsible for the Hartford Convention, was moribund. It never regained vitality.

There followed the "Era of Good Feeling," as it has always been termed, parties having ceased for a few years to assert themselves on

well-organized national lines. Mr. Monroe was widely experienced and excellently qualified, but not a heaven-born leader of men, or a masterful statesman in his hold upon the assembled representatives at Washington. His Secretary of State, John Quincy Adams of Massachusetts, had been trained by his father from boyhood for a public career, had filled diplomatic posts in several European countries while still very young, was a man of great learning, of eloquence, and of literary skill, but not versed in the arts of political management.

The country was doing its best to recover from a struggle that had taxed public and private resources very heavily. The War of 1812 had almost paralyzed the once prosperous activities of the merchants and ocean traders of the Atlantic seaboard for three long years, and it left the government of the United States with a public debt of a hundred million dollars— which was regarded as a heavy obligation at that time. The country was too busily engaged in making up its losses and reviving its business energies, to be unduly concerned over politics. But localities and regions were asserting themselves, new sectional leaders were coming to the front, personal rivalries and ambitions were beginning to affect the general harmony, and the country was slowly preparing to divide again on partisan lines.

The War of 1812 had cut off the ordinary supply of European imported manufactures, and had laid the foundations for the great American textile industry, while reviving the Hamiltonian arguments for a protective tariff in order to build up the economic independence of the United States.

Henry Clay of Kentucky had popular gifts that were lacking in President Monroe and his Secretary of State, Mr. Adams. He was in passionate sympathy with the uprisings under General Bolivar and other Latin American leaders for the expulsion of the Spanish colonial authorities from the western hemisphere. General Jackson's experiences with the Spaniards in Florida—following the earlier crisis when the Spaniards had closed the mouths of the Mississippi to the western farmers and traders whose thousands of flatboats, keelboats, and rafts had been carrying food products and cotton to New Orleans for export—had given the West an abiding hatred of the Spanish government in its exercise of control anywhere on our side of the Atlantic.

Mr. Clay in Congress was a leader of moving eloquence, and the Monroe Administration had no reason for sympathy with Spain. The United States led the world in acknowledging the independence of the new South American republics. When the Holy Alliance, made up of the chief rulers of continental Europe, after the Congress of Vienna, had shown signs of willingness to aid Spain in the recovery of her American empire, the Monroe Doctrine was proclaimed in 1823. Jefferson had been consulted and had approved, and the South and West especially were in accord with the courageous assertion of the purpose of the United States to support the liberated portions of the western hemisphere in resisting further efforts to subject them to European imperial control.

War had awakened once more the restless, pioneering spirit; and thousands of families from the East were moving with their ox-teams, horses, and covered wagons along the main trails, or were continuing to float down the Ohio. New York in 1825 completed the Erie Canal; and while this brought western products to the East for local consumption or export, it also carried thousands of families to Buffalo whence they moved farther west, many of them carried by the new steamboats on the Great Lakes.

To look a little further back, it should be noted that the Northwest Ordinance, providing for the organization and government of the territory that was afterwards divided to form Ohio, Indiana, Illinois, Michigan, and Wisconsin, had provided that slavery should be forever excluded from that area. This had, doubtless, considerably affected the movement of population, not only in numbers, but also in respect of sentiment and character. This trend is well shown by statistics. Kentucky had about 75,000 people in 1790, and in 1800 it had three times as many—more than 220,000—while Ohio in 1800 had only one-fifth as many—about 45,000. But in 1820 Ohio had outstripped Kentucky; and in the census of 1830, while Kentucky had 688,000, her neighbor north of the river had 938,000. Indiana, with a handful of people in 1800, had almost 350,000 in 1830. Illinois, which was admitted to the Union in 1818 with about 50,000 people, had almost 160,000 in 1830.

The South was also growing rapidly, with settlers who were disposed to utilize rather than to abolish the economic institution of Slavery. Thus Tennessee, with only a fourth of the population of Massachusetts in 1800, had far surpassed Massachusetts by 1830. Georgia, Alabama, Mississippi, and Louisiana had been gaining with astounding strides between 1810 and 1830, largely by reason of the world's demand for cotton. These shifts in population through the first half of the Nineteenth Century were the most determining of all influences and factors in the ups and downs of party politics. They also were the determining causes of the Mexican War, with the territorial annexations that followed it. Finally, they supplied the causes that precipitated the Civil War, while also they furnished the men, the resources, and the large nationalistic and unifying motives that brought the war to its conclusion, with the permanent and fully accepted results of an undivided nation under adequate central authority.

The career of Abraham Lincoln could not possibly be understood apart from these facts of national expansion, and the great sectional growth of the West and the South. The same general facts, largely economic, entered as an essential element into each succeeding presidential contest. Also, they form the necessary background for the study of the political fortunes of hundreds of other men besides Abraham Lincoln, some of whose names are written in the pages of school histories, while most of them though once prominent are now forgotten.

"Young Harry of the West," as Clay continued to be called long after he had outlived the stage of boy orator and precocious statesman, was regarded as the country's rising hope, with a great future that must surely lead to the presidency. But General Andrew Jackson was the hero whose reward must come first in the estimation of the South, and this opinion was shared not only in the new communities north of the Ohio, but also to some extent in northern New England, where the

HENRY CLAY, FOR WHOM LINCOLN CAMPAIGNED
Clay, idol of the Whig party, was three times defeated for the Presidency. He ran fourth in 1824, and lost to Jackson in 1832 and to Polk in 1844. He also was a prominent candidate in 1840 and 1848, though he failed to get the nomination; and in those years the Whig candidate won. Meanwhile he served conspicuously in public office for nearly forty years—in the House of Representatives, as Secretary of State, and as United States Senator. Above is a campaign poster of 1844.

plain farming folk had as yet hardly emerged from pioneering conditions and where the bold spirit of "Old Hickory" made a peculiar appeal. These rustic Yankees, like the rough frontiersmen of the South and West, were not only out of sympathy with the superior culture and the refined manners of the "aristocrats" who shared in the fortunes of the "Virginia dynasty," but they were almost equally in revolt against that other scholarly group identified with Boston and Cambridge, with Hartford and New Haven, and, to some extent, with New York City, of whom John Quincy Adams seemed to them an intellectual survival, even though he was not a subservient disciple of his father's political friends. The younger Adams was comfortable enough in his Democratic associations, as Secretary of State under Monroe. Also he was the best-trained man in sight for the presidency.

But the older States of the Atlantic seaboard had run the country long enough, and the new populations west of the Alleghenies were in aggressive mood. Not only did the great valley of the interior make its claim as a region, but it also had two pieces of presidential timber that loomed above all others, and these were Andrew Jackson of Tennessee and Henry Clay of Kentucky.

These two were not the only candidates by any means. President Monroe himself was inclined to favor his Secretary of the Treasury, a substantial and experienced citizen of Georgia, William H. Crawford. John C. Calhoun of South Carolina, and De Witt Clinton of New York, had their supporters. The plan of a congressional caucus was discarded. The more general practice employed in 1824 was that of the naming of favorites by State legislatures. Thus Clay was named by Kentucky and afterwards by Missouri, Ohio, Illinois, and Louisiana. General Jackson, first presented by a local mass convention in Tennessee, was named by many groups and bodies throughout the country. The Legislature of South Carolina presented Mr. Calhoun. Mr. Crawford was endorsed by the Legislature of Virginia. The New England States through their Legislatures were formally for Adams, although in the subsequent election popular sentiment favored some of the other candidates.

Election methods were by no means uniform at that time, presidential electors in several States being chosen by the Legislatures. There was no clear majority of electoral votes for any candidate, and, under the Constitution, three names had to be referred to the House of Representatives for final choice. Some of the Clay electors had shifted ground, so that Jackson, Adams, and Crawford were the names referred to the House. The electoral votes had stood: for Jackson 99, John Quincy Adams 84, William H. Crawford 41, Henry Clay 37.

Mr. Clay was himself Speaker of the House at that time and very popular. Upon his friends rested the responsibility of throwing the decision either way, as between Jackson and Adams. The representatives of thirteen States supported Adams, seven were for Jackson, and four for Crawford. Chief Justice Marshall administered the oath to Mr. Adams on March 4, 1825, and Andrew Jackson, who was then a Senator, promptly offered his congratulations. But General Jackson did not forgive Henry Clay, who could, if he had so chosen, have influenced his friends in Congress to vote for the candidate who had undoubtedly received a considerable plurality of the popular vote,

and who had received 99 votes as against 84 for Adams in the returns of the presidential electors. Clay became Secretary of State, and was unjustly accused of having made a previous bargain with the friends of Adams.

This situation arose half a dozen years before Abraham Lincoln had attained his majority, and had begun to take his local place as a young man greatly concerned about politics. But it created passionate differences which lasted for many long years; and even the children of the West, taking their views from the excited talk of their elders, became violent partisans of Andrew Jackson or devoted admirers and followers of Henry Clay. It happened that Lincoln—not so much through accidents of family or environment that determined the party allegiance of most citizens, as because of admiration for Clay's brilliant speeches, and natural agreement with his views —became an avowed supporter of Clay. As the anti-Jackson elements became coalesced in the new Whig party, Lincoln was soon known among his neighbors as an active and consistent Whig politician.

It is always interesting to note in studying American politics how the careers of eminent public men have overlapped. Thus Jackson, who was born in 1767, was fighting at the age of fourteen as a Revolutionary soldier in the Virginia campaign that resulted in the victory of Washington and Lafayette and the surrender of Lord Cornwallis at Yorktown. In Tennessee he had become a lawyer holding local positions, then rapidly a member of Congress, a United States Senator and a Supreme Court Judge of the State, while Washington and the elder Adams were still occupying the presidential chair. It was later that he had conquered the Creek Indians, and had become a Major-General in the War of 1812.

After Jackson's crowning success in defeating the British at New Orleans in 1815, he had taken a leading part in the acquisition of Florida by purchase from Spain, and he had become our first Governor of the new Florida Territory. In 1823 he went back to the United States Senate, in which, for a year or two, he had also served a quarter of a century earlier. In popular opinion, he was destined to become

THE GRAND NATIONAL CARAVAN MOVING EAST

Andrew Jackson, though unsuccessful in the campaign of 1824, was elected four years later and re-elected in 1832. This is a cartoon of the Jacksonian era. The banners proclaim the conquering hero: "Sound the trumpet, beat the drums." "Honor and gratitude to the man who has filled the measure of his country's glory." Jackson is astride the leading horse, with Vice-President Van Buren behind him. Jackson was the first President from a State other than Massachusetts or Virginia. He was born in western North Carolina, and had practised law at Nashville, Tennessee.

President sooner or later; and Congress was doubtless more scheming than wise in refusing to elect him in 1824. Jackson defeated Adams in 1828, and Clay in 1832. Though Clay was nominated again in 1844, changed conditions gave the victory to Polk. In 1848 the results of the Mexican War demanded a military hero rather than a seasoned statesman, especially a statesman who, like Clay or Webster, had been vigorously opposed to the war policy of President Polk, and had thought our invasion of Mexico unjustified, high-handed and inspired by unworthy motives. Lincoln loved Clay not less, but favored a Whig soldier.

THE LOG CABIN IN WHICH ANDREW JACKSON LIVED

In 1804, after Jackson had been Congressman, Senator, and Tennessee judge, he purchased a plantation near Nashville. The log cabin on that plantation was his home for fifteen years, and still remains near the mansion that is shown on page 46.

CHAPTER V

Lincoln's First Taste of Politics and War

*The presidential careers of John Q. Adams and Andrew Jackson—
Lincoln announces his candidacy for the Legislature, serves in the
Black Hawk War, and is defeated at the polls*

LINCOLN ATTAINED his twentieth birthday while John Quincy Adams had still nearly a month remaining of his single term in the White House. It would be wholly against the probabilities that Lincoln was not already politically-minded. He was "talking politics" every day, and trying to learn to express himself, in the arguments of his Hoosier community at the post office, the blacksmith's shop and the country store. He had become a reader of newspapers; and these were a repository of political literature of high educational value. Undoubtedly he was seeing the lithographed cartoon posters that even then were finding distribution throughout the country.

The disappointment of the Jacksonians in 1825 had intensified a feeling that was even more strongly exhibited in the rural neighborhoods of the West than in the towns and cities of the East, where people were more generally occupied with business and private affairs. The newspapers, as I have already intimated, were strikingly different from those of our generation. Lacking telegraphic news and with comparatively little development of the art of local reporting, the press was heavy and documentary. President's messages and formal addresses were

JOHN QUINCY ADAMS
Sixth President of the United States

Before his election, in 1824, Adams had been United States Senator from Massachusetts; Minister to Holland, Germany, Russia, and England; and Secretary of State under Monroe. He became President when Lincoln was sixteen and served until Lincoln was twenty. From 1831 until his death in 1848, Adams the former President served as a member of the House. He died in his seat there, and Lincoln—then also a member—represented the Illinois delegation at the funeral.

given ample space. And it should be said that nothing could have been better reading for the young student of politics than the perfectly phrased messages of President Adams, and the speeches of his brilliant Secretary of State, Henry Clay. Lincoln's tendency from the very beginning had been to associate himself with the intellectual and rational minority, rather than with the more emotional masses that had naturally rallied around the banners of Jackson, fully convinced, and asking for no high arguments in the sphere of statesmanship.

The inaugural address and the four annual messages of President Adams are state papers that will always stand as models. Along with clarity and beauty of style, they expounded policies with moderation of tone but with firmness of logic, and they set forth the facts of government finance and the nation's public business in a succinct but adequate manner. Above all, they handled many diplomatic and international situations with an ability that no statesman anywhere in the world in that day could have surpassed. Adams and Clay were the strongest supporters of the new South American republics, and were sending diplomatic representatives to the old Spanish cities that had now be-

A CARTOON OF 1828, WHEN ADAMS AND JACKSON WERE OPPOSING CANDIDATES
A circular letter dated "Centreville, July 19, 1828," was alleged to have urged supporters of John Quincy Adams to persuade doubtful voters, and to have "at least six strong and courageous men at the polls." This cartoon is the answer of the supporters of Andrew Jackson. It shows a voter, who maintains that he is doubtful, being dragged and pushed to the voting place by six Adams men. Adams himself, in the window, remarks: "Let us not be palsied by the wishes of our constituents." Jackson behind the tree at the right, says: "Let the people's unbiased will prevail."

come republican capitals. They were endorsing the Pan-American Congress that leaders in Central and South America had called to assemble at Panama.

Two foremost lines of domestic policy were ably presented by Adams, one being that of the steadily enlarging program of internal improvements, particularly highways and canals, under government aid and direction, while the other was the policy of increasing the rates of certain tariff schedules. Successive advances in average tariff rates had already made it clear that the country had abandoned the pretext of levying customs duties for revenue only. It was building higher tariff walls, behind which our "infant" industries could find protection against British and other foreign goods. This protective policy was generally favored in the West, and it found many adherents in the older states of the North Atlantic, where manufacturing had begun to equal shipping and ocean-borne commerce in the profitable employment of labor and capital. But this protective policy was strongly opposed in Virginia, the Carolinas and Georgia, and also in the newer cotton states of the lower South.

Very little manufacturing on a commercial basis had been attempted in the South, although plantation and household industries for local supply were common. The South wished to sell its cotton, tobacco, and other products in Europe at good prices and to bring return cargoes of textiles and other manufactured goods, bought at better prices than those of New England, New York or Pennsylvania, where mills and factories enjoyed the advantages of a protective tariff.

In 1828, toward the end of the Adams administration, there was enacted a new tariff measure which came to be designated by its critics as the "Tariff of Abominations." The Jacksonian Democrats held the protective tariff to be unconstitutional in principle, and sectionally discriminatory and unjust in its actual provisions. Taking this view of the tariff, for consistency's sake they also assailed the policy of internal improvements at federal expense, declaring it to be contrary to the meaning and intent of the Constitution. Thus the lines were actually forming for a definite readjustment of parties. There were leaders of the first rank on both sides, and there were differences of opinion about important matters. Both of these things are requisite to the existence of strong and continuing parties.

During Adams's entire term, his administration lacked majority support in the Senate. At first he had strength in the House of Representatives; but in the ensuing Congressional election the Jacksonians captured the House. The factional spirit was kept alive especially by the determination of the Jackson men to right the wrong of Jackson's previous rejection by the House.

About some occurrences of that time there was no partisan disagreement. Lafayette had come to the United States as the nation's guest, and was sent back to France in September, 1825, on the frigate *Brandywine* after a protracted sojourn of more than a year. For more than forty years following his youthful services as an officer under Washington in the Revolutionary War, Lafayette had played an important part in the political affairs of France.

The country, aglow with enthusiasm for the achievements of Washington and his compatriots, was linking the name of Bolivar, the great South American liberator, with those of Washington and Lafayette. Adams was officially eulogizing the heroes of the Greek Revolution, and the nation was in a mood for assertion and self-congratulation. It would be a dull and unwarranted conception of Abraham Lincoln and his Indiana environment at that time, to suppose that

they were not as ardently affected by Lafayette's visit, by the freeing of South America, and by the struggle of the Greeks against the Turks, as were the citizens of Virginia or other eastern States. These matters were part and parcel of the educational outfitting of Abraham Lincoln.

There was no doubt about the selection of candidates in 1828. Adams was running for a second term by the common consent of all his supporters, and there was no formality of any kind that gave him a party nomination. Jackson, on the other hand, was put in nomination by the legislature of his own State of Tennessee three years before the election was actually held. Various other State legislatures, caucuses, and local political groups, endorsed Jackson's nomination from time to time. It was only necessary to conciliate the friends of Mr. Crawford in Virginia, Georgia, and elsewhere; and this was done by the adroit Mr. Van Buren of New York, who made a Southern tour on behalf of Jackson as the undisputed candidate of the Democratic party.

It is interesting to note that by this time the choice of presidential electors had become a matter of popular vote in every one of the twenty-four States then existent except in South Carolina, where the legislature continued to appoint the electors. It is also to be observed that eighteen States chose their electors on a general State ticket, which is now our universal practice. On the other hand, four chose their electors by districts (which is by far the more suitable and desirable plan), these four being Maine, New York, Maryland, and Tennessee.

Jackson received nearly 55 per cent. of the popular vote and Adams more than 45 per cent. But majorities were so distributed among the States and districts as to give Jackson 178 votes in the electoral college and John Quincy Adams only 83. Adams carried all the New England States strongly, with New Jersey and Maryland. The Jackson majorities in New York, Ohio, Indiana and Kentucky were not large. In Louisiana it happened also that the voting was almost even, but otherwise Jackson swept the South overwhelmingly. In Illinois, also, Jackson's vote was double that of Adams, this being largely due to the more rapid development of the southern part of the State. The author of a judicious narrative history of the United States very popular more than half a century ago, characterized President Jackson's personality, and set forth his policies in so fair a summary that I find it well to quote his statement at length. Says John Clark Ridpath:

The new President was a military hero. But he was was more than that; a man of great native powers and inflexible honesty. His talents were strong but unpolished; his integrity unassailable; his will like iron. He was one of those men for whom no toils are too arduous, no responsibility too great. His personal character was strongly impressed upon his administration. Believing that the public affairs would be best conducted by such means, and to reward his friends for their party service, he removed nearly seven hundred officeholders, and appointed in their stead his own political friends. This practice came to be known as the Spoils System. It was adopted by Jackson's successors and was continued till after the Civil War.

In his first annual message the President took strong ground against rechartering the Bank of the United States. Believing that institution to be both inexpedient and unconstitutional, he recommended that the old charter should be allowed to expire by its own limitation in 1836. But the influence of the bank, with its many branches, was very great; and in 1832 a bill to recharter was brought before Congress and passed. To this measure the President opposed his veto; and since a two-thirds majority in favor of the bill could not be secured, the proposition to grant a new charter failed.

The year following Jackson's veto of the bank bill was one of great excitement on account of his determination to remove the government deposits from the old bank. This he accomplished through his secretary of the treasury. The bank officials were greatly chagrined at this bold action of the President, and by withholding their customary loans from other banks and business firms, they brought on a financial crisis of wide extent. Thousands of people petitioned the President to replace the deposits, but he was inflexible and refused to

LAFAYETTE AT THE HERMITAGE

When the Marquis visited the United States in 1824, nearly half a century after he had aided the Revolutionary army, he was widely acclaimed and remained for a year. He is here shown calling upon the hero of the Battle of New Orleans, at Jackson's home near Nashville, while on an extended steamboat tour of the sparsely settled region west of the Alleghenies. This was before Jackson's election as President and just after his first campaign.

be moved, declaring that any institution that had the power to disturb the business of the country to such an extent had no place in a republican government. Jackson won in the end and the United States Bank ceased to exist at the expiration of the old charter.

The reopening of the tariff question occasioned great excitement in Congress and throughout the country. In the session of 1831-32 additional duties were levied upon manufactured goods imported from abroad. By this act the manufacturing districts were again favored at the expense of the agricultural States. South Carolina was specially offended. A great convention of her people was held, and it was resolved that the tariff law of Congress was unconstitutional, and therefore null and void. Open resistance was threatened in case the officers of the government should attempt to collect the revenues in the harbor of Charleston. In the United States Senate the right of a State, under certain circumstances, to nullify an act of Congress was boldly proclaimed. On that issue occurred the famous debate between the eloquent Colonel Hayne,

Senator from South Carolina, and Daniel Webster, of Massachusetts, perhaps the greatest master of American oratory. The former appeared as the champion of State rights, and the latter as the advocate of constitutional supremacy.

But the question was not decided by debate. The President took the matter in hand and issued a proclamation denying the right of any State to nullify the laws of Congress. But Mr. Calhoun, the Vice-President, resigned his office to accept a seat in the Senate, where he might better defend the doctrines of his State. The President, having warned the people of South Carolina against pursuing those doctrines further, ordered a body of troops under General Scott to proceed to Charleston, and also sent thither a man-of-war. At this display of force the leaders of the nullifying party quailed and receded from their opposition. Bloodshed was happily avoided; and in the following spring the excitement was allayed by a compromise. Mr. Clay brought forward and secured the passage of a bill providing for a gradual reduction of the duties complained of until, at the end of ten years, they should reach the standard demanded by the South.

The Jacksonian times were turbulent and the administration, as a New England author once expressed it, was "one which those who enjoy a quiet life can never dwell upon with pleasure." Jackson ran the government with a high hand and believed that, as the personal choice of the people, he was ordained to have his own way. He scorned consistency, and he was not sensitive to the discord that his activities produced. But he built up the Democratic party in what have since been many of its distinctive characteristics. It has been more personal in its tone, and rather more inclined to make politics a business, than the opposing party.

The same New England historian declares of Jackson: "His adoption of the principle first formulated by Marcy, that 'to the victors belong the spoils of the enemy,' was applauded and approved. He degraded national politics to the level of a game wherein the shrewdest and the strongest, rather than the best and the wisest were to come off the victors; yet he merely extended the operation of a principle that had long been dominant in the affairs of the great States of New York and Pennsylvania, and gave to a great majority of the people of the country a government of a sort which they preferred to that which had preceded it. Thus he attracted more than he repelled; he pleased more of the men of his generation than he offended; and when the appeal was made to the voters to pass judgment upon his doings, a compact, enthusiastic body of his supporters confronted a disorganized and discordant opposition."

It was in the thick of this Jacksonian ferment that Abraham Lincoln, the young citizen, stepped forth to begin his career as Abraham Lincoln the public man. He decided very sensibly to begin by announcing himself a candidate for the Illinois State Legislature. He had returned from his second flatboat voyage to New Orleans, landing at St. Louis

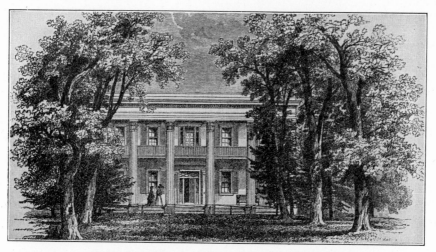

THE HERMITAGE—HOME OF ANDREW JACKSON

In his youth Jackson was forced to struggle with poverty. He was born near the line between North and South Carolina, in 1767, and grew up in a log cabin, as other frontier people did in those days. He studied law and became a substantial citizen in eastern Tennessee (then a part of North Carolina), even before the War of 1812 brought him fame and the Presidency. A log cabin continued to be the Major-General's home, however, until 1819. Then he built the mansion shown above, on his plantation near Nashville. From 1829 to 1837 he occupied the White House; and from that time until his death in 1845 he again lived at the Hermitage.

and walking from that point back to his home. These experiences had accounted for the first half of the year 1831. For the next few months, Lincoln occupied himself variously, utilized opportunities during the winter to make local friends, and improved his knowledge of English grammar and diction. His village of New Salem was some fifteen or twenty miles from Springfield, and Lincoln was destined before long to become a citizen of the larger place.

Meanwhile, his river experiences had interested him deeply in the question of transportation as affecting the development of his vicinity. Steamboats were coming up the Illinois River in increasing numbers, and Lincoln was studying the possibility of some improvement in the Sangamon River, a branch of the Illinois, that would enable small steamboats of light draft to come up as far as Springfield.

However unimportant this would seem nowadays, the idea was highly plausible at that time, and strong in its appeal, because of the lack of railroads and the necessity of teaming over the soft prairie wagon trails, with black mud to the hubs in wet weather. Most decidedly Lincoln was for internal improvements. He made his first announcement of candidacy for the Legislature about March 1, 1832. Because I like the phrasing of that announcement, and because of what one may read between the lines in view of all that had happened to crystallize Lincoln's opinions, I am taking the liberty to separate the sentences for better emphasis:

ANDREW JACKSON
Seventh President of the United States

As the head of Tennessee volunteers who had defeated the Creek Indians, Jackson's military genius was recognized by appointment as a Major-General in the regular army in 1814, and eight months later he won the Battle of New Orleans. He received the largest vote for President in 1824, but since he lacked a clear majority, with four candidates running, the election was thrown into the House, and Adams was chosen. Four years later Jackson overwhelmingly defeated Adams for the Presidency, and four years after that he was re-elected over Henry Clay.

"Fellow-citizens: I presume you all know who I am. I am humble Abraham Lincoln.

"I have been solicited by many friends to become a candidate for the Legislature.

"My politics are short and sweet, like the old woman's dance.

"I am in favor of a National Bank.

"I am in favor of the internal improvement system, and a high protective tariff.

"These are my sentiments and political principles.

"If elected, I shall be thankful; if not it will be all the same."

This announcement was followed at once by an extended statement which was printed as a hand-bill for distribution throughout the county. Lincoln had completed his twenty-second year. His address was in admirable style, and it discussed various topics with a careful weighing of words and a quality of practical wisdom that suggest the writings of Benjamin Franklin. It argued for a carefully considered policy of internal improvements, and very properly appealed to the local constituency by a discussion of their own problems of communication. He wrote intelligently on behalf of measures for the more general diffusion of education. "Upon the subjects of which I have treated," he declares, "I have spoken as I have thought. I may be wrong in regard to any or all of them, but, holding it a sound maxim that it is better only sometimes to be right than at all times to be wrong, so soon as I discover my opinions to be erroneous, I shall be ready to renounce them." In this first document, Lincoln's reasonableness shines forth.

He concludes with the following characteristic paragraph:

> Every man is said to have his peculiar ambition. Whether it be true or not, I can say, for one, that I have no other so great as that of being truly esteemed of my fellow-men, by rendering myself worthy of their esteem. How far I shall succeed in gratifying this ambition is yet to be developed. I am young, and unknown to many of you. I was born, and have ever remained, in the most humble walks of life. I have no wealthy or popular relations or friends to recommend me. My case is thrown exclusively upon the independent voters of the county; and, if elected, they will have conferred a favor upon me for which I shall be unremitting in my labors to compensate. But, if the good people in their wisdom shall see fit to keep me in the background, I have been too familiar with disappointment to be very much chagrined.

I have been at some pains to compare this first announcement of Lincoln as a candidate for an important office with the statements made by Theodore Roosevelt when, soon after his graduation at Harvard, he entered practical politics as a candidate for the New York Legislature. He was also aged twenty-two when he made his appeal for votes some fifty years later. And I have had in mind the political expressions of other young men of education and opportunity, as they were entering upon a public career. I have not discovered that any one of them showed better reasoning processes, or a firmer grasp of principles and of the policies that he had chosen to espouse, than Abraham Lincoln.

The State election was to occur in August; and in April Governor Reynolds of Illinois called upon General Neale of the State militia to organize volunteers for a campaign against the Sac, Fox, and Winnebago Indians, who were under the leadership of a famous chief known as Black Hawk. Many of these Indians still occupied territory which had been ceded by them to the United States more than twenty years earlier. Now that settlement was requiring their removal, they took to the war path. The call was printed at Springfield on April 19th and Lincoln joined a company that was at once organized. It was evidence of his prestige and his hold upon the young men of the neighborhood that he was promptly elected captain, as they marched to the area of disturbance. Troops of the United States Army had also appeared on the scene and the militia had little fighting to do. Lincoln's adventures as a soldier in 1832 were soon ended, the companies being mustered out after a few weeks.

Such an experience, however, had some value in giving personal confidence to a young man who had determined upon a course that was to lift him out of humble and precarious occupations as a private citizen. and launch him upon a political and professional career. Undoubtedly Lincoln would have made a good soldier and a meritorious officer if the occasion had brought him to the test.

Although we have no clear record of it, he must have made numerous speeches throughout the county in the two months pre-

GENERAL ATKINSON'S VICTORY OVER BLACK HAWK
This is a crude representation, after the manner of the times, of the decisive battle of the Black Hawk War, in 1832. Lincoln was not present, though he had re-enlisted in a company of independent scouts after his own volunteers—who had chosen him Captain—had been mustered out.

THE NATION'S BULWARK: A WELL-DISCIPLINED MILITIA
A Philadelphia caricature of 1829

Under the laws of the new State of Illinois, every able-bodied man between 18 and 45 was required
to drill twice a year or pay a fine of one dollar. Lincoln might have drilled with such a squad.
When the Indians under Black Hawk invaded northwestern Illinois, in 1832, Lincoln responded to
the call for volunteers and was elected Captain; but he was never under fire.

ceding the vote for presidential electors. There
was the more reason for making speeches,
because the national campaign had set in with
remarkable vigor. The Democrats had nominated Jackson for his second term, and the
"National Republicans," as the party of Clay
to which Lincoln adhered was now called,
had held the first regular convention of a
major party. They had nominated Henry
Clay for the Presidency with great enthusiasm. A subsequent rally of the "Young Republicans" had been held, to endorse the Clay
ticket; and this young men's gathering
adopted a ringing platform. This was the
first party campaign platform of which we
have any record. The example has been followed by party conventions ever since. The
Young Republican movement was as active
in Illinois as elsewhere, and Lincoln was one
of its leaders in his own neighborhood. His
brief announcement of principles was simply
a re-echoing of the platform of the men who

were there and elsewhere supporting Clay.

Jackson's victory was, of course, to have
been expected. The people took affairs into
their own hands, and henceforth for a long
time they governed through parties. Previously the government had been that of a body
of representative men sent to Congress from
whose numbers Cabinets were recruited, diplomatic agents selected, and judges elevated
to the federal bench. Jackson was at odds
with this Washington element of the trained
and representative public men. For one
thing, he believed in the direct election of
Presidents by the people. This was natural
in view of the fact that he had been the victim of the complicated electoral college in
1824, followed by the arbitrary preference of
Congress for Adams early in 1825. He was
opposed to banks and their money power, but
so were the plain people at large. He had the
habit of success and he was regarded by the
untutored masses as an invincible hero. As

a character in history we can appreciate Jackson's good qualities and find much to attract us in his powerful and self-reliant personality. Lincoln was not bitter or personal in his partisanship, but he reasoned thoughtfully against most of Jackson's positions. He had chosen his views and affiliations so firmly that they sufficed for the future.

By way of keeping convenient record of the campaigns in which Lincoln was active it may be noted that the National Republicans held their convention at Baltimore on December 12, 1831, this being eleven months previous to the election. Several Southern States had no delegates, but there was a credentials committee and the convention was not a mere mass meeting. Henry Clay was nominated unanimously, and John Sargeant of Pennsylvania was named for the Vice-Presidency. In lieu of a platform the convention issued an address strongly attacking the Jackson administration. It was at Washington in May, 1832, that the young men's ratifying convention was held, which adopted a platform in a series of ten resolutions. After defense of the protective policy and that of internal improvements, came a resolution upholding the authority of the Supreme Court and another defending the Senate in the exercise of its functions. The attitude of Jackson as regards all these subjects was criticized, as was his partisan removal of officials.

The Democrats met in convention at Baltimore on May 21, 1832, and endorsed by acclamation the general demand of the party for Jackson's renomination. On its second day the convention adopted a rule to the effect that in voting for President and Vice-President "two-thirds of the whole number of votes in the convention shall be necessary to constitute a choice." Under this rule Martin Van Buren was nominated for the Vice-Presidency. The popular vote was divided in the same proportions as in the previous election, Clay receiving about 45 per cent. and Jackson about 55. In four or five of the Southern States no Clay electoral ticket was in the field. When the electoral votes were counted, Jackson had received 219 and Clay 49. Again Lincoln's young State of Illinois went strongly for Jackson, this time about three to one.

Lincoln himself was beaten in his local contest, but on analysis it appears that, although failing to gain the office, his canvass had been a most remarkable success. The county was extensive and several thoroughly well-known and mature lawyers were among the thirteen candidates for the Legislature. The county was entitled to four, and those coming in at the top of the list were elected under the Illinois statutes. The triumph of Lincoln as a beginner in politics lay in the fact that his own voting district of New Salem disregarded party lines altogether and gave him 277 votes out of a total of 280 that were cast.

BORN TO COMMAND

OF VETO MEMORY

HAD I BEEN CONSULTED

KING ANDREW THE FIRST.

THE JACKSONIAN ERA IN AMERICAN POLITICS
Jackson was the first President to have serious and prolonged difficulites with Congress and the other arms of the government. He acted promptly and firmly when South Carolina passed the ordinance nullifying the tariff in 1832, and with equal promptness in vetoing the bill renewing the charter of the United States Bank. Jackson is here portrayed as trampling upon the Constitution and the laws. Bitter as was the opposition he met, it was exceeded by the popular enthusiasm he aroused.

This State election was held early in August, three months before the national election and not many days after Lincoln's return from his absence on military duty. His speaking through the county for Clay therefore came later, and was a thing apart from his own canvass. As showing his popularity among his neighbors on personal grounds it is recorded that in November the same precinct gave Jackson 185 and Clay only 70. But for Lincoln's influence it is certain that the Clay vote would have been much smaller. The four men elected to the Legislature were well-known citizens of Springfield and other places in the county. Among the nine who failed, Lincoln stood fourth, with nearly as many votes as those who ranked above him. He had made an excellent start and had become known thoughout the county.

The biographers are well occupied with interesting details of Lincoln's experiences following his military and political adventures of the year 1832. New Salem had been ill-chosen as the site for a growing town. Lincoln joined another man in carrying on a general store, but this venture proved financially disastrous in the end. But associated with it was Lincoln's appointment as postmaster in May, 1833, and he held the office for three years. Furthermore, he was appointed a deputy county surveyor for his portion of a county that contained two thousand square miles. The great tariff and nullification debates had taken place at Washington, and the messages of Jackson were published in the local paper at Springfield. Calhoun had resigned from the Vice-Presidency to take his place as a South Carolina Senator; and the speeches of Webster, Calhoun, Clay, and others, were appearing in the newspapers quite unabridged.

Lincoln was now a public man, permanently committed to the National Republican or so-called "Whig" positions, and he was studying the arguments with care and absorption. To have regarded him at this time as an ignorant, half illiterate backwoodsman would be to mistake trifling external things for essentials. Mr. Nicolay, his Secretary

THE RATS LEAVING A FALLING HOUSE

In 1831, as a result of a dispute among their wives, the Cabinet of President Jackson offered their resignations. Four of them had been known as the "busy B's"—Berrien, Branch, Van Buren, and Barry—and it is these four whose faces appear in this drawing.

in after life, characterizes Lincoln as he was at the moment when, in 1834, he decided to run again for the Legislature. Says Mr. Nicolay:

He could certainly view his expectations in every way in a more hopeful light. His knowledge had increased, his experience broadened, his acquaintanceship greatly increased. His talents were acknowledged, his ability recognized. He was postmaster and deputy surveyor. He had become a public character whose services were in demand. As compared with the majority of his neighbors, he was a man of learning who had seen the world. Greater, however, than all these advantages, his sympathetic kindness of heart, his sincere, open frankness, his sturdy, unshrinking honesty, and that inborn sense of justice that yielded to no influence, made up a nobility of character and bearing that impressed the rude frontiersmen as much as, if not more quickly and deeply than, it would have done the most polished and erudite society.

This election of 1834 was mainly a State affair, with a Governor to be chosen as well as a Legislature, though Congressmen were also to be elected. There were pending various questions having to do with public improvements in the development of the State. Again there were thirteen candidates for the lower house, and Lincoln took time to make a popular canvass. This time the highest vote was for a man named Dawson, credited with 1390, and Lincoln came next with 1376. The other two successful candidates were each of them more than 200 votes behind Lincoln. For a young man of twenty-five, without money or family influence, living in a decaying hamlet rather than at the center of the county, this was a victory of renown. It fixed Lincoln's position as a public man.

Here was one of the most promising young men of the United States, because of a rare combination of qualities. Without school advantages and without as yet having actually entered upon the study of law, he had become a careful reasoner about the questions that statesmen were discussing. He had been taking an extension course, so to speak, under Adams, Clay, Marshall, and Webster, without ignoring the arguments of Jackson, Calhoun, Hayne, Van Buren, and many others. Yet his knowledge of human nature and his shrewd, practical way of making personal contact, had been demonstrated in his campaign methods.

One of the four who were elected to the Legislature from Sangamon County in 1834 was a Springfield lawyer, regarding whom Lincoln afterwards made the following statement, referring to himself in the third person:

Major John T. Stuart, then in full practice of the law, was also elected. During the canvass, in a private conversation he encouraged Abraham to study law. After the election, he borrowed books of Stuart, took them home with him, and went at it in good earnest. . . . In the autumn of 1836 he obtained a law license, and on April 15, 1837, removed to Springfield and commenced the practice, his old friend Stuart taking him into partnership.

The hardest blow that befell Lincoln in his early manhood was the death of the refined, intelligent and charming girl, Ann Rutledge, to whom he had become engaged after returning from the Black Hawk campaign. The wedding was to have occurred as soon as Lincoln had been admitted to the Bar and had found it possible to assume family responsibilities. Her death occurred in August, 1835. For a time this bereavement seems to have broken Lincoln's spirit and to have affected his hold upon life. But recovery came with more determined effort to forget himself in his studies and his varied occupations.

SET-TO BETWEEN THE CHAMPION OLD TIP & THE SWELL DUTCHMAN OF KINDERHOOK 1836

The champion is William Henry Harrison, whose back is toward the reader. His second is Western Lad, and his bottle-holder is Old Seventy-Six. The Kinderhooker is Martin Van Buren, who faces the reader. Andrew Jackson seconds Van Buren, and the bottle-holder is "Little Amos [Kendall] of the Post-Office."

CHAPTER VI

Lincoln Becomes a Lawmaker

*Douglas a fellow member of the Illinois Legislature—Lawyers in the
politics of 1836—Lincoln a foremost Whig leader in his State—He
joins in a program of public improvements*

THE NEXT YEAR of major politics was
1836, when Lincoln was again elected
to the Legislature in spite of the fact
that he was a Whig in a Democratic State and
district. He had become acquainted with
many representative men of Illinois, and he
was the most active and influential of the
group who succeeded in securing the transfer
of the capital from Vandalia to Springfield,
this decision having been made during the ensuing session in 1837. Lincoln's removal to
Springfield and his beginnings as a lawyer are
of that same date. His leading part in the legislative contest over the capital location had
made him a Springfield favorite. He had now
taken up the definite career, as lawyer and
politician, that was to lead on to his own election as President just twenty-four
years after that of Martin Van
Buren in 1836.

In his legislative canvass, Lincoln
increasingly displayed that remarkable combination of the statesman's
seriousness and the politician's
shrewdness which at once inspired
confidence and brought popular support. Much of the tradition that
dwells upon his poverty, his shabby
clothes, his uncouth manners and his
inferiority in other aspects, may be
traced to his own habit of rather
humorous self-deprecation. The
Whig leaders were twitted by Democratic stump speakers upon their
"riding in fine carriages, wearing
ruffled shirts, kid gloves, massive
gold watch-chains with large gold
seals, and flourishing heavy gold-
headed canes," to use Lincoln's own
words in characterizing the charges
of an opponent. Lincoln exposed this
Col. Taylor as himself an example of

the ostentatious persons he had described as
typical Whigs. In contrast, Lincoln drew an
exaggerated picture of himself, as having once
worked on a flatboat at wages of eight dollars
a month, wearing shrunken buckskin breeches;
and, as a Whig, he added, "If you call this
aristocracy, I plead guilty to the charge." It
is well to remember that Lincoln was obliged
to sugar-coat his unpopular Whig affiliations
and his highly intelligent arguments with the
reassuring humor of the frontiersman. But
his humor, and his readiness in amusing the
rural audiences at the expense of a less worthy
antagonist, were merely incidental features of
his political campaign.

The best testimony for Lincoln's qualities
of mind and character at this time when he

THE OLD ILLINOIS STATE CAPITOL AT VANDALIA

When Lincoln was first elected to the legislature, in 1834, Vandalia
was the capital city. This particular building was erected in the summer of 1836, by local enterprise and without authorization. In
February of the following year, largely through the efforts of
Lincoln, the legislature voted to make Springfield the capital. The
Vandalia structure was last used as the Capitol in 1839, but is still
in use as a county courthouse.

53

was twenty-seven years old, is to be found in the meager but thoroughly convincing record that remains to us of his own words. On June 21, 1836, in the midst of the campaign, he wrote a letter to Colonel Robert Allen that—in perfect form and diction, but above all in its fine sense of personal honor and public responsibility—would have done credit to any statesman in American history. The letter in full is as follows:

New Salem, June 21, 1836.

Dear Colonel:—I am told that during my absence last week you passed through this place, and stated publicly that you were in possession of a fact or facts which, if known to the public, would entirely destroy the prospects of N. W. Edwards and myself at the ensuing election; but that, through favor to us, you would forbear to divulge them. No one has needed favors more than I, and, generally, few have been less unwilling to accept them; but in this case favor to me would be injustice to the public, and therefore I must beg your pardon for declining it. That I once had the confidence of the people of Sangamon county is sufficiently evident; and if I have since done anything, either by design or misadventure, which, if known, would subject me to a forfeiture of that confidence, he that knows of that thing and conceals it, is a traitor to his country's interest.

I find myself wholly unable to form any conjecture of what fact or facts, real or supposed, you spoke. But my opinion of your veracity will not permit me for a moment to doubt that you, at least, believed what you said. I am flattered with the personal regard you manifested for me; but I do hope that on more mature reflection you will view the public interest as a paramount consideration, and therefore determine to let the worst come.

I assure you that the candid statement of facts on your part, however low it may sink me, shall never break the ties of personal friendship between us.

I wish an answer to this, and you are at liberty to publish both, if you choose.

Very respectfully,

A. Lincoln.

Col. Robert Allen.

Sangamon County in this election was entitled to seven members in the lower House and two in the State Senate. It happened that the successful candidates were tall men, and they became known in the county and in the State as the "Long Nine," Lincoln being called the "Sangamon Chief," being the tallest of the group. It was the strategy of the Long Nine that secured the removal of the State capital. One of this group, Robert L. Wilson, said afterwards: "When our bill, to all appearance, was dead beyond resuscitation, and our friends could see no hope, Lincoln never for a moment despaired, but collecting his colleagues in his room for consultation, his practical common-sense and his thorough knowledge of human nature made him an over-match for his compeers and for any man I have ever known."

In view of the later prominence of the two men as political opponents, it is to be noted that Stephen A. Douglas—who was then only twenty-three years old but a Democratic politician and debater who had become as prominent in Morgan County as Lincoln had in Sangamon—was a member of this Legislature. Douglas vigorously opposed Lincoln in the struggle over the removal of the capital to Springfield.

Having left Vermont at fourteen for New York State, Douglas had later drifted on to Ohio. Following the rivers southward, then northward, in quest of a place where he might settle and become a lawyer, he had finally found his opportunity at Jacksonville, Illinois, and had been admitted to the Bar just before his twenty-first birthday. As a lad in the East, Douglas had been an ardent Jackson Democrat; and he seems to have brought with him from his six years in Ontario County, New York, and at the Canandaigua Academy, what were known then as the Albany ideas of party organization.

The headmaster of strategy and tactics of this New York school of Democratic politics was Martin Van Buren. He had long used his trained skill as a political manager in Jackson's interest. He was born at Kinderhook, a town on the Hudson River south of Albany, December 5, 1782, and had been admitted to the Bar at the age of twenty-one. He had filled various offices, and had been Attorney-General of the State. Beginning in 1821 he had served six years in the United States Senate and had then been elected Governor. He had been Secretary of State in Jackson's administration, and in August, 1831, he was sent as Minister to England.

Printed & Published by E.Jones.   128 Fulton Street N.York.

A DUEL.

This cartoon of the campaign of 1836 shows Henry Clay piercing Martin Van Buren, the Democratic nominee, with a sword labeled "tariff." Clay, though the most prominent Whig, was not the nominee of his party that year. The choice had fallen to Gen. William Henry Harrison, who stands at the left. At the extreme right is Andrew Jackson, then President, encouraging his protégé, Martin Van Buren. In the November Election, Van Buren defeated Harrison.

Arriving in London in September he was *persona grata,* but the Senate's refusal in January to confirm his appointment compelled his return. During Jackson's second term Van Buren was Vice-President of the United States, and he was Jackson's choice for the succession to the Presidency.

"Old Hickory's" views were law for the Democracy, but it required vigorous effort on Jackson's part to enforce that law in favor of Van Buren. The New York lawyer was not widely popular on his own account, but he was accepted as Jackson's lieutenant. Jackson's own State of Tennessee favored Senator Hugh L. White, and the Alabama Legislature had followed Tennessee. Jackson promptly countered the mutinous drifts by demanding a national convention; and in this he was successful. It was held at Baltimore in May, 1835, almost a year and a half previous to the election. The two-thirds rule was again adopted, for reasons rather specious than fundamental. All opposition had been beaten down and Martin Van Buren was unanimously nominated.

The Whig opposition to the Jackson-Van Buren dynasty was not homogeneous, and it was not considered feasible to hold a convention and to run the risk of failure to agree upon a candidate. It was thought by Whig politicians that the only possible way to beat Van Buren lay in encouraging several favorite sons to take the field by States or sections. Enough electoral votes might thus be secured to keep Van Buren from having a majority of the whole. Thus the election would be thrown into the House, where Jackson himself had been beaten twelve years earlier.

The leading Whig candidate was General William Henry Harrison of Ohio. The Legislature of that State, however, had expressed its preference otherwise and had nominated Judge John McLean. Daniel Webster was the foremost Whig of New England, and Massachusetts proceeded to nominate him. Judge Hugh L. White was running in Tennessee and elsewhere; and South Carolina, of course, would not support Jackson's candidate. Calhoun and Jackson had been bitter antagonists over the Nullification issue; and it was Calhoun's influence as Vice-President that had prevented the Senate's approval of Van Buren's appointment to London.

Mr. Van Buren received a slight popular majority over all the Whig candidates taken together. In the electoral college his vote was 170, while that of William Henry Harrison was 73. There were 26 electoral votes for Hugh L. White, and 14 for Daniel Webster (cast by Massachusetts). South Carolina electors voted for W. P. Mangum of North Carolina. Van Buren had carried all of New England except Vermont and Massachusetts. He had carried New York, Pennsylvania, Virginia, North Carolina, and most of the States farther south. Harrison had been successful in Vermont, New Jersey, Delaware, Maryland, Kentucky, Ohio, and Indiana.

Van Buren had also won Illinois, obtaining about 18,000 votes as against 15,000 for Harrison. The young Douglas had, of course, been an ardent Van Buren man in this successful campaign, and he was soon rewarded with what was then a lucrative and important federal position—that of Register of the Land Office at Springfield.

STEPHEN A. DOUGLAS

Douglas was four years younger than Lincoln. Both participated in the campaign of 1836, Lincoln supporting Hugh L. White and Douglas speaking for Van Buren. Both, in addition, were themselves elected to the Illinois Legislature, Lincoln for his second term. Douglas was born in Vermont in 1813, moving to Illinois at the age of twenty and being admitted to the bar. Previous to his election to the legislature, in the campaign with which this chapter is concerned, Douglas had been State's Attorney. After his legislative experience he served as a judge of the Supreme Court of Illinois. A later portrait of Douglas will be found on page 194.

Success in gaining political leadership and in securing elective or appointive office is a matter of personal qualities, but it is also affected profoundly by circumstances of time and place. Douglas had arrived in Illinois without acquaintance or credentials in 1833. He had secured pupils and taught a select school for a few months at Jacksonville, while studying the Illinois statutes, obtaining admission to the Bar, and beginning to practise in the lower courts. Yet within four years he was a leading member of the Legislature and a rising man in the political councils of the party that was in power in the State as well as in the nation. Lincoln, on the other hand, had lived in Illinois for only seven years. He also had made his own way without extraneous advantages of any kind.

Douglas in his school days in New York State had been the leading debater on the Democratic side, and all the more aggressively a supporter of Jackson and Van Buren because the Academy and the community were somewhat dominated by the anti-Masonic and Whig doctrines of that time. He had grown strong in his own convictions as the leader of the minority in his school. He

WHIG BAZAAR.

Publ ᵈ by H.R.Robinson, 52 Courtlandt St: N. York.

Van Buren, whom the cartoonist pictures as seeking to purchase a wig, had in the previous year defeated the Whig candidates for the Presidency. This is a poster caricature dated 1837, Van Buren's first year in the White House, which is remembered largely as a period of economic disturbances and financial panic. The dealer refuses to sell Van Buren a wig, but recommends Conservative oil for bald Democratic heads.

was gaining his reward rapidly in Illinois by finding his talents useful in a county and in a State where the Democrats were in majority. Lincoln, by way of contrast, had adopted Whig principles in his teens, and had gained in moral courage and mental power by a steady uphill fight on the unpopular side. He had gone to the Legislature regardless of parties, first, because of his own popularity, and second, because of his strong advocacy of certain State policies that were in accord with the speculative boom that was then prevailing in Illinois, as in other western States.

Both Lincoln and Douglas would have risen to eminence in any case; but their progress would have been less rapid in older communities, where they would have been overshadowed by middle-aged leaders. Wil-

liam Henry Harrison had gone from Virginia to Ohio in early days, and was heading for the Presidency. Jackson had left North Carolina at the right time to make his way in Tennessee from one position to another, until he had established his reign at Washington. Henry Clay had been born near Richmond, Virginia, in 1777 and—under circumstances similar to those that affected Douglas later in Vermont, his father also having died when he was a small boy—he overcame hardships, studied law, and was admitted to the Virginia Bar at the age of twenty.

But Clay proceeded at once to Lexington, Kentucky, where he began law practice in 1797. He was on hand in time to take part in forming the constitution of Kentucky, and in 1803, about five years after his arrival in the new State, he was an influential member of the Legislature. His political advancement in the State and in the nation during the next ten or twelve years was so rapid as to have been almost without parallel in our history, in view of his youth, except in the case of two or three men in the Revolutionary period, notably Alexander Hamilton.

We have had many other examples of the rapid political advancement of young lawyers appearing on the scene at the right moment in the formative periods of States still farther west. Thomas H. Benton as a lad had gone from North Carolina to Tennessee, and had passed on across the Mississippi to make his distinguished political record as a citizen of Missouri. Young men in older States, ready to begin life for themselves, had become eminent as lawyers, governors, and senators by settling at the fortunate time in Wisconsin, Minnesota, and Iowa. The same thing was true of Nebraska and Kansas. A generation later, hundreds of young lawyers found opportunity for the rapid realization of political ambitions by arriving opportunely to take part in the settlement and development of North Dakota, South Dakota, Montana, Washington, Idaho, Wyoming, Colorado, Nevada, Oklahoma, New Mexico, and Arizona. How Colonel Frémont's timely presence in California in the days of the Mexican War had catapulted him upon a meteoric career, is a story that will have its brief space in another chapter of this work, because Lincoln's career became involved with that of the picturesque explorer.

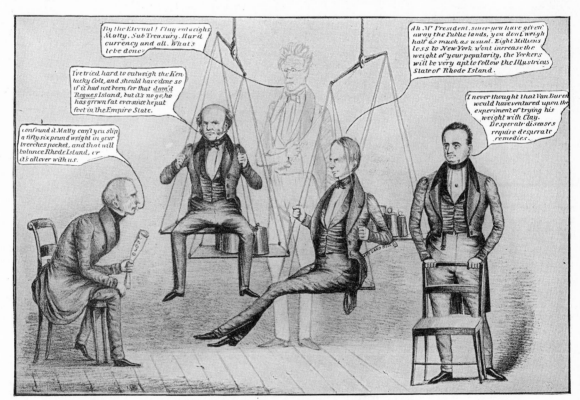

WEIGHED & FOUND WANTING.
OR THE EFFECTS OF A SUMMERS RAMBLE.

In the scales are Van Buren, at the left, who was then President, and Clay leader of the Whigs. At the right stands Daniel Webster, Senator from Massachusetts. The ghostlike figure in the background is Jackson, Van Buren's predecessor and guiding hand. This cartoon and the one on the opposite page are of the campaign of 1840, circulated in the interest of Clay—who did not, however, receive the Whig nomination. Both Van Buren and Clay in their "loop" conversations refer to Rhode Island. It was in this year that the cities of Rhode Island began to revolt against the domination of the agricultural districts. The climax of that revolt, known as Dorr's Rebellion, came two years later, when a "suffrage legislature" assembled, with Thomas W. Dorr as "Governor."

THE MEETING at SARATOGA.
*Like Boxers thus before they fight,
Their hands in friendship they unite.*

Henry Clay is here shown calling upon President Van Buren at Saratoga, in the President's home State of New York. "Like boxers thus before they fight, their hands in friendship they unite." At the left are Daniel Webster and Gen. William Henry Harrison, who with Clay were the outstanding political opponents of Van Buren in the campaign year 1840. They are commenting upon the cheering reception to Clay—"first always in the service of his country and great even among the greatest." The men in the background are supposed to be Clay followers who had pledged themselves to let their hair grow until they saw their idol in the White House. Saratoga, noted for its carbonated medicinal springs, was then a most fashionable resort, and leaders of all parties were visitors in the vast Saratoga hotels in the summer of 1840.

These observations in passing are the more relevant, since conditions familiar to older men, whose memories carry them back to the decades following the Civil War, have virtually ceased to exist, and might easily be overlooked by younger students of our political annals. "Native sons" are numerous enough now in the Western States to assert their prior claims over newcomers. But in Lincoln's time, and for a quarter-century after his death, it was still a practical thing for the youthful lawyer and politician to go West, establish himself in an infant community, and "grow up with the country." This is just what Lincoln and Douglas were doing, as each of them began life in the great State of Illinois at the age of twenty-one.

I am the more strongly impelled to make these remarks, because it remains a fashion of many writers, and of still more Lincoln's Birthday orators, to present their hero as an obscure man, with little prospect or hope of rising to fortune and fame, until he was almost fifty years old. But to have led in the selection of the permanent capital of his State while in his middle twenties; to have established himself in that capital city as a lawyer, steadily advancing in the esteem of the judges and fellow-practitioners; to have become one of the chiefs of his party in the Legislature and in State and local conventions, all well before his thirtieth year, was not to have been obscure or unpromising. In fact, Lincoln's third decade was marked by solid success.

It is to be remembered, further, that an American politician's rise to fame on the national plane is much affected by the question whether or not he belongs to the dominant party in his own State. If Lincoln had been a Democrat in 1836, his political advancement would have been much more rapid. Douglas happened to have that advantage. Mr. Dolliver and Mr. Cummins, who had gone to Iowa as young Republican lawyers from the same general region of western Pennsylvania and West Virginia, rose to the highest rank in State affairs and in the United States Senate. But there were two equally gifted young Democrats who could make no political headway in so strongly Republican a state as Iowa; and in due time one of them went to San Francisco and the other to St. Louis, each finding admission promptly to places of influence and distinction. As a Whig in a Democratic state, Lincoln made his way remarkably well.

To catch the spirit of the times, it should be noted that after the completion of New York's Erie Canal, in 1825, there was a veritable craze for canal building in Ohio, Indiana, and Illinois; that steamboats were multiplying on the Great Lakes, with Chicago rapidly growing; that river traffic also was booming, with the States of the corn-and-wheat-belt feeding the plantations of the lower South, while railroads were being projected everywhere with state and local aid. Lincoln would have been a rather solitary pessimist if he had not shared in the enthusiasm of the people of Illinois for these modern improvements. He had always been a be-liever in the policy of promoting the development of the country by government aid. He was even credited with having said that it was his ambition "to become the De Witt Clinton of Illinois."

As a candidate for re-election, he had made the following statement in June, 1836: "Whether elected or not, I go for distributing the proceeds of the sales of the public lands to the several States, to enable our State, in common with others, to dig canals and to construct railroads without borrowing money and paying interest on it." In the ensuing session of the Legislature he took a foremost part in promoting a program of public improvements that went too far in pledging the credit of the State. The optimism of that immediate period of land speculation, and of currency inflation through the unrestrained activity of State banks, was about to face a terrible blow in the nation-wide panic of 1837.

It is evident that Lincoln's constituents were not disposed to censure him for his part in creating the State debt, for they readily elected him again in 1838 and in 1840, and would have continued to do so if he had cared to serve longer than through eight continuous years. His party voted for him as Speaker of the House in 1838 and again in 1840; but the Whigs were in the minority, and he remained as active floor leader for his party. Although he had originally declared his preference for Hugh L. White as the Whig candidate for President in 1836, he was willing to join other Illinois Whigs in supporting William Henry Harrison.

A SCENE ON THE OLD ERIE CANAL—FROM AN EARLY ENGRAVING

A Definite Position on the Slave Question

The contest over slavery in free Illinois—Van Buren the first President to discuss slavery—Lincoln takes a courageous stand—Crusading Abolitionists, and their persecution

THE JACKSON POLICIES were at stake, and Lincoln was as strongly opposed to them in 1836 as he had been in 1832. The question of slavery was not an overshadowing issue at that time, and the Whig party still had its hold in some of the slave States. But the agitators on both sides were promoting discord, and in one way or another the subject forced itself to the front.

The points in his own career that Lincoln thought it worth while to set down in June, 1860, for the use of a friend who was proposing to write a brief campaign biography, are especially valuable as showing what he himself regarded as important. The question of slavery had come forward in the Legislature, in consequence of the spread of the Abolitionist movement. It is to be remembered that southern Illinois lay between the slave States of Kentucky and Missouri, and that a large majority of the State's early settlers were from slaveholding communities.

Under the Ordinance of 1787, Illinois, following Ohio and Indiana, was admitted as a free State. But, later, there had been serious attempts to assert the sovereignty of the State and to repudiate the guaranty of the Northwest Ordinance. In short, it was proposed to authorize the holding of slaves in defiance of the national limitations under which Illinois had been allowed to enter the Union. These attempts had been defeated; and with the rapid settlement of the northern and central counties from the Eastern States, there was no longer any danger that Illinois would legalize slave-holding. For some years, however, the anti-slavery clause of the State constitution had not been rigidly enforced in the southern counties. As evidence of this fact I have noted a table in the "American Almanac" for the year 1836. It gives the number of slaves in the several States according to the first five census enumerations. Illinois had 168 slaves in 1810; 917 in 1820; and 747 in 1830. But in this last year they were called "indentured colored servants."

This change of designation had followed the defeat of the pro-slavery movement by

LINCOLN, THE ILLINOIS STATESMAN
This portrait is of the period of the debates with Douglas, in 1858. It shows the man who had been Assemblyman, Congressman, presidential elector, and was emerging as a national leader in that most critical period of the nation's history.

WORSHIP OF THE NORTH

no wide margin in a popular referendum vote in 1824. But the Legislature had always remained pro-slavery in sympathy; and early in 1837, with Lincoln serving his second term, a committee had reported a set of resolutions "highly disapproving abolition societies" and otherwise catering to the sentiment then gaining control of the Democratic party, the object being to promote harmony at the opening of the Van Buren administration which began on March 4, 1837. Lincoln and five other members of the Legislature had voted against the resolutions, the large affirmative vote indicating the prevalent state of mind. The resolutions as adopted were not drafted with discrimination.

Lincoln was no fanatic at that time, or at any subsequent turn in the slavery discussion, but he had formed distinct views and he thought it well to put them on record. Accordingly, he drew up a protest and caused it to be entered on the Journal of the House in the proceedings of March 3, 1837. I have not seen it elsewhere noted that, with his fine instinct for timeliness in political action, he had presented this protest on the very eve of

"WORSHIP OF THE NORTH"

was the first of a series of "Confederate War Etchings" engraved on copper by Adalbert John Volck of Baltimore, during the war. There were twenty-nine in that series, once known, though now almost forgotten. But there were other Volck caricatures, even more striking, which have been unknown because never published hitherto, and are presented in these volumes almost seventy years after they were drawn.

The Lincoln head at the corner of the Chicago Platform, in this cartoon, is similar to Volck's clown caricature on page 12. At the left of the platform is Henry Ward Beecher, with the sacrificial knife. Charles Sumner bears a torch. Below is Horace Greeley, carrying a censer. In the middle foreground is Benjamin F. Butler, the Northern general so execrated in the South. Grouped around the Lincoln bust are Stanton, Seward, and other members of the Cabinet. General Scott and General Halleck are conspicuous. The statue is that of John Brown. Harriet Beecher Stowe is kneeling on a copy of "Uncle Tom's Cabin." Other well-known personages of the war period are in the picture.

They believe that the Congress of the United States has no power under the Constitution to interfere with the institution of slavery in the different States.

They believe that the Congress of the United States has the power, under the Constitution to abolish slavery in the District of Columbia, but that the power ought not to be exercised unless at the request of the people of the District.

The difference between these opinions and those contained in the above resolutions is their reason for entertaining this protest.

Only one other member of the Legislature was willing to join him in signing this memorandum, but Lincoln was already thinking in national terms as he was studying the debates of the closing session of Jackson's last Congress, and he was not cringing to local prejudice. He was definitely going on record as against Van Buren's position.

In his inaugural address, delivered on the day following the presentation of Lincoln's protest, Van Buren repeated a statement that he had previously made defining his attitude toward slavery as a public issue. He was the first President who had presented the subject of slavery to Congress in an official message. Referring to the difficulties that the forefathers had met and overcome, he remarked: "The last, perhaps the greatest of the prominent sources of discord and disaster supposed to lurk in our political condition was the institution of domestic slavery. Our forefathers were deeply impressed with the delicacy of this subject, and they treated it with a forbearance so evidently wise that in spite of every sinister foreboding it never, until the present period, disturbed the tranquillity of our common country." After appealing to the spirit of "generous and fraternal feeling amidst the violence of excited passions," Van Buren proceeded as follows:

Perceiving before my election the deep interest this subject was beginning to excite, I believed it a solemn duty fully to make known my sentiments in regard to it, and now, when every motive for mis-

Van Buren's inauguration. Since Lincoln twenty-three years later, in referring to this protest, declared that it "briefly defined his position on the slavery question; and so far as it goes, it was then the same as it is now," I may well quote it in full at this point:

Resolutions upon the subject of domestic slavery having passed both branches of the General Assembly at its present session, the undersigned hereby protest against the passage of the same.

They believe that the institution of slavery is founded on both injustice and bad policy, but that the promulgation of Abolition doctrines tends rather to increase than to abate its evils.

representation has passed away, I trust that they will be candidly weighed and understood. At least they will be my standard of conduct in the path before me.

I then declared that if the desire of those of my countrymen who were favorable to my election was ratified, "I must go into the Presidential chair the inflexible and uncompromising opponent of every attempt on the part of Congress to abolish slavery in the District of Columbia against the wishes of the slave-holding States, and also with the determination equally decided to resist the slightest interference with it in the States where it exists."

He regarded the fact of his election as authorizing his belief that these views on slavery were approved by "a majority of the people of the United States, including those whom they most immediately affect," and he nailed his pro-slavery flag to the mast with the declaration that "it now only remains to add that no bill conflicting with these views can ever receive my constitutional sanction."

My readers will perceive, therefore, that the Lincoln protest was directed squarely at the Van Buren position, and was not primarily concerned with the opinions of the Illinois Legislature. Neither Lincoln nor Van Buren had referred to the question of slavery in the new States of the Louisiana purchase, simply because the Missouri Compromise of 1820 was still accepted as having settled that issue. Arkansas had just been admitted as a slave State (June, 1836), Missouri having entered the Union in 1821. The practical question had to do with the District of Columbia, with Van Buren inflexible in his support of slavery, while Lincoln favored its abolition whenever the anti-slavery inhabitants of the District should be numerous enough to show a majority to that effect.

A WENDELL PHILLIPPIC
Wendell Phillips became the foremost orator in the anti-slavery cause, after his speech at Boston in 1837 in protest against the murder of the Rev. E. P. Lovejoy by a pro-slavery mob in Alton, Illinois. He later abandoned a law career, for he would not abide by an oath to uphold the Constitution as then interpreted by the courts against the rights of slaves as human beings.

It is enlightening to have Lincoln's protest of 1837 in mind when studying his bill, introduced in Congress more than ten years later, for the gradual abolition of slavery in the District of Columbia.

There had been something distinctive and rare in the calmness and naturalness with which Lincoln had taken his isolated position in the Illinois Legislature when he entered his protest of March 3, 1837, on the slavery question. A young man already so skilled in the arts of the popular politician, who nevertheless insisted upon the expression of his own convictions on questions of statesmanship without the slightest thought of temporizing, was likely to go far in influence and leadership—unless, indeed, his convictions were so erroneous in their nature that intelligent voters could not be gradually drawn to his side. There was intense feeling, and the mob spirit was abroad in the country; yet Lincoln set forth his principles and reasoned upon them with as little show of passion as if he were demonstrating his favorite problems in Euclid (for he had learned to like the logical symmetry that he had discovered in his study of geometry).

A few weeks earlier in that same year he had delivered a prepared address before the Young Men's Lyceum of Springfield. His subject was the perpetuation of our political institutions. It has been characterized by some of his biographers as an artificial and stilted piece of rhetoric, in no way to be compared with his later utterances as regards literary style. I may merely make the comment that there are advantages in studying Lincoln at first hand. The address is an admirable piece of writing, and nothing better has ever been said upon the danger of acquiesence in the actions of mobs whether in Maine or in Mississippi or Louisiana. He recounted facts of an ominous kind, showing the prevalence of lynching and the activity of mobs. He found in the agitations over slavery a widespread disposition to deal summarily with Abolitionists, while already in the North there was lawless activity against the enforcement of fugitive slave laws.

The address contains remarkably acute observations on the conditions that were shifting the motives and objects of popular hatred and passion. The long Revolutionary struggle had tended to unite American sentiment, and had done much afterwards to hold the country together in maintaining its new institutions. "I mean." said Lincoln, "the powerful influence which the interesting scenes of the Revolution had upon the passions of the people as distinguished from the judgment." And he proceeded as follows:

By this influence, the jealousy, envy and avarice incident to our nature, and so common to a state of peace, prosperity, and conscious strength, were for the time in a great measure smothered and rendered inactive, while the deep-rooted principles of hate, and the powerful motive of revenge, instead of being turned against each other, were directed exclusively against the British nation. And thus, from the force of circumstances, the basest principles of our nature were either made to lie dormant, or to become the active agents in the advancement of the noblest of causes—that of establishing and maintaining civil and religious liberty.

He found that there was danger lest we should invoke passion in our domestic matters and he declared that our temple of liberty must now be upheld by "other pillars, hewn from the solid quarry of sober reasoning." Those who have been discussing prohibition enforcement, would do well to read the following paragraphs from this speech of Abraham Lincoln to young men of his home town, delivered just sixteen days before his twenty-eighth birthday:

When I so pressingly urge a strict observance of all the laws, let me not be understood as saying

LIBERTY, EQUALITY, FRATERNITY

A cartoon by John Leech, in the London *Punch*, 1848, "dedicated to the smartest nation in all creation." England, having provided for the liberation of slaves in the sugar-growing West Indies as early as 1833, was inclined to jibe at American ideals of liberty. For years Brother Jonathan, or "Columbia"—representing the United States—was almost never pictured in *Punch* without a whip. John Leech and John Tenniel were the outstanding English cartoonists of their time. Both drew for *Punch*, their careers overlapping. In later chapters of this work there are many other drawings by Leech and by Tenniel.

there are no bad laws, or that grievances may not arise for the redress of which no legal provisions have been made. I mean to say no such thing. But I do mean to say that although bad laws, if they exist, should be repealed as soon as possible, still, while they continue in force, for the sake of example they should be religiously observed. So also in unprovided cases. If such arise, let proper legal provisions be made for them with the least possible delay, but till then let them, if not too intolerable, be borne with.

There is no grievance that is a fit object of redress by mob law. In any case that may arise, as, for instance, the promulgation of abolitionism, one of two positions is necessarily true—that is, the thing is right within itself, and therefore deserves the protection of all law and all good citizens, or it is wrong, and therefore proper to be prohibited by legal enactments; and in neither case is the interposition of mob law either necessary, justifiable, or excusable.

The Juvenile Department chronicled various unfortunate incidents in connection with the lives of children
of slaves—in this cut, the auction block.

The Ladies' Department paraphrased the slogan "Am I
Not a Man and a Brother?" adopted by the first abolition society late in the preceding century.

DEPARTMENT HEADINGS IN GARRISON'S "LIBERATOR" DURING 1832

In short, Lincoln stood firmly for law enforcement, or better still for obedient acceptance of law until in response to public opinion the law had been changed. Primarily,
it was the abolition question that was arousing the intensity of lawless passion that Lincoln deplored. The American Anti-Slavery
Society had been formed in 1833, and its
agents were traveling all over the country
organizing local societies. They were demanding "immediate" abolition, and since this
was obviously impossible it was producing a
kind of friction that moderate men regarded
as deplorable. The institution of slavery was
not to be uprooted by the Abolitionists of

that date, but they had a right to hold meetings and to discuss public policies; and the
breaking up of their meetings by mob violence everywhere was the thing that Lincoln
had calm courage to denounce.

Riots and mobs were as prevalent against
the Abolitionists in New England as anywhere else. George Thompson, the Scotchman who had secured British emancipation
in the West Indies, had come to Boston in
1834 and had delivered lectures at various
places for a year on the gradual emancipation
policy that had been put into effect by British
legislation. This would have seemed harmless enough, but Thompson had been obliged

VOL. I.]   WILLIAM LLOYD GARRISON AND ISAAC KNAPP, PUBLISHERS.   [NO. 24.

BOSTON, MASSACHUSETTS.]   OUR COUNTRY IS THE WORLD—OUR COUNTRYMEN ARE MANKIND.   [SATURDAY, JUNE 11, 1831.

The anti-slavery movement got well under way in 1832, with the establishment of a weekly
newspaper called the *Liberator*. It was founded and edited by William Lloyd Garrison, devoted
to chronicling the evils of slavery, and continued publication until the end of the Civil War.
This slave-auction heading was used during its first year.

THE ABOLITION GARRISON IN DANGER, & THE NARROW
ESCAPE of the SCOTCH AMBASSADOR.

A pro-slavery poster depicting an actual occurence. William Lloyd Garrison, editor of the
Liberator, was dragged through the streets by a Boston mob, with a rope tied around his neck;
and George Thompson, a Scotchman who had been influential in securing British Emancipation
of slaves, narrowly escaped such treatment. At that time abolitionist doctrines were almost as
unpopular throughout the North as they were in the South.

to use disguise to save his life in escaping from Boston mobs in November, 1835.

Nothing could better illustrate the atmosphere in which Lincoln's Lyceum address denounced mob law, nor does any circumstance throw more valuable light upon the filing of Lincoln's protest in the Legislature on March 3, than a tragic occurrence in Illinois only eight months later. A Presbyterian minister, Elijah P. Lovejoy, had established an Abolition newspaper at Alton, Illinois, in the strong pro-slavery environment of the southern end of the State. A mob, on November 7, 1837, sacked and destroyed his printing office, and shot and killed Mr. Lovejoy.

Abolition agents found that it was inviting death to penetrate the southern States with their demand for "immediate" freeing of the slaves. But they adopted the practice of sending their pamphlets and newspapers throughout the South in the mails. This aroused so much opposition that President Jackson in his annual message to Congress, December, 1835, had advocated the passage of a law to exclude Abolitionist publications from the mails. Such a bill was actually introduced, and Van Buren in his capacity as a candidate for the Presidency, being called upon to express himself, had come out in favor of the pending amendment of the postal laws. The bill to that effect was not carried to final passage; but the individual States and the local postmasters were allowed to rifle the mails at their own discretion, and thus Abolitionist publications were confiscated in the South and to a great extent elsewhere. With this spirit abroad in the country, it is obvious that the Abolitionist petitions, demanding that the District of Columbia be made free, were without effect and of no influence.

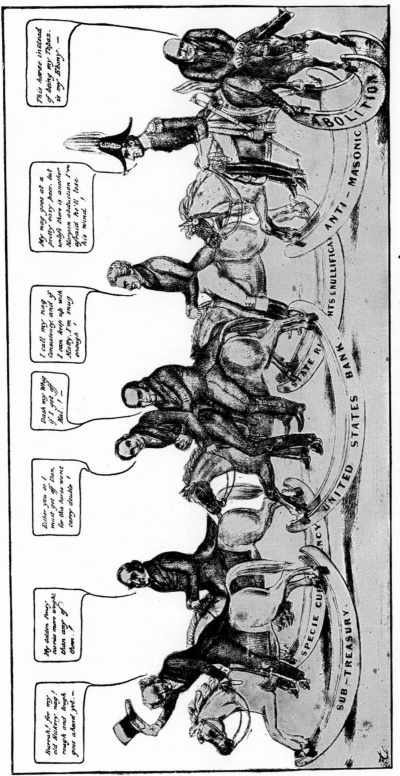

ALL ON HOBBIES, GEE UP, GEE HO!

Here are the leaders of American politics in 1838, each portrayed as riding his particular hobby—a President, a former President, four distinguished Senators, and a military idol. On the first hobby-horse is the President, Martin Van Buren, who was then advocating a Sub-Treasury system in place of the United States Bank. The second rider is Thomas H. Benton of Missouri, who was the chief supporter in the Senate of the financial policies of Van Buren. He rides his "Golden Poney." Benton was known as "Old Bullion" because of his fight for hard money against paper inflation. On the third horse are Henry Clay and Daniel Webster, who succeeded in defeating in the Senate the fiscal policies of Van Buren. Riding the hobby "State Rights and Nullification" is John C. Calhoun, who four years earlier had first maintained in the Senate that his State of South Carolina could nullify a federal tariff. The rider in military uniform, on the Anti-Masonic horse, is William Henry Harrison, hero of the Battle of Tippecanoe and of the War of 1812. He had been the candidate of the Whigs in opposition to Van Buren, in 1836, and had also accepted the nomination of the Anti-Masonic party which had come into existence as a result of the mysterious disappearance of William Morgan of New York, who had threatened to divulge the secrets of the Masonic order. On the last hobby-horse, Abolition, is John Quincy Adams, former President and then a member of the House of Representatives, who had assumed leadership in opposition to all measures fostering slavery. In 1836, Adams was perhaps the first to assert that slavery could be legally abolished by the exercise of the war powers of the Government.

Emancipation Projects ⊷ Lincoln's Plan

*He proposes gradual emancipation in the District of Columbia—The
African slave trade—British, French and Latin-American methods
for liberation of the Negroes*

LINCOLN NEVER CEASED to think that the methods of the Abolitionists were disrupting, harmful, and dangerous. But with his calm logic he also studied the subject of slavery in the Federal District. After Van Buren's inflexible stand on that question, subsequent Presidents (Harrison, Tyler, and Polk) had regarded that particular issue as settled, and had said nothing about it. In his inaugural address, March 4, 1845, Mr. Polk—who was, of course, a pro-slavery President—had confined himself to this single sentence in his allusions to slavery: "It is a source of deep regret that in some sections of our country misguided persons have occasionally indulged in schemes and agitations whose object is the destruction of domestic institutions existing in other sections—institutions which existed at the adoption of the Constitution."

Since Lincoln held to his own views on this question with such tenacity and consistency, I think it well at this point to refer to his position in Congress in 1849. It was still his opinion that if slavery were to be regarded as a subject with which each State might deal, it would be reasonable to regard the District of Columbia as a distinct entity, in which the residents might properly have some voice on such a question. The District of Columbia had been originally formed from territory ceded by Maryland and Virginia, in both of which slavery existed. Congress had full jurisdiction over the District, and could therefore abolish slavery if it so desired.

Van Buren had held, quite illogically, that slavery must continue in the District until representatives from the slave States were willing to have it abolished. Anti-slavery men, on the other hand, held that it was the duty of free-state majorities in Congress to convert the District into a free-state Territory. Lincoln, elected to Congress in 1846 and retiring on March 4, 1849, found Congress still under the spell of pro-slavery sentiment, but he was not content to return to private life without again putting himself on record. Accordingly he introduced his bill for gradual abolition in the District of Columbia. The careful provisions of his scheme undoubtedly represented his opinions as to steps that ought to be taken at some future time to eliminate slavery south of Mason and Dixon's line, with the acquiescence of the Southern States one after another.

Before explaining Lincoln's bill, it may be well to present in a summary way the statistical

THE MANIFEST DESTINY OF SAMBO
Whether North or South was to win the long continued argument, the Negro for years bore the brunt of it. Lincoln's plan of 1849 would have abolished slavery for all Negroes born thereafter. This cartoon of the War period. by Stephens in *Vanity Fair*, uses Lincoln and Davis to represent the opposing viewpoints of North and South. Davis has been tossed in the air.

69

facts regarding white and black population in the District of Columbia.

Although, ever since the removal of the capital to Washington in 1800, the population of the District had been growing steadily, there was nothing to cause a proportionate growth in the number of slaves. Obviously, the Government could not hold slaves, and could not use them as laborers or in any capacity whatever. The hundred square miles of the District had been occupied by farmers and by inhabitants of the two villages of Georgetown and Washington. Twenty-five per cent. of the 14,000 inhabitants were slaves in the year 1800. The total number of slaves in 1820 was 6,377, this being less than 20 per cent. of the total population of 33,000. The enumerations of 1830, 1840, and 1850 showed a rapid dwindling of the slave population of the district, so that when Lincoln introduced his bill in 1849, the slaves were barely 7 per cent. of a total count of about 51,000.

The host of new Government clerks that Jackson had invited to Washington, and that had been considerably increased year after year, until the growth of public business in the Mexican War had brought a fresh access of civil and military dependents upon the public treasury, were not the class of people who kept slaves. Adoption of a plan of grad-

ual emancipation would have made little practical difference to anybody domiciled in the District, because the few slave owners would have been fully compensated, and could afterwards have employed all the colored help they needed on their own terms.

But the District was Southern in origin and tradition, and the people were pro-slavery even though they had no slaves. The South was in strong control in all departments of the government, and the slavery leaders would tolerate no discussion of emancipation in the District because such a step would be regarded as in some measure a victory for the abolitionists and a foreshadowing of the larger movement that was to demand national emancipation.

Lincoln's bill was introduced on January 16, 1849. The first section provided that certain persons should never henceforth be held in slavery within the District. This applied to slaves not already owned by residents of the District, and to unborn children. The second section permitted those coming into the District in official character to bring and retain their domestic servants, without being in any way affected by the proposed measure. The third section, relating to children born of slave mothers after January 1, 1850, provided that they should be held for service as apprentices until they had attained a certain age, being allowed suitable support and education.

The fourth section provided that the slaves already in the District should know no change unless the owner should consent to emancipate them, in which case a Government Board consisting of high officials should determine the full value, and give the owner an order on the Treasury, while giving the slave a certificate of freedom. The fifth section empowered and required the local authorities "to provide active and efficient means to arrest and deliver up to their owners

THE AMERICAN SLAVERY QUESTION—A GERMAN VIEW

This Cartoon from *Kladderadatsch,* the Berlin humorous weekly, bears the following explanatory caption: "The Northerner wishes to get rid of the black man and can do it; but the Southerner can not. Whereupon there arises between the Brothers Jonathan such a tremendous noise that Europe is unable to get cotton to stop up her ears. In the background is Brazil, where the blacks are obtaining the mastery over the whites."

all fugitive slaves escaping into said District." Section six specified details for the submission of the bill to local vote of free white male citizens, the President of the United States being authorized to canvass the result and, in case of a majority in favor of the act, to give it effect by issuing his proclamation.

In a speech at Peoria, Illinois, some five years later, Lincoln referred to the situation that had existed at Washington in the following terms:

The South clamored for a more efficient fugitive slave law. The North clamored for the abolition of a peculiar species of slave trade in the District of Columbia, in connection with which, in view from the windows of the Capitol, a sort of negro livery stable, where droves of negroes were collected, temporarily kept and finally taken to Southern markets precisely like droves of horses, had been openly maintained for years.

There had actually been introduced in Congress a more drastic proposal for abolition, and it had been bitterly debated. The Lincoln proposal was offered as a substitute for the radical measure that had no possible chance to secure approval. Nothing could have been more considerate of Southern feelings than the proposal of the Whig from Illinois; but the debate had already been too acrimonious for any sort of compromise. The Lincoln measure had many secret friends but few outspoken ones. Nothing came of it at the time, yet much was to come of it later; for it was to stand as evidence of the depth and breadth of Abraham Lincoln's understanding.

He was furnishing a platform upon which wise and prudent men, North and South,

THE LAND OF LIBERTY—A BRITISH VIEW IN 1847

A "holier than thou" attitude is evident in all the cartoons of *Punch* in the years preceding the Civil War. At the moment this one was published (December, 1847) the army of General Scott had reached Mexico City and the one-sided conflict was ended, leaving the impression abroad that Uncle Sam had been bullying a defenseless neighbor. The cartoonist here is Richard Doyle, known as Dickie Doyle, whose initialled signature includes the outline of a dicky-bird.

might in due time have come together for the solution of a problem that was threatening division of the Union. He believed in gradual emancipation on an orderly plan, for the economic and social well-being of both races. He also held to the sane and practical view that full compensation out of the Federal Treasury would be highly expedient, entirely fair, and a good investment from every standpoint. The facts that Lincoln held these statesmanlike views while still in his twenties, that he later set them forth in Congress when he was exactly forty years old, and that he adhered to them in 1860 at the age of fifty-one when elected President, formed a part of that record which in later times came to be understood, alike by descendants of the rabid Abolitionists and by progeny of the blinded eulogists of slavery as a divine institution. Wendell Phillips complimented Lincoln by calling him "the slave hound of Illinois;" and we shall later see what Southern Democrats called him in 1860, when it dawned upon their minds that he was destined to be elected President because their own party had split asunder on the slavery issue.

Early in the century the United States and Great Britain, with other countries of con-

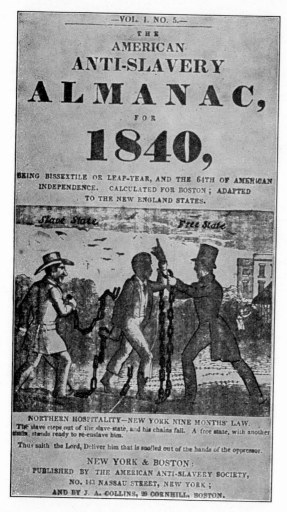

NORTHERN HOSPITALITY—NEW YORK NINE MONTHS' LAW.
The slave steps out of the slave-state, and his chains fall. A free state, with another chain, stands ready to re-enslave him.
Thus saith the Lord, Deliver him that is spoiled out of the hands of the oppressor.

NEW YORK & BOSTON:
PUBLISHED BY THE AMERICAN ANTI-SLAVERY SOCIETY,
NO. 143 NASSAU STREET, NEW YORK;
AND BY J. A. COLLINS, 25 CORNHILL, BOSTON.

The pages of this yearbook were filled with extreme and exaggerated cases of cruelty to slaves. In this cover design attention is called to a law in New York which operated against the rights of Negroes even in a free state.

tinental Europe, had joined in efforts to suppress the bringing of new cargoes of slaves from Africa. Spain had not yet assumed this attitude, and Cuba as a Spanish possession became the great slave mart of the western world. Slave-traders of all nationalities persisted in the horrible practices of kidnapping on the African coast. By evading the American and British naval patrol they brought fresh cargoes to the Spanish colonial possessions. From Cuba and other islands, and from ports on the Spanish mainland including those of Mexico, slaves by the scores of thousands were being smuggled into the United States to meet the insatiate labor demands of the cotton planters, who were opening new fields in Alabama, Mississippi, and Louisiana.

These conditions on the lower Mississippi made profitable markets for wheat, corn, pork, and beef, from the farms of Ohio, Indiana, Illinois, and Missouri, with supplies of many other kinds in demand for plantation use. This river trade, steadily growing, had something to do with the persistence of Illinois sentiment against the Abolitionists, and in favor of the prosperous relations that existed between the free-labor agriculture north of the Ohio River and the Missouri Compromise line, and the slave-labor agriculture of the lower South. Lincoln understood this motive, and he had no proposals to make that could possibly affect detrimentally the exchange of commodities between the wheat-and-corn belt and the cotton States of the lower Mississippi.

But looking to the future, and planning with the far-seeing vision of a man who knew that such questions had to be settled by decisions rather than by avoidance and neglect, he had come to firm conclusions. The United States Government must in due time act where it had exclusive jurisdiction, and must leave it to the slave States, each for itself, to deal with slavery within its own bounds, exactly as various northern States had previously done. There was no flaw in Lincoln's reasoning.

For example, New Jersey's State Act to abolish slavery bore the date of April 18, 1846, this being the year of Lincoln's election to Congress. It is true that slavery had been

FUGITIVE SLAVES ESCAPING NORTH

Lincoln's plan of 1849, for abolishing slavery within the District of Columbia, yielded to the South in its provision that fugitive slaves should be arrested and delivered up to their owners. This is one of the original drawings for Harriet Beecher Stowe's "Uncle Tom's Cabin," published in 1852. The book did more to arouse abolition feeling in the north than anything else up to the time of John Brown's raid. Its sale was probably greater than that of any book previously published in the United States except the Bible.

naturally dwindling in New Jersey, so that from about 12,500 slaves in the year 1800, the number had declined to 2,254 by the census of 1830. New York's action had come earlier; and the 20,000 slaves of 1800 were reduced to a few more than 10,000 in 1820, and had disappeared in the next decade, leaving only 75 in 1830. Massachusetts had abolished slavery before 1790, and Maine, New Hampshire, and Vermont had speedily followed; but Rhode Island and Connecticut had been more tolerant, and a handful of slaves was still enumerated in those States as late as 1830 and 1840. Maryland, of course, was an important slave State, and Delaware maintained slavery until the Civil War. Lincoln believed that if we set the example of gradual emancipation by popular consent in the District of Columbia, with full compensation to such slave owners as were ready to manumit their bondsmen, we would do much to allay fear in the South. This plan might also pave the way for an ulti-

mate change of status in the cotton belt—a change that could not come about in a hurried fashion without disastrous consequences.

It is well, moreover, to remember that all intelligent Americans, North and South, were fully aware of the position of the slavery question in other countries. Nearly four years before Lincoln recorded his views in the Illinois Legislature—namely, in August, 1833—an act providing for emancipation in the British colonies was carried through the House of Commons and promptly accepted by the House of Lords and the Crown, under the leadership of Lord Grey who was then Prime Minister. Ten years earlier the English Anti-Slavery Society had been formed, and its propaganda had met with violent opposition on the part of the sugar planters in the West Indies, with various supporting interests in Great Britain. But the agitation against slavery in the British Parliament had steadily gained in strength until it had won its victory.

It is not to be argued that British ethical standards were higher than those that prevailed in America. It merely happened that the British Islands themselves had no slaves, and very few people in Great Britain had personal reasons for accepting the views of a handful of rich slave-owners and sugar planters in distant islands. It was typical of English methods that a series of measures intended to ameliorate slave conditions should have been adopted before emancipation was proclaimed in 1833.

Furthermore, there was nothing abrupt or confiscatory about the English plan of emancipation. The sum of a hundred million dollars was appropriated at the outset, from which planters could be compensated. All slaves were to be designated as "apprentices," and to be held in bondage for seven years, giving service to their former owners in lieu of maintenance. This rule did not apply to children under the age of six, who were made free at once. The law provided that full freedom for all former slaves should take effect in August, 1840. But as it afterwards turned out, the plan of indentured apprenticeship worked badly, and could not be enforced under conditions existing in the West Indies. So complete abolition was hastened, and it came to pass in 1838, with payment to owners on adjusted terms.

This English example naturally had its influence upon American minds, and doubtless it provided Lincoln with some of the ideas that took form in his plan for the District of Columbia. It is also to be noted as a significant fact that the Provisional Government of France, that superseded the Royal Government of Louis Philippe and that initiated

the Second Republic in 1848, had promptly proclaimed and carried into effect a plan of immediate emancipation throughout the French colonies.

Within our own Hemisphere, emancipation movements had been the order of the day. Thus Mexico, having secured her independence, had abolished slavery by decree in September, 1829, so that Texas was a free-soil State in the Mexican Republic when the American settlers expelled the Mexicans and established the Republic of Texas. Furthermore, New Mexico and California were free-soil areas when we occupied them at the outbreak of the Mexican War. The government at Buenos Aires had adopted a plan of slow abolition, by giving freedom to all children born in slavery after a certain date in the year 1813. The Republic of Colombia had arranged that all young slaves should be made free on their eighteenth birthday, beginning with the month of July, 1839.

Slavery, of course, in one form or another continued to exist in darkest Africa, in the Turkish Empire, and in various parts of Asia. But otherwise there remained no important areas in which slave labor was employed under modern economic conditions, excepting only the slave-holding portion of the United States, the Spanish Island of Cuba, and the great Portuguese Empire of Brazil. I am recording these readily accessible facts and dates as a mere matter of convenience, in order that they may be brought into comparison with Lincoln's protest of 1837 at Springfield, and his bill of 1849 for gradual emancipation in the District of Columbia. Lincoln, himself, of course, was fully aware of these British,

COMMEMORATING THE ABOLITION OF
SLAVERY BY GREAT BRITAIN IN 1834
*An anniversary medal, in the
H. Russell Drowne collection*

A SLAVE MARKET SUCH AS LINCOLN SAW FROM THE WINDOWS OF THE CAPITOL
AT WASHINGTON WHILE A MEMBER OF CONGRESS

This is another of the original drawings for "Uncle Tom's Cabin"

French and Latin-American projects for Negro emancipation. The world at large was abandoning the slavery system, as not only inconsistent with prevailing ideas of liberty and the inherent rights of man, but also as economically obsolete. Brazil, in 1850, had definitely stopped importations; so that Cuba was left as the sole *entrepot* for slave cargoes.

SOME SIGNIFICANT DATES IN LINCOLN'S FIRST THIRTY YEARS

1809—Abraham Lincoln is born on a farm near Hodgenville, Kentucky, February 12th.

1815—Battle of New Orleans, won by Gen. Andrew Jackson.

Battle of Waterloo, ending Napoleon's power in Europe.

Lincoln receives his only formal schooling from Zachariah Riney and Caleb Hazel, in a Kentucky country school.

1816—The Lincoln family moves to a farm on Little Pigeon Creek, near Gentryville, Spencer County, Indiana.

Indiana admitted as a State.

1818—Illinois admitted as a State.

1820—Missouri admitted as a Slave State under a compromise arrangement prohibiting slavery in the remainder of Louisiana Territory to the north.

1825—John Quincy Adams elected President by the House of Representatives. John C. Calhoun elected Vice-President.

1828—Andrew Jackson, Democrat, elected President, Calhoun continuing as Vice-President.

Lincoln makes his first trip to New Orleans, on a flatboat down the Ohio and Mississippi.

1830—The Lincoln family moves from Indiana to a farm near Decatur, Macon County, Ill.

1831—Lincoln makes a second trip to New Orleans. Upon his return he settles at New Salem, in Sangamon County, Illinois, becoming a clerk in a grocery store.

1832—Andrew Jackson re-elected President, with Martin Van Buren Vice-President.

Lincoln serves for two months as Captain of Volunteers in the Black Hawk War, though not in actual fighting.

Lincoln is a candidate for the Illinois Legislature, losing by a narrow margin. Later he campaigns for Henry Clay.

1832—South Carolina, led by John C. Calhoun, refuses to accept the new Tariff, claiming a right to nullify Federal law.

1833—Chicago incorporated as a town, with 135 inhabitants.

Lincoln appointed postmaster at New Salem and assistant surveyor.

1834—Lincoln is elected to the Illinois Legislature as a Whig.

1834-41—Lincoln's service in the Illinois Legislature.

1836—Van Buren elected President.

1837—Financial panic throughout the country.

Legislature votes removal of State capital from Vandalia to Springfield, largely through Lincoln's efforts.

Lincoln removes to Springfield and enters a law partnership with John Todd Stuart.

A mob kills Elijah P. Lovejoy at Alton, Ill.

1839—Capital moves to Springfield.

CHAPTER IX

A Crisis in National Banking

*Lincoln is licensed to practise law, moves to Springfield, and is
married—President Jackson denounces the National Bank—Lincoln
qualifies as an authority on banking*

LINCOLN HAD BEEN licensed to practise law
in the fall of 1836 and had taken up his
home at Springfield in April, 1837,
where he was accepted as a partner by his
friend, Major John T. Stuart, who had also
served in the Legislature, and had political
ambitions, along with
character and ability. It
was in the following
year, 1838, that Stuart
was nominated for Con-
gress by the Whigs of the
district, with the boyish
and diminutive Douglas
(he was not much more
than five feet in height)
named by the Democrats
as his opponent. It was a
strenuous and bitter can-
vass, thirty-four great
counties being grouped at
that time in this one congressional district. Stuart
was fully six feet tall
and a heavier man than
Lincoln; and the contrast
between him and Douglas
was as striking as that
which was afforded in
the famous Lincoln-
Douglas senatorial contest
twenty years later.

Douglas at this time
was only twenty-five years old, but he was
already a man of mark, an orator and
debater of striking promise, and a most adroit
campaigner and vote-winner. Stuart was the
victor by a majority of 35 in a total of 36,000.
If Douglas had contested the election in the
Democratic House at Washington he probably would have unseated Stuart; but he could
not afford the expense or time involved and

MRS. LINCOLN: AN EARLY PORTRAIT
Mary Todd of Lexington, Kentucky, had come
to Springfield, Illinois, to live with her married sister. There she met Lincoln, for her sister's husband was a fellow-member of the
Legislature. They were married at Springfield
on November 4, 1842.

he accepted his defeat. This was made easier
for him by the gift of a federal office.

Lincoln, who was naturally active in supporting Stuart's campaign, could not think of
national politics on his own account at that
time. He had an indebtedness to pay off resulting from the failure of his
earlier mercantile ven-
ture, and he had yet to
establish himself as a lawyer. It should be said that
Stuart was re-elected to
Congress in 1840, and
that, during the four years
of his membership of the
House at Washington,
Lincoln remained at
Springfield as active partner in the law firm.

Also in both of the
election years of 1838 and
1840, Lincoln was making
his own canvass for the
Legislature, while Stuart
was running for Congress.
Since the Legislature had
now left Vandalia and
come to the new capital at
Springfield, Lincoln could
keep his law office open
while taking his full share
in the work of the law-
making body of the State.

With his partner coming and going between
Springfield and Washington, Lincoln enjoyed
the sense of personal contact with national
affairs. We may anticipate by noting that
he declined a renomination for the Legislature in 1842, his private affairs absorbing
his attention at that time. For, in the election
month of November, 1842, he was married to
Mary Todd, the daughter of Robert S. Todd,

of Lexington, Kentucky. A few months later he was making a long step forward in his professional and business career by accepting a partnership offered him by Stephen T. Logan, who stood at the very head of the Bar of Illinois as a trial lawyer. Certainly from this time on we may disregard the notion that Lincoln was an altogether obscure and unpromising person. He was excellently married, well settled, and steadily making his way.

The extensive literature that has come into existence regarding Lincoln's marriage, his domestic affairs, and like matters of a private and personal nature, is of varying merit. Most of it has no important relation to his political career.

THE HOUSE WHERE LINCOLN WAS MARRIED

When Abraham Lincoln and Mary Todd were married, on November 4, 1842, the ceremony took place in this red-brick residence at 441 South Second Street, Springfield. It was the home of Mrs. Lincoln's sister, Mrs. Ninian W. Edwards. Mr. Edwards' father was the third Governor of Illinois. In this house, also, Mrs. Lincoln died in August, 1882.

LINCOLN'S HOME IN SPRINGFIELD

In 1844, two years after his marriage, Lincoln bought this house at Eighth and Jackson Streets. It had been built in 1839. Though not conspicuous, it was classed as one of the town's better houses. Here he lived for seventeen years, until he moved into the White House. After the death of Mrs. Lincoln, in 1882, the house passed to the President's son Robert, who turned it over to the State of Illinois. It is visited by many thousands each year. Oak, hickory, and black walnut all entered into the construction of this modest residence.

The same sort of natural curiosity pursues the life-story of every man who happens to become famous. Biographers of a certain school expend undue effort in meddling with privacy. Happily, not many writers about Lincoln have found it possible to ignore the record that he was making year by year as a citizen of Illinois, as one of the ablest practising lawyers in the history of America, and as a political leader and thinker of rare sagacity. Certainly nothing in his family life had crushed his spirit, or had spoiled a tempered reasonableness not equalled in the record of any other young American politician of his generation. Douglas also was a man of first-rate talents, and he had genuine convictions and tested courage. But Douglas had the common failing in political debate of misrepresenting opponents, of playing upon his audience by appeals to prejudice, and of employing palpably sophistical arguments. Lincoln, on the other hand, always manifested the utmost endeavor to state a case fairly, to recite facts without garbling, and to give clearly and with logical precision the reasons that convinced him.

JOHN T. STUART   STEPHEN T. LOGAN   WILLIAM H. HERNDON

John Todd Stuart, Lincoln's first partner (1837-41), was a cousin of the Mary Todd who in 1842 became Mrs. Lincoln. Stephen T. Logan, who had been a judge of the circuit court, was senior partner from 1841 to 1844. William H. Herndon remained as junior partner until Lincoln's death.

LINCOLN'S THREE LAW PARTNERS

That Lincoln was making numerous speeches showing this quality, we have every reason to believe. Few of them have survived as evidence of his intellectual development in the Van Buren period. But fortunately we have one speech which in the very nature of the case could not have been a departure, either in substance of doctrine or in method of reasoning, from many others that he made in early public life, for his platform efforts were always consistent.

The speech to which I refer was delivered in December, 1839. It was printed in pamphlet form, and happily a copy was still in existence and available when Nicolay and Hay were compiling the Lincoln papers in 1894. I shall make some analysis of the speech, because it deals wholly with national questions, and exhibits Lincoln as a student of those problems of banking, currency, and financial administration that were even more central in the public mind during Van Buren's administration than was the slavery question.

The original bank of the United States, devised in 1791 by Alexander Hamilton as fiscal agent of the government, had served its purpose, had fallen into disfavor, and at the end of its charter period had been transformed into a Philadelphia bank with a Pennsylvania charter. A second United States Bank had been established by Madison and his financial advisers in 1816, to take care of the enlarged treasury operations growing out of the War of 1812. The management of this bank may have been guilty of mistakes of one kind or another, and it encountered political prejudice. However worthy or otherwise it may have been, the Jacksonian Democrats were furiously and fanatically opposed to extending its chartered existence. Jackson dealt it a fatal blow when he withdrew the government's deposits from the central bank of the United States, and from the branches in leading American cities. He had already in July, 1832, vetoed a bill that had passed Congress, under the leadership of Daniel Webster and Henry Clay, for an extension of the bank's charter for another term of years from the date of its expiration in 1836.

Jackson especially objected to the combination of public and private functions that had made possible the ownership in Great Britain of a large part of the stock of the Bank of the United States. In his message of December, 1835, Jackson continued to denounce the spirit of monopoly that had been exemplified both in the conception and in the methods of the Bank of the United States. With too much

THE STATE CAPITOL AT SPRINGFIELD, WHEN LINCOLN
WAS IN THE LEGISLATURE

During Lincoln's eight-year service as an Assemblyman in Illinois, the Legislature met
first at Vandalia and later at Springfield. The Vandalia State House is shown on page 53.
Lincoln had been a leader in the movement to make Springfield, in his own county, the
capital of the State. This building was first occupied in December, 1839, and Lincoln
attended sessions here until March, 1841. Meanwhile he had moved to Springfield, and
was practising law there. By 1876 a larger State House had been constructed, and since
then this building has been used as the court house of Sangamon county.

optimism, he descanted upon the smooth going
that the Treasury had experienced for a year
in doing its business through "the use of the
State banks, which do not derive their charters
from the General Government and are not controlled by its authority." "All the wants of
the community," he added, "in relation to exchange and currency are supplied as well as
they have ever been before." Referring to the
evils of an unchecked paper system, Jackson
declared that "the management of the revenue
can be made auxiliary to the reform which the
Legislatures of several of the States have already commenced in regard to the suppression
of small bills."

And so General Jackson continued to paint
a most cheerful picture; but—alas for Jackson's self-confidence and belief in the value of
his victory over that centralized monster the
Bank of the United States—a storm was impending, the violence and wreckage of which
has hardly ever been equalled in the history of
American currency and banking. A recent
historian of obviously anti-Jackson convictions, sums up the results of the Treasury's
experiment in using State banks, in the following sentences:

It was Van Buren's misfortune that the storm
which Jackson had called from the sky, by his reckless use of high explosives, burst just as Jackson
reached shelter and as the "Magician" stepped forth
to take the great rain-maker's place. The terrible
panic of 1837 began when the administration was
but two months old—a direct consequence of the
financial disorder produced by Jackson's war on
the Bank. The enforced liquidation of the greatest
monetary institution in the country; the transfer of
the public funds to banks much weaker and far
more loosely managed than the Bank of the United
States; a wild speculation induced by the excessive
note-issues of state banks which had a fictitious
capital only; and the inability of the banks to re-
spond when called upon to refund the sums intrusted
to them, under the law for "depositing" the surplus
revenue with the States—such were the events
which brought about the suspension of specie payments on the 10th of May, 1837.

Obviously Mr. Van Buren could not continue to use State banks; and it would have been politically impossible to reverse the party position and establish a third Bank of the United States. The banks had with virtual unanimity suspended specie payments about two months after Van Buren's inauguration.

Congress was called in special session, and on September 4th the President transmitted to it a message of great length, analyzing the country's financial difficulties, and making remedial proposals. Speculation of all sorts had been so reckless for two or three years that reaction had become inevitable. This had been stimulated by redundant issues of paper money. First, it was recommended "to separate the fiscal operations of the government from those of individuals or corporations." Mr. Van Buren observed that neither in England nor in the United States had a central bank been able to prevent an undue expansion of credit and the evils that flow from it. He regarded banking as a private business that should be carried on by bankers for the convenience of commerce and trade. As a result of President Van Buren's reasoning there was introduced a measure creating a so-called Sub-Treasury system, under which the Government should become the custodian of its own funds.

It was typical of the universal interest in these questions of finance and currency that there should have been protracted public discussion, during a series of evenings, in the

THE APOLOGY   MEDIATION   SATISFACTION

FRANCE PAYS THE SPOLIATION CLAIMS, FOR DAMAGE TO UNITED STATES COMMERCE DURING THE WARS OF NAPOLEON

The French King Louis Philippe is at the right, with the English King William IV acting as mediator with President Jackson. At the left is Martin Van Buren, then Vice-President, who had arranged the settlement while Secretary of State in 1831. France had been dilatory in making payment until President Jackson assumed a vigorous position in 1834.

CAUCUS on the SURPLUS BILL.

Published June, 1836, by the Proprietor. H.R.Robinson, 48 Courtlandt Street, New York.

President Jackson, at the left, deliberates over a bill passed by Congress, lending surplus Government moneys to the States. Van Buren, at the right, had already been nominated by the Democrats as Jackson's successor. In the center is Levi Woodbury, Secretary of the Treasury.

Hall of the House of Representatives at Springfield in December, 1839. Mr. Douglas had spoken against the revival of the United States Bank, and had defended the Van Buren Sub-Treasury scheme. He had taunted and defied the Whigs to meet his arguments. Mr. Lincoln accepted the challenge, meeting it with his habitual aim at the major issue. "The subject heretofore and now to be discussed," he began, "is the sub-treasury scheme of the present administration, as a means of collecting, safekeeping, transferring, and disbursing the revenues of the nation, as contrasted with the national bank for the same purposes. Mr. Douglas has said that we, the Whigs, have not dared to meet them, the Locos, in argument on this question. I protest against this assertion." He then proceeded, with as

much care to reason philosophically and to avoid clap-trap and partisanship, as if he had been preparing a brief for the Supreme Court.

"Of the sub-treasury then," said Mr. Lincoln, "as contrasted with a national bank for the before enumerated purposes, I lay down the following propositions, to wit: (1) It will injuriously affect the community by its operation on the circulating medium. (2) It will be a more expensive fiscal agent. (3) It will be a less secure depository of the public money." Mr. Lincoln then proceeded to show how the national bank by its ordinary operations had kept money in circulation. "By the sub-treasury," he remarked, "the revenue is to be collected and kept in iron boxes until the government wants it for disbursement; thus robbing the people of the use of it, while the government does not itself need it, and while the money is performing no nobler office than that of rusting in iron boxes. The natural effect of this change of policy, everyone will see, is to reduce the quantity of money in circulation."

Mr. Van Buren had provided for the collection of the revenues in gold and silver in his recommendations for the pending sub-treasury bill. Mr. Lincoln showed that this would prove an advantage to a favored class, and detrimental to the general public, because it would draw into the strong boxes of the sub-treasury more than half of all the gold and silver dollars in the United States. As an argument for his Illinois hearers, he further demonstrated that the government's land offices in the western States and Territories were absorbing most of the available money of the people, and that the Van Buren proposals would so enhance the purchasing power of money as to double or treble the price of public land and thus make almost insurmountable the difficulties "that poor people now encounter in procuring a home."

As regards the working of a national bank under normal conditions, Mr. Lincoln held that it could take reasonable care of contractions and expansions, and provide a safely elastic volume of currency. He admitted that it could not be expected to regulate the currency when it was under official attack, "crippled and thrown into death convulsions by the removal of the deposits from it, and other hostile measures of the government against it." And there followed this wise and significant sentence: "We do not pretend that a national bank can establish and maintain a sound and uniform state of currency in the country, *in spite of* the national government; but we do say that it has established and maintained such a currency, and can do so again, *by the aid* of that government; and we further say that no duty is more imperative on that government than the duty it owes the people of furnishing them a sound and uniform currency."

I may not pause to review Lincoln's facts and figures set in array to prove that it would be more expensive to operate the sub-treasury system than to handle the public revenues through a national bank. So much loss had been incurred through the failure of the State Banks that Mr. Lincoln proceeded at length to discuss the question of relative security for the public money. He alluded to many defalcations on the part of government officials that had occurred in operating the custom houses, the land offices and the mints; and he predicted further defalcations at the hands of officials who might have the public funds under their control if the sub-treasury system were adopted. He made an ingenious argument to show that, human nature being what it is, banks would be preferable custodians for public funds.

The pending sub-treasury bill provided for four Receivers-general, at New York, Boston, Charleston and St. Louis, through whose hands most of the rev-

Entered according to Act of Congress, in the year 1837 by H.R. Robinson, in the Clerk's Office of the District Court of the United States, of the Southern District of New York

WHO'LL HAVE THE SPECIE?—

President Van Buren is showing very little respect for the British Bulldog and the French cock, in a situation growing out of the suspension of specie payments in May, 1837—only two months after the inauguration of the new President.

Draw'd off from Natur by Zek: Downing, Neffu to Major Jack Downing.

THE DOWNFALL OF MOTHER BANK.

Printed & Publ.d by H.R.Robinson; 52 Courtlandt St.t N-York.

President Jackson was opposed to the National Bank and in 1832 vetoed a bill extending its charter. But since the Bank had four years to live, Jackson in 1833 ordered his Secretary of the Treasury to withdraw Government funds. The Major Jack Downing, appearing in the two cartoons in this chapter, was a fictitious character, the name under which Charles Augustus Davis wrote satirical letters on politics. The name was revived in the Civil War period.

enues would flow. Lincoln compared these treasury branches with the branches of the national bank located at the same places, and attempted to prove that funds under the active operation of banks would be actually safer than if they were lying idle until needed for disbursement under the custodianship of government officials.

Next Lincoln undertook to argue the disputed question of the constitutionality of a National Bank; and this he dealt with by the familiar logical method of the *reductio ad absurdum*. In short, he showed that the government funds had to be handled in one way or another, and held that if the Van Buren way was constitutional, the way of Hamilton and that of Madison and his advisors must be equally so.

Leaving these arguments as to the theory and practice of banking and currency systems, Lincoln came to concrete disputes over government expenditures that had been included on previous evenings in the allegations of Messrs. Douglas and Lamborn. Comparisons of the costs of the government under different administrations had been made by these Democratic debaters, using methods to which resort is always a temptation when politicians discuss finance. Mr. Lincoln went into an elaborate review of particular objects of expenditure, the most important of these being the War in Florida against the Seminoles, that had been protracted and of course unduly extravagant, as wars have usually been.

Mr. Douglas had excused the expenditures of 1838, which had been large beyond precedent in a year of peace, by saying that ten million dollars of that expenditure "was a contingent appropriation, to prosecute an anticipated war with Great Britain on the Maine boundary question." Lincoln characterized this statement not only as untrue but supremely ridiculous. "First," he declared, "the ten millions appropriation was not made until 1839, and consequently could not possibly have been expended in 1838; second, although it was appropriated, it has never been expended at all."

Mr. Lamborn had insisted that "the difference between the Van Buren party and the Whigs was that although the former sometimes erred in practice, they were always correct in principle, whereas the latter are wrong in principle." To give this a more telling effect with the audience, Lamborn had said: "The Democrats are vulnerable in the heel, but they are sound in the head and the heart." This gave Lincoln the opportunity to relieve his serious argument on banks, currency and financial administration by touches of humor and of well-merited ridicule. Lamborn, further, had boasted that, in view of the results of the Congressional elections in 1838, every State in the Union would vote to give Van Buren a second term in the Presidential election of 1840.

Such boastful predictions afforded Lincoln the chance for a peroration, in which he employed a soaring and artificial style of oratory, meant to impress the audience and to show that he too could use figures of speech and build rhetorical sentences with as much fluency as Douglas himself, whenever he might choose to depart from his better manner of unadorned but more admirable diction. Politicians and preachers of that day were also the public entertainers.

THE MODERN BALAAM AND HIS ASS

President Van Buren comes into office as successor to President Jackson, the expression, "I shall tread in the footsteps of my illustrious predecessor," being a quotation from Van Buren's inaugural address. In two cartoons on these facing pages we see the Democratic donkey.

NEW EDITION OF MACBETH. BANK-OH'S! GHOST.

As the successor to Jackson in 1837, President Van Buren inherited a financial situation which culminated in the worst panic the country had experienced. He is here explaining to the Ghost of Commerce that he did not cause the panic.

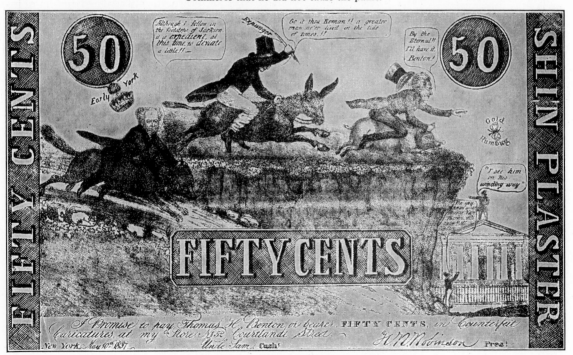

A SHINPLASTER CARICATURE OF MAY, 1837

Van Buren had been inaugurated and he is shown here speeding downhill while Senator Benton and Jackson are chasing the Gold Humbug. Benton had been Jackson's chief supporter in the Senate in the banking crisis. This imitation shinplaster is signed by H. R. Robinson, who published many of the poster caricatures of the period.

CUTTING DOWN THE HICKORY TREE

"Old Hickory," Andrew Jackson, is being disturbed in his Sub-Treasury crow's nest by William Henry Harrison, who swings his reform axe while Clay and Webster pull on the rope. The second crow, falling from the nest, is Martin Van Buren.

Our form of government has from the beginning made popular these difficult questions of taxation, monetary standards, banking, currency, and the financial methods and functions of government. Such topics have always been discussed, not merely at Washington and not alone at the state capitals, but at every country cross-roads from one coast to the other. This fact has been viewed with concern at times in our own country and with amused criticism by European financial authorities. But it could not have been otherwise and in the long run it has not been harmful. The United States alone has been able to bring economic questions of this kind into the sphere of serious even if not always highly intelligent discussion, in every community.

Lincoln had listened to the raging torrents of local argument. He had studied carefully the masterly discussions of Webster, Clay and others following the lines laid down by Hamilton and his successors. He had also given attention to the very able—although somewhat

fallacious—arguments of Jackson, Van Buren, and their principal supporters, against the aristocratic and monopolistic tendencies of a central bank, acting as fiscal agent for the government and regulating currency in the interest of normal business as against inflation. Reading these arguments and observing the course of affairs in his own State and throughout the country, Lincoln had assumed positions that are demonstrated in the experience of the nation to have been safe and sound.

Our western thinker and leader was destined twenty-two years after this Springfield debate of 1839 to assume national responsibility. He was to have in his own hands the executive control of financial transactions swollen by war from a modest stream to a vast river. It was therefore of consequence that he should in an earlier period have adopted principles that were capable of serving for his guidance in emergencies. Otherwise he might not have been able to navigate the stormy waters. He had to deal with many men of strong will in the two Congresses and the Cabinet, and with currents of public opinion that could not be wholly disregarded. There had to be compromises, and some temporary inflation was inevitable. But Lincoln's policies gave us a thoroughly reformed banking system which later on made possible a full resumption of specie payments with no repudiation and without violent deflation.

Lincoln's arguments of 1839 show that he would have been fully alive to deficiencies in our banking and currency system that resulted in the work of the Aldrich Commission and in the modified plans that gave us in 1913 the Federal Reserve System with its central board and its twelve regional reserve banks. Lincoln's national bank system of 1864 remained, while Van Buren's sub-treasury system was abolished in favor of those principles that Lincoln had set forth when defending active banks as public depositories. After more than sixty years we had come back to a system that Lincoln as a young man, aged thirty, had set forth in sound principle in 1839, in general accord with the ideas and aims of Alexander Hamilton in providing a scheme of banking and financial administration.

CHAPTER X

The Boisterous Harrison Campaign

*An Indian fighter is elected President—Harrison's genuine qualifica-
tions—Lincoln demonstrates ability as a stump speaker and a talent
for party organization*

IN HIS MEMORANDUM of 1860, summariz-
ing in condensed fashion the facts of his
political career, and speaking in the third
person, Lincoln remarked: "After 1840 he
declined re-election to the Legislature. He was
on the Harrison electoral ticket in 1840, and
on that of Clay in 1844, and spent much time
and labor in both those
canvasses." Since he al-
ways used the emphasis of
understatement when re-
ferring to his own achievements, we might need no
further evidence to con-
vince us that Lincoln took
a leading part in Illinois on
behalf of the Whigs in
these two memorable cam-
paigns for the Presidency.
His own seat in the Legislature had been secure, regardless of party.

Martin Van Buren,
whom the cartoonists of
the opposition were always
disparaging as a mere subordinate of Jackson, and
whom they contemptu-
ously designated as
"Marty" or "Matty," had
shown himself a President
of high character and distinguished ability. He
stood revealed as a statesman, a leader of his party,
a man of intellect, cautious
but eventually courageous,
a master of forcible yet
graceful English diction.
There had been enough to
justify Lamborn and
Douglas, debating a year

MARTIN VAN BUREN
President of the United States, 1837-1841

For twenty years following 1821, Van Buren
served almost continuously in high office:
United States Senator, Governor of New
York, Secretary of State, Minister to England (rejected by the Senate), Vice-President,
and President. He had aided materially in
Jackson's election in 1828 and became Jackson's political protegé and heir. After one
term in the White House Van Buren was
defeated by Harrison in 1840 and was an
unsuccessful aspirant for a third Democratic
nomination in 1844. In 1848 he was the candidate of the Free Soil party. He was born
at Kinderhook, New York, in 1782 and died
there in 1862, at the age of eighty.

before the election of 1840, in their enthusiastic laudation of Van Buren when meeting Lincoln and others in the forensic tilts at Springfield. Lamborn's prediction that Van Buren
would carry every State in 1840 was the
typical expression of those Democrats who
believed in their party, in its policies, and in its
presidential leader and
who abhorred the Whigs
and all their ways and
works. They thought that
the great voting public
could never be induced to
reverse itself, and to place
in power the aristocrats
and financiers of the East,
led by men like Daniel
Webster of Massachusetts,
with their western fellow-
worshippers at the shrine
of plutocracy, like Clay in
Kentucky, Harrison in
Ohio, and Abraham Lin-
coln in Illinois.

The Democrats had in-
deed lost ground in the
mid-term elections for
Congress in 1838; but they
thought this merely a temporary set-back. They re-
nominated Mr. Van Buren,
whom they called the "Little Magician," in a glow
of enthusiasm and with no
opposition whatever, Ten-
nessee and even South
Carolina having at length
resumed full party co-op-
eration.

No such thing as a Na-
tional Democratic Com-
mittee had been invented;

87

and the Democrats in the New Hampshire Legislature took it upon themselves to issue a national call for a convention to meet at Baltimore on May 4, 1840. It was to some extent informal, but three-quarters of the States were regularly represented. Mr. Van Buren was unanimously renominated, and the convention decided to leave the Vice-Presidency to be settled in the electoral college. It adopted a platform of nine brief, terse, and unambiguous resolutions—such a platform as might well be studied by platform committees in our own times.

This Democratic platform of 1840 was for strict construction of governmental functions; against internal improvements at federal expense; unfriendly to a protective tariff; opposed to a United States Bank as calculated to place the business of the country "within the control of a concentrated money power;" opposed to all efforts to induce Congress to interfere with questions of slavery; and, finally, it reiterated the Democratic tenets which made our land "the asylum of the oppressed of every nation"—an eager bid for the Irish, German and foreign-born vote.

The National Whig Convention had taken time by the forelock and had met at Harris-

burg, Pennsylvania, five months earlier than the Democratic gathering at Baltimore. Henry Clay was still the popular leader of the Whigs. He was sixty-two years old, and had been in the forefront of politics and statesmanship for more than thirty years. He would have been the logical nominee, and the party doubtless came short of its highest duty to itself and to the country in its failure to designate him to make the contest against Van Buren in 1840. But the Whigs at that time were not well knit together in point of convictions, their one strong point of agreement consisting in their opposition to the "Loco-Focos," as for a few years they chose to term the Democrats.

Clay's views were too positive for the Southern Whigs, and his personal affiliations were temporarily in disfavor (he happened to be a Free-Mason) in Eastern States, then stirred feverishly by the fanatical delusions of the "anti-Masonic" and "Know-Nothing" movements. The convention at Harrisburg held an informal vote as a test of actual preference, and found Clay in the lead. The first regular ballot gave Clay 103, William Henry Harrison 94, and General Winfield Scott 57. After a number of ballots the Harrison vote grew to 148, and Clay's fell to 90, whereupon the convention accepted the Harrison nomination "in a whirlwind of enthusiasm."

John Tyler of Virginia, who had become momentarily popular with the Clay elements of the party, was selected for the Vice-Presidency. His record was not that of the orthodox Whigs, but he was agreed upon without opposition. The convention was, like so many later ones, under the sway of the short-sighted and fallacious idea that it might strengthen the ticket in the South by setting up a balance against the sturdy old hero of the anti-slavery Northwest, Tyler himself being an aristocratic planter and slave-owner.

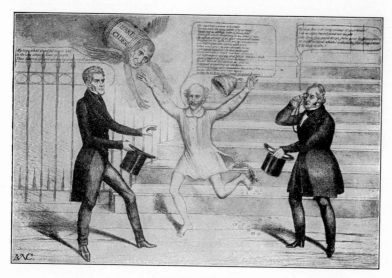

MATTY'S DREAM

President Martin Van Buren dashes down the steps of the White House and in pseudo-Shakespearian language recounts a dream in which he felt himself crushed in a cider press by fiends in the shape of cider barrels. Calhoun (at the left) and Benton try to reassure him. This is a poster cartoon of the campaign of 1840. All the cartoons in this chapter, except the last one, favor Harrison.

POLITICAL JUGGLERS LOSING THEIR BALANCE

President Van Buren had been nominated for a second term by the Democrats, and General Harrison was the Whig Candidate. Amos Kendall and Francis P. Blair, the most prominent members of "Jackson's Kitchen Cabinet," were credited with being the real managers of the Democratic party in the Jackson-Van Buren era. Harrison in the above cartoon is upsetting the Democratic regime so long in power. The log cabin and cider barrel played a prominent part in the campaign of 1840. Someone had said that Harrison was more at home in his log cabin with a barrel of cider than he would be in the White House—and the intended slur was turned to good account by the Whigs.

General William Henry Harrison was born in the famous home of his ancestors, at Berkeley on the James River, in Virginia. He was the son of the Benjamin Harrison who was a Revolutionary leader and a signer of the Declaration of Independence. Young William Henry after studying at Hampden-Sidney College entered the army with a lieutenant's commission at the age of eighteen, and found himself serving as aide-de-camp to General Anthony Wayne in his campaigns against the Indians of Ohio in 1792 and the following years. Such intelligence, capacity and courage did Harrison exhibit in those trying times of frontier settlement and Indian warfare, that he was made Secretary of the vast Northwest Territory in 1798 at the age of twenty-five. The next year he was serving as Territorial Delegate at Washington.

For many years, until 1812, he was Governor of the Indiana Territory, which until 1809 included Illinois and Wisconsin. In his capacity as Governor he lived for some time at the old French village of Vincennes. Also, for years, he was Superintendent of Indian Affairs; and although he was not ruthless

THE NORTH BEND FARMER *and* HIS VISITORS

Pilgrimages to General Harrison's home at North Bend, Ohio, were a feature of the campaign of 1840. This group of visitors represents merely the imagination of the artist and publisher; they are all Democrats, and Harrison was the nominee of the opposing Whig party. At the left of the group are Francis P. Blair, editor of the Washington *Globe,* and Postmaster-General Amos Kendall, the two principal advisers of the Democratic administration. The next figure is that of Andrew Jackson, former President. Then comes Martin Van Buren, President and candidate for a second term. Blair is stating that he will report in his paper that he found Harrison drinking and reading abolition tracts, which will kill him politically. Jackson declares it to be "a dirty job; I don't like it." Van Buren characterizes Harrison as an old fool to live in a log cabin and plow his own ground; "look at me, I roll in riches and live in splendor and laugh at the dear People whom I gull." Harrison himself asks his visitors to accept the fare of the log cabin. "I have no champagne but can give you a mug of good cider and clean beds." Note the fastidious costumes of the visitors and the plain garb of the host.

or aggressive against the resident tribes, he was compelled to protect settlers and to enforce land treaties.

This made him one of the heroes of border warfare against hostile Indians, the difficulties of the situation being intensified by the fact that intriguing British garrisons had been kept in occupation at Detroit in defiance of the terms of the Peace Treaty of 1783. The serious fact that the British were supplying the Indians with guns and ammunition, and keeping them stirred up against the Americans for fully twenty years, was well known to Harrison. This situation became greatly aggravated, as the country was going through the period of increasing disagreement with Great Britain that resulted in the War of 1812. That

the high-spirited pioneers had endured so much was due to their lack of numbers..

Early in 1811, Congress had forbidden all trade with Great Britain and her colonies; and the war spirit was even more prevalent in the West than elsewhere. Unquestionably the British had armed the great Chief Tecumseh and his formidable warriors with fresh supplies of musketry, powder and ball. Thus General Harrison's victory over Tecumseh at the battle of Tippecanoe Creek in November, 1811, was regarded as the opening of a justifiable war, the closing episode of which was Jackson's great victory at New Orleans.

Incidentally, it is to be noted that Harrison's victory which gave him the favorite title of "Tippecanoe" was fought fully half a year before war against Great Britain was actually declared, while the Battle of New Orleans was fought two weeks after the peace treaty had been signed. These two victories had created for their respective heroes that popular availability that carried both of them in due time to the White House.

Harrison's genuine qualifications, however, had resulted from a lifetime spent in the conduct of public affairs, while he served as the guiding spirit in the settlement and political organization of the Northwestern States. His Indian fighting, it may be noted, had not completed his military experience. Commissioned as a Major-General, he recaptured Detroit, drove the British across the line into Canada, and defeated General Proctor in a severe fight on British soil, October 5, 1813. After the War of 1812, General Harrison held public

WILLIAM HENRY HARRISON
Ninth President of the United States

Harrison's early career was in the army, from which he resigned in 1798 at the age of twenty-five. He then became Governor of Indiana Territory, a region including Indiana, Illinois, Wisconsin, and Michigan. An Indian uprising in 1811 and the War of 1812 brought him back into the army, and he earned promotion to the rank of Major-General. After that he made his home in Ohio, and was elected to the House of Representatives and to the Senate. Twice he was the Whig candidate in opposition to Van Buren, being defeated in 1836 and successful in 1840. He died April 4, 1841, after only one month in the Presidency.

WILLIAM HENRY HARRISON
NINTH PRESIDENT OF THE UNITED STATES
INAUGURATED MARCH 4th 1841   DIED APRIL 4th 1841

Reproduced from a colored lithograph widely circulated at the time of Harrison's death in 1841. He was the first President to die in office. In subsequent chapters will be found other lithographs commemorating the deaths of Presidents John Quincy Adams and Andrew Jackson—the three indicating a prevailing custom.

offices in Ohio, and represented that State in the United States Senate from 1824 to 1828. President John Quincy Adams and Secretary of State Clay then induced him to go to the Republic of Colombia as United States Minister, to support the policies of that administration, following the enunciation of the Monroe Doctrine and the Pan-American Congress at Panama, and to advance American interests along the lines that lay so clearly in the ambitious plans and programs of Henry Clay.

The situation was altogether changed, however, by the election of Jackson to the Presidency, this resulting in the recall of Harrison from South America in 1829. After almost forty years of strenuous occupation in public capacities, he was glad to retire to his farm at North Bend, Ohio, near Cincinnati.

Harrison, who is springing the trap with the aid of a hickory limb and a bale of cotton, actually carried all the States listed and several others. He received a total of 234 electoral votes, against 60 for Van Buren.

prising to a modest, well-seasoned old gentleman who had never posed as a hero or a popular leader. The outburst of noisy appreciation that exhibited itself in demonstrations of all kinds throughout the country was due rather to circumstances and conditions than to Harrison's personal magnetism or qualities of statesmanship, although he was a suitable and worthy candidate. He was four years older than Henry Clay, and ten years older than his opponent, President Van Buren.

I have made it clear that Harrison was a man of sound judgment, good sense, and vast administrative and military experience. He had been identified with the beginnings and the later development of the series of States north of the Ohio River. In some sense he was the embodiment of the principles of the Northwest

Six years later, however, the exigencies of Whig politics invaded his quiet and pleasant life in the Ohio Valley, and dragged him into the limelight as a Presidential candidate. His defeat by Van Buren in 1836 had put an end to the visiting delegations that admired his livestock and his crops, and it allowed him a further term for repose and contemplation. But again in 1840 he was found the most available candidate for the Whigs, and what had been a relatively calm adventure on the seas of presidential politics was now to be followed by a second one of a much more tempestuous and exciting character.

The pilgrimages to North Bend in 1840 were somewhat like those of the famous "front porch" campaign of McKinley in 1896. The visible evidences of Harrison's amazing popularity were sur-

The Little Magician raising the spirit of Santaclaus,
a la Der Freischutz.
HUESTIS & Co. 104 NASSAU STREET, NEW-YORK.

Van Buren, because of his undeniable astuteness as a politician, was known as "The Little Magician" and as "The Kinderhook Fox," from the name of his home town in New York.

Ordinance. Harrison, like Lincoln, was an anti-slavery man, while Tyler his running-mate was by residence, by private interests and by habits of thought a Southern partisan in the steadily widening breach that the slavery question was producing. Like Clay, Lincoln and all the leading Western Whigs, Harrison stood for internal improvements at national expense, believed in protective tariffs, and held unshaken views in favor of a National Bank of the United States. His nomination, however, was distinctly for the purpose of catching votes, because in the minds of the masses he had always been remembered as a hero of the last war against the British. The Whig slogan of that season was "Tippecanoe, and Tyler too!"

In their campaigning, the Whigs had taken

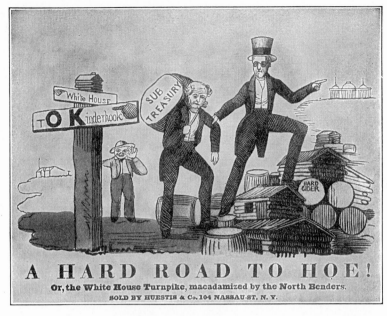

A HARD ROAD TO HOE!

Or, the White House Turnpike, macadamized by the North Benders.

SOLD BY HUESTIS & Co. 104 NASSAU-ST, N. Y.

During Van Buren's term as President came the panic of 1837, precipitated largely by acts of his predecessor and of Congress. Van Buren's own plan for a sub-treasury system had been rejected by Congress in 1837 but was adopted in July, 1840, in the height of the campaign. The Whigs made the panic an issue.

a leaf out of the book of their Democratic opponents. In short, they had undertaken to appear as the party of the people. Harrison suited them as a candidate, for the very reason that he was not too clearly identified in the public mind with those unpopular views held by the "aristocrats" and "monopolists" regarding banks and the enlargement of federal functions. The Whig parades and spectacular demonstrations, exhibiting log cabins on wheels, cider barrels, and other things suggestive of frontier exploits and experiences, were the unprecedented and long-remembered features of the campaign.

As it happened, Van Buren was too much the scholarly, mild-mannered, peace-loving gentleman to make a strong appeal to the rip-roaring masses of the American electorate of 1840. When the

The People's Line--Take care of the Locomotive

Sold at 104 Nassau, and 18 Division Streets, New-York.

The railroad was still something of a novelty, and was a favorite subject for cartoonists. The face on this locomotive is that of Harrison, while Van Buren (then President, and a candidate for re-election) is on "Uncle Sam's cab."

THE NORTH BEND GAME COCK

The successful Whig campaign of 1840 was marked by
new methods which aroused popular enthusiasm—mass
meetings, parades, slogans. "Tippecanoe and Tyler Too,"
the cry of this game cock, has not yet been forgotten.

Mr. Beveridge finds that although Lincoln
spoke all over the State, frequently traveling
and debating with Douglas, his best work in
that fight of 1840 was in organizing county
Whig committees everywhere, and seeing that
they divided their counties into small districts,
checking up all the voters and working on the
doubtful cases. While we have less information than we should wish, we know enough
to elaborate extensively Lincoln's own brief
statement that he "spent much time and labor"
in the campaign. I should be disposed to
attach great importance, from Lincoln's own
standpoint, to his twofold undertakings in
that year of politics. His biographers—in the
lack of accessible data—have not drawn upon
their imaginations.

As a stump speaker Lincoln had now demonstrated maturely his amazing ability to
dwell upon principles, and to deal broadly with
facts and statistics, while at the same time he
was adapting himself in spontaneous fashion
to the moods of popular audiences, responsive
to their liking for amusing anecdotes and
clever retorts. But, besides this, he had demonstrated his talent for party organization,
and for those careful and thorough methods
that are now the familiar practice of all party

votes were counted, only seven States were
carried by Van Buren, while nineteen States
gave majorities for the Harrison electors. The
popular majorities were not large, but they
were well distributed. Of the 294 electors,
Harrison received the vote of 234, while Van
Buren had only 60.

Lincoln had hoped to be one of the 294
members of the Electoral College of 1840,
upon whom devolved the constitutional responsibility of selecting a President. He was,
indeed, one of the five men on the Whig electoral ticket of his State. But Van Buren carried Illinois by a popular majority of nearly
2,000 votes, in a total vote of 93,000. The
total vote in 1836 had been only 33,000, and
the relative Democratic majority had been five
times as great. This comparison shows not
only that Illinois was growing rapidly in population, but that this growth was of a kind that
was building up the Whig party as against the
Democrats.

HARRISON'S HOME IN VINCENNES, INDIANA

Where he lived as Governor of Indiana Territory from
1801 to 1811, when he defeated the Indians in the famous
battle of Tippecanoe and was placed in command of troops
in the Northwest during the War of 1812.

GOING UP SALT RIVER

President Van Buren stands on the bank while Clay, Webster, and Wise ride the Harrison horse—
with the familiar barrel of hard cider—up the river that signifies political defeat.

machines. He was taking his natural place as the strongest and most responsible party leader in a rapidly developing State that was fast assuming a pivotal character.

THE RESIDENCE OF WILLIAM HENRY HARRISON AT NORTH BEND, OHIO

After a career of twenty years as Governor of a vast region known as Indiana Territory, and following subsequent service in Indian uprisings and the War of 1812, Harrison had settled down to the life
of a farmer in Ohio. For nearly thirty years thereafter he lived at North Bend, in Hamilton County,
on the Ohio River, in the southwestern corner of that State. In this house, also, William Henry
Harrison's grandson, Benjamin Harrison (President from 1889 to 1893), was born in 1833.

CHAPTER XI

A President Without a Party

Lincoln warns against injurious partisanship—Tyler becomes President through the death of Harrison, and abandons Whig doctrines—The Cabinet, except Webster, resign

EARLY IN 1841 Lincoln's service in the Legislature had come to an end. Mr. Beveridge—himself a product of Illinois and Indiana, with talents similar to Lincoln's in point of capacity for the firm grasp and lucid presentation of principles, and also for the use of the methods of practical politics — has gone more thoroughly than preceding biographers into the study of Lincoln's career in the State Legislature. No one could have appreciated more fully than Mr. Beveridge the possibilities for training in all the tasks of government that lay in the work of the Legislature of a great State in its formative period.

It is probably true that in the fundamentals of statesmanship Mr. Lincoln had acquired a more valuable experience by virtue of his four terms in the Legislature than he would have gained at Washington if he had served those same two-year periods in Congress. At Washington, he would have been drawn more closely into the details of federal government and the personalities of party controversy. He would doubtless have attained a national reputation earlier. But, remaining in

Illinois, he was in a position to study national questions with more calmness and detachment. He was actually debating these issues with a better grasp of underlying principles than was shown by other public men of Illinois who were representing the State at Washington. They were so close to daily maneuvers that the dust of conflict was in their eyes. To change the figure of speech, they could not always see the woods for the density of the undergrowth in which they were entangled.

When it came to matters of public business, there was much to be learned in dealing with the immense number of questions always pending in the Illinois Legislature. It has often been observed as regards European politics that the really responsible statesmen of small countries have had a broad and also a profound development of character, capacity and wisdom, such as one seldom finds in the official groups of a great empire. Mr. Beveridge has done well, therefore, to study the records at Springfield, and to make extensive research into the part that Lincoln had taken previous to 1843 in the gov-

JOHN TYLER
President of the United States, 1841-1845

When William Henry Harrison died, after only a month in the White House, Tyler became President and served for the remainder of the term. He was the first Vice-President thus to be elevated to the presidency. He was a Virginia lawyer who had been elected to the legislature at the age of twenty-one, and whose public career had included service as Representative in Congress, Governor of Virginia, and United States Senator. His had always been a stormy political career, and in the presidential office he was repudiated by the party which had elected him. He presided over the Peace Convention called by Virginia in February, 1861, in a futile effort to avert the impending crisis. When Virginia seceded from the Union in 1861 Tyler was elected to the Confederate House of Representatives, but died early in the following year before taking his seat.

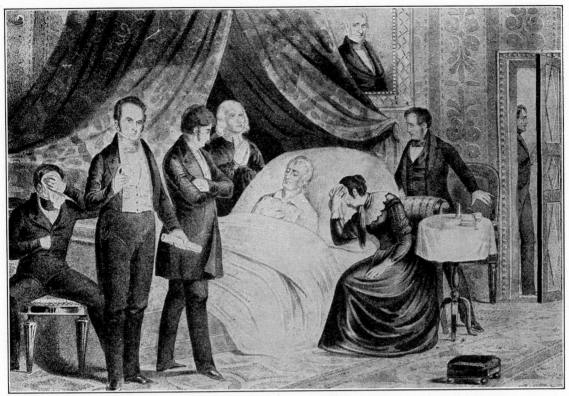

Tho' Ewing Sec of Trea   Dan'l Webster Sec of State   Physician   Rev Dr Hawley   President Harrison   Niece   Nephew   E Granger Post Master Gen'l

DEATH OF HARRISON, APRIL 4. A.D. 1841.

I wish you to understand the true principles of the Government. I wish them carried out I ask nothing more

Entered according to Act of Congress A.D. 1841 by N. Currier in the Clerks office of the Southern Dist of New York

William Henry Harrison died of pneumonia one month after his inauguration, the first President to die in office. The persons grouped about his bedside are: Thomas Ewing, Secretary of the Treasury; Daniel Webster, Secretary of State; the physician; the Rev. Dr. Hawley; the President's niece and nephew; and in the doorway Francis Granger, Postmaster-General. The painting on the wall is a portrait of the President himself. This death scene is reproduced from a large lithograph in possession of the author, which was widely circulated throughout the country for framing and hanging in the homes of Harrison's admirers, especially in Ohio and the West.

ernmental affairs of the State of Illinois.

The campaign for the Presidency in the year 1844 had begun as soon as the votes were counted in 1840. The Democrats were both surprised and angry at the sweeping success of Harrison. Far from abandoning their defeated candidate, they rallied with remarkable conviction and enthusiasm about the trailing banner of Van Buren. The Democratic members of practically every Legislature in the Union held caucuses within a few weeks and announced their support of Van Buren for 1844. This was happening while the kindly and competent little gentleman from Kinderhook, New York, was serving the four months that remained of his term in the White House after the shock of his defeat.

The Whigs, on the other hand, having gained their victory were awaiting the fourth of March, 1841, for which date they were planning a tremendous demonstration at Washington on Inauguration Day. Jackson had loaded the civil service with Democrats; and the growth of public business had given Van Buren opportunities to appoint many more of the faithful, who were eager to feed from the public crib. Naturally, the Whig henchmen were similarly greedy and expectant. They were arriving at Washington by every means of conveyance, to be on hand with their applications for jobs.

The only state paper attributable to President Harrison in the four brief weeks of his Chief Magistracy was his conciliatory and dignified inaugural address, with its allusions to Roman history, and its air of sage and reflective benevolence. In that document he deprecated the use of the veto power by Presidents, and begged parties to take a less violent attitude toward one another. A toilsome public career of half a century had left his physical vitality impaired; and the pressure of his new responsibilities was beyond his limited power of endurance. He died on April 4, exactly a month after he had taken the oath of office.

It might prove to be well in every presidential year if both major parties should take to heart President Harrison's warning against the evils of excessive partisanship. Several sentences in his address should be kept current as a legacy to party leaders, not only in the United States but in all other democratic countries. "To me it appears perfectly clear," said President Harrison in referring to party strifes then resounding throughout the land, "that the interest of the country requires that the violence of the spirit by which those parties are at this time governed, must be greatly mitigated, if not entirely extinguished, or consequences will ensue which are appalling to be thought of. If parties in a republic are necessary to secure a degree of vigilance sufficient to keep the public functionaries within the bounds of law and duty, at that point their usefulness ends. Beyond that they become destructive of public virtue, the parent of a spirit antagonistic to that of liberty, and eventually its inevitable conqueror."

Of Mr. Lincoln it may be said, as of President Harrison, that his partisanship was never of a destructive character, but always subordinated to his regard for the welfare of the country. Moreover, it was always so expressed as to keep the friendly good-will of his fellow-citizens regardless of party lines.

In the session of the Illinois Legislature that came to an end March 1, 1841, three days before Harrison's inauguration, there had been a terrific struggle over legislation reorganizing the judiciary of the State, intended to throw that co-ordinate branch of the government into subjection to the personal and political objects of the Democratic majority in the law-making body. A debate lasting many days, in which men of remarkable ability and of future fame took leading parts, was characteristic of the discussions of institutional problems that were training many others besides Abraham Lincoln in western legislatures.

Finding themselves unable to break down the Democratic majority that was forcing this unsound measure upon the State, a group of Whig members issued "An Appeal to the People of the State of Illinois." Mr. Lincoln was one of the six members of the committee on behalf of the Whigs of the Legislature who prepared and sent out the address. Messrs. Nicolay and Hay present the document as of Lincoln's authorship. In any case, it represented his sentiments; and—quite apart from its extended review of the exact situation then existing as regards the present and prospective organization of the law courts of Illinois—it contains a plea for the dignity and the high functions of an independent judiciary. It might well be republished from time to time, in view of attacks upon the Federal courts and the occasional injection of politics into the selection of judges and the organization of judiciary systems under the several State governments. As a warning against undue and injurious partisanship in the affairs of the State, especially at a time when economic conditions had been so desperate by reason of the panic of 1837, the following sentences, attributed to Lincoln, may well be compared with those which I have quoted from President Harrison's address:

It was not expected by you that the spirit of party would take the lead in the councils of the State, and make every interest bend to its demands. Nor was it expected that any party would assume to itself the entire control of legislation, and convert the means and offices of the State, and the substance of the people, into aliment for party subsistence. Neither could it have been expected by you that party spirit, however strong its desires and unreasonable its demands, would have passed the sanctuary of the Constitution, and entered with its unhallowed and hideous form into the formation of the judiciary system.

The Vice-President, John Tyler, had not yet arrived at Washington from his home in Virginia when the members of the Harrison

REQUESTING HIM TO RESIGN.

Tyler—who is portrayed here as stepping out of the presidential chair—was elected to the Vice-Presidency in 1840 as a Whig, and almost immediately became President through the death of Harrison. But he had supported Jackson in 1828, had been the vice-presidential nominee of disaffected Democrats in 1836, and his principles were largely Democratic. After he had vetoed important bills passed by the Whig majority in Congress in 1842, the party disclaimed him and the Cabinet resigned. This is a cartoon put out by the supporters of Henry Clay during the presidential campaign that followed. Clay had led the Whigs in Congress, in framing the legislation that Tyler vetoed, and he became the party nominee for President. Clay did not step into the presidential chair, however, as this cartoonist had indicated, for he lost the election. James K. Polk, who stands at the left of the platform, was elected President. Next to him is his running-mate for Vice-President, George M. Dallas, and at the extreme left is Andrew Jackson, idol of the Democratic party.

Cabinet announced to the country the death of the President. Mr. Harrison had made Daniel Webster of Massachusetts Secretary of State; Thomas Ewing of Ohio, Secretary of the Treasury; John Bell of Tennessee, Secretary of War; John J. Crittenden of Kentucky, Attorney-General; George E. Badger of North Carolina, Secretary of the Navy; and Francis Granger of New York, Postmaster-General. It has been said of him that in selecting these gentlemen for the heads of departments, he had "singled out for members of his official household, regardless of their rivalries, the statesmen who had stood in the front ranks of the government opposition during the past twelve years."

It must not be supposed that Harrison had slighted Henry Clay, his disappointed rival for the nomination. He had originally planned that Clay should be Secretary of State, and that Webster, who had served as chairman of the Senate Committee on Finance, should head the Treasury Department. Harrison had actually gone to Frankfort, Kentucky, soon after his election, to confer with Clay and to offer him the leading position in the Cabinet. But Clay declared that he preferred to remain at his post of leadership in the Senate, and urged that Webster was the massive and powerful Whig statesman whose abilities ought to be recognized by appointment as Secretary of State. Mr. Crittenden was the junior Senator from Kentucky, and it has been said that he entered the Cabinet as a sort of proxy for the real head of the Whig party. John Bell of Tennessee had been a Jackson Democrat, but had drifted—through earlier support of Judge White—into affiliation with the Whigs.

John Tyler's assumption of the Presidency afforded the first occasion for the discovery that it might be well for political parties to be sure they know their man when they are selecting a running-mate for a presidential nominee. Mr. Tyler was an excellent gentleman, and his address to the people of the United States upon taking office was reassuring, espe-cially upon the point of the "spoils system." He promised to remove no incumbent who had faithfully and honestly acquitted himself of the duties of his office, except in cases of active and objectionable partisanship. But President Tyler immediately found it requisite to focus his attention upon the ever-recurring questions of fiscal policy. He supported the repeal of the Sub-Treasury law (which, how-ever, was re-enacted five years later under President Polk, in 1846). But he declined to favor the chartering of a new central Bank of the United States, unless with severe and un-precedented restrictions. He asserted his con-victions in his veto message, August 16, 1841, when he refused to approve "an act to incor-porate the subscribers to the Fiscal Bank of the United States," which had originated in

THE MAN WOT DRIVES THE CONSTITUTION

Published by Jno CHILDS, No 4 Wall St New York.

The cry that the other side was trying to destroy the Constitution was raised continuously by both parties during this period. Clay had to his credit two famous compromises by which disunion had been averted, and was yet to have a third. With his running-mate in the campaign of 1844, Theodore Frelinghuysen, he is here driving to Washington. The vehicles in difficulties are those of Tyler, then President, and Van Buren, former President. Neither Tyler nor Van Buren, however, was nominated. It was Polk as victor who drove in style to the White House on March 4, 1845.

GREAT PRESIDENTIAL STEEPLE CHASE OF 1844

Coming in — Odds 10 to 1 on Old Kentucky.

This poster was published early in the season, before the nomination. Van Buren—the second horse—was not chosen by the Democrats. His place in this presidential race was taken by Polk, and Polk won. The horses, from left to right, represent: Henry Clay, the Whig nominee; Martin Van Buren; John C. Calhoun, who is throwing his rider; President Tyler, "old Veto, stuck in the mud" on the river bank; and Cave Johnson, then a member of Congress from Tennessee and later Polk's Postmaster-General. Horse-racing was a universal diversion, with a race track in almost every county, east, west, and south.

the Senate under Clay's leadership and had passed both houses.

Mr. Tyler declared that he had been elected Vice-President with the full knowledge that he had always been opposed to the use of banks of any kind, national or state, for the government's fiscal operations. Two days after the veto, Secretaries Ewing, Bell, Crittenden, and Badger resigned from the Cabinet, with Granger at once following. Webster, who took the view that the foreign relations of the country were not involved in the disputes over the bank bill, alone kept his post. Mr. Tyler was getting his seat in the saddle. He meant to be President in his own right, and not be the rubber-stamp for a government by Harrison's surviving Cabinet. It was evident that he must either form his own Cabinet, or else subject himself to the domination of statesmen who would have been in perfect accord with Mr. Harrison, who had selected them, but who

could not sharply reverse their mature views of financial policies to oblige an accidental President.

Mr. Tyler, moreover, had at once surrounded himself with a group of admirable and scholarly Virginia gentlemen who were called his "kitchen cabinet;" and their private influence at the White House had not pleased the official Whig Cabinet. Mr. Webster, who was hoping to settle the Northeast boundary dispute with Great Britain, concerned himself as little as possible with the Cabinet upheavals. As between President Tyler and Secretary Ewing, it was in point of fact a question as to which one ought to be responsible for the financial policies. Ewing knew more about finance, but Tyler was the constitutional executive; and he established a precedent that has been maintained. The new Cabinet selected by Tyler was made up of men not so conspicuous as those who had resigned. Webster held on for nearly two years longer, but left the Cabinet in May, 1843. He had lost influence with his own party, while disagreeing with Tyler.

Never at any time during the Tyler administration did the Cabinet situation become stabilized. Two members of the Cabinet were killed by the explosion of a gun on a naval vessel on Chesapeake Bay. Southern Democrats were named to fill one vacancy after another. Ultimately, John C. Calhoun of South Carolina was offered the post of Secretary of State, and James K. Polk was invited to enter the Cabinet. For some reason Polk declined. But Calhoun accepted, though with evident hesitancy because he had his own presidential aspirations, and he did not wish to be committed to the renomination of President Tyler.

I have brought forward these names, and given due attention to the Washington situation, because the men and the measures of the Tyler period were of vital interest to Lincoln, who was preparing to take a great part in the campaign of 1844. The self-assertion of President Tyler, and his unqualified dissent from the doctrines and positions of the Whig party to which he had owed his election, resulted in the further strengthening of Henry Clay as the pre-eminent national leader of the Whig party, and by far the most influential statesman of the entire country. Lincoln had always been a devoted admirer of the brilliant Kentuckian, and was preparing to do his utmost to aid in the nomination of Clay and his election to the Presidency.

THE HUNTER OF KENTUCKY.

Henry Clay, of Kentucky, and Theodore Frelinghuysen of New Jersey, Whig nominees for President and Vice-President in 1844, are pictured as ridding the country of the most prominent Democrats. The reader will have noticed that all the cartoons in this chapter, dealing with the campaign of 1844, are pro-Clay. Those in the previous chapter, concerned with the campaign of 1840, similarly favored the Whig candidate, Harrison. Doubtless the Whigs were the better patrons of the publishers of these lithographed poster caricatures.

CLEANSING THE A UGEAN STABLE.

The Whigs are doing the cleaning. Clay and Frelinghuysen, candidates for President and Vice-President, are tossing their Democratic opponent out of the window. Henry A. Wise, then a Whig Congressman from Virginia, afterwards Democratic Governor of Virginia, is refusing entrance to Madam Texas. But this election of 1844 had a different result; the Democrats won, Polk was elected, and Texas was admitted to the Union in 1845. Calhoun holds the Kinderhook Fox, Van Buren.

CHAPTER XII

Clay Loses His Third Campaign

*Polk emerges as the first "dark horse" candidate—Texas and Oregon
the issues, in an era of expansion—Lincoln explains his opposition to
the annexation of Texas*

LINCOLN WAS NOW READY to go to Congress, but there were other capable and aspiring Whigs who were practising law at the State capital and seeking political honors. He had been married in 1842; and such were the connections of his Kentucky bride that it was repeated everywhere, throughout Sangamon County and the several other counties that formed the Congressional district, that "Abe Lincoln had married into the aristocracy." Furthermore, the religious denominations were playing politics, and Lincoln was not a member of any church. His wife's family connections were with the less popular denominations, the Episcopalians and the Presbyterians. The so-called "Campbellites" (more properly known as the Disciples or Christians) held the foremost place among the plain people, and the Methodists, of course, were hardly less numerous. J. J. Hardin was a strong and able candidate, while Edward D. Baker was also a man of ability who had the advantage of the Campbellite support.

Perhaps Lincoln was too confident; but, in any case, Sangamon County gave its preliminary preference to Baker, and appointed Lin-

POLITICAL COCK FIGHTERS.

During the early part of the campaign of 1844 Clay seemed certain to win over Polk, because of his vastly greater reputation and wide personal popularity. This poster caricature places Clay on top in the contest. In the background, are from left to right: Webster, Tyler, Van Buren, Calhoun, Benton, and Jackson, with the man at the extreme right not identified.

coln as one of the delegates to the district convention to work for Baker's nomination. Lincoln's old home, the village of New Salem, was now in the county of Menard, which had been formed by a division of the original Sangamon County. Menard's first choice in the convention was its old resident, Lincoln. But the convention compromised by nominating the third candidate, J. J. Hardin, disappointing the two active rivals, Baker and Lincoln. It came to be understood by candidates, and perhaps throughout the district, that the Whigs were to give these three aspirants successive terms at Washington. Baker came second in the sequence, and was elected in 1844, while Lincoln was obliged to wait for his turn until 1846. Mr. Beveridge is in his element in recounting Lincoln's ups and downs in that period as an aspirant for Congressional hon-

ors. We shall see, as our narrative proceeds, that Lincoln lost nothing by waiting.

He was, however, drawn deeply into the presidential struggle of 1844. John Tyler's course had served to strengthen the hold of Clay upon the Whigs of the country, while the Democrats had not been harmonized by the strange proceedings of a President who had been elected on the Whig ticket but had shown strong Democratic leanings without becoming a follower of Jackson and Van Buren. Among the Whigs every doubt about the nomination of Henry Clay had disappeared; and no party was ever more united or more ardent in the support of a presidential candidate.

The Whigs met at Baltimore on the first of May, 1844. This was the most complete and symmetrical national convention that had ever been held by either party. All business was transacted in a single session, Clay having been nominated by acclamation with no other name presented. Several ballots resulted in the choice of Theodore Frelinghuysen for Vice-President. This time the Whigs knew both candidates thoroughly, and commended them, with full confidence in their devotion to Whig principles. The third and fourth resolutions were eulogistic first of Henry Clay and then of Mr. Frelinghuysen. The Whig doctrines were all summed up in the second resolution; and since Lincoln was making his way forward in public life on this platform

HENRY CLAY.
NOMINATED FOR
Eleventh President of the United States.

The reader will notice an ingenious device in this campaign portrait which explains what appears to be an erroneous statement that Henry Clay was the eleventh President of the United States. In the original lithograph, considerably larger, the eye more readily discovers two additional words in the caption, on a line by themselves: "Nominated for." The device appealed to the confident admirers of a candidate, and to the thrifty who after election—if their candidate won—found it easy to eliminate the two words in small type and hang the portrait on the walls of the home during the Presidential term. The colored lithographs reproduced in these early chapters are all from the private collection of the author.

JAMES K. POLK.
FREEDOM'S CHAMPION.

Polk was elected President in this campaign of 1844. When the Democratic convention, after eight ballots, had failed to choose between Van Buren and Cass it turned to Polk—the first "dark horse" in the history of the Presidency. He was born in North Carolina in 1795 and educated at the State University. But early in his youth the family moved into Tennessee and the future President began to practice law there in 1820. Three years later he was elected to the legislature and in the following year was sent to Congress. He served in the House for seven terms, the last two as Speaker, and was then chosen Governor of Tennessee, in 1839. His administration as President was notable for the winning of the war with Mexico and the settlement of the Oregon boundary dispute with England. Polk died at Nashville in 1849, three months after his term expired.

we may well quote the plank in full. It stands recorded as follows:

Resolved that these principles may be summed up as comprising: A well regulated currency; a tariff for revenue to defray the necessary expenses of the government, and discriminating with special reference to the protection of the domestic labor of the country; the distribution of the proceeds from the sales of the public lands; a single-term for the Presidency; a reform of executive usurpations; and generally such an administration of the affairs of the country as shall impart to every branch of the public service, the greatest practical efficiency, controlled by a well-regulated and wise economy.

It was remarked in the previous chapter that after Mr. Van Buren's defeat in 1840, Democratic caucuses throughout the nation had at once declared their intention to nominate him again in 1844. This purpose had not been abandoned, and the real head of the Democratic party was to have been pitted against the actual leader of the Whigs. But something happened, as a bolt out of clear sky, that shifted the issues and caused the rejection of Van Buren. The Democrats brought a "dark horse" to the front for the first time in our presidential history, and wrecked Henry Clay's life-long ambition to serve a term in the White House.

On the twenty-second of April, President Tyler had sent to the Senate a treaty with the Republic of Texas, providing for the annexation of that imperial domain by the United States. The United States had acquired some

pretentions as to Texas in making the Louisiana Purchase of 1803, Spain and France not being in agreement over the line between French and Spanish possessions in North America. But when we acquired Florida by purchase from Spain in 1819 we definitely relinquished our claims to Texas. Meanwhile, Mexico had been successful in its struggle for independence; and by the Treaty of Cordova, between Mexico and Spain (February, 1821), Texas with Coahuila had become one of the constituent states of the federated republic of Mexico.

After the Missouri Compromise of 1820, Southern leaders had begun to look enviously toward Texas as their one great opportunity to extend slave territory. Many land grants in Texas were sought for, and some large ones

MATTY MEETING THE TEXAS QUESTION.

Martin Van Buren, who had been elected President in 1836 and defeated by Harrison in 1840, was a receptive candidate for a third nomination in this year 1844. He had a majority on the first ballot, in the convention, but failed to receive the necessary two-thirds vote. He had declared against the annexation of Texas and thus alienated some Southern support. Madam Texas in this cartoon is a fearful creature, in contrast with the attractive person shown on the opposite page. All the men here are Democrats. Van Buren ("Matty" being a nickname from Martin) is being prodded by Andrew Jackson. Texas is carried on a platform by Senators Benton and Calhoun. At the right are the convention nominees for President and Vice-President, James K. Polk and George M. Dallas.

VIRTUOUS HARRY, OR SET A THIEF TO CATCH A THIEF!

Texas had revolted from Mexico in 1836 and established itself as an independent republic. The question of admission to the Union, or annexation, was the leading issue of the campaign of 1844. Polk and Dallas, the Democratic nominees, declared for annexation, while Clay and the Whigs were against it as not fair to Mexico. In this poster caricature Clay is represented as refusing to have anything to do with Madam Texas and gamblers, horse-racers, and licentious profligates. The Quaker retorts: "Softly, softly, friend Harry. Thou hast mentioned the very reason that we cannot vote for *thee!*" Clay was widely accused of being fond of all the relaxations and amusements of his day. Lincoln was a Presidential Elector on Clay's ticket in Illinois in this campaign of 1844, and he spoke for Clay and against the annexation of Texas not only in his own State but in Indiana as well.

were obtained by Southern Catholics on the ground of religious sympathy, Mexico being under dominant Roman Catholic control. Both Clay and Van Buren, as Secretaries of State— the first in 1827 and the second in 1829—had offered increasing sums of money to Mexico for the purchase of Texas, but without results. This Texas question was leading us directly into two great wars, first that which President Polk directed against Mexico, and second that which President Lincoln waged for the preservation of the Union and the restoration of the Stars and Stripes in Texas as everywhere else; therefore it may be worth our while to record several convenient dates and facts.

For a dozen years after the Mexican independence of 1821, Southern land-seekers and adventurers of a filibustering tendency had been forcing their way into Texas. In 1833 Texas separated from Coahuila and set itself up as a full State in the Mexican federal system. But two years later a dictatorship was in power at Mexico City, state sovereignty was annulled by the Mexican Congress, and all the state constitutions were declared nonexistent. This gave Texas its welcome opportunity to secede and proclaim its independence.

General Sam Houston, another of the young men from older sections who were seeking fame and fortune by leadership in law, pol-

SILAS WRIGHT
Received the Democratic nomination and declined. Member of New York State Senate, 1823-27, of federal House of Representatives, 1827-29. United States Senator, 1833-44. Governor of New York, 1845-46. Died in 1847, at the age of fifty-two.

THEODORE FRELINGHUYSEN
Whig nominee. Senator from New Jersey, 1829-35. Mayor of Newark, 1836-39. Chancellor of New York University, 1839-50. President of Rutgers College in New Jersey, 1850-62. Died in 1862, at the age of seventy-five.

GEORGE M. DALLAS
Democratic nominee, elected. Mayor of Philadelphia, 1828. Senator from Pennsylvania, 1831-32. Minister to Russia, 1835-39. Vice-President, 1845-49. Minister to Great Britain, 1856-61. Died in 1864, at the age of seventy-two.

NOMINATED FOR VICE-PRESIDENT IN THE CAMPAIGN OF 1844

itics, and amateur soldiery in frontier communities, was the commander of the Texas troops that after a short campaign of four or five weeks defeated a much larger Mexican army led by the President and Dictator, General Santa Anna himself. As a war prisoner, the Mexican leader was ready to sign a treaty acknowledging the independence of the Republic of Texas. Having done this, he was allowed to go to the United States, and after some months he returned to Mexico. The treaty that he had signed was not ratified.

With the incoming of President Van Buren in March, 1837, the United States recognized the independence of Texas and set up diplomatic connections. England and France took similar steps. Acquiring independence had cost Texas a good deal of money, and the resources of the young republic were too little developed to give assurance of solvency. The Mexican population of Texas had been very small, and Americans were running the experimental republic. An immediate attempt to secure annexation (in 1837) had some Southern support, but failed at Washington.

But the Texans in due time discovered that they possessed an almost infallible remedy for American reluctance in the matter of annexation. They held possession of an area of 265,780 square miles, all but a small percentage of which was public domain in full control of the Texas Congress. Nothing was easier than to issue land warrants in great numbers and to dispose of them throughout the southern half of the United States. As an able writer puts it, the owners of these warrants "were at once converted into advocacy of Texas annexation."

In 1843 it was asserted by a Virginia Congressman that if we delayed to annex Texas, Great Britain would be given the opportunity; and we would have no grounds for complaint if we had undertaken to play the part of dog in the manger. General Jackson was still living, and in March of that year he wrote a letter strongly advocating immediate annexation.

It had been planned to hold the Democratic convention as early as December, 1843, with Van Buren's nomination thus far uncontested. But it was postponed until May 27, 1844, and meanwhile candidates were boldly questioned as to their stand on the Texas question. Van Buren had the courage to part company with his old mentor, Andrew Jackson, and he declared himself opposed to annexation in a letter of April 20th. Clay had taken the same ground in a letter dated three days earlier. The convention made Van Buren's nomination impossible from the outset by adopting the two-thirds rule that had governed the two preceding conventions.

The annexation treaty had been negotiated and concluded on the part of the United States by Tyler's Secretary of State, the eminent John C. Calhoun of South Carolina. This was on April 12th, and the Van Buren letter was written on April 20th, two days before President Tyler sent the treaty to the Senate. Mr. Van Buren's letter was not, however, given to the public until the 27th, exactly a month before the meeting of the Baltimore convention. Tyler may have thought that this would promote his own candidacy, while the faithful Van Burenites regarded the whole affair as devised by Calhoun. Thus the leading organ of the Van Buren Democrats declared—referring to Calhoun—"It is the last card of his desperate competitor, who has been playing for twenty-five years for the Presidency with the frenzy of a gamester."

Van Buren still had strength, and he would have been nominated on the first ballot but for the adoption of the two-thirds rule, the Southern votes favoring the rule while most of the Northern ones were against it. As Mr. Stanwood remarks, "the conclusion is inevita-

JOHN C. CALHOUN

As Secretary of State, Calhoun negotiated the treaty annexing Texas in the year 1844. It was promptly rejected by the Senate, became an issue in the campaign, and was then approved by the Senate on March 1, 1845, just before the end of Tyler's administration. Calhoun had been a distinguished member of the House, 1811-17; Secretary of War under Monroe, 1817-25; Vice-President with John Quincy Adams and Andrew Jackson, 1825-37, resigning; Senator, 1832 until his death in 1850, with the exception of a year as Secretary of State during the administration of President Tyler.

ble that they, the Northern delegates, were willing that he should be sacrificed, but that they did not quite venture to appear with daggers in their own hands." Van Buren on the first ballot received 134 votes out of 151 from the Northern States, while there were only 12 votes for him out of 105 from the South. He had a clear majority of 26 over all other candidates put together. But he lacked 32 votes of the necessary two-thirds. Lewis Cass of Michigan was second with 83, Richard M. Johnson of Kentucky had 24, James Buchanan of Pennsylvania 4, Levi Woodbury of New Hampshire 2, Commodore Stewart of Pennsylvania 1, and John C. Calhoun of South Carolina 6.

On the second day of the convention, a new name appeared as the eighth ballot was taken. Van Buren had 104, Cass 114, and James K. Polk of Tennessee 44. The New York chairman, acting upon instructions, thereupon withdrew the name of Mr. Van Buren and the large New York delegation swung over to Polk. We are told that a "stampede" followed with the result that every delegation changed its vote and Polk was unanimously nominated.

Senator Silas Wright of New York was named for Vice-President but refused, this being perhaps the only case of the kind previous to the declaration of Governor Lowden of Illinois at Cleveland in 1924. Senator Wright held the views of Mr. Van Buren; but George M. Dallas of Pennsylvania—who was ultimately selected and became Vice-President—in due time stood with the South on the Texas question. A flourishing Texas city bears his name and reminds us of the campaign of 1844.

The platform took a lofty tone and ridiculed the "factitious symbols" (referring to the log-cabins, the rowdy parades, and the hard-cider orgies of the Harrison campaign), and it made appeal to "the intelligence, patriotism and dis-criminating justice of the American people." With a preliminary sentence or two the plat-form of 1840 was readopted. Then followed a resolution against the distribution of the proceeds of the sale of public lands and an-other approving of the veto power, "which has thrice saved the American people from the corrupt and tyrannical domination of the Bank of the United States."

Next came the really significant plank upon which the campaign was destined to turn. It reads as follows: "Resolved, that our title to the whole of the territory of Oregon is clear and unquestionable; that no portion of the same ought to be ceded to England or any other power; and that the reoccupation of Ore-gon and the reannexation of Texas at the earliest practicable period are great American measures, which this convention recommends to the cordial support of the Democracy of the Union." A resolution expressing esteem for Martin Van Buren was, of course, entirely sincere. The party had set itself to great business, and it had made its nomination of candidates to accord with understandings of the platform.

A minor party asserted itself in this cam-paign, that of the Abolitionists, who formed what they called the Liberty party, and they named James G. Birney for President and Thomas Morris of Ohio for Vice-President. They adopted a platform of exceedingly great

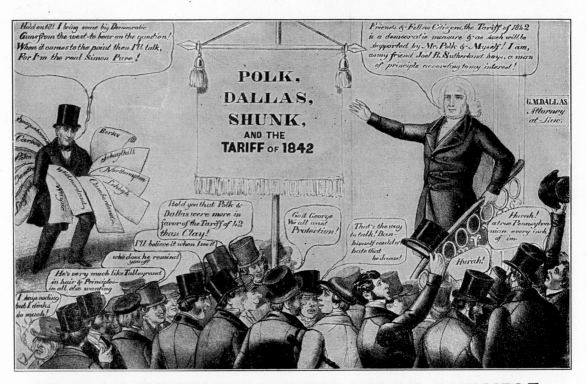

POLITICAL JESUITISM-OR INTEREST VERSUS PRINCIPLE.

The two principal figures in this cartoon are Pennsylvanians. At the left is Francis R. Shunk, suc-cessful Democratic candidate for Governor. At the right is George M. Dallas, nominee for Vice-President, put on the ticket to strengthen Democratic chances in the North. The tariff of 1842, which Dallas is shown as endorsing, was a Whig measure strongly opposed by the Southern Democrats. It raised the rates provided by the compromise of 1833, and was widely approved in the North. Two years after this election, when Dallas as Vice-President was presiding in the Senate, he cast the deciding vote to secure the passage of the Democratic tariff of 1846, by which tariff rates were reduced. He thus offended the protectionist industries of his own State of Pennsylvania.

WHIG APPEAL FOR AN EXCUSE.

Theodore Frelinghuysen, nominee for Vice-President on the Whig ticket, is dressed in academic robes with his head in the clouds. At this time he was Chancellor of the University of New York. He appeals here for "an excuse for teaching free-trade doctrines to students in the University, and tariff doctrines to the Whig party, who think it all important." Clay, seated at the dice table in front of President Tyler, suggests: "Never give up, Freely. Do as I did when Walker proved, according to Roosevelt's Mode of Protecting Domestic Industry, that the tariff cannot give protection while we have bank paper to raise prices and induce excessive imports and give foreign nations a bounty— blackguard them when you cannot answer."

length devoted exclusively to the slavery question. Mr. Birney was a southern man who had formerly owned slaves in Kentucky and Alabama, but had gone north and established an anti-slavery paper in Ohio.

Mr. Clay held that we were boldly facing two wars at the same time, one with Great Britain, over the Oregon dispute, and the other with Mexico, that country never having acknowledged the independence of Texas. To assert both territorial claims at the same time was to place ourselves in a position that meant the sacrifice of one or the other, with the possible loss of both. But counsels of prudence meant nothing to the embattled Democrats in 1844. Reckless statesmanship sometimes inflames public opinion to the point of equal recklessness.

Clay was the most popular public man the country has ever produced, while Polk— against whom nothing could be said—had no personal hold and was unknown to the masses. He had been Speaker of the House at Washington for four years, but more recently he had twice been defeated for the governorship of Tennessee. Like most early Tennesseans, he had been born in North Carolina; but he had been elected to the Tennessee Legislature in 1823 at the age of twenty-eight. He was in his fiftieth year when he entered upon the Presidency, March 4, 1845.

The popular vote for presidential electors gave 1,377,243 for Polk, and 1,299,062 for Clay. In the electoral college, however, Polk's vote was 170 and Clay's 105. Maine, New Hampshire, New York and Pennsylvania had gone Democratic. Clay, on the other hand, had carried North Carolina, Kentucky and Tennessee. Of the four Western States, Clay had carried Ohio; but Michigan, Indiana and Illinois had gone for Polk and Dallas. Majorities in most States had been very small.

If the Abolitionist vote for Birney in New York had been cast for Clay, it would have turned the thirty-six presidential electors to what was the real anti-slavery side; and this alone would have been sufficient to make Henry Clay President. Similarly, the Abolitionists defeated Clay in Michigan, and practically also in Indiana. Their wrong-headedness and folly had thus brought on the Mexican War, with a series of consequences that plunged us inevitably into the terrible abyss of the war between the States.

Mr. Beveridge says that "when the campaign came on the ardor of the Whigs knew no bounds. 'Redeem the country,' 'restore pros-

perity' and, louder than all else, 'Hooray for Clay,' were the war-cries of the Whigs. The Democratic slogans were 'Texas,' 'Oregon,' 'Manifest Destiny,' 'Forward,' 'To the West,' and, above all, that stirring, militant demand, 'Fifty-four Forty or Fight'—'War rather than to yield to Great Britain any part of the vast domain below that line, every foot of which, the Democrats claimed, belonged by right to the United States.' Indeed, as a practical influence on voters, American title to the Oregon country was quite as strong a political force in the campaign of 1844 as the annexation of Texas. Already long trains of covered wagons were making their way to the far Northwest."

Lincoln, as we have already said, was one of the Whig nominees for Presidential elector; and we have sufficient evidence as to his assiduous efforts to promote Whig success. It is to be regretted that his extemporaneous

POLK VERSUS WOOL; OR THE HARRY-CANE
This is a high-tariff Whig cartoon, directed against a free-trade candidate. Polk, the Democratic nominee for President in 1844, is being assailed by the woolly ram, and the tools of various manufacturing industries that favor a protective tariff. In his predicament the cartoon makes Polk say: "It is my opinion that wool should be duty free."

TARIFF AND TEXAS: TWO ISSUES OF 1844

For the industrial sections of the North a protective tariff was far more important than the acquisition of Texas. In this cartoon Clay rides his sea-shell chariot, flying the tariff banner, in triumph to the White House. Polk and Dallas, the Democratic candidates, together with Senator Benton, float on the Texas bladders. Van Buren is left to sink or swim by himself.

speeches were not reported for our benefit, and that if any had been carefully written out by him they had disappeared too soon for use by Nicolay and Hay and have not been discovered by more recent biographers. Francis F. Browne, in his valuable "Everyday Life of Abraham Lincoln," informs us that "Lincoln canvassed Illinois and a part of Indiana during the campaign, meeting the chief Democratic speakers, and especially Douglas, in debate. While in Indiana he visited the home of his boyhood and met old friends." He made a campaign; but we have no details.

At this time it seems undoubtedly true that Lincoln had never met Henry Clay and had never heard him speak. It was two years later, when Lincoln was an expectant candidate for Congress, that he went to Lexington, heard Clay speak at a public meeting, and visited the great party leader at Ashland. Mr. Clay had known, of course, for years of Lincoln's Whig activities in Illinois, and especially

his support of the Clay-Frelinghuysen ticket of 1844. Dr. William E. Barton, in his excellent life of Abraham Lincoln, prints for our benefit a letter of Lincoln's written in October, 1845, in which he analyzes in his characteristic way the defection of the New York supporters of the Birney ticket. "If the Whig Abolitionists of New York," writes Lincoln, "had voted with us last fall, Mr. Clay would now be President, Whig principles in the ascendant and Texas not annexed; whereas, by the division, all that either had at stake in the contest was lost." In a later part of this epistle, Lincoln makes observations on Texas and the slavery question that are so typical of his mentality and so important as looking to his future lines of reasoning and action, that I am glad to quote a long paragraph in full:

But I will not argue further. I perhaps ought to say that individually I was never much interested in the Texas question. I never could see much good to come of annexation, inasmuch as they were

NOT A DRUM WAS HEARD NOR A FUNERAL NOTE
AS HIS CORSE TO THE RAMPARTS WE HURRIED—
NOT A LOCO DISCHARGED HIS FAREWELL SHOT
O'ER THE DITCH WHERE OUR HERO WE BURIED.

It is Van Buren, the Fox, who is being buried. He had served only one term in the White House, being renominated in 1840 but defeated by Harrison, and failing to receive his third nomination in this year 1844 because of his opposition to the annexation of Texas. The grave-diggers are Clay and Webster; the horse, Andrew Jackson; the driver, President Tyler; and the mourners, Benton and Calhoun. With the exception of two words—*Loco* instead of *soldier,* and *ditch* in place of *grave*—the poetry is the first verse of Charles Wolfe's "Burial of Sir John Moore."

already a free republican people on our own model. On the other hand, I never could very clearly see how the annexation would augment the evil of slavery. It always seemed to me that the slaves would be taken there in about equal numbers, with or without annexation. And if more *were* taken because of annexation, still there would be just so many the fewer left where they were taken from. It is possibly true, to some extent, with annexation, some slaves may be sent to Texas and continued in slavery that otherwise might have been liberated. To whatever extent this may be true, I think annexation an evil. I hold it to be a paramount duty of us in the free States, due to the Union of the States,

ASHLAND, THE HOME OF HENRY CLAY

Our illustration is from an old print, showing Ashland as it appeared at about the time when Lincoln visited Henry Clay.

and perhaps to liberty itself (paradox though it may seem), to let slavery in the other States alone; while, on the other hand, I hold it to be equally clear that we should never knowingly lend ourselves, directly or indirectly, to prevent that slavery from dying a natural death—to find new places for it to live in, when it can no longer exist in the old. Of course I am not now considering what would be our duty in cases of insurrection among the slaves. To recur to the Texas question, I understand the Liberty men have viewed annexation as a much greater evil than ever I did; and I would like to convince you, if I could, that they could have prevented it, without violation of principle, if they had chosen.

DEATH OF HENRY CLAY, JUNIOR, IN THE MEXICAN WAR

Although the Whigs and their presidential candidate, Henry Clay, had opposed the annexation of Texas and the beginning of the Mexican War, they supported the war loyally after it had begun. Speaking in the House on July 27, 1848, Lincoln said: "You have constantly had our votes here for all the necessary supplies. And more than this, you have had the services, the blood, and the lives of our political brethren in every trial and on every field. . . . Clay and Webster each gave a son, never to be returned."

CHAPTER XIII

War with Mexico — The Oregon Crisis

*Lincoln is nominated and elected to Congress—Admission of Texas
as a State results in war with Mexico—Disputes with England over
the Oregon boundary*

STARTLING CHAPTERS in the history of American expansion were writing themselves in the news of the day, and Lincoln was eager to be at Washington in the thick of these great affairs. Having been disappointed in his hopes of a nomination in 1842 and again in 1844, he took unwonted pains in advance of the district convention of 1846 to forestall the possible competition of his able and popular rival, J. J. Hardin. Baker regarded himself as under agreement to step aside in favor of Lincoln. Hardin had previously served a term, and Baker was now the incumbent. For some time it was doubtful what steps Hardin would take, but at length he announced his candidacy. He proposed to Lincoln that they should hold what we would now call a primary election throughout the district, to name the candidate by direct choice of Whig voters. But Lincoln refused, and declared that he was satisfied with the convention system by which Hardin and Baker had been named in succession.

So assiduous was Lincoln's canvass, and so thorough his organization work, that Hardin withdrew before the convention was held; and on May 1, 1846, Lincoln was nominated, with no other name presented. The platform took the orthodox Whig positions on the tariff and the bank question, but ignored the new and acute issues that were agitating Washington and the country.

Ten days after Lincoln's nomination on May 1st, President Polk sent a message to Con-

FAIR ROSAMOND; OR THE ASHBURTON TREATY
From *Punch* (London), November, 1842

Before the Northwest boundary was settled, the Northeast boundary—between Maine and Nova Scotia—was fixed by the Ashburton treaty. Great Britain sent Baron Ashburton as special commissioner, while the United States was represented by Daniel Webster, Secretary of State. It is worth noting that this treaty also provided that each nation should maintain a squadron on the coast of Africa for suppression of the slave trade. The cartoon shows America, in Indian costume, demanding that Britannia must choose between the treaty cup and the war dagger. Its inspiration is the story of the fair Queen Rosamond, who was forced by her husband to drink from a cup which was in fact the skull of her father.

ciates was almost universal. President Tyler had been able to secure the passage of a joint resolution authorizing the admission of Texas as a State, and he returned it to Congress with his approval only a short time before the inauguration of Mr. Polk as his successor in March, 1845. The Texas Congress had later accepted the proposal with unanimity, and within a few months Texas had adopted a State constitution. Soon after the session of Congress opened at Washington in December, 1845, this Texas constitution was ratified, and the admission of Texas was completed by virtue of a proclamation issued by President Polk on December 29th.

If there had been no slavery question to engender party strife and to arouse sectional apprehensions, there could have been little doubt anywhere as to the propriety of the annexation of Texas by the United States. After ten years of actual control by the American settlers, Mexico—torn by revolution and without stable leadership—could never have regained Texas. The Mexicans could have done little with the empty expanses of Texan territory, even if they had been able to assert by force the claims of a nominal sovereignty. President Polk attempted to conciliate them, and to negotiate a fair adjustment of differences. He sent Mr. Slidell of Louisiana as a special ambassador to Mexico, but wholly without avail. Slidell was not received or heard.

The objections of anti-slavery men and Whig leaders to the policies that led us into

PETER CARTWRIGHT
Lincoln was elected to Congress in 1846, his Democratic opponent being this famous itinerant Methodist preacher. Cartwright had been a member of the Legislature in 1828 and 1832, and was twenty-four years older than Lincoln. He had long played a leading part in building up the Methodist Church in the Middle West. Cartwright was 87 when he died, in 1872.

gress explaining the failure of his effort to conciliate Mexico, and Congress declared that a state of war existed by the act of Mexico. On May 13th Polk issued his War Proclamation. The decision was popular, and volunteers were ready to enlist beyond all possible need. The call for fifty thousand found six times that number responding at once. Mr. Beveridge gives a graphic account of the resistless enthusiasm for the Mexican War that swept the country throughout the summer of 1846, while Lincoln was running for Congress against the famous Peter Cartwright who had been nominated by the Democrats.

Everybody in the West had been familiar with the thrilling events—the Alamo tragedy, for example—in the brief struggle for the independence of Texas in 1836; and the fellow-feeling for Sam Houston and his Texas asso-

TEXAS COMING IN

This is a cartoon of the campaign of 1844 which accurately foretold events. It was not until the following March that Texas actually was invited into the Union; and it shows Polk welcoming Texas from the White House side of Salt River. In cartoons of this period Salt River represents defeat. The five Whig leaders pulling on the rope have not been able to stay the progress of the steamboat Texas. From left to right they are: Clay and Frelinghuysen, candidates for President and Vice-President; Daniel Webster; Henry A. Wise, a member of Congress from Virginia; and one man who is not identified. Astride the barrel in Salt River is William Lloyd Garrison, declaring that he will not keep company with Clay, an unholy man and a blackleg. It was, indeed, the loss of the Abolition vote—which went to James G. Birney—that brought about the defeat of Clay.

the Mexican War could not be viewed lightly. But as for the war itself, it seems a fair contention that the Mexicans were the aggressors in the military sense, and brought on the clash for which the West in the summer of 1846 was enthusiastic without regard to party. American expansion was the theme that made the Mexican War so popular, and the slavery problem was virtually forgotten for the moment, in the ardor for territorial gain.

Lincoln took the platform, with other speakers of both parties, at war rallies in Springfield. Since he and his circuit-riding Methodist opponent, Mr. Cartwright, were of similar views upon the war and upon several other subjects (Cartwright being no believer in slavery), the contest was not bitter. Lin-

coln had a remarkable campaign manager in his young law partner, William H. Herndon, who remained his close friend as well as his business associate through all the remaining years, and who became one of his biographers. As Beveridge remarks: "The contest was one of personal popularity and party organization, in both of which Lincoln had an immense advantage over the truculent old Methodist preacher. Many Democrats thought that a minister ought not to run for political office; the Democratic workers were indifferent, and the organization loose and inefficient. Indeed, early in the campaign, the Democratic leaders gave up the contest, and that party cast only 42 per cent. of the total vote."

It was, of course, quite impossible for President Polk to fight the British Empire while he had a war with Mexico on his hands. The most telling slogan of his electoral campaign had been "Fifty-four Forty or Fight." The subsequent literature of the Oregon question has grown to be voluminous. But the main facts can be readily stated and easily understood.

Boundary questions will not settle themselves, and they must either be subjected to the costs and hazards of war, or else worked out by the bargaining methods of diplomacy. The United States had come into possession of a long stretch of Atlantic coast line, with difficulties in fixing exact terminal points both northward

VAST AREAS ACQUIRED DURING POLK'S ADMINISTRATION

First came the annexation of Texas in 1845, just as Polk was being inaugurated. This resulted in war with Mexico and the acquisition of all that unpopulated region lying between Texas and the Pacific which later became the States of California, Nevada, Utah, Arizona, and parts of Colorado and New Mexico. For that territory the United States paid Mexico $15,000,000. Even while war with Mexico was being waged, there came a dispute with Great Britain over the Oregon country, resulting in the compromise line shown on this map. The United States claim was founded upon the explorations of Captain Gray and of Lewis and Clark, strengthened by the acquisition of Spanish, French, and Russian rights. In 1818 the United States had entered into an arrangement with Great Britain for joint occupation, which lasted until 1846 when the Oregon country was permanently divided between them.

THIS IS THE HOUSE THAT POLK BUILT

From *Yankee Doodle*, a humorous weekly published in New York for about two years beginning with October, 1846. It was frankly opposed to the Mexican War and ridiculed the statesmanship of President Polk.

and southward. Webster had remained in the Tyler Cabinet in order to complete the negotiations with Lord Ashburton over the Northeast boundary—to fix the line between Maine and Nova Scotia, and to divide the Great Lakes. We had earlier avoided a war with Spain, and had settled the Southeast boundary by purchasing the whole of Florida under the terms of the Treaty of 1819.

We were sweeping westward, and were inevitably facing the prospect of a coast line on the Pacific, that might prove as extensive as that which we had confirmed on the Atlantic by successful diplomacy.

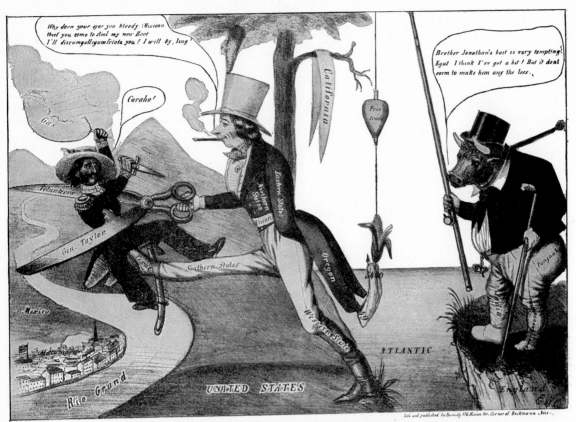

UNCLE SAM'S TAYLORIFICS

This is a New York lithograph of 1846, which portrays Great Britain—the John Bull of the cartoonists—literally as a bull instead of the traditional burly Englishman. Uncle Sam, or Brother Jonathan, is here crossing the Rio Grande into Mexico with his armies, while John Bull finds the moment opportune to fish for that portion of Oregon lying between 54° 40″ and 49°—which did, indeed, become English territory by the treaty of 1846. This is an excellent example of the lithographic poster caricatures of E. W. Clay, whose initials are seen in the lower right corner, and whose work appears more often than that of any other artist in the illustrations of this and nearby chapters.

While Lincoln was making his campaign in the summer of 1846, Commodore Sloat of our Pacific Squadron was occupying California, without any Spanish forces to make serious trouble. General Kearny, who was then stationed at Fort Leavenworth, Kansas, was at once placed at the head of an expedition that marched across the country and occupied New Mexico, which then included Arizona. John C. Frémont, a young officer of the regular army, had for several years been exploring Oregon and the Northwest; and he was conveniently at hand, in that historic summer of 1846, to share California honors with Admirals Sloat and Stockton.

It was already certain, in view of the vic-tories that General Zachary Taylor had been winning in the northern states of Mexico, that the war must result in complete American victory. With Texas already ours, we would inevitably carry a southern boundary straight to the Pacific, retaining New Mexico and California. This southern line would have to be adjusted in detail, as a part of the peace agreement, when the Mexicans were ready to lay down their arms.

But the Mexicans refused peace overtures in 1846; refused again after Taylor had defeated them overwhelmingly at Buena Vista in February, 1847; and they continued to reject reasonable American terms after General Winfield Scott had landed an army at Vera

WHO'S AFRAID?
Punch's first cartoon on the Oregon question,
April 12, 1845.

Sir Robert Peel, British Premier, is ready for a duel with
President Polk. King Louis Philippe of France is pictured
as supporting the American President. The Democrats in
1844 had made a campaign issue of the Oregon boundary,
declaring that the title of the United States to the whole
region was clear and unquestionable. Polk, their candidate for President, was successful and in his inaugural address in March, 1845, he asserted the claims of the United
States in terms suggesting the possibility of war. This
cartoon from *Punch* was England's unofficial answer.

promotion of Britain's commercial interest in
securing free-trade with a new cotton-growing
country. Moreover, the hold of Mexico upon
California was of the very slightest, and
the British had their aspirations, well-known
and long-standing, in that direction, about
which there is no possible reason to speak
reproachfully.

As for our Northwestern claims, we had
already made it certain by explorations, by
the establishment of a fur-trading post at the
mouth of the Columbia River, and by the beginning of permanent settlements, that we
should be able to hold Oregon as the first
stretch of American territory on the Pacific.
We had reached an understanding with Russia that the Czar's government would not assert claims south of the parallel known as
"Fifty-four Forty." The Spaniards, followed
by the Mexicans, had never claimed anything
north of the forty-second degree of latitude,
this being the present northern line of California. The British, meanwhile, were carrying on a considerable fur-trade through private agencies in this stretch called the "Oregon Country," that lay between the northern
California line at "Forty-two" and the Rus-

Cruz and had marched over
the mountains to the capital.
Scott's victory at Chapultepec, and his occupation of the
City of Mexico, brought the
war to an end in the middle
of September. The Treaty of
Guadaloupe - Hidalgo was
signed on February 2, 1848,
and thereby the United States
made permanent acquisition
of New Mexico and California, paying a considerable
sum of money.

It should not be supposed
that these American transactions of the years from 1845
to 1848 had been unobserved
in Europe. There were British influences working to
keep Texas from joining the
United States, in obvious

WAR! OR NO WAR!
"Ike! I say the 49th, and let's settle it amercably."
"No Sir-ree. I goes for the hull of Oregon or none—I do, and don't do
ner-thin else."

(This is a hint to the effect that belligerency over the Oregon question was
largely bluster. We reproduce it from a lithograph published at New York in
April, 1846, at the height of the crisis.)

"WHAT! STRIKE YOUR OWN FATHER!"   TEACHING GRANDMOTHER BRITANNIA TO SUCK EGGS

"YOUNG YANKEE-DOODLE," AS HE SEEMED TO THE ENGLISH
DURING THE DISPUTE OVER OREGON

Two cartoons from London *Punch,* March, 1846.

In the first sixty years of *Punch,* from 1841 to 1901, two really great artists stood out among others who contributed to its political success. In the earlier period it was John Leech, in the later period John Tenniel, their careers overlapping in the '50s. To both in turn came the opportunity to stand up for John Bull and ridicule Uncle Sam during international crises. The reader should remember that the cartoonist of *Punch* was a member of its editorial board, reflecting its deliberate opinion. He was never embarrassed by the caution that often tempers the language of the editorial writer.

Two of the cartoons on this page bear the signature of John Leech, and the third was evidently drawn by him. They set forth the opinion prevalent in England when America was shouting "Fifty-Four-Forty or Fight," from which position we receded when we accepted the boundary of Forty-nine degrees. James Buchanan, as American Secretary of State, and Richard Pakenham, special British envoy, arranged a compromise settlement that was submitted to the Senate by President Polk in June, 1846, and duly ratified by the Senate.

RIDICULOUS EXHIBITION; OR, YANKEE-DOODLE PUTTING HIS
HEAD INTO THE BRITISH LION'S MOUTH.

From *Punch,* May 2, 1846.

sian line at "Fifty-four Forty." This area, claimed in part by the British and claimed *in toto* by the Americans, included what are now the States of Oregon and Washington and the Canadian province of British Columbia.

Douglas had held that to allow the British any part of this area was to submit to a violation of the Monroe Doctrine. In their platform of 1844 the Democrats had declared firmly for the uncompromising occupation of the whole Oregon country. In his first message to Congress, December 2, 1845, President Polk had dealt at great length with the subject, explaining that in view of compromises that had previously been offered, he had endeavored to settle the dispute by carrying the line of the forty-ninth parallel straight to the Pacific coast. But on British refusal President Polk had withdrawn the offer and had asserted American title to the entire Oregon territory.

He advised the scrupulous observance of the agreement that had been made for the temporary joint occupation, but he proceeded to reassert the Monroe Doctrine as applicable to the Oregon situation. Two months later President Polk had sent to Congress correspondence that seemed to make it clear that, upon their own frank admission, the British were arming in preparation for an American war. Congress proceeded at once to authorize the President to give the necessary twelve months' notice for the ending of the joint occupation of Oregon. Whereupon the British Ambassador, on June 6, 1846, agreed to accept what had been a repeated American offer—namely, the extension of the forty-ninth parallel to the seacoast, leaving Vancouver's Island to the British. There was still a Whig majority in the Senate, and the Whigs wisely and prudently advised President Polk to accept the offer. This was accordingly done, the business reached its conclusion smoothly and promptly, and the last step was taken on July 17th with exchange of ratifications at London.

Thus President Polk had been sensible enough to lay aside extreme claims in the Northwest, while he had been reasonable and moderate in his treatment of Mexico in the adjustment of the new Southwest boundary.

Since campaign talk is not always consistent, much less impartial, in its verdicts, one cannot quite blame Lincoln and his Whig supporters for

THE GREEDY BOY.

VICTORIA—YOU GREEDY YOUNG YANKEE! YOU WON'T LEAVE A CRUMB FOR LITTLE FREDERICK ALBERT.
LOUIS PHILIPPE—SOYEZ TRANQUILLE MA CHERE; YOU ARE VARY FOND OF INDIAN BONBONS, AND I LOAF VARY MOSH ZE TABAC D'ALGIERS MYSELF   WE SHALL MOSH BETTER BOTH BE QUIET.

Frederick Albert was Victoria's son, then five years old, later Edward VII. Louis Philippe was King of France from 1830 until he was forced to abdicate as a result of the revolution of 1848. His remark about Indian bonbons, in the caption above, refers to Britain's war against the Sikhs, lasting from 1845 to 1849 and resulting in the annexation of the Punjab. This cartoon is from *Yankee Doodle*, New York, November, 1846.

ULTIMATUM ON THE OREGON QUESTION.

The young Queen Victoria is on her throne, and the conversation with President Polk has reference not only to the Oregon boundary but to the opening of Britain's ports to American grain free of duty. Victoria claims it as a friendly act, while Polk asserts that it was done only to save England from starvation. The famine in Ireland occurred at this time, which explains the presence in this drawing of Daniel O'Connell, the Liberator. As for Oregon, Victoria declares that she offered to settle by arbitration. Polk replies that he too offered to arbitrate but Victoria refused. Now he will not arbitrate. If Victoria agrees to his demands for the whole region he is willing to negotiate. General Bunkum, at the right, blusters loudly, while at the left the Duke of Wellington, hero of the Battle of Waterloo thirty years earlier, urges the British lion "up and at 'em!" This is an extraordinary cartoon, again the work of E. W. Clay, showing a situation under Polk which might easily have led to war with England while we were still engaged in war with Mexico. It was in this year that Lincoln was elected to Congress and began to participate in international affairs.

turning the tables on the Democrats. This Oregon settlement had been announced in the very height of the Congressional campaign, and Whigs twitted Democrats unmercifully upon having so hastily retreated after their "Fifty-four Forty or Fight" war-cry. The unthinking masses wanted no compromises with England, and so they turned to the support of Lincoln and other Whig candidates, although it had been Clay himself and the Whig Senate that had encouraged Polk and had ratified the British agreement.

Lincoln was easily elected over his opponent; and he afterwards regretted that he had been so modest and so lacking in political foresight

as to have declared that he would be content with a single term. This was the only Whig district in Illinois, and it was sending able men, one after another, each for a single term. It was thus depriving itself of the prestige that would have resulted from keeping the same man at Washington long enough to make himself felt in committees and on the floor of the House. But in these matters there are compensations that appear in the retrospect.

It was almost a year and a half after his election in 1846 before Lincoln took his seat on the opening day of the first session of the new Congress in December, 1847. Douglas had been elected to Congress as a Democrat in an adjoining district in 1842 and 1844, with Hardin in one term and Baker in the next term as his colleagues from Lincoln's Seventh Illinois District. In 1846 Douglas was elected for a third term, on the same day that Lincoln was chosen for his first and only term in Congress. Lincoln had continued to meet Douglas in debate from time to time, and their careers were moving along parallel lines so far as Illinois was concerned, although Douglas with his aggressive personality and his brilliancy in debate was already making his mark at Washington as a champion of Democratic policies.

So rapid, indeed, was Douglas's advancement that instead of taking his seat in the House with the Illinois delegation, he appeared at the other end of the Capitol and took the oath of office as a Senator of the United States from Illinois, when Congress opened on the first Monday of December, 1847. The Democratic Legislature at Springfield had conferred this honor upon the rising young leader of their party, who was then only thirty-three years old. Lincoln was nearly six years older, being some weeks short of thirty-nine when he took his seat as a member of Congress.

POLK, IN HIS DREAM, SWEARS NEVER TO ABANDON HIS OREGON DEMANDS

Books on the table in the White House bedroom indicate that the President had been reading "The Art of War" and a life of Napoleon, as well as Calvin's works and a thesis on practical piety. The devilish apparition hides behind a mask of Andrew Jackson, and demands of Polk "never to take your toe off that line should you deluge your country with seas of blood, produce a servile insurrection, and dislocate every joint of this happy and prosperous union!" Attracted by the noise of the nightmare are three members of President Polk's cabinet: George Bancroft, the historian, who was then Secretary of the Navy; James Buchanan, Secretary of State, with the candle, who detects a strong smell of brimstone; and Robert James Walker, Secretary of the Treasury and author of the Walker Tariff of 1846, who holds the tariff bill under his arm and declares the President to be patriotic even in his dreams. The cartoon is dated April, 1846.

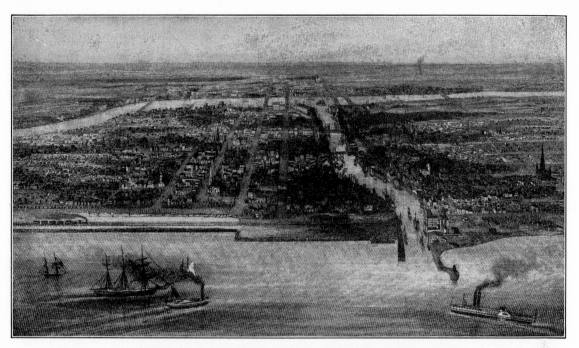

CHAPTER XIV

Lincoln, the Congressman

He attends a great river and harbor convention at Chicago—Some noted biographers of Lincoln—His personal appearance—A speech against Cass for President, on the floor of the House

IN THE LONG INTERVAL after his election, Lincoln had ample time to adjust his own private affairs, although he followed the course of history-making events, as the Mexican War proceeded, with the closest attention. The year 1847 was one of almost unprecedented interest in the settlement and development of the great West. President Polk had not been satisfied to occupy himself with his war to the southward and his territorial acquisitions and boundary adjustments on the Pacific Coast. He had dealt rapidly with various domestic issues. He had proceeded to urge a reduction of tariff rates, justified not only on constitutional grounds but to meet increased war expenditures. Among other executive activities was his veto of a River and Harbor appropriation bill. This had caused great dissatisfaction, in view of the country's eagerness for improvements required by the expansion of national territory, the growth of internal and external trade, and the western movement of population that was stimulating steamboat traffic on the Great Lakes and on the rivers of the Mississippi Valley. A great River and Harbor Convention was called to meet at Chicago, July 5, 1847, in protest against the veto.

125

No such gathering, official or otherwise, in point of numbers and of representative interest, had ever before been held in the United States. We have an account of the convention in Dr. Barton's life of Lincoln, this biographer being the first to make note of the fact that Lincoln attended that great meeting as a delegate from Sangamon County. Mr. Beveridge gives a still more detailed account of this notable occasion that was important enough to bring Horace Greeley, Thurlow Weed, and many other leading Whig journalists from New York and elsewhere to the growing city on Lake Michigan, besides Whig statesmen, business men, and promoters of all sorts. The Eastern visitors traveled on the Great Lakes in splendid steamboats, and wrote glowingly of their first trip to the magnificent West. Southern delegates came north on the Mississippi

LINCOLN'S FAVORITE CANDIDATE FOR THE PRESIDENCY IN 1848

Though the honor of entering Mexico City fell to General Scott, Zachary Taylor was the real hero of the Mexican War through his victories at Resaca de la Palma, Monterey, and Buena Vista. In the year following the war he was nominated as the Whig candidate for the Presidency and was elected. Congressman Lincoln spoke for Taylor not only throughout Illinois but in New England, particularly at Worcester and Boston. This is a sketch of General Taylor made by a lieutenant of artillery at the battle of Palo Alto.

steamboats, making a short land trip from a river point to Chicago.

Mr. Beveridge observes that this convention gave Lincoln his first personal contact with men of nationwide prominence from other States. The chairman of the convention, for instance, was Hon. Edward Bates, of St. Louis, whom Lincoln was to appoint Attorney-General in his first Cabinet of March, 1861, almost fourteen years later. While Lincoln was noting everything with intense interest, he was not wholly unobserved himself. He even took the floor and made a brief speech, in reply to the famous New York lawyer, David Dudley Field (attending as a spokesman for President Polk), who had disagreed at some point with the convention's formal resolutions. Mr. Beveridge tells us that Horace Greeley, writing of the convention for his own paper, the New York *Tribune,* remarked that "Hon. Abraham Lincoln, a tall specimen of an Illinoisan, just elected to Congress from the only Whig district in the State, was called out, and spoke briefly and happily in reply to Mr. Field." This incident reminds me that David Dudley Field took an active part in the hidden wire-pulling at Chicago in the Convention of 1860 that defeated Seward and resulted in Lincoln's nomination.

No such demonstration had ever been made in support of Lincoln's life-long dogma of Internal Improvements as a national policy; and the tall Congressman-elect was imbued with fresh vigor by all that was said and done in this convention. Mr. Beveridge shrewdly suggests that Whig policies along economic lines at this time were in full harmony with the expansive mood of the country, and that the Democratic opposition to internal improvements, still stubbornly maintained as a party doctrine, played a more important part than has been usually recognized in the Presidential victory gained by the Whigs in 1848.

Dr. Barton observes that the River and Harbor Convention had put Chicago upon the nation's map. "It did more than any previous or subsequent assembly to link the fortunes of the great State of Illinois with the North and East." Dr. Barton continues as follows: "It must have been a very illuminating event to

IDA M. TARBELL

While an editor on the staff of *Mc-Clure's,* Miss Tarbell began a study of Lincoln's career which resulted in the publication of a two-volume Life in 1900—then the most important Lincoln biography that had appeared since that of Nicolay and Hay. Revised editions have followed.

© Bachrach

ALBERT J. BEVERIDGE

Himself a lawyer, statesman, and orator of the Middle West, Senator Beveridge had devoted years of intensive research and labor to a Life of Lincoln when his own death in 1926 ended the story. Two volumes carry Lincoln to the debates with Douglas in 1858.

© Underwood

WILLIAM E. BARTON

A Congregational minister long resident in Illinois, author of half a hundred volumes in various fields of literature, Dr. Barton has made himself an authority on Lincoln. His two-volume Life was published in 1925; and "The Lineage of Lincoln," in 1929, adds new information.

THREE FAMOUS BIOGRAPHERS OF LINCOLN

Lincoln. It was probably his first view of the Great Lakes. It was his first important reminder that, while he was elected from central Illinois, he, as the only Whig member of Congress from the State, must find his political support thereafter largely in the newer portion of the State, where the Whigs were more largely in control. It must have reminded him, and he was soon to be rudely reminded again, that Chicago and northern Illinois with her, was thenceforth to be reckoned with as an important political, as well as economic, factor."

I may pause to remark that biographers encounter difficulties that they do not always explain to their readers. They are conscious that in any given period the important man who is the subject of their inquiries must have been doing something or going somewhere. But too frequently they can find no trace of his activities. Their hero had kept no diaries; nor had the wife, or the law-partner, or any other intimate associate, performed the daily offices of a Boswell. Herndon and Lamon, who survived to write Lincoln biographies,

knew a vast deal about his concerns and his movements that it never occurred to them to include in their volumes of reminiscence. Strictly contemporary biographers, writing about a man who has attained eminence under their own eyes, are more likely to record trivial things in a somewhat disparaging and apologetic manner, and to exploit their own philosophies of life and character, than to give us an orderly arrangement of the plain, precise facts that are so obvious to them that they leave them fatally unrecorded.

Nicolay and Hay were duly objective and informative in their ten-volume history of Lincoln and his times. But they made no thorough research into the earlier periods of his life, because as his secretaries at the White House, in daily contact with him, it was their chief business to deal with the vastly important Presidential years. Their first volume covers everything up to the Frémont-Buchanan campaign of 1856, and the second volume carries the reader through the campaign of 1860, with Lincoln elected, Secession movements

THOMAS NAST'S CONCEPTION OF LINCOLN

Though always exceedingly friendly, Thomas Nast, like all the other cartoonists, rarely presented Lincoln in the dress of a statesman. In this cartoon of July, 1861, after Lincoln had become President, we see the tradition of shabby attire still maintained. The other figure in the cartoon is Jefferson Davis, the period being one of confidence in the North that the Confederacy would not last.

for us our estimates and opinions than to give us specific facts that would have aided us in arriving at our own judgments. Miss Tarbell in 1894 began to make first-hand inquiries that resulted in substantial additions to our knowledge of Lincoln's youth and his private life. Dr. William E. Barton, in researches that were still continuing in 1929, had made further distinct additions to our knowledge of the Lincoln family and its migrations, and to our understanding of Lincoln's development as a public man.

Finally, Mr. Beveridge in two posthumous volumes, appearing in the autumn of 1928, brought his notable Life of Lincoln to the point of an unfinished chapter on Lincoln's campaign for the Senate in 1858 and his debates with Douglas. Without haste and with untiring industry, aided by the best historical scholars and with the resources of public li-

well under way, and the country waiting in suspense for Buchanan's retirement and Lincoln's inauguration on March 4, 1861. The remaining eight volumes are devoted to the four years of Lincoln's first term, his re-election, and the culmination of the war, followed by his assassination, a few weeks after the delivery of his famous second inaugural address.

It would have been fortunate for us, in our natural desire to know the life story of the most eminent American since Washington, if the men who were Lincoln's associates in the long years previous to 1856 had been as modestly intelligent in their subsequent biographical work as were his White House secretaries. They supplied us, indeed, with much information for which we are thankful; but after the manner of men who were lawyers rather than historians, they were more concerned to shape

LINCOLN AS THE CARTOONISTS FIRST PICTURED HIM

This sketch of Lincoln in Springfield, in the period of his election to the Presidency, is used here to illustrate a prevalent eastern conception of the Illinois statesman, poorly clad, in short-waisted, swallow-tail coat and thin pantaloons. Compare it with the actual portrait on the opposite page. Lincoln's visitor in this cartoon is Artemus Ward, the sketch accompanying an account the humorist wrote of "A Visit to Abe Lincoln," for *Vanity Fair*.

braries and private collections at his disposal, Mr. Beveridge proved at length and in detail a thesis that I had long held without access to all the supporting facts. It was this: that the Lincoln of 1861-5 was merely the Lincoln of the thirty previous years, trained and developed in the school of experience, educated through constant study of current history and the movements of American life, and tested by the trials and emergencies of a crisis toward which events had been carrying the nation. Lincoln, as well as other men, had been preparing unconsciously for the impending conflict.

Thus Lincoln as Beveridge saw him, like his long-time rival Douglas, was a political thinker, a man versed in the arts of practical politics, and a recognized leader of what was suddenly becoming in 1847-8 the dominant party. He was well equipped to have a share in the nation's councils at Washington when he entered upon his term of service, with the Mexican War in progress, absorbing the attention of the people, who supported it with ardor.

Mr. Beveridge, like Mr. Barton, holds the view that Lincoln had probably never visited Chicago or seen Lake Michigan before his attendance at the River and Harbor Convention. The opinion found some support in a quotation that Mr. Barton gives as a footnote, from the Chicago *Journal* of July 6, 1847. This item, printed at the moment when Lincoln was in Chicago, derives its greatest value from the evidence it furnishes of the high opinion in which Lincoln was held even then in the rising metropolis on Lake Michigan. Let us promote the paragraph to the place that it deserves in the main text:

Abraham Lincoln, the only Whig Representative to Congress from this State, we are happy to see in attendance upon the convention. This is his first visit to the commercial emporium of the State, and we have no doubt his first visit will impress him more deeply, if possible, with the importance, and inspire a higher zeal for the great interest of, River and Harbor improvements. We expect much from him as a Representative in Congress, and we have no doubt our expectations will be more than realized, for never was reliance placed in a nobler heart and a sounder judgment. We know the banner he bears will never be soiled.

THE EARLIEST PORTRAIT OF LINCOLN
Authorities differ as to the exact date of this daguerreotype, but it is known to be of the period of Lincoln's election to Congress in 1846 or shortly thereafter. He was then about thirty-seven years old. The portrait was first published in 1895, through the courtesy of the President's son, the late Robert T. Lincoln.

The reporter might have been mistaken as regards the "first visit." Lincoln had visited New Orleans twice as a young man, had practised law in numerous counties, had canvassed Illinois and Indiana in presidential campaigns, and was looking to the future with ambitions that could only be realized through his state-wide acquaintance with the people and the interests of Illinois. He had long been an apostle of improvements to benefit navigation and commerce. I should prefer to find some statement in Lincoln's own words before accepting the view that he had never seen Chicago until a year after his election to Congress. An eminent lawyer, politician and Congressman-elect residing at Albany, New York, might in earlier life have visited New York City more than once, with his name on hotel registers but with no interview or flattering paragraph in the metropolitan newspapers. There were similar reports as to Grover Cleveland's unfamiliarity with New York City and Washington, when he emerged in national politics. I raise the point about Lincoln in Chicago not as vital in itself, but as illustrating the difficulties that biographers encounter in dealing with so simple a fact as the question when Lincoln first saw the metropolis of his own State, the city in which he was to be nominated for the Presidency thirteen years after the River and Harbor Convention.

It is true that he had arrived in Illinois from southern Indiana, a region in which the newspapers of Cincinnati, Ohio, and Louisville, Kentucky, were then as now the more familiar organs of current intelligence and opinion. And at Springfield, as one of his contemporaries has told us, a Louisville newspaper continued to be his favorite daily source of amusement as well as information. But it is also undoubtedly true that he was a reader of Chicago newspapers, and we know that he came later into touch with Mr. Medill and the Chicago *Tribune*. His own immediate organ was the *Sangamo Journal,* published in his home city of Springfield, whose opinions echoed his own views, and for which he often wrote editorials on major topics as well as upon State and local questions of legislation and partisan politics.

It is recorded that Lincoln in 1846—presumably after, rather than before, his election to Congress—had made the journey from the capital of Illinois to Lexington (the capital of Kentucky), for the sole purpose of hearing Clay make a speech; and we are told that Clay invited Lincoln to remain

LEWIS CASS, DEMOCRATIC NOMINEE FOR THE PRESIDENCY IN 1848

Born in New Hampshire in 1782, Cass moved with his family to Ohio when he was about eighteen and was admitted to the bar there in 1802. Member of the Assembly, federal marshal, colonel of militia in the war of 1812, brigadier-general in the regular army, Governor of the Territory of Michigan, Secretary of War in Jackson's Cabinet, Minister to France, Senator from Michigan—such had been the imposing career of Lewis Cass when he was defeated by Gen. Zachary Taylor in the campaign of 1848. He returned to the Senate, became Secretary of State in the Buchanan Cabinet, supported the Northern cause during the Civil War, and died in 1866.

and make him a visit at Ashland, the invitation being accepted. That he had never made the short trip from Springfield to Chicago until a year later than his visit to Clay at Lexington, is somewhat difficult to believe.

Neither am I quite satisfied to accept every detail of the reminiscences of certain persons who in advanced years describe minutely such things as Lincoln's costume on particular occasions. If Greeley or the Chicago *Journal* had found anything strikingly unusual, their comments would probably have given us that impression. It may be doubted whether his friend and admirer, Elihu B. Washburne, could remember with precision, forty years later, just what clothes Lincoln wore at the River and Harbor meeting in 1847. It is set down, however, in his reminiscences that Lincoln's costume consisted of a "short-waisted, thin, swallowtailed coat; a short vest of same material, thin pantaloons, scarcely coming down to his ankles; a straw hat; and a pair of brogans with woolen socks."

It was mid-summer and hot weather, and Lincoln had come across the prairies by stage-coach. Many of us have attended mid-summer conventions in Chicago, and have seen countless statesmen content to wear shirts and thin trousers only. We will readily believe that Lincoln cared nothing for costume, and did not pose magnificently like Henry Clay or Lewis Cass. But we need not feel sympathetically sorry about his clothes as if that had been a matter that was subjecting him to cruel embarrassment. We may, indeed, decline to think that Elihu Washburne had the eye of a tailor. He merely had his conceptions of the dignity of the presidential office, and he was seeking contrasts as in old age he remembered Lincoln in the days of informality on the prairies, when men could afford to be careless about clothes. Mrs. Lincoln was of the Kentucky "quality," and would have had her influence in such matters. We must admit, however, that Mr. George Grey Barnard had found some justification, in the reminiscences of various people besides Elihu B. Washburne, for the unstatesmanlike costume that has caused criticism of his heroic statue of Lincoln as a young man. The cartoonists of 1860 were only too ready to accept the tradition of a badly dressed, shabby Lincoln, as so many of the caricatures presented in these pages must attest beyond dispute.

The rumors regarding Lincoln's manner and personal appearance seemed to have a certain value as political assets in 1860, and they were encouraged rather than contradicted by Lincoln's supporters. There was enough truth to give some color of veracity to the hundreds of tales that came into circulation about the phenomenal frontiersman of shambling figure, awkward manners, and ill-assorted raiment who had defeated a conventional statesman like Seward in the Chicago Convention. I might quote additional costume descriptions, suspiciously like that of Mr. Washburne, in the reminiscences of other survivors of Lincoln's early period, some of these fixing the same weird costume as of the year 1832, fifteen years before the Chicago meeting of 1847, and just after Lincoln had returned from the Black Hawk War to make his first appeal as candidate for the Legislature. Lincoln's own habit of poking fun at himself in stump speeches, in order to pave the way for a sally of mild ridicule directed against an opponent, helped, of course, to sustain the legends of his incomparable uncouthness.

It was only a few months after he had taken his seat in Congress that Lincoln was a delegate to the Whig convention at Philadelphia that nominated General Zachary Taylor for the Presidency. The Democrats were in the field with Hon. Lewis Cass of Michigan as

BARNARD'S STATUE OF LINCOLN

Erected in Cincinnati in 1917, George Grey Barnard's heroic statue gained high praise for artistic merit and encountered criticism for portraying a Lincoln in unstatesmanlike costume, possessed of extraordinary hands and feet. But Barnard had been meticulous in his search for exact measurements and models. When a replica of this statue was later presented to Manchester, England, the principal address was made by Alton B. Parker, who had been the Democratic candidate for the Presidency in 1904.

their candidate. Curiously enough, both of these nominees had participated in the Black Hawk War, with General Lewis Cass commanding the improvised expedition, and Colonel Zach Taylor, who had been an army officer

CASS & HIS CABINET IN 1849.

A lithograph poster issued during the Presidential campaign of 1848, in which Lewis Cass, the Democratic nominee, was defeated by his Whig opponent, General Zachary Taylor. This is not a confident, friendly cartoon put out by the supporters of Cass, for the group—although a distinguished one—is discussing the spoils of the election and the error of the Whigs in deserting Clay. Cass himself, for example, as a President addressing his Cabinet, remarks: "Gentlemen! We stand on the Democratic Platform, that is, to Reward our Friends. Rewarding of enemies and deserting of friends is what caused the breaking-up of the Whig party." The members of this imaginative Cabinet are (beginning at the left) Amos Kendall of Kentucky and Levi Woodbury of New Hampshire, who had both been members of the cabinets of Jackson and Van Buren; John C. Calhoun of South Carolina, Thomas H. Benton of Missouri, Sam Houston of Texas, and William Allen of Ohio, the last four being prominent Democratic members of the Senate.

for twenty-four years and had served well in the War of 1812, on hand to do the real fighting. If Lincoln as a captain of raw militia had little contact with the gallant Taylor in that brief experience, he did not hesitate to match his own career as an Indian fighter with that of the Democratic candidate for the Presidency, of whom he had never thought highly.

Congress remained in session for some time after the presidential conventions had been held; and late in July the tall Whig member from Illinois (who had quickly attained unusual prominence for a new Congressman in spite of later assertions to the contrary) indulged in a strictly political speech on the floor

of the House. He undertook to attribute sound Whig principles to his own military candidate Taylor, who had never been in politics, while reviewing at length the opinions and the career of Lewis Cass as a man with military as well as political background—a hero of the William Henry Harrison victories in the War of 1812 and, later, an Indian fighter in the Black Hawk War of 1832.

A Georgia member of Congress, Mr. Iverson, on the previous day had accused the Whigs of having deserted all their principles and "taken shelter under General Taylor's military coat-tail." Whereupon Lincoln asked his colleague if he did not know that his own

A WAR PRESIDENT.

Manifest Destiny.

New Mexico.
California Chihuahua.
Zacatecas. MEXICO. Peru.
Yucatan, Cuba.

GAS

PROGRESSIVE DEMOCRACY.

AS LINCOLN AND THE WHIGS PICTURED THE DEMOCRATIC CANDIDATE IN 1848

Though he had been in public office for thirty-five years, Lewis Cass retained the title of General from the War of 1812. In a speech upon the floor of the House of Representatives, quoted in this chapter, Lincoln ridiculed the military record of Cass in a spirit quite similar to that which is evident in this cartoon. Here, and in another cartoon on page 154, we see also a temptation prevailing at the time to play upon the similarity of the words *Cass* and *gas*.

party had run the last five presidential races under General Jackson's coat-tail, and that they were now running the sixth under the same cover. Finding himself in his element with the give-and-take of a stump debate proceeding on the floor of the House, Lincoln ran on in the following vein:

Yes, sir, that coat-tail was used not only for General Jackson himself, but has been clung to, with the grip of death, by every Democratic candidate since. You have never ventured, and dare not now venture, from under it. Your campaign papers have constantly been "Old Hickories," with rude likenesses of the old general upon them; hickory poles and hickory brooms your never-ending em-

blems; Mr. Polk himself was "Young Hickory," "Little Hickory," or something so; and even now your campaign paper here is proclaiming that Cass and Butler are of the true "Hickory stripe." Now, sir, you dare not give it up. Like a horde of hungry ticks you have stuck to the tail of the Hermitage lion to the end of his life; and you are still sticking to it, and drawing sustenance from it, after he is dead.

Lincoln explained that he was using figures of speech that he would not have been the first to introduce, but he was meeting the gentleman from Georgia on his own ground. He was perhaps without an equal anywhere in his ability to find pithy anecdotes and allusions with which to enliven political debate. He then proceeded to treat Cass's military record with scathing ridicule:

He (Cass) was not at Hull's surrender, but he was close by; he was volunteer aid to General Harrison on the day of the battle of the Thames; and as you said in 1840 Harrison was picking huckleberries two miles off while the battle was fought, I suppose it is a just conclusion with you to say Cass was aiding Harrison to pick huckleberries. This is about all, except the mooted question of the broken sword. Some authors say he broke it, some say he threw it away, and some others, who ought to know, say nothing about it. Perhaps it would be a fair historical compromise to say, if he did not break it, he did not do anything else with it.

By the way, Mr. Speaker, did you know I am a military hero? Yes, sir; in the days of the Black Hawk war I fought, bled and came away. Speaking of General Cass's career reminds me of my own. I was not at Stillman's defeat, but I was about as near it as Cass was to Hull's surrender; and, like him, I saw the place very soon afterward. It is quite certain I did not break my sword, for I had none to break; but I bent a musket pretty badly on one occasion. If Cass broke his sword, the idea is he broke it in desperation; I bent the musket by accident. If General Cass went in advance of me in picking huckleberries, I guess I surpassed him in charges upon the wild onions. If he saw any live, fighting Indians, it was more than I did; but I had a good many bloody struggles with the mosquitoes, and although I never fainted from the loss of blood, I can truly say I was often very hungry.

Mr. Speaker, if I should ever conclude to doff whatever our Democratic friends may suppose there is of black-cockade federalism about me, and therefore they take me up as their candidate for the Presidency, I protest they shall not make fun of me, as they have of General Cass, by attempting to write me into a military hero.

It must not for a moment be supposed that Lincoln was making himself conspicuous in Congress by buffoonery or by partisanship on low levels. This very speech, with its paragraphs of rather undignified personality in reply to Iverson's even less dignified attack upon the Whigs, was in all its major portions composed of a worthy and intelligent, even though partisan, review of political issues. Doubtless the speech was made with the principal object of distribution as a campaign document in Illinois. Ever since that date, Congressmen in presidential years have been making political speeches on the floor at Washington, and using the franking privilege to give them circulation in their home States or elsewhere. It is worth observing that even in a partisan speech, like this one for the plaintiff in the case of Taylor against Cass, Lincoln always built his argument upon bed-rock principles.

A CONTEMPORARY CARICATURE OF CASS

This was published in one of the first issues of *Yankee Doodle*, in 1846, and harmonizes with the characterization made by Lincoln in the political debate of 1848 which is quoted on page 133. Text accompanying the drawing makes slighting reference to Cass on his hobby-horse, with particular relation to the withdrawal of the Democrats from their extreme demands in Oregon.

THE CAPITOL AT WASHINGTON, WHEN LINCOLN WAS A MEMBER
OF CONGRESS

After the British had burned it in 1814 the Capitol was rebuilt according to the original plan. This engraving shows it as it appeared during the years from 1827 until 1851. Then the construction of extensions at each end was begun, and these were completed—with the new dome—in 1863, during Lincoln's Presidency.

CHAPTER XV

Washington in Polk's Time

Lincoln's first journey to Washington—His distinguished contemporaries in Congress, and the contacts he formed there—A period of political and social revolt in Europe

THERE WAS PUBLISHED in 1917 a volume entitled "Uncollected Letters of Abraham Lincoln, Now First Brought Together by Gilbert A. Tracy with an introduction by Ida M. Tarbell." Mr. Tracy who had been a clerk in the War Department from 1863 to 1868 had afterwards, as Miss Tarbell informs us, become a Connecticut farmer who collected Lincoln material and gradually found enough letters that had not appeared in previous collections of Lincoln's "Complete Works" to justify a supplementary volume. I make this allusion rather conspicuously because Mr. Tracy's efforts illustrate the fact that the biographers of great men can never be definitive, to the last detail.

Letters of French officers and soldiers who served under Rochambeau and Lafayette in the Revolution, now found from time to time in the garrets of old French homes, afford fresh glimpses of George Washington as man and soldier. Similarly, we learn details about the Revolutionary War from the re-discovered diaries and letters of Hessians and other Germans who were fighting on the British side. Lincoln's days were not those of stenographers or of carefully filed carbon copies of correspondence. John Hay's presence in the White House as one of the group of men composing Lincoln's personal staff was due to the fact that, besides other qualifications, this youth had acquired the then novel accomplishment of shorthand writing.

We may anticipate nothing further about Lincoln of a startling character. But that some items of worth-while information may yet come to light, especially in letters written by various people as they had been brought

135

VOLUNTEERS FOR TEXAS

This is a New York poster caricature bearing the date of
May, 1846. It had been the asserted privilege of the
effete East to ridicule the militia of the newer States and
the volunteers for Indian wars; and that privilege was
exercised also in respect to the Mexican War. Both cartoons on this page express derision of the warlike West.

into contact with Lincoln, may be expected as
a matter of course. Lincoln himself doubtless
wrote hundreds or even thousands of letters
that were destroyed, many of which would
have been of literary, historical, and biographical value.

Mr. Beveridge informs us that Mr. and Mrs.
Lincoln, with their son Robert, now in his
sixth year, on their journey to Washington
"went by way of St. Louis, up the Ohio on a
steamboat to Pittsburgh, and thence by rail to
Baltimore and Washington." In Mr. Tracy's
volume there appears a letter from Lincoln to
a correspondent on a matter of litigation, written October 19, 1847. In that letter he says:
"Unfortunately for my attending to the business you sent, I start for Washington by way
of Kentucky, on next Monday."

Since Congress was not opening until December 6th, the Lincoln family were allowing
themselves a margin of about six weeks. This
letter raises a proper question for an investi-
gator like Mr. Barton to answer by his methods
of research. I am not able to discover that
any writer has really found out anything in

detail about this first trip of Abraham Lincoln
to the nation's capital as a member of its
law-making body. I make this seemingly unimportant allusion for two reasons. First,
because it shows a single instance among almost countless ones where the zealously pursuing biographers find the trail completely
broken. The more significant reason, however, lies in the contrast afforded between this
trip of Lincoln in his official capacity from
Springfield to Washington in the autumn of
1847, and the journey he made between these
two capitals as President-elect for his inauguration of March 4, 1861.

Mr. Beveridge bases his statement that the
Lincolns went to Washington by way of St.

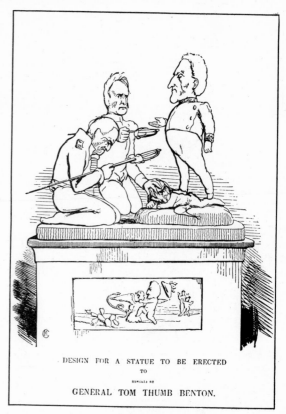

DESIGN FOR A STATUE TO BE ERECTED
TO
HIMSELF BY
GENERAL TOM THUMB BENTON.

It was not a far cry, in the days of the Mexican War,
from political leadership to command of armies in the
field; and the veteran Senator from Missouri, Thomas H.
Benton, who had been a colonel in the War of 1812, was
seriously considered by President Polk as commander of
the American forces in Mexico or as chief of staff issuing
orders from Washington. Benton is here pictured standing
on the prostrate, one-legged Mexican dictator, Santa Anna,
while Generals Scott and Taylor offer him their swords.
This is a cartoon from *Yankee Doodle*, a comic periodical
published in New York.

ROUGH AND READY LOCOMOTIVE AGAINST THE FIELD.

General Taylor, who was strictly a military man all his life until elected to the Presidency, had been nicknamed "Old Rough and Ready" because of his somewhat careless manners. In contrast, General Scott, nominated four years later, was derisively called "Old Fuss and Feathers." This cartoon appeared early in the campaign of 1848. It shows President Polk on the White House steps, with General Taylor and Lewis Cass engaged in the presidential race. In the distance is General Scott, pictured as hurrying to President Polk with the much delayed treaty of peace that had been negotiated by Nicholas Trist, Assistant Secretary of State. Trist's peace mission in Mexico was at first a failure, though he remained until finally, in February, 1848, the treaty was signed.

Louis upon some remark that was afterwards attributed to Mrs. Lincoln. It is hard to discover anything that this latest authority has overlooked, but apparently he had not read a letter that Lincoln himself wrote from Washington in February to a Mr. Welles, that appears in Tracy's collection. It had to do with an earlier letter containing money that had somehow been lost. Lincoln was to have delivered it personally in St. Louis. The letter to Mr. Welles proceeds as follows:

To make it more secure than it would be in my hat, where I carry most all my packages, I put it in my trunk. I had a great many jobs to do in St. Louis; and by the very extra care I had taken of yours, overlooked it. On the Steam Boat near the mouth of the Ohio, I opened the trunk and discovered the letter. I then began to cast about for some

safe hand to send it back by. Mr. Yeatman, Judge Pope's son-in-law, and stepson of Mr. Bell of Tennessee, was on board, and was to return immediately to St. Louis from the Mouth of Cumberland. At my request he took the letter and promised to deliver it.

Incidentally it is to be noted that the letter further spoke of Mr. Yeatman's unquestionable character, and of Lincoln's fear lest some "pickpocket on the boat may have seen me give him the letter and slipped it from him." It was typical of Lincoln's consideration that he called upon Mr. Yeatman in Washington about the lost letter, and thought it natural enough that "never seeing the letter again, he would never think of it."

All this makes it clear that Lincoln had his circle of friends in St. Louis, and affairs of

ALEXANDER H. STEPHENS
When Lincoln came into the House, in 1847, Stephens—though three years younger—had already been a member, from Georgia, for two terms. They became close friends. During Lincoln's term as President, Stephens served as Vice-President of the Confederacy. After the War he was again a Georgia Congressman at Washington.

JEFFERSON DAVIS
Serving his first term in the House, from Mississippi, Davis in 1846 resigned to become a Colonel in the war with Mexico. From 1847 to 1851 he was a member of the Senate. Later he was Pierce's Secretary of War, and again a member of the Senate. In February, 1861, he was elected President of the Confederate States. He died in 1889.

ROBERT TOOMBS
A Representative from Georgia, 1845-53, and Senator from 1853 to 1861, when the South seceded, Toombs was made Secretary of State in the Confederate Cabinet of Jefferson Davis. He resigned after a few months to become a Brigadier-General in the Southern army. Toombs, Stephens, and Lincoln were all Whigs in 1848.

THESE MEN LINCOLN KNEW WHILE A MEMBER OF THE HOUSE, AND LATER THEY
HELD THE THREE MOST PROMINENT OFFICES IN THE CONFEDERACY.

one kind or another to occupy him in that city. With weeks on his hands, we may reasonably infer—in view of Lincoln's earlier letter saying that he was "going to Washington by way of Kentucky," and remembering the further fact that Mrs. Lincoln's own friends and relatives were living in that State—that the journey was again broken by visits *en route*.

This, to be sure, is a sidelight of no great candlepower; but it may help the reader to understand that the too ready assumption that Lincoln was obscure, unknown, and untravelled even in his own section of the country, is merely based upon the failure of later biographers to find letters long ago destroyed, and the failure of earlier biographers to record what they supposed to be commonplace and uninteresting.

As regards Mr. Lincoln's service in Congress, it is more important to consider that experience as lifting him finally to the plane of national politics, than to give especial weight

to his sayings and doings as a Congressman. This was the first House for many years that was not organized and controlled by the Democrats. There was a small Whig majority, due to various causes but not due to any marked reaction against Polk's Mexican policy, and the war for territorial expansion.

The Speakership was conferred upon the Hon. Robert C. Winthrop of Massachusetts, an excellent representative of Harvard training and Boston culture. It is not likely that Mr. Winthrop's memories of Lincoln as a Congressman, revived in after years, could have been much softened to accord with the sentiment of a nation in mourning for the martyred President. Referring to Lincoln in Congress, Mr. Winthrop said: "I recall vividly the impressions I then formed, both of his ability and amiability. We were old Whigs together, and agreed entirely upon all questions of public interest. I never lost my personal regard for him. For shrewdness and

THOMAS HART BENTON

Participation in the War of 1812 brought Benton into contact with the new country west of the Mississippi, and he settled at St. Louis in 1815. Previously he had practiced law in Tennessee and had been elected to the State Senate there. When Missouri was admitted in 1821, Benton was sent to the United States Senate. For thirty years thereafter he dominated the politics of Missouri and was one of the Senate's most conspicuous leaders. Opposition to the Clay-Webster compromise of 1850 brought about his retirement.

DANIEL WEBSTER

After serving ten years in the House, not continuously, Webster was elected to the Senate from Massachusetts in 1827 and there became one of the great statesmen and orators of all time. From 1841 until 1845 he was Secretary of State under Harrison and Tyler, and from 1850 until his death in 1852 he occupied that office under Fillmore. With those exceptions his career in the Senate extended over a quarter of a century. He shared the leadership of the Whig party with Clay through a long period, but never received a Presidential nomination.

sagacity, and keen practical sense, he has had no superior in our day or generation."

The Lincoln family lived in a boarding-house that stood where now the Library of Congress occupies the square east of the Capitol grounds. Eight or ten Congressmen sat at the same table and became Lincoln's personal friends. Perhaps his best friend in Congress was Alexander H. Stephens of Georgia, a Whig member who afterwards became Vice-President of the Confederacy. In a letter to Herndon a few weeks after the opening of the session, Lincoln said that Mr. Stephens had just concluded "the very best speech of an hour's length" he had ever heard. Writing in later years, Mr. Stephens said: "I knew

Mr. Lincoln well and intimately. We were both ardent supporters of General Taylor for President in 1848. Mr. Lincoln, Toombs, Preston, myself, and others formed the first Congressional Taylor Club, known as the 'Young Indians,' and organized the Taylor movement, which resulted in his nomination."

It may be well at this point to quote further from this account by Mr. Stephens, because that statesman was under no temptation to compose a eulogy. "Mr. Lincoln was careless as to his manner and awkward in his speech, but possessed a very strong, clear, vigorous mind. He always attracted and rivetted the attention of the House when he spoke. His manner of speech as well as of thought was original. He had no model. He was a man of strong convictions, and what Carlyle would have called an *earnest* man. He abounded in anecdote. He illustrated everything he was talking about by anecdote, always exceedingly apt and pointed; and socially he kept his company in a roar of laughter."

As the sole Whig member from Illinois, Lincoln was regarded at Washington as head of the party in that State, just as Douglas, then in the Senate, was the recognized chief of the Illinois Democrats. Politicians will readily understand that these party conditions gave Lincoln, as a new member at Washington, a more favorable position than he might otherwise have secured. He had his reasonable share of committee appointments, and enjoyed the kind of recognition that brought him into close contact with many public men.

Having only the minor responsibilities that a new member incurs, he was able to cross frequently to the Senate chamber, and listen to men whose names had been long familiar to him, men whose speeches he had been reading since boyhood. At the same time he was acquainting himself with the personalities of younger men, who were destined to play a great part in the Civil War period. Among

A DAUMIER CARTOON OF THE YEAR 1848

For eighteen years Louis Philippe had been King of France; but the revolution of February, 1848, brought about his abdication and the proclamation of a republic. This cartoon by Honoré Daumier— perhaps the greatest French caricaturist of all time—shows Louis Napoleon, nephew of Napoleon I, as a candidate for the presidency of France in 1848. Though at first rejected, the French Assembly did elect Louis Napoleon as president of the Republic. Just four years later he had so shaped events that he was proclaimed Emperor. This same Louis Napoleon who became President of France while Lincoln was in Congress was thus Emperor of the French during Lincoln's Presidency, as Napoleon III. He was the son of the elder Napoleon's brother Louis. The French revolution of 1848 was the signal for an outbreak of popular movements throughout Europe. In Austria, Hungary, and Germany there were resignations, new governments, and reforms.

THE REPUBLICAN PARTY GOING TO THE RIGHT HOUSE.

The year 1848 witnessed the launching of democratic uprisings in France, Germany, and Hungary; and in the United States the same period saw the rise of various social movements destined to attract wide attention. The abolition movement is dealt with in subsequent chapters of this book. Others that might be mentioned were the beginning of the demand for woman's rights, the action of Maine in 1846 that began the march of prohibition, the establishment of the Mormon Church in Utah in 1847, and such brief experiments as the socialistic colony at Brook Farm, Massachusetts. When the Republican party was founded, in 1854, it was often asserted by its opponents that radical groups made up its principal strength. In a later chapter there is a poster caricature showing Frémont receiving a long line of such visitors in 1856, while here we reproduce a similar one seeking to show that their support went to Lincoln in 1860. He is carried on a rail by Horace Greeley.

the veterans were Daniel Webster of Massachusetts, John C. Calhoun of South Carolina, Thomas H. Benton of Missouri, and Lewis Cass of Michigan (Clay was temporarily out of the Senate, but was soon to return). Calhoun had been Tyler's last Secretary of State, but was back at his old seat in the Senate. James Buchanan, on the other hand, had left the Senate to become Polk's Secretary of State. The eminent William L. Marcy of New York was now serving as Secretary of War, and Robert J. Walker of Mississippi was Secretary of the Treasury.

Among the new members of the Senate sworn in on December 6th with Douglas was a man who had suddenly achieved amazing popularity as a hero of the Mexican War. This was Jefferson Davis of Mississippi. Davis had been a member of the House of Representatives, but at the outbreak of the war had hurried back to his own State to serve as Colonel of a famous volunteer regiment, the "Mississippi Rifles." Joining General Taylor's expedition, this regiment had won deserved fame; and Davis shared honors with General Taylor by his valor at the Battle of Buena Vista. The volunteer regiment was no longer needed, and Davis returned as the idol of his State and with the plaudits of the country.

A vacancy caused by the death of Senator Spaight enabled the Governor of Mississippi to honor Col. Jefferson Davis by appointing him to the Senate for the remainder of the term. The Mexican War was by no means finished, and a strong element among the extreme Southern leaders was urging President Polk to increase the regular army, push the conquest of Mexico to the point of overwhelming victory, and annex the entire Mexican area, or, at least, all of the states of northern Mexico. Also, Calhoun and the Southern men were already openly planning for the extension of slavery to the territory that was to be annexed.

These questions were being forced upon Polk and his administration, and they were at the heart of schemes and intrigues within the Democratic party as the forthcoming presidential convention was approaching. In these senatorial discussions, and in the more confidential councils of the Democratic leaders, Jefferson Davis was playing a great part. It is a notable circumstance that among the members of this Congress sitting in the Senate chamber were Douglas of Illinois and Bell of Tennessee, who were to head Presidential tickets in 1860, with Davis who was to be President of the Confederacy, Hannibal Hamlin of Maine, who was to be Lincoln's running mate, and Gen. Sam Houston who, when the crisis came, could not abandon the flag of the country that had added the Lone Star of Texas to the star-spangled banner. From New York was John A. Dix, who also, like Sam Houston, lives in history for his devotion to the flag.

Sitting in the House with Lincoln was the historian John G. Palfrey of Massachusetts,

while another eminent historian, George Bancroft, was then serving as Polk's Secretary of the Navy and literary mentor, and was about to be sent to London as United States Minister at the Court of St. James's. In the House, besides Stephens, who was to become Vice-President of the Confederacy, the Georgia delegation included Howell Cobb and Robert Toombs, both of whom later became pillars of the southern edifice. There were many others, Northern and Southern, who were to attain their wider fame at the time when Lincoln himself came into supreme command.

Most noteworthy as a link with the past was John Quincy Adams, who had served for many years in the House of Representatives after his retirement from the Presidency. Lincoln in his youth had been familiar with Adams's great state papers; and he was now hearing "the Old Man Eloquent," who was unrivalled in erudition as well as in oratorical graces, among the members of the lower House. Adams, who was then in his eighty-second year, was taking part in a somewhat acrimonious partisan discussion over suspending the rules to vote the thanks of Congress to various political war heroes, when he was fatally stricken with paralysis. Lincoln was present, voting "Nay" with Adams; and thus he "witnessed the death-stroke of one of the preeminent men of the nation, an outstanding figure in American history," to quote from Beveridge's excellent account. Lincoln was appointed on the Committee of Arrangements for the funeral of John Quincy Adams.

Lincoln was at Washington in a period that might well have stimulated the intellectual processes and aroused the imagination of a man far less gifted. For the United States, the great story of the Nineteenth Century was to turn upon events associated in one way or another with the Mexican War. Old men who re-

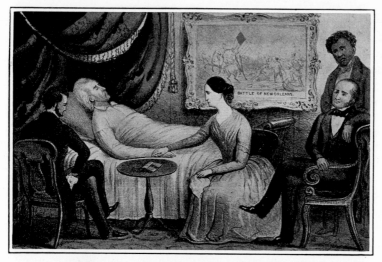

DEATH OF GEN.ʸ JACKSON,

born, March 15ᵗʰ 1767, and died June 8ᵗʰ 1845, in his 78 year

Andrew Jackson remained the guiding spirit, if not the actual head, of the Democratic party from his retirement in 1837 until his death in 1845. At this deathbed scene are Major Lewis, an intimate friend; Andrew Jackson, Jr., his adopted son; his daughter-in-law; and George, the Negro servant, whose own grave is near that of the General, in the Hermitage grounds.

membered Washington, and who had known intimately the group composed of the elder Adams, Jefferson, Madison, Marshall, and many others of their generation, were still in public life and their voices were heard in debate, on one side or on the other, in the contentious discussions of the Polk administration.   Men of middle age, like Lincoln, Douglas, and Jefferson Davis, were stepping to the front and boldly assuming responsibility.

With the foreign legations at Washington—European and South American—and with political upheavals taking place in many countries, Lincoln as a constant student of newspapers was acquiring a new fund of international information.   On April 3, 1848, President Polk had sent a special message to Congress accompanied by documents, announcing the overthrow of the French Monarchy.   "The world has seldom witnessed," said Mr. Polk, "a more interesting or sublime spectacle than the peaceful rising of the French people, resolved to secure for themselves enlarged liberty, and to assert in the majesty of their strength the great truth that in this enlightened age man is capable of governing himself."

Four months later, Polk sent a message nominating Mr. Donelson of Tennessee to be "Envoy Extraordinary and Minister Plenipotentiary of the United States to the Federal Government of Germany."   The outburst of liberalism in Germany was indeed short-lived, and unsuccessful in its apparent results, even though profound in its historical influences. Its failure resulted in the emigration to the United States of many young men of university culture and military training, who were afterwards to become leaders in the Middle West and to take high civil and military positions in Lincoln's administration.   The Hungarian revolution, and many other movements were arousing similar interest in the United States.   Kossuth in Hungary and Garibaldi in

JOHN QUINCY ADAMS
SEIZED WITH A FIT IN THE HOUSE OF REPRESENTATIVES FEB? 21ST 1848

Soon after the expiration of his term as President, in March, 1831, John Quincy Adams returned to Washington as a Representative in Congress from Massachusetts, and served in that office for seventeen years. On February 21, 1848, he was stricken with paralysis while in his seat and died two days later. Lincoln was then a member of Congress and was present at the moment. He was one of the committee that went officially to Massachusetts to attend the funeral.

Italy were names that in due time became familiar in every American household.

Along with the stirring of the spirit of democracy throughout the world, there were social and economic movements with which American newspapers were dealing at length. Mr. Greeley's New York *Tribune,* of which Lincoln had become a regular reader, was especially interested in all this radical efflorescence.   A considerable group of journalists, like Greeley himself and his brilliant lieutenant Charles A. Dana, Henry J. Raymond, and others who were rising to literary eminence, had been more or less touched by the particular

LAMARTINE.   CAVAIGNAC.   LOUIS-NAPOLEON.   YOUNG PARIS.

THE JUDGMENT OF PARIS

While the people of the United States were electing a President in 1848, the voters of France were similarly engaged. The monarchy had failed in February, a constitution had been adopted, and a President was to be chosen on December 4th with a term limited to four years. There were three candidates: Lamartine, the poet, whose eloquence had gained for him a prominent place in politics; Cavaignac, Minister of War, who had played a leading part in the revolt, and who expected to be chosen President; and Prince Bonaparte, nephew of Napoleon. The magic of the name Napoleon carried the election; and Louis Napoleon ruled France for twenty-two years, first as President and afterward as Emperor. The cartoon is by Richard Doyle, published in *Punch* (London) in October, 1848.

type of socialistic gospel known as Fourierism, especially as practised in the famous Brook Farm Colony. Albert Brisbane, father of Arthur Brisbane, was the philosophic exponent in America of those doctrines of social uplift through groups living in association like one large family. Along with Abolitionism, new cults and queer societies were springing into being everywhere in the country.

Such movements were ridiculed in the lithograph posters of the day, and a few years later the Democrats were accusing the new Republican party of harboring all the cranks and radicals, of every stripe, that had emerged in the intellectual turmoil of the Forties and early Fifties. Meanwhile, the illustrators, especially those who worked for the lithographers, whose presses were now busy in New Orleans, in Cincinnati, and other places in the West and South as well as in Philadelphia, New York, Hartford and Boston, were flooding the country with their conceptions of the battles and

the heroes of the Mexican War. And let us remember that with all these caricatures and pictorial efforts Lincoln was quite as familiar as are any public men of our own day with the cartoons of Berryman in the Washington *Star,* Darling in the New York *Herald - Tribune,* Rollin Kirby in the *World,* or McCutcheon in the Chicago *Tribune.* A few years later Lincoln was to know the cartoons of Nast, and the powerful political satire of John Tenniel in *Punch.*

On December 12, 1848, President Polk transmitted to the Senate the following message, which could not have escaped Lincoln's attention:

"I nominate Second Lieutenant Ulysses S. Grant (since promoted First Lieutenant), of the Fourth Regiment of Infantry, to be First Lieutenant by brevet, for gallant and meritorious services in the Battle of Chapultepec, September 13, 1847, as proposed in the accompanying communication from the Secretary of War."

Robert E. Lee also was especially distinguished as an officer in the Mexican War, and George B. McClellan was another young officer cited for meritorious services, who, with many other older and younger officers that I may not here pause to mention by name, were to attain far greater military distinction on one side or the other in the Civil War. It was a part of Lincoln's preparation for his future duties, as commander-in-chief of our armies and navies, that he had in 1848 become so familiar not only with the exploits of General Taylor and General Scott, but also with the deeds and qualities of many younger soldiers, both regulars and volunteers.

CHAPTER XVI

Lincoln a Leader in the Politics of 1848

*He advises Zachary Taylor on his campaign—A three-party fight
that defeats Cass and elects Taylor, the Whig candidate—Lincoln
speaks in Massachusetts*

O F LINCOLN'S SPEECHES, votes and activities in the Thirtieth Congress, we have a sufficiently complete record to form our own opinions. In the longer perspectives, that record seems to have more significance than historians and biographers have, as a rule, attached to it. We learn from it not so much what he achieved, of the extent of his growing influence upon the course of legislation and politics, as what he had become, in his convictions and in his competency as a public man. The wholly absorbing topic of the period was the Mexican War. Like everyone else in both Houses, with negligible exceptions, Lincoln voted the necessary supplies to carry on the war, and stoutly defended the Whigs against their political opponents when any questions were raised as to lack of war zeal, or evasion of patriotic duty.

But Lincoln had entered Congress as a staunch partisan, with as strong prejudices against President Polk as he had entertained against President Tyler. And he was committed to the Whig view of the Mexican War as an unnecessary enterprise, deliberately provoked by Calhoun and Southern leaders for territorial acquisition. He thought of it as an enterprise undertaken to counter-balance the Free States of the rapidly developing Northwest. He was ready to challenge President Polk on points of accuracy as to the ownership of that particular strip on the Texas frontier, the invasion of which by Mexican soldiers had, according to the President's message, precipitated a conflict that Texas and the United States had done nothing to incite. Lincoln had been in Congress only two weeks when he introduced a series of resolutions calling upon Polk to specify the exact spot where the outrages had occurred.

On January 12, 1848, about a month after he had taken his place, Lincoln made a speech in defense of his belief that the war with Mexico "was unnecessarily and unconstitutionally commenced by the President." He was following up in this forensic effort his previous resolutions, and he dealt at length with the geographical facts regarding the boundaries of Texas. He was frank enough to say: "If the President can show that the soil was ours where the first blood of the war was shed—that it was not within an inhabited country, or if within such that the inhabitants

GENERAL Z. TAYLOR
"ROUGH & READY"

Lincoln's choice for the Presidency in 1848 was General Taylor, though he had not lost his admiration for Henry Clay; and Lincoln spoke for Taylor not only in his own State of Illinois but at Boston, Worcester, and elsewhere in Massachusetts, by invitation from the local Whig leaders. General Taylor was the hero of Palo Alto, Resaca de la Palma, Monterey, and Buena Vista.

had submitted themselves to the civil authority of Texas or of the United States, and that the same is true of the site of Fort Brown—then I am with him for his justification. In that case I shall be most happy to reverse the vote I gave the other day."

It may be noted that Mr. Beveridge, himself a Republican with strong Whig proclivities, fully accepts the verdicts of several recent historians, among them Channing, Rives, Smith, and Stephenson, who justify the Mexican War and support Polk as against the prejudiced attitude of Lincoln and his fellow-Whigs. Beveridge declares that these historians "demolish the old Whig and Abolition theory of the Mexican War, which until recent years was accepted by writers—the theory that it was a war of conquest instigated by the slave power, begun and waged by a powerful and grasping nation against a small and weak country for the purpose of seizing territory to extend the domain of slavery."

Later on in the same speech Lincoln made certain challenging observations regarding the continuance of the war, which had been "going on for some twenty months." He remarked that "the President now claims about one-half of the Mexican territory, and that by far the better half so far as concerns our ability to make anything out of it." His point was that Taylor had already conquered the states of northern Mexico, which were very scantily populated. In those regions we might promote American settlement, while the rest of Mexico was densely inhabited and would not be for us a desirable acquisition. He failed to see that the only way to bring the Mexicans to terms, and thus to end the war, was to occupy the Capital and compel a settlement.

Polk's actual terms were liberal to Mexico. Both countries would have been better off, in the long run, if while we were about it we had annexed by purchase a zone extending some distance south of the Rio Grande, with a parallel of latitude for the boundary line, on the plan of our Oregon settlement that took the Forty-ninth parallel for the division. Rivers seldom form satisfactory boundaries.

These territories of northern Mexico were not adapted to cotton-growing, and would not have invited the American slave system. For laborers they would have continued for a time to utilize Mexican peons, but they would have been settled eventually by sturdy Americans.

I have already alluded to Lincoln's political speech of June 30, 1848, after General Taylor and Lewis Cass had been made the opposing nominees for the Presidency. This was one of the telling addresses of that campaign. Lincoln also was listening to his colleagues, and was sending partisan Whig speeches made by many fellow-members to his friends and constituents in Illinois. We find him suggesting what he thought to be the best practical positions for his somewhat puzzled candidate,

PLUCKED:

THE MEXICAN EAGLE BEFORE THE WAR!　　OR　　THE MEXICAN EAGLE AFTER THE WAR!

The war with Mexico was short and one-sided. General Taylor from the Texas border, and General Scott from the Gulf port of Vera Cruz, invaded Mexico without a single reversal. Taylor's victories came first, followed by Scott's march to Mexico City, the two campaigns lasting from May, 1846 to September, 1847. It is interesting to compare this cartoon with one quite similar which appears later in these pages, showing the American eagle at the beginning and at the end of President Buchanan's administration.

General Taylor, to take with regard to public questions. In the first place, he held that the old contention favoring a National Bank had better be ignored, as a lost cause. He foresaw that a tariff revision was coming, with a view to more revenue to meet the war debt; but wished that Taylor would demand that tariff modification be made "with due reference to the protection of our home industry."

"As to the Mexican War," added Lincoln (for Taylor's guidance), "I still think the defensive-line policy the best to terminate it." He then puts these words, suppositiously, in Taylor's mouth: "In a final treaty of peace we shall probably be under a sort of necessity of taking some territory. But it is my desire that we shall not acquire any extending so far South as to enlarge and aggravate the distracting question of slavery." Finally, in this memorandum, he advises that Taylor should express the view that legislation ought to be left to Congress "uninfluenced by the executive in its origin or progress, and undisturbed by the veto unless in very special and clear cases." It will be remembered that Jackson, Van Buren, Tyler, and Polk, had all been assertive heads of the Government, urging their policies upon Congress and the country, and using the veto power freely and without reluctance.

In July, Lincoln made a Taylor speech on the floor of the House reviewing precedents in the use of the veto power, putting a platform of principles under General Taylor's feet, and challenging General Cass's record on the "Wilmot Proviso." Mr. Wilmot, a Democrat of Pennsylvania, had earlier presented a famous resolution to the effect that slavery should not be permitted in any territory that might be acquired as a result of the Mexican War. Lincoln as a member of the Post Office Committee, and as an expert in matters of land laws and western settlement, had been active in Congress in dealing with domestic issues relating to extension of postal service, sale of public lands, and support of internal transportation and other improvements. The country was excited about California and Oregon, and was negotiating for control of the Panama route, with the view of building

GENERAL SCOTT REVELLING IN THE HALLS OF THE MONTEZUMAS.

A New York cartoon, not too friendly, published at the time of the occupation of the Mexican capital by Gen. Winfield Scott, commander of the United States Army, in September, 1847. A decisive battle at Churubusco had been followed by an armistice. Then hostilities were resumed, and Chapultepec—guarding Mexico City—was captured on September 13th. On the next day General Scott was "revelling in the halls of the Montezumas."

a trans-isthmian railroad and perhaps ultimately a ship canal to unite the oceans.

General Winfield Scott was also a Whig, and had for a long time been regarded as of presidential caliber. But there were reasons of immediate availability that seemed to Lincoln to make the choice of General Zachary Taylor preferable. It was with regret that he could not join in supporting his long-time party chief, Henry Clay; but he felt that this would be a political mistake. Clay remained the party's mentor and pre-eminent statesman, with his crowning efforts for national harmony yet to be made, two years later in the Senate. Taylor's personal position was that of a man who had not originally believed in marching an American Army to the Rio

Grande. But he had obeyed orders, and had thereby made himself a first-class military hero. This was in spite of his opinion that war might have been avoided if we had been less ready to meet the Mexican forces on the field of battle. Such a record gave Taylor a peculiar availability. The anti-war men could back him on his sentiments, and the war party loved him for his successes on the battlefield.

The Democrats held their convention first, meeting at Baltimore on May 22d. They regularized party methods for the future by fixing the number of delegates as equal to the electoral vote of each State. They appointed a National Democratic Committee, and again they adopted the two-thirds rule.

The unity of the convention was affected by

DESERTION OF HENRY CLAY.

(AFTER VANDERLYN'S PICTURE OF CAIUS MARIUS.)

The Kentucky Senator in every campaign from 1824 to 1848 was either a leading candidate or actually nominated for the Presidency. It was his misfortune that in the two elections carried by the Whigs the nomination had been tendered to a more available candidate, brought forward by war. Clay was "deserted" by his party in the year 1848, according to this cartoon from *Yankee Doodle;* he was "assassinated," according to a similar cartoon reproduced on page 151.

a sharp cleavage in New York between the upstate followers of Van Buren and Silas Wright and the elements that centered in Tammany Hall. The former had become known as "Barn-Burners," someone having suggested that in their zeal for uplift and reform they were like the farmer who had burned his barn to get rid of the rats. The other faction was known as "Hunkers" and was led by Mr. Marcy, Polk's Secretary of State, and supported, as I have said, by Tammany Hall. They were called "Hunkers" because they were said to be hunkering, or hankering, for the offices. In those days the Whigs called Democrats in general "Loco-Focos."

This rather far-fetched designation grew out of a lively row in Tammany Hall in the year 1835. The so-called "Equal Rights" men, radical Jacksonians opposed to Tammany, had gone to Tammany Hall to attend a Democratic mass-meeting, and to oppose certain Tammany nominations. The Tammany men had slipped out of the hall and turned off the gas-lights. The Equal Rights men supplied themselves with candles, and passed around boxes of the new so-called "Loco-Foco" matches, a chemical invention which had just come into use. I am taking space to explain these designations, because they were used constantly in the campaigns of that period, and also because it is necessary to understand them in order to catch the meaning of many of the contemporary cartoons.

The Whigs had fallen into the habit of calling all Democrats "Loco-Focos," Lincoln himself constantly using that term in his political correspondence. But in the Baltimore Convention of 1848, the terms "Hunker" and "Barn-Burner" were applied specifically to the two factions in New York State. Each of the two appeared with a full delegation. The Hunkers had been favored rather than the Barn-Burners with appointments by President Polk. Neither faction was satisfied with the convention's action, taken after two days of argument. It was decided by a close vote to allow each to cast half the votes to which New York was entitled, both delegations being seated. Barn-Burners indignantly withdrew and the Hunkers sulked. Their quarrel was carried to election day, and it resulted in a tremendous New York plurality for General Taylor. The national outcome turned upon the New York vote, as has been the case in several presidential elections since 1848.

Candidates in abundance were brought forward at Baltimore, but Lewis Cass of Michigan was the favorite from the start. On the first ballot he had 125 votes, James Buchanan 55, Levi Woodbury of New Hampshire 53, John C. Calhoun 9, with scattering votes for two or three others. Cass was nominated on the fourth ballot with 179, Buchanan having 33, Woodbury 38. President Polk would have welcomed a renomination, but he had originally declared himself a one-term man; and there was no disposition to overrule what he had said in 1844. Since General Cass, like the other candidates, was against the Wilmot Proviso, and was considered one of the "Northern men with Southern principles," it was regarded as tactful to choose a man of striking personality and distinguished career, an altogether shapely and solid piece of presidential timber. General William O. Butler of Kentucky was nominated for the Vice-Presidency.

The platform justified the Mexican War, praised the army, congratulated the new French Republic and glorified "this grand political truth: of the sovereignty of the people and their power and capacity for self-government which is prostrating thrones and erecting republics on the ruins of despotism in the Old World." In one terse resolution the platform praised the Democratic party for its continued success in defeating efforts to create a national bank, for its prevention of the distribution of the proceeds of land sales, for its management of currency and monetary conditions and for "the noble impulse given to the cause of free-trade by the repeal of the tariff of 1842, and the creation of the more equal, honest, and productive tariff of 1846." Certainly this was a vigorous and unambiguous platform, following in sequence a number of equally frank and well-written Democratic platforms that were in contrast with the growing tendencies of the Whig party to conceal its lack of unity on points of principle.

GENERAL ZACHARY TAYLOR
Twelfth President of the United States

Though the Whigs had opposed the idea of war with Mexico they supported it vigorously when it came, and later they nominated its two outstanding military leaders as their candidates for the presidency—Taylor in 1848 and Scott in 1852. Taylor was born in Virginia in 1784, and went into Kentucky with his family while still a child. He entered the army in 1808, came out of the war of 1812 as a Major, rose through the rank of Colonel to Brigadier-General in the Black Hawk and Seminole Indian wars, and as commander of the southern division of the western military department was the obvious choice to lead the expedition into Mexico in 1846. He was elected President two years later, when a Louisiana planter, but died in office on July 9, 1850, sixteen months after inauguration.

Lincoln, as we have already discovered, was present at the Whig national convention at Philadelphia, opening on the seventh of June. General Taylor, like Henry Clay, his chief competitor for the nomination, was a Southern slave-holder. He had long been identified with the American army, and he was sixty-four years of age, having been born in Orange County, Virginia, November 24, 1784. He was the favorite of Louisiana, and had been put in nomination by a convention of the people of that State, regardless of party, many months before the convention date. Similar endorsements in Alabama and other Southern communities attested Taylor's popularity. He seemed inclined at first to make an independent run; but in casting about for a party he concluded that he was, after all, "a Whig though not an ultra one."

Henry Clay had outlived some of the issues with which he had been most strongly identified; and the Whigs, finding themselves on the unpopular side of the Mexican War, felt it necessary to choose for their standard-bearer a war-hero whose valorous deeds might serve them as a bridge. In the Philadelphia convention of June 7th Taylor was nominated on the fourth ballot. He had 111 votes on the first, against 97 for Henry Clay, 43 for General Winfield Scott (whose home was in New Jersey), 22 for Daniel Webster, 2 for John McLean of Ohio, and 4 for John M. Clayton of Delaware. On the final ballot, the vote stood Taylor 171, Clay 32, Scott 63, Webster 14. At each ballot Taylor had received votes from every one of the States; and the convention accepted him with enthusiasm.

Rivalry for the Vice-Presidency lay between Millard Fillmore of New York and Abbott Lawrence of Massachusetts, with Fillmore successful on the second ballot. This ticket, "Taylor and Fillmore," was not the sort that great statesmen like Daniel Webster and Henry Clay could view with emotions of satisfaction. But it was a vote-getting selection, as the event proved, and it served the purpose for which it had been named.

There were all sorts of sporadic attempts at the founding of new parties in 1848, previous to the two big conventions. The so-called "Native Americans" had launched a move-

THE AVAILABLE PARTY TRYING TO GET THEIR VILLANY ENDORSED BY THE VERY MAN THEY HAVE ASSASINATED

There was some doubt whether Henry Clay would support General Taylor after he himself had been passed over by the convention. In this cartoon Clay refers to the fact that Taylor was refusing to state his position on any of the important questions of the day. At the left of his three visitors is William V. Brady, then Mayor of New York, and at the right is John J. Crittenden, who in that year 1848 served first as Senator from Kentucky and later as Governor. The note that they present reads: "Mr. Clay: We have called on you to humbly request that you will state to your friends that you approve of the Philadelphia convention and that you endorse General Taylor as a good Whig."

THE ASSASINATION OF THE SAGE OF ASHLAND.

Henry Clay would have been the obvious choice of the Whigs in 1848 had the war with Mexico not brought forward General Taylor. The vote-getting qualifications of the military leader outweighed those of the statesman, and Clay was once more disappointed. His first bid for the presidency came in 1824, when he was one of four candidates no one of whom received a majority; and Clay, being then Speaker of the House, helped to elect Adams. In 1832 Clay was the nominee of the National Republican party, defeated by Jackson. In 1840 the Whig nomination that he expected was given to General Harrison. In 1844 he was nominated by the Whigs and defeated by Polk largely because he opposed the annexation of Texas. In 1848 the Whig nomination was given to General Taylor. Clay is designated here as the Sage of Ashland, that being the name of his estate near Lexington, Kentucky. Shakespeare's tragedies were popular on the American stage; the elder Booth was at the height of his career. The assassinators are thus found to be repeating lines used by the conspirators in "Julius Caesar."

ment, and the Abolitionists, meeting in New York City, had nominated John P. Hale of New Hampshire. These smaller affairs, however, were afterwards absorbed to some extent in a coalition movement which included New York Democratic Barn-Burners, Ohio anti-slavery men both Democrats and Whigs, and especially the anti-slavery Whigs of Massachusetts. This movement, with strong leaders, was not to be despised. It came to be known by the term "Free Soil," from the brave motto on its banners: "Free Soil, Free Speech, Free Labor, and Free Men."

Ex-President Van Buren (whose opinions were now rapidly taking a Northern complexion) somewhat reluctantly accepted the Free Soil nomination for the Presidency. Charles Francis Adams of Massachusetts (son of John Quincy Adams and afterwards Mr. Lincoln's Minister to England), was nominated for Vice-President. If this was as yet a relatively small party, it had leaders more eminent than the nominees of either of the great parties, and it had adopted a powerful platform, most of which was devoted to a series of pronouncements on the subject of slavery. At the tail of the series of resolutions was the following: *"Resolved*: That we inscribe on our banner, Free Soil, Free Speech, Free Labor and Free Men, and under it we will fight on, and fight ever, until a triumphant victory shall reward our exertions."

The popular vote for the Taylor ticket was 1,360,000, that of the Cass ticket 1,220,500, while the Van Buren Free Soil ticket had exactly 291,263. This vote for the third party seemed small—ten or eleven per cent. of the total poll. Yet the rivalry between the two famous Democrats Cass and Van Buren gave the State of New York to the Whigs, thereby electing Taylor President of the United States. The popular vote in New York was 218,603 for Taylor, 120,510 for Van Buren, and only 114,318 for Cass. The Van Buren ticket drew almost enough Democrats, though not quite,

to carry Lincoln's State of Illinois for the Whig ticket. Largely on grounds of personal popularity, Taylor carried Delaware, Florida, Georgia, Kentucky, Louisiana, Maryland, North Carolina, and Tennessee, all of these being slave-holding States that might under more normal conditions have gone Democratic. Cass carried Virginia, but by a very narrow margin. Ohio, Indiana, Illinois, Michigan, Wisconsin, and Iowa all went Democratic, and gave their electoral vote to Cass. The main result seemed rather a curious reversal of the sectional tendencies that were so soon to exhibit themselves.

Although the Free Soil movement did not poll a large aggregate vote, it was decidedly stronger in Massachusetts and Vermont than the regular Democratic ticket, as I have just shown that it was in New York. Its impor-

POLITICAL GAME OF BRAG SHEW OF HANDS.

Brag, a card game similar to poker, was frequently used as a subject for these cartoons. The four players around this table are two Whigs and two Democrats. Taylor, facing the reader, has won the Whig nomination with three aces or bullets. Clay rises and announces that his own bluff game has failed. At the left of the picture is Calhoun, lending encouragement to Cass, the Democratic nominee. At the right are President Polk, seated, and his Secretary of State, James Buchanan.

MARRIAGE OF THE FREE SOIL AND LIBERTY PARTIES.

Martin Van Buren, not having been at all anxious to accept the Free Soil party's nomination for the presidency, could not have been particularly pleased when his candidacy was endorsed by the much more radical abolitionist Liberty party. Pushing Van Buren forward in this cartoon is Horace Greeley, editor of the New York *Tribune*. Reading the marriage service is Benjamin F. Butler of New York, not to be confused with the man of the same name who became a Civil War general and Governor of Massachusetts. The Butler in this cartoon had been Van Buren's law partner and a member of the cabinets of Jackson and Van Buren. For most of his life an enthusiastic Democrat, he was beginning to disapprove of some of that party's policies, and joined the new Republican party in 1856. He was the father of William Allen Butler and grandfather of Charles Henry Butler, both distinguished lawyers.

tance lay in the fact that it was the beginning of the break-up of the Whig party. Mr. Barton reminds us that in Massachusetts it was led by men of the highest distinction, among whom he names Henry Wilson, Charles Francis Adams, Anson Burlingame, John A. Andrew, E. Rockwood Hoar and John G. Palfrey. Mr. Beveridge adds the names George Frisbie Hoar and Richard Henry Dana, and further reminds us that "nearly all men of letters in Massachusetts supported the new party— Whittier, Longfellow, Lowell." These were men who, at a later time, surrounded Lincoln in the forefront of the Republican party.

At this time, however, Lincoln as an orthodox Whig was fighting the "bolt" of the Free Soilers from the party of Webster and Clay.

He was one of several speakers from New York and States further West, who were invited to take the stump in Massachusetts, and he accepted promptly. There has been a somewhat prevalent impression (due perhaps to the dramatists and rhapsodists who translate Lincoln from the prairies to the White House, with twenty years ignored) that Lincoln had never spoken in the East until he delivered the Cooper Union Speech in 1860, immediately after which he made a few addresses in New England. But on September 13, 1848, he attended the Whig convention of Massachusetts at Worcester, and delivered before the delegates a long evening address.

His main object in Massachusetts was to check the Free Soil revolt, on the ground that

Whig victory would really be better for the cause of the anti-slavery men than the election of Cass on a pro-slavery platform. As it turned out, however, the third party movement, by splitting the Democrats in New York, was the instrument by which Lincoln's candidate won the election. Similarly, the split availed to increase the Whig plurality in Massachusetts. Barton says that Lincoln spoke in Boston on September 15th, and at Lowell on the following day. In the next week he made addresses at Dorchester, Chelsea and Dedham—where he "evoked so much enthusiasm that his audience was unwilling to have him leave for Cambridge, where he spoke that night." Leaving Cambridge, he spoke again in Boston with William H. Seward of New York, the eloquent statesman who was in 1860 to be his foremost rival for the

nomination, and who became his Secretary of State. The two men became well acquainted on this occasion, and Lincoln was impressed by Seward's earnestness and tone of prophecy.

As a speaker, Lincoln was undoubtedly a favorite that year in Massachusetts. Reasons of his own led him to decline many further invitations to canvass in the East. He returned to Illinois by way of Niagara Falls and Lake Erie, and stopped at Chicago, where on October 6th he made a two-hour campaign speech. Anticipating events, it may be noted that Lincoln appeared again in Chicago by official invitation on July 25, 1850, to deliver a commemorative address on President Taylor, who had died in office July 9th. This memorial address was brought to light and published by Mr. Barton some seventy years after it had been heard by the leading men of Chicago.

THE DEMOCRATIC FUNERAL OF 1848.

In this year Martin Van Buren, twice the standard-bearer of the Democrats, had somewhat reluctantly accepted the nomination of the so-called Free Soil party, causing a split in the Democratic ranks which was fatal to the party's chance of success. This Whig cartoon shows Van Buren the fox and Cass the gas-bag, carried by pall-bearers Houston, Benton, and Calhoun—all Democratic Senators. President Polk, whose term was expiring, is being carried by Allen, Kendall, Woodbury, and Worth—the first three being Democratic Senators and the last a Major-General second in command to Taylor and to Scott in the war with Mexico.

In the campaign of 1852 the Democrats brought forward Franklin Pierce of New Hampshire as their candidate for President. This cartoon throws more light upon the prohibition movement, then under way, than upon the personal qualities of Pierce, who is pictured here as needing the support of a tree. Maine—represented by the man on horseback, scolding the New Hampshire presidential nominee—had been the first State to abolish the sale of liquor, in 1846. Vermont had followed in 1852, the presidential campaign year. Pierce's own State of New Hampshire did not adopt prohibition until 1855, and abandoned it in 1902.

CHAPTER XVII

Lincoln Returns to Private Life

He considers government posts in the Land Office and Oregon—The Compromise of 1850—The nominating convention and presidential election of 1852

PRESIDENT TAYLOR, though born in Virginia, had for a long time been a resident of Louisiana where he owned a large sugar plantation and several hundred slaves. He is credited with having been a good business man, well-trained in methods of practical efficiency, both by the conduct of his private affairs and also by the responsibilities of a long career in the army. He came to Washington with preconceived ideas of the constitutional rights of the slave-holding States, but he was no victim of the metaphysics of Calhoun and the theorists of that school, nor was he committed to the practical policies of the slavery expansionists like Cobb, Toombs, and Davis. He was a man of little education, but of reasonable mentality; and he soon came to understand the futility of the Southern purpose to force slavery upon new communities that did not want it and were determined not to have it.

The rush to California from all parts of the world, gold having been discovered at the very moment of the signing of the treaty with Mexico, promptly resulted in a statehood movement; and a convention in California formed an anti-slavery constitution with the unanimous vote of the delegates. The demand on the part of slave-owners that they should be given the right to go to these new regions and carry their archaic institution with them, was purely theoretical in view of the facts. The census of 1850 showed that California already had a population of 92,597, and there was not a single slave enumerated, although there were 965 free persons of color.

Neither was there a single slave in the territory of New Mexico, it may be pertinent to note, where there were 17 free Negroes and a total white population of 61,530. In the Utah Territory, afterwards subdivided to form several States, there were exactly 26 slaves and 24 free Negroes. Kansas, Nebraska, the Dakotas, and other portions of the new Northwest were still in the condition of a wilderness area not yet opened for settlement. This wild territory was closed to slavery by the Compromise of 1820. It offered almost no possibility of ever coming under the slave system, with the exception of its extreme southern portion, that was in the near future to be marked off as the Territory of Kansas.

Being a man of poise and common sense, Taylor quickly perceived, after he had become President, that the carrying of slavery into the new country acquired from Mexico, quite apart from fine-spun theories, was out of the question as a concrete proposal. In the first place, the new territories belonged to the United States as a whole; and an overwhelming majority of the people of the country were opposed to slavery extension. In the second place, there were no prospective cotton and sugar plantations in any of these new areas. There was nothing that tempted the pioneers

and prospectors to encourage slavery and set up the local slave codes that cumbered the statute books of the old Slave States.

The lower South, in its new enthusiasm for wealth and prosperity under an economic system that would brook no thought of alternatives, began to revive the long suspended project of annexing Cuba. It was the idea of the Gulf States that they might convert that rich island of tobacco and sugar plantations into three or four American slave states. We had bought Florida in 1819, and Taylor's Secretary of State—John M. Clayton of Delaware—was now concluding the Clayton-Bulwer Treaty relating to a trans-Isthmian canal. Cuban annexation was logical, and it was tempting for other reasons than the strengthening of the slave system. President Taylor, however, took firm ground against schemes to force this Cuban project. He showed his sincerity by his efforts to prevent the filibusters from provoking Cuban insurrections. He advised Congress to admit California as a Free State, and this was done on September 9, 1850, exactly two months after Taylor's death.

The return of a Whig administration had compelled Taylor, in spite of himself, to give more attention to the demands of office-seekers than to questions of statesmanship. Not only were the federal offices at Washington sought by Whigs who urged the immediate dismissal of many thousands of Democratic incumbents, but federal appointments in all the States—postmasterships and the like—occupied most of the time and energy of Whig politicians, who were demanding of Taylor that he should consult them about questions of local patronage. As regards the State of New York with its tangle of factions, Taylor expected at first to rely upon the counsel of Vice-President Fillmore. But before long he preferred the guidance of William H. Seward, who had just entered the Senate, where he took his place at once as a powerful leader of the more progressive and advanced Whig element.

Lincoln, as I have remarked, had found Washington a congenial center of life and of public work. He had not been long in Congress before he wrote home to his partner Herndon as follows:

It is very pleasant to learn from you that there are some who desire that I should be reelected. I most heartily thank them for their kind partiality; and I can say, as Mr. Clay said of the annexation of Texas, that "personally I would not object" to a reelection, although I thought at the time, and still think, it would be quite as well for me to return to the law at the end of a single term. I made the declaration, that I would not be a candidate again, more from a wish to deal fairly with others, to keep peace among our friends, and to keep the district from going to the enemy, than for any cause personal to myself; so that, if it should so happen that nobody else wishes to be elected, I could not refuse the people the right to send me again. But to enter myself as a competitor of others, or to authorize any one so to enter me, is what my word and honor forbid.

The old line Whigs, with Lincoln himself still standing pat as a party regular and conservative, were now beginning to disintegrate everywhere; and this was true of the Seventh Congressional District of Illinois. His young partner, Herndon, wrote frequently to warn him that the new generation was beginning to resent "the stubbornness and bad judgment of the old fossils in the party who were constantly holding the young men back." It was to Judge Stephen T. Logan that Lincoln had been virtually committed as his successor; and Logan was duly nominated. But the voters declined to elect him. It was by no means certain that Lincoln's readiness to be continued in Congress would have kept him there, even if Logan had withdrawn and the local convention had tendered Lincoln the renomination that he coveted. Logan was a worthy candidate, but the old party lines had so shifted that Lincoln himself might have been defeated at the polls, in spite of his personal hold upon the voters.

Retiring Congressmen have a notorious appetite for appointive office; and Lincoln, who deserved so well of the Taylor-Fillmore administration, thought that something fairly good ought be his if the proper strings were pulled. On that subject he wrote: "I believe that, so far as the Whigs in Congress are concerned, I could have the General Land Office almost by common consent; but then Sweet and Don Morrison and Cyrus Edwards all want it, and what is worse, while I could

JOSHUA, COMMANDING THE SUN TO STAND STILL.

Until a few weeks before his death in 1850, Senator John C. Calhoun of South Carolina continued his struggle for the right of an individual State to settle its destiny independently of the will of the others. First this doctine of State Rights and Nullification had to do with the tariff, but in later years it applied particularly to slavery. In this cartoon the sun represents the abolition press. Calhoun, as Joshua, issues his command: "Sun of intellectual light and liberty, stand ye still, in masterly inactivity, that the nation of Carolina may continue to hold Negroes and plant cotton till the day of Judgment!"

easily take it myself, I fear I should have trouble to get it for any other man in Illinois." While really wanting the office very much for himself, Lincoln was making his candidacy conditional upon his inability to secure it for Cyrus Edwards. Political influences at length gave the position to Justin Butterfield, a Chicago lawyer, who had supported the Mexican War when Lincoln opposed it. Furthermore, Logan was somewhat disaffected because he thought that Lincoln's anti-war record was the principal cause of Whig defeat in the Congressional fight. Lincoln's opponents seemed everywhere to be gaining at his expense, and some of his old friends clearly felt that he had been playing a double-face game in the matter of appointments. He was by no means a happy Whig, as he returned to Springfield.

The burdens of office were too much for honest old Zachary Taylor, and he died on July 9, 1850, having served sixteen months, or one-third of his term. Even if Lincoln had succeeded in obtaining the appointment that seemed to him so desirable, he would have held it at most only during Fillmore's administration of less than three years, since all such posts were filled with still another set of new men when the election of Franklin Pierce over General Scott brought the Democrats back into power.

Furthermore, Lincoln would have found the administrative detail of the Land Office uncongenial to a man who had never had any experience in managing an organization like this, with its systematic routine. A bureau head in Washington is a subordinate person, who does not talk politics in hotel lobbies or take the stump from time to time as a party orator. Such a post would have been manifestly unsuited to so self-ordered and independent a personage as Abraham Lincoln. He had always been greatly interested in public policy as affecting the Western lands; but as Commissioner of the Land Office the Congressional committees would have failed to consult him. They would instead have been in communication with his superior, the Secretary of the Interior. It was merely that he and Mrs. Lincoln liked Washington life.

WILLIAM RUFUS KING

Elected Vice-President on the ticket with Franklin Pierce in 1852, he died in April of the following year. He was a North Carolinian by birth (1786), but had moved into Alabama in 1818, becoming one of that State's first United States Senators. In that office he served for thirty years until his election as Vice-President, interrupted only by a period as Minister to France under President Polk.

This Interior Department was a brand-new creation, and President Taylor had made Thomas Ewing of Ohio its first head. Fillmore two months after he entered the White House gave the Interior portfolio to Alexander H. H. Stuart of Virginia. These changes would have found Abraham Lincoln merely a bureau head in a department of rotating appointees, with no mortgage on his own job. The whole episode indicates—what many other evidences go to prove—that Lincoln at that time, and for a few years afterwards, was drifting rather than choosing, in so far as external details of his career were concerned.

Regardless of his own inclinations, however, circumstances were compelling one decision after another that proved fortunate in the end.

It is an honorable thing for a man fit for the representative tasks of law-making and government to work for the realization of his ambitions. But there are times when it is the better plan to resume the paths of private life contentedly, and let the office seek the man. Mr. Barton, following many other biographers, declares: "Though President Taylor did not see fit to offer him the Land Office in Washington, his successor, President Fillmore, did offer him the Governorship of Oregon." Mr. Barton continues as follows: "Lincoln was sorely tempted to accept. He anticipated little joy in Springfield. There was much that was irksome to him in the practice of law. He did not care much to be Governor of the Territory, but he reflected that before

JOHN PARKER HALE

Free Soil candidate for the Presidency in 1852. Hale was a New Hampshire Democrat who found himself in bitter strife with his party by opposing slavery. He served first in the House, beginning in 1843, then in the Senate, of which he was a member while running for the Presidency. He retired from the Senate in 1865 to become Minister to Spain. Hale was one of the organizers of the Republican party.

long Oregon would be a State, and that the territorial governor would stand a chance of being one of the first Senators. Mrs. Lincoln vetoed this proposition. She had no intention of going to live in Oregon. If she could not live in Washington, Springfield was the next best thing. Her home was there and her friends were there, and she had more faith than Lincoln had just then in his political future."

Nicolay and Hay state unequivocally that it was Taylor not Fillmore who "offered Mr. Lincoln the Governorship of Oregon," upon what they regard as ample authority. Mr. Joseph H. Barrett in his important work published in 1904, entitled "Abraham Lincoln and His Presidency," went straight to the files at Washington, and discovered that Lincoln was not in fact offered the Governorship of Oregon, but rather that on August 9, 1849, a duly certified commission was issued to him, appointing him *Secretary* of the Oregon Territory, the Governorship on the same date having been awarded to Hon. Joseph Marshall of Indiana. Both commissions were returned, and were placed in the archives marked "declined."

MILLARD FILLMORE
President of the United States, 1850-1853

Fillmore became President through the death of Zachary Taylor, and served for slightly less than three years. He was a lawyer of Buffalo, N. Y., born in 1800, and entered public life at the age of twenty-eight as a member of the Legislature. He was then elected to Congress, serving four terms, becoming chairman of the Ways and Means Committee which framed the high protective tariff of 1842, and retired in the following year. In 1848 he was elected Vice-President, and on July 9, 1850 stepped into the presidency. He failed to secure a renomination, but in 1856 he was the candidate of the American or Know Nothing party, receiving a considerable popular vote, but carrying only the State of Maryland.

art who became Secretary of the Interior)—that for the mere cost at government expense of a trip to Oregon Lincoln might hope to return, also at government expense on transcontinental mileage account, as United States Senator. California had hastened to make the lucky John C. Frémont one of its two first members of the United States Senate; but the idea that Lincoln might arrive at high office in Washington by way of the Oregon Trail, was probably never entertained by him for a moment.

He was aware, though some of his biographers have not considered the fact, that Oregon in 1850 was by no means ready for statehood. The population by the census of that year counted in the Oregon Territory (containing an area three or four times as large as the later State of Oregon) was only 13,294. In point of fact the date of favorable action at Washington on the admission of Oregon was February 14, 1859; and no Oregon Senator had an opportunity to take his seat until December 5th of that year, with the presidential campaign of 1860 already begun in its preliminary movements. Lincoln, of course, could

Mr. Beveridge, with his especial aptitude for political facts and their bearings, discovered in his own way that it was Fillmore and not Taylor who had issued the commission, and that the office in question was the Secretaryship. In most of the biographies there is the assumption—readily traced to Lincoln's Illinois friend Stuart (not to the Virginia Stu- not have regarded Oregon as offering any hope of political advancement.

That Lincoln ever thought of abandoning his own State of Illinois I cannot believe. He and Douglas had already set their stakes once and for all. Each had "gone West to grow up with the country" and had fully proved the advantages of his location. It happened that

HENRY CLAY AND HIS WIFE

Reproduced from an original Brady photograph owned by
the author. While a practising lawyer at Lexington, Kentucky, Clay married Lucretia Hart, daughter of a respected
and well-known resident of that city. They had eleven
children, six daughters and five sons. The daughter named
for her mother died at the age of fourteen. The son
named for his father was killed in the war with Mexico.
A married daughter died at the age of twenty, another
died while Clay was on his way to Washington to become Secretary of State. We make no effort here to call
the roll in full; his private life was in some respects as full
of disappointments to him as was his political career.
While still a member of the Senate, Clay died in 1852 at
the age of seventy-five, having been in public life more
than half a century.

Douglas as a Democrat was in the Senate, and
in the public eye. Lincoln, belonging to the
minority party, was relegated to private life. I
cannot be completely convinced by the testimony that is heaped up to prove that this return to his law practice had filled Lincoln with
unspeakable gloom and disappointment.

Such are the paradoxes of politics that
Douglas, not Lincoln, was just then in the less
enviable situation. For Douglas was where
he must form opinions rapidly, and answer
for them to the entire country. In retirement
from office for a few years, he could have
studied situations and assumed his positions
more deliberately. It was his very place of
eminence in the Senate that led him to a mistake that precipitated conflicts within the
Democratic party, by virtue of which he lost

to Buchanan in 1856. Lincoln's exclusion from
public life gave him opportunity to recon-
sider his ground, and to resume the leadership
for which he was prepared when the old Whig
position had become no longer tenable. The
Republican party of his State in due time
found him in accord with its advanced
views. Moreover, in the midst of his disappointment about the Land Office position, he
was not without recognition and honor on the
part of the Illinois Whigs. Mr. Barrett states
the case as follows:

A United States Senator was to be chosen at the
next session of the Illinois Legislature, but a Whig
majority in that body was not among the possibilities of the time. Lincoln was voted for by the
Whig members for that office when the election
came off, while the more effective vote of the Democratic majority was given to General James
Shields, who had resigned his place as Commissioner of the General Land Office to go to the war,
had been shot through the body on a Mexican battlefield, and had come back a military hero, who
could easily distance all political competitors.

Lincoln had only to wait, practising his profession with increased prestige, and studying
the course of public events with serious purpose to find high ground from which he could
look to the country's future regardless of what
lay behind. With all his ambition, and his
consciousness that he had the power to stand
with the ablest men of both parties, he had
never risen wholly above the early sense of
disadvantage. His frequent moods of depression and melancholy had plagued him with
what in the pseudo-scientific jargon of our
day is called the "inferiority complex." In
"the invaluable discipline of defeat," as Beveridge observes, Lincoln was to forget himself
in order to fight the battles of his country. It
is not my purpose in these pages to dwell at
length upon his private fortunes in this period,
nor shall I yield to the temptation of making
an elaborate review of the political events that
were following each other so swiftly in the
days that were now closing upon the long careers of Clay, Webster, and Calhoun.

In his excellent school history, Professor
Muzzey comments upon the brilliancy of the
United States Senate as it assembled in Decem-
ber, 1849. "There met for the last time,"

says Mr. Muzzey, "the great triumvirate of American statesmen, Clay, Webster, and Calhoun—all three born during the Revolutionary War, and all so identified with every public question for a generation that to write the biography of any one of them would be to write the history of our country during that period." He then cites the names of Benton, Cass, Bell, Douglas, Davis, Seward, Chase, and Hale, "the last three being the first pronounced anti-slavery delegation in the Senate."

The Missouri Compromise of 1820 which had fixed a dividing line between Slave States and Free States to be formed out of the Louisiana Purchase, had stood for thirty years. But the Mexican War had reopened the discussion. There were differences about California, New Mexico, Texas, the District of Columbia, and the fugitive slave laws. In what was termed his Omnibus Bill, Clay attempted to secure harmony. He proposed California's admission as a free state, and the division of the New Mexico area on the Thirty-seventh parallel, leaving the slavery question to the choice of the settlers. He was readjusting Texas boundaries with compensation, and abolishing the slave trade (but not slavery itself) in the District of Columbia. He was proposing a new and more effective law for the recovery of runaway Negroes.

Calhoun made his final plea for the South on March 4, 1850, five weeks after the Clay bill had been introduced, and died before the end of the month. Webster's great speech was on the 7th of March, and he supported Clay's bill. He thought the Wilmot Proviso unnecessary, because he knew that slavery would never invade the plains and mountains of the areas in dispute. Webster spoke as a statesman, but was denounced in Massachusetts as a moral reprobate by the impatient Free-Soilers. Seward, now in the Senate from New York, appealed to what he called the "higher law" of the anti-slavery movement. Salmon P. Chase of Ohio, who like Seward was to hold high rank in Lincoln's Cabinet, opposed the Compromise as a weak and vain concession to the aggressive slave-holders. President Taylor, the Louisiana planter and slave-owner, had been won over to Seward's

WINFIELD SCOTT.
WHIG CANDIDATE FOR
Fourteenth President of the United States,
FROM DAGUERREOTYPE.

Abandoning a law career at the age of twenty-one, Scott entered the army with the rank of Captain in 1808 and remained in active service until he retired, at the age of 75, in the first year of the Civil War. The War of 1812 brought him opportunity for distinguished service, and when war with Mexico came in 1846 he was commander of the army and as such entered Mexico City to receive the surrender of Santa Anna. In 1852 he was nominated by the Whigs for President, but was overwhelmingly defeated by the Democratic candidate, Franklin Pierce. This portrait is reproduced from a colored lithograph campaign poster; note the words in small type "Whig candidate for" which precede the line "Fourteenth President of the United States."

high views against the extension of slavery, and he would probably have vetoed the Clay Compromise. But the bill was passed several weeks after his death, and President Fillmore signed it. The Compromise was on its face a victory for the South. In reality it was a *modus vivendi* that added not an acre to slave territory in the new parts of the country, that took at least a small step toward improvement in the District of Columbia, that gave California immediate admission as a Free State, and that made fugitive slave laws odious by providing for their enforcement.

If Lincoln had not much to say in public about the Compromise of 1850, he made a fine *apologia* for Clay in a memorial address at Springfield in July, 1852, immediately after the death of the great Kentucky statesman. He defended Clay from the attacks of extremists on both sides, and made it appear that on the whole Clay's life had been devoted to the cause of human liberty, with Negroes not excepted in his view from the human race.

President Fillmore had promptly taken his stand as a Whig of orthodox views, and he dispensed with Taylor's Cabinet. He made Webster Secretary of State, Thomas Corwin of Ohio Secretary of the Treasury, and John J. Crittenden of Kentucky Attorney General, with changes in all the other Cabinet places. Although Fillmore somehow failed to write

his name boldly upon the pages of history, Mr. James Ford Rhodes, our foremost authority upon that period, pronounces the following verdict: "When Fillmore withdrew from the presidential office, the general sentiment proclaimed that he had filled the place with ability and honor. The country abounded with prosperity; the administration was identified with the Compromise and the Compromise had now become very popular. . . . In a just estimate therefore of our Vice-Presidents who have become Presidents, we should class Fillmore with Arthur, and not with Tyler and Johnson."

Both parties were preparing for the presidential contest of 1852. General Cass was still in the field for the Democratic nomination, while Buchanan, Douglas and Marcy were all favored by their friends. The convention met

DOUGLAS　　　　　PIERCE　　　　　CASS　BUCHANAN　　　　MARCY　DICKINSON HOUSTON

POLITICAL HYPOCRISY.

Disappointed Candidates congratulating Gen' Frank Pierce on his nomination for the Presidency.

Pierce, who stands on the Democratic platform, had not been a prominent candidate for the nomination. These other men had been his rivals in the convention, particularly Stephen A. Douglas, who steps forward from the left, and Lewis Cass and James Buchanan, who advance toward Pierce from the other side. The three men at the right of the picture are William L. Marcy, who became Pierce's Secretary of State; Daniel S. Dickinson, Senator from New York, and Sam Houston.

SOLICITING A VOTE.

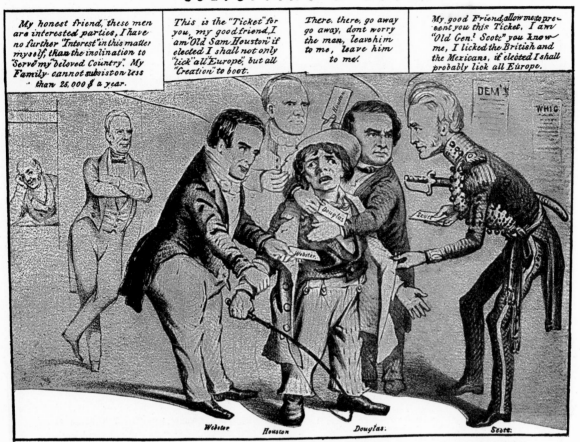

The major political question of slavery had presumably been settled by the Compromise of 1850, and the campaign of 1852 was being fought largely around the personalities of the leaders. The two most conspicuous Whig candidates were Daniel Webster, then Secretary of State, and General Scott, who actually received the nomination. The two Democrats in this cartoon are Sam Houston, who had been President of Texas and was then Senator, and Stephen A. Douglas, Senator from Illinois, already an acknowledged leader of his party and destined to figure largely in cartoons in subsequent chapters of the present work. Franklin Pierce of New Hampshire, who received the Democratic nomination, does not appear in this pre-convention cartoon. He had not been a conspicuous candidate until the convention chose him to end a deadlock. In offering this harassed voter his own ticket, General Scott says: "You know me. I licked the British and the Mexicans. If elected I shall probably lick all Europe." Webster is made to appear most interested in the $25,000 salary.

at Baltimore, June 1st. Incidentally, to show how names may repeat themselves in Democratic politics, John W. Davis of Indiana was permanent chairman. After the two-thirds rule had been adopted, it was evident that Cass and Buchanan, far in the lead, would defeat one another. Cass slowly lost, and on the twenty-ninth ballot Douglas and Buchanan were neck and neck. On the thirty-fifth ballot, Cass was far in the lead, but Virginia trotted in a dark horse named Franklin Pierce of New Hampshire. On the forty-eighth ballot, Marcy was in the lead, with Cass and

Pierce coming next and with Douglas and Buchanan trailing in the rear. Then came a stampede for Pierce, and everything was over. This result had been planned, in view of the prospect that no conspicuous candidate could be chosen. The platform was consistent with its predecessors, and it specifically upheld the Compromise of 1850.

The Whig convention at Baltimore, on the 16th of June, found Mr. Fillmore in favor with the Southern delegates and General Winfield Scott the leading candidate of the North. Webster's 7th of March speech had brought

GREAT FOOTRACE FOR THE PRESIDENTIAL PURSE ($100,000 AND PICKINGS) OVER THE UNION COURSE 1852.

For sale at N⁰ 2 Spruce St N.Y.

Daniel Webster is conspicuous in three of the cartoons of this chapter. A distinguished Senator and member of two Cabinets, he had shared the leadership of the Whig party with Henry Clay. Unlike Clay, Webster never received the party's presidential nomination. He came nearest to it in this year 1852, after his support of the Fugitive Slave Law had been looked upon as a bid for Southern support. The other runners in this race are General Scott, who was later nominated by the Whigs, and Franklin Pierce, who had already received the Democratic nomination. The purse of $100,000 represents the four-year income from the Presidency at that time. It might be added here that both Webster and Clay died in the period after the Whig convention and before the election. Webster's death came at his Massachusetts home, Marshfield, on October 24th, while Clay had died in Washington on June 29th of this year 1852.

him Southern favor, but only as next choice after Fillmore. The Northern faction won in the end, but it was on the fifty-third ballot, and by a very small majority. A rather colorless platform was adopted, ending with a harmony resolution beginning as follows: "That the series of acts of the Thirty-second Congress, the act known as the Fugitive Slave Law included, are received and acquiesced in by the Whig party of the United States as a settlement in principle and substance of the dangerous and exciting questions which they embrace." This was adopted by a vote of 212 to 70. With both parties agreed on the most dangerous issue, the Democrats had a clear advantage, and the Whigs were fighting their last campaign as a major party.

The growing anti-slavery sentiment of the North was not satisfied with the platform; and General Scott was not regarded as a statesman, or a leader in the field of politics. The ticket of Pierce and King received 254 electoral votes as against only 42 for the Whig ticket of Scott and Graham. Scott carried Massachusetts, Vermont, Kentucky, and Tennessee. All the other States were carried by Pierce. The popular majorities were, however, so small that if the scanty vote for the Free-Soil ticket headed by John P. Hale of New Hampshire had been added to the Scott vote, the two sides would have been almost even in the balloting. Hale received nearly 150,000 votes—about half as many as had been cast for the Free Soil ticket four years earlier.

Lincoln, of course, supported the Whig ticket and made speeches for Scott; but since he regarded Democratic victory as inevitable, he threw himself with less zeal than usual into a campaign that seemed to have no great principles at stake. To quote Lincoln's own summing up, in the third person: "In 1852 he was upon the Scott electoral ticket, and did something in the way of canvassing, but owing to the hopelessness of the cause in Illinois, he did less than in previous presidential campaigns."

Sometimes the busiest, happiest, and most prosperous years of a public man's life are those that are filled with private occupations between periods of political activity. Most of the biographers touch scantily upon Lincoln's life at this time. The exception is Mr. Beveridge, who is not content merely to tell us that

Lincoln was engaged for about five years, from 1849 to 1854, in the building up of his law practice. He informs us that Lincoln "spent at least six months of every year away from Springfield riding the circuit, and he was the only lawyer that attended the courts in every county seat. . . . Court was held in the various counties from the middle of March to the middle of June, and again from early September until the first of December. For more than three years after his Congressional term the Eighth Circuit comprised fourteen counties, Sangamon, Tazewell, Woodford, McLean, Logan, DeWitt, Champaign, Vermilion, Piatt, Edgar, Shelby, Moultrie, Macon, and Christian. It was nearly 140 miles long by almost 110 miles broad, nearly one-fifth of the entire area of the State."

PAP, SOUP, AND CHOWDER.

A poster caricature of the campaign of 1852, after the Democrats had nominated and while the Whigs were taking fifty-three ballots. Pierce, the Democratic nominee, rides unmolested to the White House, on horseback, while the three Whig leaders eat their favorite food. President Fillmore, carried on the shoulders of the editor of the New York *Mirror*, eats Government Pap, a synonym for patronage, and expresses regret that he will not be renominated. General Scott, supported by Horace Greeley, editor of the *Tribune*, eats soup. It is said that he once left his office to take "a hasty plate of soup" and never lived down the phrase. Scott's progress toward the White House is interfered with by the Southern voter who tugs at his arm and seeks the candidate's views regarding the Fugitive Slave Law. Daniel Webster, carried by James Watson Webb, editor of the New York *Courier and Enquirer,* eats chowder, said to have been his favorite dish.

CHAPTER XVIII

Birth of the Republican Party

The older statesmen pass on, Lincoln's contemporaries assuming control—Social conditions in the South—The Kansas-Nebraska bill and its important sequel

THE OLD LEADERS were now for the most part gathered unto the Fathers. Jackson had died in 1845, the year before Lincoln's election to Congress. John Quincy Adams had fallen at his post, and Lincoln had accompanied the body to its resting place in Massachusetts. Calhoun had taken part in the Compromise debate of 1850, another man reading his speech for him as he sat near in mortal illness, and the end came within a month. Clay's death had followed in June, 1852, and Lincoln had delivered a memorial oration. Daniel Webster died at Marshfield October 25, 1852, five months after his unsuccessful attempt to win the Whig nomination, and four months after the death of Clay. Van Buren was still living at Kinderhook, and he survived until 1862, a firm supporter of Lincoln's administration, but not a leading figure in the great drama after the Compromise of 1850.

Lincoln's contemporaries were now in full responsibility. The two Democrats of most brilliant parts were Stephen A. Douglas of Illinois and Jefferson Davis of Mississippi. They were orators who would have commanded attention in any age. Each of them had the energy and the courage of men born to lead. Emerging from the ranks of the conservative

166

FRANKLIN PIERCE
*Fourteenth President
of the United States*

In the Democratic convention of 1852, which nominated him for the Presidency, Pierce's name did not appear until the thirty-fifth ballot. He had been a member of the House for two terms beginning in 1833, and then served almost a full six-year term in the Senate, retiring in 1842 to his home at Concord, New Hampshire, to practice law. At the outbreak of war with Mexico he enlisted as a private but was commissioned a Colonel of militia and promoted to be a Brigadier-General. He was again in private life when the presidential nomination made him a national figure. In the November election Pierce carried all the States except four.

Whigs, and impelled by the course of events to accept high commands in the new Republican party, were Seward of New York and Chase of Ohio, each with profound anti-slavery convictions, great attainments as lawyers, and political and forensic talents of a high order.

Douglas and Davis had been longer in the Senate, while Seward and Chase were new arrivals but in full maturity of intellect and training.

With Webster gone, a new type of public man was coming forward in Massachusetts, scholarly and accomplished, but intense and intolerant. Webster and Clay had partaken of the broad and generous spirit of comprehension that made Washington the common denominator, in the earlier periods of discord as between followers of Hamilton and Jefferson. Charles Sumner, John P. Hale, and other leaders of New England were even less tolerant and sympathetic than Seward.

No set of men so little understood the South as the extreme Abolitionists. They saw the wrongs of slavery, and they would not compromise with evil. Less rabid men like Seward, in the North and East, were combating a false and impossible sectional attitude, and they did not sufficiently analyze the nature and causes of this Southern solidarity.

ORNITHOLOGY.

Two Great Birds of the United States, not described by Audubon.

Genus. Turkey cockeyus cum Fuss and Fetheribus — ✣ *Genus. Gamecockius Granitestatei..*

The game-cock of the Granite State, Franklin Pierce, was wrong in his challenge that Scott could not cross the Mason and Dixon Line; for although the Whigs carried only four States in this year 1852, two of them were Kentucky and Tennessee. The turkey represents General Scott, "Old Fuss and Feathers" being a nickname applied to him in contrast to "Old Rough and Ready," which had characterized his brother officer and predecessor as presidential candidate of the Whigs, General Taylor. The cartoonist here asserts that John James Audubon, the great American naturalist who had died in the preceding year, had failed to describe this particular turkey and this game-cock in his monumental work "The Birds of America."

There were three great population elements in the South. The first was composed of the educated and cultured community, planters, property owners, and social elements that represented Anglo-Saxon civilization. A much larger element, numerically, was made up of the non-slaveholding farmers, the mountaineers, and the so-called "poor whites," many of whom were descended from indentured English servants and misdemeanants of the colonial period. These people, in the main, had always been political followers of their more prosperous neighbors, and were largely Jeffersonian, in so far as they were aware of the existence of social and political doctrines. The other great population element comprised several million African slaves, who found slavery cruel and unbearable in many of its aspects, yet who were so bound by their sense of domestic attachment and loyalty to the superior class, upon whom they were dependent, that when the final test of war came they proved themselves to be the most devoted Southerners of any class whatever, in view of facts and motives that might have provoked them to insurrection.

The clearer truth of history, as now it begins to reveal itself, shows that the consolidated Southern position was due to many things besides slavery. There was the love of land and the Anglo-Saxon instinct for pioneering and territorial extension. There was strong individualism, and the sense of personal right that helped to explain the wholly indefensible view that a slave-owner ought to be allowed to take slaves into new national territory. This

A BORDER RUFFIAN OF THE DARKEST DYE

The two illustrations on this page are reproduced from a book published in New York in 1856, entitled "The War in Kansas," by G. D. Brewerton. The one reproduced above bears the following descriptive caption: "The white man quickened his pace, but Caesar overhauled the panting fugitive, who surrendered at discretion, at the same time begging for his life."

tific discussion of the historical trends of modern industry and labor. Unfortunately, economic history had few students before 1850. Webster was perfectly right in his 7th of March speech when he explained that it would be needless further to irritate the South, in its present state of feverish excitement, by prohibiting slavery in advance of settlement in regions where slavery in the very nature of things—soil, climate, and topography— could never gain a lasting foothold.

Illinois was so placed as to have peculiar advantages for the development of leaders who might mediate between the dangerous and fanatical sectionalism of the changing South and the no less dangerous and reckless crusading spirit that was slowly but surely win-

claim was asserted, with passionate intensity, regardless not only of such national decisions as that of the Ordinance of 1787, but also regardless of the verdicts of the new communities themselves.

Anyone who has studied speculative land movements, whether in Iowa and the Dakotas, or in Florida and Southern California, ought to comprehend the sheer greed and ferocity of the land, cotton, and slave speculation that had created a state of social delirium in Alabama, Mississippi, and Louisiana. The Southern churches had suddenly discovered that slavery was a divine institution, and its maintenance the chief duty of applied religion.

Those were not the times when men could be made to listen to the calm and scien-

THE BORDER RUFFIANS EXTRICATE THE FREE STATE ARTILLERY

This contemporary cartoon makes the artillery quite harmless in its appearance. But the heated political discussion over the admission of Kansas did result in actual war, in 1856. Partisans from adjoining slave and free states had rushed into the territory, each side seeking to frame the State constitution.

LIBERTY THE FAIR MAID OF KANSAS_IN THE HANDS OF THE "BORDER RUFFIANS"

The leaders of the Democratic party are here blamed for high-handed methods used in Kansas in 1856. President Pierce is in the center of the group. At the left, with patched trousers, is William L. Marcy, Secretary of State. The man with watch in hand is James Buchanan, who had returned from his post as minister to Great Britain and was to be elected President later in the same year. Standing behind the maid representing Kansas is Lewis Cass, who became Buchanan's Secretary of State. At the extreme right is Senator Douglas, with an unfamiliar beard. As chairman of the Senate Committee on Territories, Douglas was author of the Kansas-Nebraska bill of 1854, which—instead of legislating slavery into any territory, or excluding it—had left the people free to regulate domestic institutions in their own way. This squatter sovereignty principle brought on the disorder in Kansas but eventually it proved itself efficient.

ning the North to the anti-slavery movement as a holy cause. Illinois had two leaders touched with genius and rising to greatness. Lincoln, with a few years of fortunate opportunity in private life to readjust his views, was preparing to lead the North, while trying to restrain its angry expressions and to sooth its aroused temper. Douglas, far too conspicuous in the Senate for unobserved meditation, was obliged to do his thinking on his feet. He was acting under the minor compulsions of the Senate's committee business, rather than upon well-chosen lines of major policy.

Douglas had come to Illinois from Vermont, with his schoolboy record as a militant Jacksonian Democrat. Party exigencies had brought him into relation with the Southern Democratic leaders, without which his ambitions for promotion would have been in vain. By heredity and instinct Douglas was always more the Northern man than was Lincoln.

With Virginia and Kentucky background, Lincoln's residence until manhood was in a part of Indiana populated by Southerners. He married, also, into a family of slave-owning Kentuckians, and it was always easy for him to fraternize with Southern men. Although his family had been so poor, and his own early advantages so meager as regards education, he was in many respects like the politicians and lawyers of Kentucky, Tennessee, North Carolina, Georgia, and Virginia.

As for the State of Illinois itself, a glance at the map shows that more than half of it lies south of the northern line of Missouri, while the southern tip of it extends southward far enough to look across the Ohio to the Kentucky shore. The Northwest Ordinance had protected Illinois for freedom, but its early settlers were from the South. With the exception of the Springfield district, Illinois had always been a Democratic State, and this had permitted Douglas, as a born leader of men, to make his early appearance in the United States Senate. Lincoln had slowly but steadily made his way to the undisputed leadership of the other party in Illinois, following Henry Clay in his general positions.

Lincoln came back into politics with refreshed mind and enhanced power through a false move made by Douglas in 1854. Douglas was chairman of the Senate Committee on Territories. David Atchison, a Senator from Missouri, was a member of that committee, somewhat unscrupulous, and a daring and aggressive worker for slavery extension. To the immediate westward of his State of Missouri lay the empty prairies of what is now the agricultural State of Kansas. To the east of Missouri lay the settled and prosperous Free State of Illinois. Kansas was a part of

the unorganized region known as the Nebraska Territory. Atchison brought in a bill to organize this Territory, survey its lands, and open it to settlement. But naturally the people of Missouri, with unappeased land hunger, wanted to occupy the rich lands of eastern Kansas, and they were not willing to leave slavery behind them. They regarded it as highly detrimental to the continued existence of slavery in Missouri to be pinched in between free Illinois on the East and a free Kansas on the West, with a free Iowa on the North.

As chairman of the Committee on Territories, Douglas felt impelled to report the bill as his own. Not to have done so would have given Atchison undue influence, and would apparently thwart Douglas's ambition to secure the presidential nomination in 1856. Atchison sought to organize the whole Nebraska

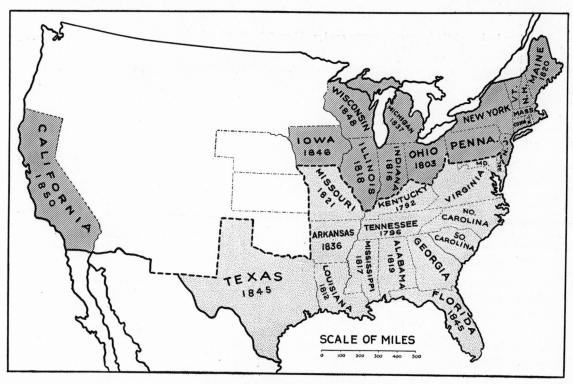

THE UNITED STATES IN 1854

In the ten-year period from 1812 to 1821, seven States were admitted into the Union: Louisiana, Indiana, Mississippi, Illinois, Alabama, Maine, and Missouri. By that time the great debate over slavery had arisen, and no States were admitted in the following fifteen years. Then Arkansas and Michigan came in, balancing each other. Florida and Texas in 1845 rounded out the southern and eastern coast line. Iowa was admitted in 1846, Wisconsin in 1848, and California in 1850. Then arose the protracted discussion over Kansas and Nebraska, which kept Douglas in the forefront and brought Lincoln back into national politics after a period of practical retirement as a lawyer in Illinois. Our map shows Slave States, shaded lightly, and Free States; and the dotted line indicates the region which later became the States of Nebraska and Kansas.

LINCOLN SHOWS DOUGLAS THE RIGHT ROAD TO THE WHITE HOUSE

Discussion over the likelihood of slavery in Kansas resulted in dissension within the Democratic party in the Free State of Illinois, and very nearly brought about Lincoln's election to the United States Senate early in 1855. He threw his support to an anti-Douglas Democrat, Lyman Trumbull, and elected him. In 1856 Lincoln declined a nomination for Governor, and named the man who was nominated and elected (William H. Bissell). Lincoln was second choice for Vice-President at the first Republican National Convention in that same year. In 1858 he was the "first and only choice" of Illinois Republicans for United States Senator, and challenged Douglas, his Democratic opponent, to a series of debates. Meanwhile the situation in Kansas had grown worse, and Douglas himself refused to condone the Administration's policy. In this cartoon from *Phunny Phellow*, a humorous political paper published at New York in the campaign of 1860, Lincoln is consoling Douglas, with the Kansas feather in his hat, and suggesting that splitting rails was a better way to become President.

country as slave territory; but this could not have been carried through Congress. As Douglas brought the bill to the floor of the Senate, there was a provision which left it to the settlers, in a territorial convention, to decide the slavery question for themselves.

Atchison, however, insisted upon an amendment which radically changed the situation as viewed in a practical light. He forced Douglas to accept the plan of an immediate separation of Kansas from Nebraska, with the further proviso that Kansas should at once be organized as a Territory by itself. The

Nebraska region proper, lying west of Iowa, was of course hopeless from the standpoint of the pro-slavery propaganda. But Kansas lay due west of Missouri, and in the same latitude as Virginia and Kentucky. The Missourians considered it the best possible concrete opening for a new Slave State.

The Kansas-Nebraska Bill passed both houses of Congress and became a law with President Pierce's signature on May 30, 1854, after five months of debate. Douglas returned from the East early in the autumn, to find Illinois deeply stirred by the breaking of the truce that both parties had so solemnly accepted in their platforms of 1852. He defended his course at Chicago on September 1st, and spoke in the State House at Springfield on October 4th. Lincoln followed at once with a reply that was well considered, and—according to several listeners—of amazing eloquence. He had, of course, been studying this Kansas dilemma for many months, and was now quite through with policies of temporizing and compromise. He was definitely in politics again, and became at once a candidate for the United States Senate against Douglas's colleague, General James Shields, who was seeking re-election.

Douglas had faced a hostile and angry throng at Chicago, and felt that his popularity had suffered in Illinois even as in states farther East. His debate in Springfield on October 4th, where his three-hour speech in the afternoon was answered in a similarly long speech by Lincoln in the evening, was not for the "Little Giant" a triumphant memory. Mr.

LYMAN TRUMBULL
Elected to the United States Senate by the Illinois legislature in 1855, with Lincoln playing the leading part. Then a Democrat, Trumbull later joined the new Republican party; but after the death of Lincoln he once more became a Democrat. He remained in the Senate for eighteen years, returning in 1875 to law practice.

Barrett says that "Lincoln was relied upon by the Anti-Nebraskans, Whig and Democratic, as a most effective champion; and his speech in turn was so masterly as to surprise both friends and opponents." Twelve days later, the two leaders spoke in debate at Peoria, and Lincoln regarded his reply to Douglas on that occasion as one of the greatest efforts of his life. His subject was the repeal of the Missouri Compromise; and he argued for the propriety of its restoration. This speech included as frank a discussion of the slavery question as any that Lincoln made in all his career.

On the contention that slavery, if left alone, would never take root in Kansas, Lincoln made the following observations in this Peoria speech of October 16, 1854:

"Let me here drop the main argument, to notice what I consider rather an inferior matter. It is argued that slavery will not go to Kansas and Nebraska, in any event. This is a palliation, a lullaby. I have some hope that it will not; but let us not be too confident. As to climate, a glance at the map shows that there are five slave States — Delaware, Maryland, Virginia, Kentucky, and Missouri, and also the District of Columbia, all north of the Missouri Com-

GENERAL SHIELDS WOUNDED
Lincoln was the Whig candidate for United States Senator from Illinois in 1855. The seat was that of James Shields, the same Springfield lawyer with whom Lincoln had nearly fought a duel fourteen years earlier. Shields had become a brigadier-general in the Mexican War, had been wounded in May, 1847, while leading his troops, and had returned to be lionized and elected to the Senate. As that six-year term was expiring, in 1855, Shields assumed a position in the slavery controversy which alienated some Democratic support, and Lincoln saw a chance that he himself might be elected. He led Shields on the first ballot, 45 votes to 41, with 13 votes scattering. But the Democrats, who were in a majority later, united upon Lyman Trumbull.

"NO HIGHER LAW."

One of the measures included in the Compromise of 1850 was the Fugitive Slave Law. It provided for the appointment of a federal commissioner in every county to decide whether or not a seized colored man was an escaping slave, the Negro's testimony not to be considered. It provided, further, that the commissioner's fee was doubled if he decided against the alleged fugitive. This Fugitive Slave Law gave effect to a provision in the Constitution, that persons held to service or labor in one State and escaping into another shall be delivered up. William H. Seward, Senator from New York, opposed this provision, and in a speech on March 11, 1850, declared that "there is a higher law than the Constitution." Daniel Webster, standing toward the right of this cartoon, apologetic rather than proud, was Clay's chief supporter in securing the adoption of the compromise measures. This is unusual among cartoons of that time, in its extreme anti-slavery character.

promise line. The census returns of 1850 show that within these there are eight hundred and sixty-seven thousand two hundred and seventy-six slaves, being more than one-fourth of all the slaves in the nation.

"It is not climate, then, that will keep slavery out of these Territories. Is there anything in the peculiar nature of the country? Missouri adjoins these Territories by her entire western boundary, and slavery is already within every one of her western counties. I have even heard it said that there are more slaves in proportion to whites in the northwestern county of Missouri, than within any other county in the State. Slavery pressed entirely up to the old western boundary of the State, and when

rather recently a part of that boundary at the northwest was moved out a little farther west, slavery followed on quite up to the new line. Now when the restriction is removed, what is to prevent it from going still farther? Climate will not, no peculiarity of the country will, nothing in nature will. Will the disposition of the people prevent it? Those nearest the scene are all in favor of the extension. The Yankees who are opposed to it may be most numerous; but, in military phrase, the battle-field is too far from their base of operations."

Younger readers should have it well in mind that United States Senators were elected by the Legislatures of the States until after the passage of the Seventeenth Amendment to

THE GREAT REPUBLICAN REFORM PARTY.

When Lincoln was the Whig candidate for Senator in 1855, the Whigs were already breaking up and a new Republican party was forming. Into that new party came Whigs, Free-Soilers, Abolitionists, and Democrats. It also attracted some radical and disaffected elements. At the head of this imaginary line greeting Frémont—the first national candidate of the Republicans—is the Negro, and behind him are a representative of the Catholic Church, a believer in Free Love, a communist, an advocate of woman's rights, and, finally, a prohibitionist.

the Constitution in 1913, which provides for direct popular election. The Illinois Legislature convened for this purpose on February 8, 1855. Lincoln and Shields were the chief opposing candidates, the uncertainty being due to the tendencies of both parties to split on the Kansas issue. Lyman Trumbull was a prominent anti-slavery Democrat, and his name was presented as a competitor. On the first ballot there were 45 votes for Lincoln, 41 for Shields, and 5 for Trumbull with 8 scattering. After six ballots, the Shields vote was transferred *en masse* to the Governor of the State, J. A. Matteson. Matteson was gaining and Lincoln was losing through several more ballots, until suddenly Lincoln made a bold move and threw enough of his strength to Trumbull to secure his election by a vote of 51 to 47.

Lincoln's election had been regarded as virtually assured, and there was disappointment among his friends. But he himself wisely and generously said that "On the whole it is perhaps well for our general cause that Trumbull is elected." And this proved to be wholly true in the reshaping of parties and in the later support, loyal and powerful, that Senator Trumbull brought to Lincoln and the "general cause."

In 1858, in his opening speech in joint debate with Lincoln, Douglas declared that there had been an arrangement in 1854 between Lincoln and Trumbull to lead their respective followers out of the two dissolving old parties into "an Abolition party under the name and disguise of a Republican party." Doubtless Douglas believed this to be true, but there is no evidence that sustains the charge. Unquestionably Douglas would have preferred to have Lincoln beat Shields or Matteson in 1854, rather than to risk Lincoln's more dangerous competition for his own seat in 1858, when otherwise he would have Trumbull confronting him.

Attention was now turning altogether away from the debate at Washington, over the Kansas bill, to the excitement of competitive colonization in Kansas itself. Since Kansas was to put the principle of "squatter sovereignty" into effect without delay, the zealots on both sides proposed to occupy Kansas with militant propagandists, rather than with ordinary pioneer farmers.

With the Kansas-Nebraska Bill came the actual founding of the Republican party. It brought together the Free-Soilers, the Whigs, all but the more violent of the Abolitionists, and a large contingent of Democrats. Historically the party may be said to have had its beginning on July 6, 1854, at Jackson, Michigan, where the name "Republican" was adopted in State convention, and where the chief plank of the platform was as follows:

"*Resolved,* That postponing and suspending all differences with regard to political economy or administrative policy, in view of the imminent danger that Kansas and Nebraska will be grasped by Slavery, and a thousand miles of slave soil be thus interposed between the Free States of the Atlantic and those of the Pacific, we will act cordially and faithfully in unison to avert and repeal this gigantic wrong and shame."

Similar movements had been springing up simultaneously in a number of States, but the Michigan meeting which nominated a full State ticket, adopted a party platform, and agreed upon the party name, is accorded the honors by political historians. The influence of the Abolitionists upon Northern opinion and upon the origins and doctrines of the Republican party may well be studied in the calm and philosophical pages of James Ford Rhodes. Meanwhile, for the latest survey of the Abolition cult in its promotion of sectional antagonism and of civil war, it is necessary to read the opening chapters of Mr. Beveridge's second volume.

Horace Greeley was soon brought into the Republican fold, with the New York *Tribune* as his personal organ, this being the most widely circulated and influential newspaper in America at that time. Some thirty Congressmen had met in Washington the day after the Kansas-Nebraska Bill had passed the House, and on their own account had taken initial steps toward the forming of a new party. The details are on record in Mr. Francis Curtis's "History of the Republican Party;" and it is enough to remark at this point that the Republicans became at once a major party organ-

A CONTESTED SEAT

The candidates in 1852 both were men who had gained distinction in the war with Mexico. Scott, who jerks away the presidential chair in this picture, was a Major-General. Pierce, on the floor, was only a Brigadier-General. The Brigadier-General won on election day.

ization, with the Whig party doomed though not yet dissolved.

The break-up of old parties was strikingly evidenced when the Thirty-fourth Congress, elected in 1854, met in December of the following year and proceeded to the choice of a Speaker. After a long struggle, Nathaniel P. Banks of Massachusetts, who had formerly been an anti-slavery Democrat, but was now an avowed Republican, secured that post of influence. With the new party winning control in one northern State after another, and now securing the Speakership of the Thirty-fourth Congress, it was so well established that one of its founders, Henry Wilson of Massachusetts, in after years looking backward over its history, and forward to consider its prospects, declared that he could see no reason why it should not last a thousand years.

Lincoln was not one of the first to announce himself a

Republican on the ruins of his old Whig party. But before the national convention of 1856 had been held, he was recognized not only as a member of the new party, but as the leading Republican of his State and of the Northwest. He had made a speech that was the greatest effort of his life, in the opinion of those who heard it, at a State convention early in 1856, that organized the Republican party of Illinois. Lyman Trumbull presided at that Convention, having passed from his position as an anti-Nebraska Democrat, along with another eminent Democratic leader John M. Palmer, to the comradeship of old Whigs like Lincoln, in the endeavor to rally Illinois against Douglas. Lincoln's swing from Whig to Republican required courage in view of local circumstances. The convention met at Bloomington late in May, and was made up of mixed and strange elements. Lincoln's thrilling speech unified the gathering and saved the day.

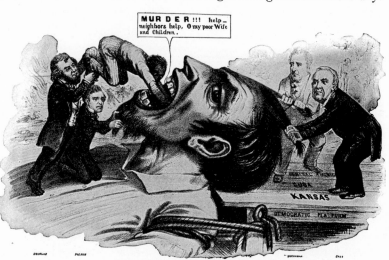

FORCING SLAVERY DOWN THE THROAT OF A FREESOILER

Free Soil advocates had their own national ticket in 1848 and 1852, but not in 1856. Here we see the four leading Democrats in the campaign of 1856. At the left are Senator Douglas of Illinois and President Pierce. At the right, pulling the Free-Soiler's hair, are James Buchanan, the successful Democratic candidate, and Lewis Cass, who was to become Buchanan's Secretary of State.

MISSOURIANS GOING TO KANSAS TO VOTE

A contemporary engraving attributed to F. O. C. Darley. It was widely understood that bands of armed men crossed into Kansas from the slave State of Missouri, taking possession of the polls and controlling the election of 1854 which resulted in the temporary ascendancy of the pro-slavery advocates. Then followed civil war and a new election three years later, with the subsequent adoption of a constitution prohibiting slavery. Darley was a Philadelphia-born artist doing important work as a book illustrator in New York, even then a member of the National Academy and later becoming internationally known.

CHAPTER XIX

The Presidential Election of 1856

*The rival colonization of "Bloody Kansas," by North and South—
Designs on Cuba meet with Republican disapproval—Lincoln takes
high rank in the new party*

SENTIMENTS ARE ALSO FACTS, regardless of their justification. Webster had declared it a fact that slave labor would never produce cotton, sugar or tobacco on the arid plains of New Mexico; but the sentiment of Massachusetts against his 7th of March speech was a harder fact than any stone wall on his farm at Marshfield. Douglas was now to find that he had underestimated the resistless force of Northern anti-slavery sentiment, as a far more real though less tangible thing than the statutes that he had been helping to make and unmake at Washington.

The Missouri Compromise of 1820 had fixed the parallel of 36° 30′ as the dividing line between the areas of freedom and slavery in the West. Douglas until lately had regarded this line as one of the irrevocable fixtures, comparable with the charter of freedom for States north of the Ohio in the Ordinance of 1787. This Missouri Compromise had allowed the single State of Missouri to be admitted with slavery, but had expressly declared that otherwise slavery should be kept south of the specified parallel of latitude.

Through the influence of Jefferson Davis, who was then Secretary of War and by far the ablest and most influential member of President Franklin Pierce's Cabinet, and also at the instance of Southern Senators, Douglas

177

had substituted the Kansas-Nebraska Bill for the earlier bill that dealt with Nebraska as undivided. The assurance of President Pierce that he would sign the new bill, which included specifically the repeal of the Missouri Compromise, had been secured in advance. To understand the situation, readers must keep in mind the fact that Kansas lay north of the parallel 36° 30′, and had therefore been guaranteed as free territory by the Compromise of 1820, which had been universally accepted. To justify himself, Douglas took the ground that by the Compromise of 1850 a new principle had been adopted, that of permitting the territories to decide for themselves, thus replacing the old scheme of a fixed line that should forever separate free soil from slave soil.

This, however, had not been so understood in 1850; for Douglas himself at that time had declared the Missouri Compromise to be "canonized in the hearts of the American people as a thing which no ruthless hand would ever be reckless enough to disturb." No one had thought that the law of 1850 affecting New Mexico and Utah was to be applied far eastward to the organization of Kansas, the status of which had been ordained in the law of 1820.

It must not be supposed that Douglas argued weakly or insincerely. He held his own against Senators of the highest ability, and carried his bill to its final passage in May, 1854, when it became a law with President Pierce's approval after a debate of five months. On its face, this was a great parliamentary triumph for Douglas. But like Webster four years earlier, he had taken positions for which Northern disapprobation was bitter enough to have burned him at the stake. Mr.

HARRIET BEECHER STOWE
The author of "Uncle Tom's Cabin" was the daughter of Lyman Beecher, the sister of Henry Ward Beecher, and the husband of Calvin E. Stowe—all distinguished clergymen. Most of her life was spent in New England, but from 1832 to 1850 (when she was twenty-one to thirty-nine years of age) she lived in Cincinnati. Her father was president of Lane Theological Seminary there, and her husband was a professor in the same institution. Mrs. Stowe's observations of slave life, upon which her book was based, resulted from this long residence in Cincinnati, lying just across the Ohio from the slave State of Kentucky.

Muzzey remarks that "Douglas was denounced as a turn-coat, a traitor, a Judas, a Benedict Arnold, who had sold himself to the South for the presidential nomination." He was burned in effigy so frequently that he himself said he could "travel from Boston to Chicago by the light of the fires." It was declared that "485,000 square miles of territory that had forever been dedicated to freedom were opened to the slave-holder."

Yet Douglas doubtless foresaw that under his plan of squatter sovereignty not a mile of this area would actually become the abode of legalized slavery, unless in the merely transitional stages of Kansas settlement. His arguments were ingenious, and in the perspectives of three-quarters of a century, they appear by no means contemptible. But they offended both legal and moral principles, according to the prevailing sentiment of the North, and they blighted the promising political career of the ambitious Douglas.

In 1852 Mrs. Harriet Beecher Stowe had written "Uncle Tom's Cabin," a novel that intensified still further the moral indignation against slavery as a social and domestic institution. It is stated that when Mrs. Stowe was presented to President Lincoln in the White House ten years later he remarked as he greeted her: "So this is the little woman who brought on this big Civil War!" For a time the new fugitive slave law of 1850 had seemed to be effective, and to reduce if not wipe out completely that system for aiding slaves to cross the North to the Canada border known as the "Underground Railroad." But now, the States officially began to nullify the law. By local statutes, administrative measures and judicial proceedings they tried to thwart completely the efforts of Federal officials to aid Southern owners in the recovery of their escaped bondmen. This Northern nullification was hardly different in legal principle from the action of South Carolina in nullifying the tariffs of 1828 and 1832.

The rival colonizing movements were set on foot with no delay whatever. The New England Emigrant Aid Society was promptly organized, to assist picked young men to settle in Kansas; and the present city of Lawrence bears the name of the Boston merchant who gave money and aid to the emigrant movement. The city of Atchison, on the other hand, bears the name of the Missouri

LITTLE EVA AND UNCLE TOM

(An illustration from the original edition of "Uncle Tom's Cabin")

The publication of "Uncle Tom's Cabin" in 1852, and its amazing sale, contributed materially to the popular agitation in the North against slavery. Its author was Harriet Beecher Stowe. The story is that of Uncle Tom, a slave who after long service for kindly and sympathetic owners is sold into a life of cruelty and suffering. Little Eva was this first master's daughter. There are dramatic incidents where husband and wife in the slave cabins are parted forever, where the escaping young wife with her child in her arms is pursued across the ice of the Ohio River by bloodhounds, where slaves are beaten by overseers, and Uncle Tom himself dies from the effects of a whipping.

Senator who was the most energetic of the Southern leaders in promoting the counter-movement of occupation. With many organized and inhabited counties of western Missouri adjacent to the Kansas border, or within easy marching distance, the Missourians adopted the plan of border raids, in preference to the slower and less militant northern scheme of founding actual settlements.

From other parts of the South came volunteer bands of armed men, somewhat as the militia had risen ten years earlier to join the expedition against Mexico. Non-resident raiders organized the first territorial government, and enacted a drastic pro-slavery code. The Free Soil settlers formed a

SOUTHERN CHIVALRY — ARGUMENT versus CLUB'S.

Charles Sumner, a distinguished Boston lawyer and former Harvard professor, had been elected to the Senate in 1851 by Free Soilers and anti-slavery Democrats. He particularly opposed the Fugitive Slave Law and other Compromise measures, and on May 20, 1856, delivered a speech in the Senate on "The Crime Against Kansas." It was a severe indictment of Senator Andrew P. Butler of South Carolina, as well as of Senator Douglas. Two days later Butler's nephew, Preston S. Brooks, himself a member of the House, attacked Sumner with a cane. Penned in his seat, Sumner was beaten insensible. He was canonized as a martyr in the North, while Brooks—who resigned and was immediately re-elected—became a popular hero in the South. Sumner was seriously injured, remaining away from the Senate for three years.

MASTER JONATHAN TRIES TO SMOKE A CUBA;
BUT IT DOESN'T AGREE WITH HIM!

This is a cartoon from *Punch* (London), published in
June, 1850. During Taylor's term as President it was
widely proposed in the South that Cuba should be annexed, for sugar, tobacco, and slave territory. Filibustering expeditions under a Venezuelan adventurer named
Narciso Lopez were fitted out at Southern ports, and became the subject of *Punch's* satire. The first, in 1849, was
blocked by President Taylor. The second failed. The
third succeeded in landing 600 men in Cuba, but they
soon met defeat and Lopez himself was captured and
executed in 1851.

government of their own, and applied to Congress for the admission of Kansas as a State.
Destruction of the Free Soil town of Lawrence was at once followed by an avenging
raid—with John Brown of Ossawatomie as
the leader of a small band including his four
sons—upon a settlement of Missourians living
in his vicinity in southeast Kan-
sas. The massacre of several men
by John Brown's band, seized in
their homes at night, shocked the
North and drove the South to
frenzies of indignation.

There is an extensive literature
of the Kansas question in the annals of American politics and government, and there is also a literature that deals with local details of
this epoch of ferocious though
quite temporary civil war in Kansas. It may suffice here to remark
that the climax of the Kansas situation was reached in May, 1856,
less than a month before the first
Republican national convention
met at Pittsburgh. Senator Sumner had made a bitter speech
against the South, and he had been

beaten almost to the point of death by a South
Carolina Congressman. United States troops
had finally been sent to Kansas to keep order,
and, with protection thus furnished, the *bona-
fide* settlement by Northern men proceeded
safely and conclusively. Anticipating events,
it may be added that it was not until 1861 with
the Republicans in full power at Washington
that Kansas was finally admitted as a Free
State. But the question of slavery in that territory had continued to agitate parties through
the Buchanan administration.

Other questions, meanwhile, had also been
claiming the attention of the Pierce administration. Notable among these was the aggressive diplomacy that sought the acquisition
of Cuba. William L. Marcy of New York
was Secretary of State, Jefferson Davis of
Mississippi was Secretary of War, James C.
Dobbin of North Carolina Secretary of the
Navy, and Caleb Cushing of Massachusetts
Attorney-General. These were all able men,
with Davis by far the most masterful and energetic. There arose the incident of an American steamship, the *Black Warrior,* seized by
the Spaniards at Havana, with the South disposed to hope that it would give excuse for a
war with Spain, and justify the long-desired
occupation and retention of Cuba.

WANTED: A WHALER

The agitation to annex Cuba continued long after the failure of the
Lopez filibustering expedition. It broke out again twice during Buchanan's
administration as President. This cartoon—from *Vanity Fair* (New
York), June, 1860—shows Sam Houston, the Texas expansionist, rowing
the boat for the harpoonist.

THE "OSTEND DOCTRINE",
Practical Democrats carrying out the principle.

For Sale at N.º 2 Spruce St. N.Y.

The recent acquisition of vast regions in the West made it easy for the South to believe that the island of Cuba should also be included within the American Union. Besides, Cuba was restive under Spanish rule. As a result of this pressure, the three foremost American ministers in Europe met at Ostend, Belgium, in October, 1854, and issued a manifesto declaring that if the United States could not buy Cuba it would be justified in taking the island from Spain by force. The three diplomats were James Buchanan, minister to England; John Y. Mason, minister to France; and Pierre Soulé, minister to Spain. Above is a cartoon circulated in the presidential campaign two years later, when Buchanan was the Democratic nominee. The Republicans then sought to use against him this doctrine of justifiable force. The tramps are using the language of the Ostend Manifesto while they rob Buchanan. The one at the right, for example, takes Buchanan's hat with the statement that "its immediate acquisition is of paramount importance." Another intimates that "considerations exist which render delay exceedingly dangerous."

So strong was this feeling that President Pierce found it necessary in May, 1854, to issue a warning to "citizens of the United States and others residing therein" against "organizing and fitting out a military expedition for the invasion of the Island of Cuba."

In October, governments in both hemispheres were startled by the issuance of what was called the "Ostend Manifesto." New Orleans, in particular, had been a center of agitation in favor of the annexation of Cuba and Pierre Soulé of that city was sent to Spain as American Minister to urge upon the Spanish government the desirability of selling the Island to the United States. A sum was offered that was many times larger than that which Jefferson had paid Napoleon for the vast Louisiana area in which Mr. Soulé was born. But the Spaniards were obdurate, holding that they would rather see Cuba forever submerged

JOHN C. FRÉMONT

When the leaders of the new Republican party looked
around for a candidate in 1856, they chose the 43-year-old
Pathfinder of the West. Born in Georgia in 1813, John
Charles Frémont had become at twenty-three a professor
of mathematics and engineering in the navy. In 1842 he
entered upon the first of five exploring expeditions into the
new country west of the Rockies. When war came with
Mexico, Colonel Frémont raised a small force of volunteers
which seized and held the region that is now California.
While stationed at Washington in 1841 he had met and
eloped with Jessie Benton, the daughter of the distinguished Senator Benton of Missouri. In 1850 he was
chosen as one of the first Senators from California. In the
presidential election of 1856, as candidate of the Republican
party, Frémont received 114 electoral votes against 174
for Buchanan.

beneath Caribbean waters than to sell it at any
conceivable price.

Whereupon, John Y. Mason, American
Minister to France, and James Buchanan, Minister to Great Britain, joined Mr. Soulé for a
conference over the Cuban question at Ostend
in Belgium. Secretary Marcy and the Pierce
administration were regarded as responsible
for the Manifesto issued by this trio of Democratic diplomatists. The so-called "circular"
was in the form of a report to the Department
of State, advising that Spain's misgovernment
would undoubtedly lead to an insurrectionary
war in Cuba, proposing that the United States
should offer Spain $120,000,000, and arguing

that in case of Spain's continued refusal, the
United States would be justified in taking
Cuba by force.

It was the lingering memory of the Republican opposition to the Ostend Manifesto that
led Congress, at the instance of President
McKinley's administration, to register a
solemn disavowal of all annexation motives
when Cuba was occupied by the American
army and navy in 1898. A preliminary convention of Republicans at Pittsburgh on
Washington's Birthday, 1856, adopted a long
address to the people of the United States,
and called a nominating convention to meet
at Philadelphia, June 17th. With all the
northern States and the Territories represented, there were also delegates from the four
Slave States of Delaware, Maryland, Virginia
and Kentucky. Senator Seward of New York
was the most conspicuous man in the new
party, in the eyes of the convention. But he
did not expect success in that year, and refused
to be the candidate. Senator Chase of Ohio
and John McLean also of Ohio came next in
prominence, but for certain reasons of availability their names were withdrawn.

Colonel John C. Frémont was the only remaining candidate of national fame, and he
was unanimously nominated, following a
single informal ballot. He was picturesque
and popular, had been in the Senate from California for a short time, was a son-in-law of
that sterling old Democrat Senator Benton of
Missouri, and was nominated rather for what
we should call publicity purposes than upon any
solid basis of political experience or statesmanlike qualification.

The ballot for Vice-President gave William
L. Dayton of New Jersey 259 votes, Abraham Lincoln of Illinois 110, and the Speaker
of the House, N. P. Banks of Massachusetts,
46. Dayton was unanimously chosen, and the
new ticket was hailed with enthusiasm. The
Whigs had seldom found themselves capable
of adopting platforms that had the ring of
earnest and united conviction; but the Republicans of 1856 supported the Declaration of
Independence, declared the sovereignty of
Congress over the Territories, and added the
famous assertion that it is "both the right and

duty of Congress to prohibit in the Territories those twin relics of barbarism, polygamy and slavery." It should be noted that the Mormons had abandoned their headquarters at Nauvoo, Illinois, and had established themselves near the Great Salt Lake in Utah.

The platform made a long and detailed recital of the grievances of Kansas, for which "the administration, the President, his advisers, agents, supporters, apologists, and accessories either before or after the fact," were arraigned as guilty of "this high crime against the Constitution, the Union and humanity." Another plank demanded the immediate admission of Kansas as a Free State. It was further resolved, "That the highwayman's plea that might makes right, embodied in the Ostend circular, was in every respect unworthy of American diplomacy, and would bring shame and dishonor upon any government or people that gave it their sanction." Final resolutions demanded the construction of a railroad to the Pacific Ocean, and appropriations for rivers and harbors.

The Democratic convention had already met, this time at Cincinnati, on the 2nd of June. President Pierce was a candidate for renomination, while James Buchanan of Pennsylvania was preferred by many Northern Democrats of moderate views. Mr. Douglas was still the brilliant and popular leader, with an especial claim upon the favor of the South. Again the two-thirds rule was adopted, and again New York appeared with rival delegations, both of which were seated. Buchanan led on the first ballot with 135 votes, President Pierce had 122, Douglas 33, and Cass 5. There were seventeen ballots altogether, with Pierce eliminated on the sixteenth, when Buchanan had 168 votes and Douglas 121. The Douglas men did not hold out to take advantage of the two-thirds rule, but fell in line promptly, and on the next ballot Buchanan received the entire 296 votes.

There were many candidates for the Vice-Presidency, but John C. Breckinridge of Kentucky was unanimously chosen on the second ballot. The platform emphasized State's Rights, accepted the compromise measures of 1850 with the Fugitive Slave Act, and fell

THE DEMOCRATIC PARTY UNDER PIERCE

The followers of Stephen A. Douglas, particularly took "Young America" as a slogan because of his comparative youth; but it applied somewhat generally to the new, hot-blooded elements which were gaining control of the Democratic party. Franklin Pierce, then President, here rests on the shoulders of "Young America" while supported by Douglas on the left and by the veteran Lewis Cass on the right. This is not a complimentary cartoon, however, for Cass is made to claim that to the victors belong the spoils, and Douglas to remark that "preservation of slave property to our Aristocracy is the true test of sound Democracy." Cass had been accused of collecting salaries from the Government for three different jobs at once, and as early as 1848 Lincoln had read before Congress a series of figures intended to prove the charge.

back upon the "Kentucky and Virginia Resolutions of 1797 and 1798" as a part of the fundamental creed of the Democratic party. The Kansas-Nebraska bill was strongly endorsed, and the general principle of squatter sovereignty upheld.

A later plank declared "in favor of free seas and progressive free trade throughout the world." The right of predominant influence at Panama was asserted, and it was "resolved, that the Democratic party will expect of the next administration that every proper effort be made to insure our ascendency in the Gulf of Mexico." The administration of

There were three rival candidates in this year 1856. The poster caricature reproduced above favors ex-President Fillmore, nominee of the American or Know-Nothing party, remnant of the Whigs who had elected him Vice-President eight years earlier. Therefore Fillmore is in the lead, his carriage and horse runing smoothly and the crowd shouting "Fillmore and Union Forever". James Buchanan, nominated by the Democrats, is being carried on the shoulders of President Pierce. John C. Frémont, chosen as the first presidential candidate of the new Republican party, is last in this race, his cart being off the road and in the mire of abolition. He is being helped by Horace Greeley, at the animal's head, and by Henry Ward Beecher, at the cartwheel. Beecher entreats Greeley to jerk up the horse's head once more "and shriek for Kansas, and I'll give the wheel a pry with my rifle." But Greeley complains that "It's no use crying Kansas any more. I guess we are about used up." The rifle which Beecher is using as a lever, and the bundle of rifles which he carries in the cartoon reproduced on page 185, are allusions to an incident during the agitation over Kansas. It was said that contributions solicited from Beecher's Plymouth Church in Brooklyn were used to buy arms and ammunition for the Free State settlers in Kansas. In the November election, Fillmore was last, and not first, in the presidential race. He received about half as many votes as Buchanan, but carried the single State of Maryland.

THE "MUSTANG" TEAM

Frémont's journey to the White House is blocked by a tollgate operator who does not like the load he carries. Riding on the Republican horse are three distinguished New York newspaper editors, who did **not** agree among themselves but in varying measure supported the new party. On this mustang are: First, Horace Greeley of the *Tribune;* next, James Gordon Bennett of the *Herald;* third, Henry J. Raymond of the *Times.* Hanging to the tail of the cart is James W. Webb, who had founded the *Courier and Enquirer* thirty years earlier and was dean of them all. The cross which Frémont carries on his shoulder, in this cartoon and also the one on the opposite page, reflects the existence of rumors at the time that he was affiliated with the Roman Catholic Church.

President Pierce was endorsed, with an expression of "unqualified admiration of his measures and policy."

Although, as I have remarked in the preceding chapter, the Whig party was doomed by the sudden apparition of the Republican party, it was strong enough to take the field with a ticket of its own in 1856, and to draw votes enough away from the Frémont ticket to elect Buchanan. The Whig Convention met at Baltimore on the 17th of September, with Edward Bates of Missouri presiding. In its platform this convention resolved "that the Whigs of the United States declare as a fundamental rule of political faith the absolute necessity for avoiding geographical parties."

The Whigs looked with alarm at the two other parties, "one claiming to represent only sixteen Northern States and the other appealing mainly to the passions and prejudices of the Southern States." As in their mind "the only remedy for an evil so appalling," the Whigs offered ex-President Fillmore to head a non-sectional ticket. They praised "his justice and moderation," "his calm and pacific temperament" and his many other excellent attributes and qualifications. And thus they limited themselves to proclaiming their candidate as the embodiment of their whole political creed.

There was an enthusiastic Republican campaign in the North, but the Fillmore ticket diverted many votes. The totals gave 1,838,-169 to Buchanan, 1,341,264 to Frémont, and 875,534 to Fillmore. This Fillmore Whig ticket actually carried the one State of Maryland, where Frémont had only a handful of votes. No votes at all were reported for Frémont in eleven Southern States. When the electoral votes were counted, Buchanan and Breckinridge were found to have 174, Frémont and Dayton 114, and Fillmore and Donelson 8. Frémont had carried all of the New England States, New York, Ohio, Michigan, Wisconsin and Iowa. Buchanan, besides sweeping the South, had carried his own State of Pennsylvania. In spite of the vigorous campaign of Lincoln, Trumbull and the Republicans of that State, Illinois gave a small plurality for Buchanan, which would have been wiped out four or five times over but for the vote that went to Fillmore. In Indiana, Buchanan had a clear majority over all. Bu-

chanan also carried California, with Fillmore second and Frémont a very bad third in his own State.

Douglas had behaved with notable magnanimity. He had waived the two-thirds rule without delay in favor of his rival who had gained the majority. He had promptly proclaimed his ardent support of the ticket and platform. One of his biographers states that he sold a hundred acres of land at this time on the western limits of Chicago at $1,000 per acre, and out of the proceeds "contributed with great liberality to the campaign fund, not only of his own State, but also of Pennsylvania." His sincerity and his unselfishness carried conviction wherever he spoke.

Buchanan had been out of the country, and had not been involved in the bitter fight over

A Frémont poster of the campaign of 1856, taking its cue from the candidate's career as an explorer, and showing Fillmore and Buchanan crushed by the avalanche of States that Frémont supporters were hoping to carry. Frémont actually did win in eleven of the States designated here, but Buchanan was elected, sweeping the South and carrying California, Illinois, Indiana, Pennsylvania, and New Jersey as well. "Free Soil, Free Speech, Free Press, Free Men, and Frémont," which appears in the rainbow, was the campaign slogan of the new Republican party.

COL FREMONT'S LAST GRAND EXPLORING EXPEDITION IN 1856.

Almost continuously from 1842 to 1854 Frémont had been engaged—as a topographical engineer, under Government auspices—in exploring the vast new region lying between the Rocky Mountains and the Pacific Ocean. In 1856 he became the first nominee of the Republican party. In this cartoon Senator Seward of New York leads toward Salt River the abolition nag that bears the face of Horace Greeley, while Henry Ward Beecher carries a supply of rifles, and Kit Carson, the famous scout who often accompanied Frémont, surveys this expedition disapprovingly. Salt River, found in many cartoons in subsequent chapters, conveys the idea that the Frémont expedition of 1856 is headed toward defeat. Here again, as in the cartoon on page 182, is reference to the charge that Beecher supplied rifles to Kansas settlers: "Be heavenly minded my brethren all. But if you fall out at trifles, settle the matter with powder and ball, and I will furnish the rifles."

the Kansas-Nebraska Bill. He was more available, therefore, than either Douglas or Pierce. Buchanan alone of these three could have carried Pennsylvania. Nevertheless, if the Kansas-Nebraska measure had been withheld by Douglas until after the election of 1856, it is quite probable that he, as the real leader of the Democratic party, would have been nominated at Cincinnati. It is also more than probable that in such case he would have been elected. There would have been a growing Free Soil party in the field, but Lincoln would have remained a Whig, as would Seward in the East; and the Republican party would not have appeared in this election.

The whole situation had been changed by the Kansas-Nebraska bill of 1854; and while Douglas was still to hold the leading place in his party, he was to be the candidate in 1860 of the Northern fragment of a disrupted Democracy, with defeat inevitable at the hands of his old Illinois rival, Abraham Lincoln.

Meanwhile, Lincoln had attended the Philadelphia Republican convention as a delegate from Illinois, where, if Dayton had stepped aside, he would have been placed on the ticket with Frémont. It was fortunate that this empty honor passed him by. As usual, he was named on the electoral ticket in his State, and we know upon his own testimony that he made more than fifty speeches in Illinois and adjoining States for the Frémont and Dayton ticket. These speeches were strong and positive in tone, asserting the authority of the federal government and declaring that under no circumstances should the union be dissolved.

In an address after the election, Lincoln dwelt upon the fact that Buchanan, though victorious in the Electoral College, was in a minority of about four hundred thousand in the aggregate popular vote. "In the late contest," he declared, "we were divided between Frémont and Fillmore." And he continued as follows: "Can we not come together for the future? Let everyone who really believes and is resolved that free society is not and shall not be a failure, and who can conscien-tiously declare that in the past contest he had done only what he thought best—let every such one have charity to believe that every other one can say as much. Thus let bygones be bygones; let past differences as nothing be; and with steady eye on the real issue, let us reinaugurate the good old 'central ideas' of the Republic. . . . We shall then be able, not to declare that 'all states as states are equal' nor yet that 'all citizens as citizens are equal' but to renew the broader, better declaration, including both those and much more, that 'all men are created equal'."

THE RIGHT MAN FOR THE RIGHT PLACE.

The supporters of Fillmore offer him as a candidate of justice and moderation, without sectionalism, in contrast to the sectional appeal of Frémont in the North and Buchanan in the South. Frémont, at the left of the cartoon, characterizes Buchanan as a slave-holding villain; while Buchanan retorts that Frémont is a rascally abolitionist. Fillmore assumes the rôle of peacemaker. In this group portrait of the candidates in 1856 the portraiture is remarkably accurate. For reasons not now discoverable, the artists who drew originals for these lithographic posters—during the campaign of 1856 and that of four years later—did not sign their drawings; but it is known that many of them were the work of Louis Maurer.

THE GREAT AMERICAN BUCK HUNT OF 1856.

The buck is Buchanan, headed toward the White House. It is a poster caricature published in the interest of Fillmore, candidate of the American party, who stands on Union Rock at the right of the picture. Frémont's sectional gun has exploded, and it remains for Fillmore to bring down Old Buck with his American rifle. Meanwhile Henry Ward Beecher and Horace Greeley, who supported Frémont, are mired in the abolition bog. The divided opposition to the Democratic ticket that is expressed in this cartoon resulted in Buchanan's election.

CHAPTER XX

Lincoln and Douglas ⊶ A Supreme Debate

President Buchanan appeals for harmony—The Dred Scott decision
stirs the Northern States—A senatorial contest in Illinois results in
the most famous of all political stumping tours

WHEN JAMES BUCHANAN was inaugurated President of the United States on March 4, 1857, he congratulated himself and the country that—in spite of the excitement of the election contest—"when the people proclaimed their will the tempest at once subsided and all was calm." Proceeding with his optimistic address, he made the following observations:

What a happy conception, then, was it for Congress to apply this simple rule, that the will of the majority shall govern, to the settlement of the question of domestic slavery in the Territories! Congress is neither "to legislate slavery in any Territory or State nor to exclude it therefrom, but to leave the people thereof perfectly free to form and regulate their domestic institutions in their own way, subject only to the Constitution of the United States." As a natural consequence, Congress has also prescribed that when the Territory of Kansas shall be admitted as a State it "shall be received into the Union with or without slavery, as their constitution may prescribe at the time of their admission."

Dwelling further upon this subject, with genuine and glowing satisfaction, the new President was able to declare: "No other question remains for adjustment, because all agree that under the Constitution slavery in the States is beyond the reach of any human power except that of the respective States themselves

189

wherein it exists." And in tone of pious bene-
diction he concluded: "May we not, then, hope
that the long agitation on this subject is approaching its end."

This excellent and upright Pennsylvanian
did not dream that he was to hold the reins of
authority during the stormiest period of agitation in the history of the country. At the age
of sixty-six he had spent more than forty years
in public life. He had served in the Legislature, had been ten years in the lower House at
Washington, had been Minister to Russia in
Jackson's time, and had then sat in the Senate
for ten years, after which for four years he
was President Polk's Secretary of State. Defeated by Franklin Pierce for the presidential
nomination in 1852, he had been sent as Minister to England; and now he was to serve for
four years as President of the United States.
Few contemporary statesmen in any country
could have matched Buchanan's record for

steady advancement in official life, and for
broad experience in domestic and foreign affairs. He had administered our foreign office
during the Mexican War; and he had directed
the settlement by virtue of which we acquired vast new territories. This extension of
American jurisdiction had led to the reopening of the earlier slavery compromises.

Another veteran statesman, Lewis Cass of
Michigan, was made Secretary of State by Mr.
Buchanan. Howell Cobb of Georgia became
Secretary of the Treasury. The War Department was assigned to John B. Floyd of Virginia, and Jeremiah S. Black of Pennsylvania
was appointed Attorney-General. A Tennes-
sean, Aaron V. Brown, became Postmaster-
General. The Navy portfolio was assigned to
Isaac Toucey of Connecticut. Jacob Thompson of Mississippi was the new Secretary of
the Interior. This cabinet was meant to balance nicely the sectional situation.

THE PRESIDENTIAL CAMPAIGN OF '56

Slavery enters Kansas, breaking through the fence on the Mason and Dixon's Line and carrying on
its back the candidate of the Democratic party. The chariot is drawn by three Dough Faces, a name
given to pro-slavery Democrats of the North: Lewis Cass, of Michigan, soon to become Buchanan's
Secretary of State; Stephen A. Douglas, of Illinois, an outstanding member of the Senate; and
President Pierce, of New Hampshire, who had recognized the pro-slavery element in Kansas.
Frémont dashes forward to stop the progress of the animal. This is a Cincinnati caricature.

The Morning after the Election November 1856.

Pub! by I.Childs 84 S! 3rd St.Phil!

Horace Greeley appears conspicuously in five of the cartoons in this chapter and the preceding one. Here we see four New York newspaper editors who had supported Frémont. It is the day after election, and they are turning from Frémont to Buchanan, the President-elect. The four editors are: Horace Greeley of the *Tribune,* Bennett of the *Herald,* Webb of the *Courier and Enquirer,* and an unnamed German. Frémont rides home on horseback, declaring his loss of faith in editors, who had made him believe that "papers could do all things." At the right of the picture, in "the dark and gloomy caverns of Know-Nothingism," is Fillmore, placing upon Raymond, editor of the *Times,* the blame for an unsuccessful campaign.

Buchanan sought also to be at peace with all mankind; and almost two weeks before his inauguration he took the unusual precaution to write a letter directly to the British Foreign Minister at London. In that letter he said: "General Cass is to be my Secretary of State and no Englishman need feel the least uneasiness on this account. His anglophobia, as you used facetiously to term it, if it ever existed no longer exists. His age, his patriotism, his long and able public services, his unsullied private character and the almost universal feeling in his favor render his appointment peculiarly appropriate." General Cass was almost ten years older than Buchanan, and doubtless the President expected to direct his own foreign policy. Three of these cabinet officers were to become Secessionist leaders

before the end of Buchanan's term, and two were later to become Confederate Generals.

The turmoil of the last year of Buchanan's four-year period has somewhat obscured the earlier years; but from the very beginning there was excitement enough in the daily news. Two days after Buchanan had succeeded Pierce in the White House, came the "Dred Scott Decision" of the Supreme Court. It was not the case itself, but the elaborate opinion rendered by Chief Justice Roger B. Taney, that aroused contentious argument and sectional passion far beyond any other court decision in the history of the United States. Dred Scott was a slave in Missouri who had sojourned for some time at military posts in the Western Territory, whither his owner (an Army surgeon) had taken him. At a considerably later time, after the death in Missouri of the former owner, it was claimed on Scott's behalf that he acquired the permanent status of a free man when his foot had touched the soil of a region where slavery was not a lawful institution.

The Missouri courts had denied this contention, and the Supreme Court had confirmed the judgment of the lower Federal court in accepting the opinion of the State tribunals. The trouble was caused by the elaborate and quite unnecessary metaphysical disquisition in which the aged Chief Justice led himself along to the fallacious conclusion that a Negro as such could have no legal rights because Negroes when actually slaves were treated as chattels, and not as human beings. This was even more absurd than was the opposite contention that under the system that then existed an actual slave owned by a citizen of a slave state became a free man permanently if it could be shown that he had at some previous time been brought into a non-slaveholding territory.

Taney had been appointed by President Jackson to succeed Chief Justice Marshall, who died in 1835. He was able, conscientious, abstractly logical, and affected with that legalistic quality of mind which ignores the relationship of law to history, and works in realms of theory.

The Buchanan Administration was in no way displeased by the Court's decision, which in effect nullified all compromise enactments. Jefferson Davis and the South felt that final victory had been gained for the most extreme of Calhoun's contentions. But in the North the decision was held in abhorrence, and the

ROGER BROOKE TANEY

From 1836 until his death in 1864, Taney was Chief Justice of the United States. He was a Democrat, a Baltimore lawyer, who had been Attorney-General in the cabinet of Jackson. During Jackson's administration the personnel of the Supreme Court was entirely changed. John Marshall had broadly interpreted the Constitution for thirty-four years; but Roger Taney, who succeeded him, was a strict constructionist. His most noted decisions were in the Dred Scott case (1857) and in the denial of the right of the President to suspend the writ of *habeas corpus* even when exercising full war powers, as in 1861.

Court was assailed in language too unjust and vulgar to repeat. The Kansas issue was taken up with renewed determination on both sides. In December, 1857, a pro-slavery constitution was framed at Lecompton without authority from Congress, and ratified by a dishonest referendum. Two weeks later that instrument was repudiated overwhelmingly in a referendum vote that was relatively fair. Anti-slavery men had abstained in one case, and pro-slavery voters had largely abstained in the other. Ignoring this second referendum, Buchanan urged Congress to admit Kansas to statehood on the pro-slavery Lecompton Constitution.

But Douglas, with a vigor and courage that surprised both sides, opposed such action. He declared that his Kansas bill had contemplated an honest and not a dishonest test of the will of the people of Kansas. He denounced the Lecompton activities as fraudulent. Although the bill was passed in the Senate, with Douglas supporting the Republican minority, it was defeated in the House. A proper and legal reference of the Lecompton Constitution to a third vote of the people, by authority of Congress, resulted in its defeat by a vote of 11,000 to 2,000. Douglas was now as vituperously assailed throughout the South as, only four years earlier, he had been reprobated in the North.

It was under these conditions that Douglas returned to Illinois. A new Legislature was to be elected, and it was to choose a Senator to succeed Douglas whose term was expiring. He had entered the Senate on March 4, 1847, and was now the undisputed leader of the Northern wing of the Democratic party, while

Dred Scott, the Negro slave of an army officer, maintained that he had become free when his owner took him into free territory to live temporarily, afterward returning to Missouri. One of several suits which he brought reached the Supreme Court, and Chief Justice Taney delivered the opinion. He held that Scott was not a citizen, had no standing in the federal courts, and was only a piece of property. He went further and declared the Missouri Compromise of 1820 unconstitutional, on the ground that neither Congress nor the territorial governments could prohibit slavery in the Territories. The decision aroused intense feeling in the North. It was handed down in the first week of President Buchanan's administration, and, as the above cartoon indicates, it was an issue in the campaign three years later. The political quadrille here is composed of four candidates for the Presidency in 1860. Lincoln is in the upper right corner, and Douglas in the lower left. Above Douglas is John C. Breckinridge, of Kentucky, nominated by the Southern Democrats. Below Lincoln is John Bell, of Tennessee, candidate on a Constitutional Union ticket.

Jefferson Davis had become only less widely recognized as the most active and influential leader of the Southern wing. Douglas's candidacy for re-election was, of course, virtually unopposed in Illinois within his own party (a dissenting handful of so-called Lecomptonites merely emphasized the resistless party leadership of Douglas), and his success depended upon securing a Democratic majority in the new Legislature.

The Republicans had not yet gained predominance in the State, but they were hopeful. A Republican state convention unanimously designated Abraham Lincoln as the party's candidate for the senatorship, and hailed his position as foremost orator, thinker and politician of the anti-slavery forces of Illinois. There followed a campaign that eventually centered in the plan that Lincoln and Douglas personally adopted of holding a series of joint debates. The nation-wide fame of Douglas, who expected to be nominated for the Presidency in 1860, lent to these forensic exhibitions an extraordinary publicity outside of the State. This served Lincoln's case well, because his presence on the same platform with Stephen A. Douglas made him a national political character in the full sense.

The famous debates, however, did not begin until late in August, and the opposing candidates had already taken their positions with deliberate care. Their appearance at various places on the same platform brought immense crowds to hear them, and afforded the people of Illinois an admirable opportunity to compare the two foremost public men of the state while also providing an illustration of the means by which masses of American citizens are trained for the exercise of self-government. Horace Greeley, in a lecture on Lincoln, based upon his own personal recollections, made the following observations upon the two contending champions:

I cannot help regarding that senatorial contest of 1858, between Lincoln and Douglas, as one of the most characteristic and at the same time most creditable incidents in our national history. There was an honest and earnest difference with regard to a most important and imminent public question; and Illinois was very equally divided thereon, with a United States Senator for six years to be chosen by the Legislature then to be elected. Hereupon each party selects its ablest and most trusted champion, nominates him for the coveted post, and sends him out as the authorized, indorsed, accredited champion of its principles and policy, to canvass the state and secure a verdict for its cause. So the two champions traversed the prairies, speaking alternately to the same vast audiences at several central, accessible points, and speaking separately at others, until the day of election, when Douglas secured a small majority in either branch of the Legislature, and was re-elected, though Lincoln had the larger popular vote. But while Lincoln had spent less than a thousand dollars in all, Douglas had borrowed and disbursed in the canvass no less than eighty thousand dollars, incurring a debt which weighed him down to the grave. I presume no dime of this was used to buy up his competitor's voters, but all to organize and draw out his own; still the debt so improvidently, if not culpably, incurred remained to harass him out of this mortal life. Lincoln it was said was beaten: it was a hasty, erring judgment. This canvass made him stronger at home, and stronger with the Republicans of the whole country.

SENATOR DOUGLAS OF ILLINOIS

Douglas' second six-year term was to expire in March, 1859, and his re-election or retirement would come at the hands of a legislature to be chosen in 1858. Twice he had been a leading candidate for the Democratic presidential nomination; and when Lincoln challenged him to a series of debates he had been looking forward with confidence to his re-election as United States Senator and to a nomination for the Presidency in 1860.

If the debates are to be studied for their doctrines it is desirable to begin with two set speeches, in which the opponents had separately dealt with the questions upon which they were divided. The first of these was Lincoln's speech at Springfield before the Republican State convention, delivered in the evening of June 16th, the convention having during that day passed a resolution unanimously declaring that "Abraham Lincoln is the first and only choice of the Republicans of Illinois for the United States Senate."

Douglas meanwhile was still in Washington, the session of Congress having ended on that same date, June 16th. He remained in New York and the East for two or three weeks, and appeared at Chicago on July 9th, where he spoke upon the burning issues of the day and answered Lincoln's speech of June 16th. Referring to the arrival of Senator Douglas at Chicago, Mr. Gardner in his biography remarks: "A special train loaded with prominent citizens was dispatched to meet him. On his arrival he was greeted with tumultuous applause. He addressed the vast multitude from the balcony of the Tremont House. Thirty thousand people are said to have gathered to hear him.

He was profoundly pleased by this splendid ovation, so strikingly in contrast with the reception four years before, when his neighbors refused even to hear him in defense of his course. Among the distinguished visitors on the speakers' stand sat Lincoln."

On the following evening Lincoln spoke to the citizens of Chicago in reply to Douglas. The next appearance of Douglas was at a great public gathering at Bloomington on July 16th. At Springfield on the following day this Bloomington speech was repeated. Lincoln's turn came in the evening of that same day, July 17th, at Springfield. He had heard Douglas speak at Bloomington, and they had come together in a companionable way to the State Capital, Lincoln's home city, where Douglas also had served in the Legislature and afterwards as Register of the Land Office. The "Little Giant" was moving about the state as a conquering hero, with decorated special trains and with such evidences of personal popularity as had never been accorded before to any man in the West, not even to Henry Clay himself. He had an extremely difficult situation to meet, but he avoided all appearance of being on the defensive. He had so shaped his course at Washington that he had one form of appeal for the anti-slavery population of the northern third of Illinois, another sort of the middle section, and a third for the people of southern origin who predominated in the lower counties of the State. As an extemporaneous stump speaker, he was without rival in his own day, and he has hardly been equalled at any time.

ABRAHAM LINCOLN IN 1858

From an ambrotype made on August 25, 1858, at Macomb, Illinois, while Lincoln was in the midst of his debates with Douglas. The issue over which they fought was slavery, the prize was Douglas' seat in the United States Senate. Though Lincoln failed to win the Senatorship, he had forced Douglas to take positions which profoundly affected presidential issues two years later; and he himself gained fame far beyond the borders of his State.

Lincoln had waited several weeks before deciding how to carry on the campaign during the remaining period before the election of legislators. He had somewhat vaguely thought that perhaps Senator Douglas would propose a series of debates; but, although such a plan was not in accordance with the preferences of the Senator, it could not well be rejected when Lincoln himself on July 24th sent him a note simply asking: "Will it be agreeable to you to make an arrangement for you and myself to divide time and address the same audiences in the present canvass?"

Douglas replied on the same day, proposing a "discussion between us at one prominent point in each Congressional District in the State except the Second and Sixth, where we have both spoken and in each of which you had the concluding speech." There were nine Congressional Districts in Illinois, and thus it remained to hold seven joint debates. "If agreeable to you," continued Douglas, "I will indicate the following places as the most suitable in the several Congressional Districts at which we should speak, to wit: Freeport, Ottawa, Galesburg, Quincy, Alton, Jonesboro, and Charleston." Dates were at once arranged, with Ottawa first on the list for August 21st, Freeport six days later, Jonesboro, September 15th, Charleston, September 18th, Galesburg, October 7th, Quincy, October 13th, and Alton, October 15th. Mr. William Gardner in his brief but impartial and trustworthy survey of the life and career of Stephen A. Douglas gives an excellent picture of the two antagonists and the setting for the momentous intellectual contest that lifted each man to the dignity of his party's nomination for the Presidency two years later. Says Mr. Gardner:

Now that Lincoln has become idealized and is safely classed with the great men of all ages, his modest challenge seems like a condescension of the immortal President to his rival. It then seemed an act of temerity bordering on madness. Lincoln's friends thought it rash. Douglas's friends had no hope that his adversary would be so easily delivered into his hands.

Yet Lincoln was not a despised antagonist. He was the most prominent Republican in Illinois. But Douglas was the recognized head of a great national party, the giant of the Senate, the most resourceful American then living. Through years of desperate battling he had successfully repelled the assaults of Seward, Sumner and Chase. He had more recently encountered with equal ease all the Southern Senators. It seemed a simple task to meet this humble Western lawyer and make his friends ashamed of their senatorial candidate. Douglas did not share the pleasant illusion of his friends. Before leaving Washington, when he heard that Lincoln was nominated, he said to Forney:

"I shall have my hands full. He is the strong man of his party—full of wit, facts, dates—and the best stump speaker, with his droll ways and dry jokes, in the West. He is as honest as he is shrewd; and if I beat him my victory will be hardly won."

Lincoln was burning with jealousy. He believed himself to be Douglas's full equal in mental endowment. Fortune, he thought, with a tinge of bitterness, had dealt with them most unequally, clothing his rival with the glory of a world-renowned statesman, and leaving him to waste his powers on the obscure quarrels of litigious clients in a small town. He yearned for the opportunity to measure himself with the great Senator on a conspicuous stage.

This series of debates was a rare piece of strategy on Lincoln's part. Douglas had so long been wrapped in his senatorial toga that his greatness had become exaggerated to the popular mind of Illinois; while Lincoln had been a plain, modest lawyer, moving among the people in the daily round of routine

life. The dogmatic statement of the great Senator carried more weight than the profoundest argument or the clearest demonstration of the country lawyer. But these debates brought them to a common level. They measured their intellectual strength in the presence of the people, with all official trappings laid aside; and while no one could well be disappointed in Douglas's strength, the whole country was amazed at the unexpected power of Lincoln.

The latest, and perhaps the best balanced,

WHERE THE LINCOLN-DOUGLAS DEBATES WERE HELD IN 1858

The seven Illinois towns selected are numbered on this map in the chronological order of the debates. The heavy lines indicate Congressional districts as then laid out. There was one debate in each district except the two which included Chicago and Springfield. In those cities Lincoln and Douglas had already spoken.

LINCOLN, DOUGLAS, AND THE RAIL-FENCE HANDICAP
This campaign poster of 1860 (published in Buffalo), puts in the mouth of the diminutive Douglas
the plaintive question, "How can I get over this rail fence." Lincoln declares with assurance, "It
can't stop me, for I built it." From the black figure between the rails comes the unwelcome message, "You find me in dis yer fence, Massa Duglis."

estimate of Lincoln and Douglas, in that
rivalry on the hustings in 1858, is to be found
in the concluding chapters of Mr. Beveridge's
biography:

It may be helpful at this point to look at the combatants once more. Physically and mentally, Lincoln and Douglas were exactly opposite types.
Douglas was short and thick set, with great depth
and breadth of chest, big round face, firm wide
mouth, powerful square jaws, strong muscular
neck, large and brilliant blue eyes, a mighty head
and a deep voice. Lincoln was very tall and thin,
with narrow chest and drooping shoulders, a long,
slender, wrinkled neck, a lined and withered face,
shrunken checks, small head, and shrill voice.
Lincoln was humorous and quizzical, indifferent
to or forgetful of his clothes which never fitted,

slow of thought and action, given to moods of melancholy broken by strange and sudden bursts of fun,
and he was the best story-teller in the country.
Douglas was cordial and dignified, alert, quick, and
resourceful, careful of his dress; but he could not
tell a story or crack a joke and never tried to do so.
As speakers the quality of both men is shown by
what they said. Each was scrupulously honest, personally, although the followers of each denied that
the other was overloaded with that virtue. Both
were strong for the Union, both intensely patriotic,
facts that we shall see emerge in flaming grandeur
when the stern and decisive hour shall come.
Lincoln and Douglas were inordinately ambitious,
politically; but Lincoln had for the most part failed,
while Douglas had mounted on eagle's wings with
never a let down, never a halt. In 1858 the name
of Douglas was known to every man and woman in
the whole land, while that of Lincoln, though

familiar to Republican politicians in other States, had not been heard by the masses of the people outside of Illinois. The hold of Douglas on his followers everywhere was absolute. He was an idol to them; their devotion amounted to a frenzy; they acted as if under a spell.

It may be borne in mind that the joint debates comprised by no means all the speeches made by the candidates during the campaign season. Dr. Allen Johnson, whose biography of Stephen A. Douglas is the accepted and standard one, gives us a statement of the local conditions, and of the environment of the first of the joint debates, that is so accurate and so informing that I may well conclude this chapter by an extended quotation from a volume that is admirable as a political study and as an instance of careful historical research:

The next three months may be regarded as a prolonged debate, accentuated by the seven joint discussions. The rival candidates traversed much the same territory, and addressed much the same audiences on successive days. At times, chance made them fellow-passengers on the same train or steamboat. Douglas had already begun his itinerary, when Lincoln's last note reached him in Piatt County. He had just spoken at Clinton, in De Witt County, and again he had found Lincoln in the audience.

No general ever planned a military campaign with greater regard to the topography of the enemy's country, than Douglas plotted his campaign in central Illinois. For it was in the central counties that the election was to be won or lost. The Republican strength lay in the upper, northern third of the State; the Democratic strength, in the southern third. The doubtful area lay between Ottawa on the north and Belleville on the south; Oquawka on the northwest and Paris on the east. Only twice did Douglas make any extended tour outside this area; once to meet his appointment with Lincoln at Freeport; and once to engage in the third joint debate at Jonesboro.

The first week in August found Douglas speaking at various points along the Illinois River to enthusiastic crowds. Lincoln followed closely after, bent upon weakening the force of his opponent's arguments by lodging an immediate demurrer against them. On the whole, Douglas drew the larger crowds; but it was observed that Lincoln's audiences increased as he proceeded northward. Ottawa was the objective point for both travelers, for there was to be held the first joint debate on August 21st.

An enormous crowd awaited them. From sunrise to mid-day, men, women, and children poured into town in every sort of conveyance. It was a typical mid-summer day in Illinois. The prairie roads were thoroughly baked by the sun, and the dust rose, like a fine powder, from beneath the feet of horses and pedestrians, enveloping all in blinding clouds. A train of seventeen cars had brought ardent supporters of Douglas from Chicago. The town was gaily decked; the booming of cannon resounded across the prairie; bands of music added to the excitement of the occasion. The speakers were escorted to the public square by two huge processions. So eager was the crowd that it was with much difficulty, and no little delay, that Lincoln and Douglas, the committee men, and the reporters, were landed on the platform.

For the first time in the campaign, the rival candidates were placed side by side. The crowd instinctively took its measure of the two men. They presented a striking contrast. Lincoln, tall, angular, and long of limb; Douglas, short, almost dwarfed by comparison, broad-shouldered and thick-chested. Lincoln was clad in a frock coat of rusty black, which was evidently not made for his lank, ungainly body. His sleeves did not reach his wrists by several inches, and his trousers failed to conceal his huge feet. His long, sinewy neck emerged from a white collar, drawn over a black tie. Altogether, his appearance bordered upon the grotesque, and would have provoked mirth in any other than an Illinois audience, which knew and respected the man too well to mark his costume. Douglas, on the contrary, presented a well-groomed figure. He wore a well-fitting suit of broadcloth; his linen was immaculate; and altogether he had the appearance of a man of the world whom fortune had favored.

Mr. Sandburg, who was himself born in Galesburg, Illinois, is at his best in his anecdotal account of the great debates. He supplies much local color, and by his quotations from newspapers, East and West, he gives us a just impression of the significance that was attached to the Illinois contest. In the complete works of Abraham Lincoln there is not a line of the great speech at the Bloomington convention of 1856. It was extemporaneous, and went unreported. But in 1858 the words were taken down. "The reporters would give the country 'full phonographic verbatim reports,' newspapers told their readers." Young Robert Hitt, afterwards a prominent Illinois Congressman, was especially relied upon, and it is largely to his stenographic skill that we owe, as a great boon, our authentic record of the most famous of all forensic discussions.

CHAPTER XXI

How the Two Illinois Rivals Stood

*The gradual disintegration of the older political parties—Douglas
finds himself leader of a Democratic minority faction—Lincoln's
speech, when named for the Senate*

As I HAVE STATED in the previous chapter, Lincoln had set forth his main lines of argument in the prepared speech that he delivered before the Illinois State Republican Convention on June 16th when he was named as the party's candidate for the Senate. Douglas had carefully considered his home-coming when Congress adjourned on June 16th, and he had studied the political situation at large by spending some days in conference at New York and elsewhere. While Douglas had great advantages of reputation and prestige, and while no other politician was his equal in dealing with immediate predicaments, he was actually facing a situation that was rendered extremely difficult by shifting conditions. Lincoln stood on bed rock as regards certain fundamental principles, and also he knew exactly what he was trying to accomplish in the strategies of this particular campaign.

Douglas had deceived himself regarding the value, both momentary and ultimate, of the principles that were involved in his squatter sovereignty doctrine, as embodied in the Kan-

THE LITTLE GIANT, IN THE CHARACTER OF THE GLADIATOR

Though short in stature, Douglas possessed physical and mental solidity which earned for him the nickname of Little Giant. This poster caricature was published at Philadelphia in 1858, the year of his debates with Lincoln. The Philadelphia artist had evidently worked from a portrait taken some time previously, when Douglas wore a beard.

sas-Nebraska Bill, with its repeal of the compromise measures that had been worked out by the elder statesmen. At first Douglas had seemed to be formulating plans that the Southern extremists could heartily accept. The proposal to leave the slavery question to the settlers of Kansas to decide for themselves, taken in conjunction with the Dred Scott decision, had been too quickly acclaimed as a final victory for the slaveholders. Douglas's later attack upon the Lecompton constitution, in defiance of President Buchanan, had dismayed and angered the South, while it had puzzled the North. It brought him, for the moment, into favor with Republican leaders of the East, among them Senator Seward of New York and Henry Wilson of Massachusetts; and even Horace Greeley of the New York *Tribune* had thought that Douglas ought to be re-elected to the Senate as a reward for his fearlessness in demanding that "squatter sovereignty" should be exercised honestly, and that the anti-slavery voters of Kansas should not be tricked out of their fair part in the processes of self-determination.

199

"SIT DOWN, LINCOLN, YOUR TIME IS UP"

The artist illustrates a scene during the fourth debate, at Charleston, Illinois, on September 18th. Lincoln had been delivering his
argument with telling effect, and Douglas had lost his poise, walking rapidly up and down the platform with watch in hand and
finally calling time. In these debates each spoke for an hour and a
half, the man who opened the discussion saving a half-hour of his
time for rebuttal. Thus each man had opportunity to answer the
other from the same platform.

The obvious fact was that parties were dis-
integrating. The old Whig party was now a
thing of the past, most of the Southern Whigs
having become Democrats on the slave issue.
Most of the Northern Whig statesmen, like
Seward in the East and Lincoln in the West,
were now active in the new Republican party.
The Free-soilers, whose movement had crys-
tallized at an earlier date, had been absorbed,
for the most part, into this all-inclusive
"Black Republican" party of the North. Many
Democrats, including distinguished leaders in
various States, had marched into the Repub-

lican camp, where their adherence was
hailed with enthusiasm, and where they
were assigned posts of honor without
prejudice.

Some Eastern Republican leaders
seemed to hold the view that if the Republicans of Illinois should step aside in
favor of Douglas, the result would be
his re-election as an overwhelming
triumph and his Presidential nomination in 1860 on a Union ticket would
carry the North overwhelmingly, would
make some appeal to the South, and
would remove the disunion danger.
Douglas himself, perhaps, had entertained such ideas, until the Republican
Convention at Springfield, on June
16th, had cleared up the situation. He
had fought Whigs and Republicans in
Illinois for so many years that they
could not possibly have turned to his
support, merely to reward him because
he had opposed the admission of Kansas on the fraudulent Lecompton constitution. He now perceived that he had
to make his fight for re-election on
straight Democratic lines.

Douglas was riding two horses that
were pulling apart, and in spite of his
amazing skill he was falling between.
Republicanism was gaining in the
North, while intense sectionalism, under the leadership of a group whose
ablest strategist was Jefferson Davis,
was dominating the South.

Quite apart from the medieval dia-
lectics of court decisions, and the discussion of particular methods and compromises as regards slavery in new territories,
the plain fact stood out that the North was
infected with the anti-slavery movement, while
the South was rapidly adopting a wholly new
religion of slavery as a sacred and divine institution, to criticize which was blasphemous.

In earlier times there had not been a man
in the United States who thought of slavery
otherwise than as wrong in itself and a thing
to be abolished, although the view prevailed
in the South that the extinction of this institution must be by gradual processes, to be

THE IRREPRESSIBLE CONFLICT

LINCOLN'S FIGHT TO KEEP SLAVERY OUT OF THE TERRITORIES

This poster originated at Cincinnati, often called "Porkopolis" in those days because of its packing industry. The head of the hog is a portrait of James Buchanan, President, who had been nominated and elected upon a platform adopted by the Democratic convention at Cincinnati in 1856. Douglas (at the right) justifies the platform on the ground that it would keep slavery out of the Territories; but Lincoln declares that the slave interests had been permitted to go too far already and should be sent back where they belong. In this cartoon we see for the first time in these pages the term "irrepressible conflict," used by Senator William H. Seward of New York in a speech in the Senate on October 25, 1858, in which he referred to the antagonism between freedom and slavery as "an irrepressible conflict between opposing and enduring forces."

worked out through some future period that could not be strictly defined. A Southern Congressman, the assailant of Senator Sumner, was quoted as having admitted freely that Washington, Jefferson, Madison, and all of the early Southern statesmen were opposed to slavery; but as he proceeded to explain, either naively or cynically, the invention of the cotton gin had made all the difference in the world; and slavery had now become the essential factor in Southern prosperity—an institution to be maintained as the permanent basis of future wealth and well-being.

History was shaping itself through the passions and prejudices of two great sections of the country which were so divided in sentiment that mere political devices could not hold them

together. The more reckless of Southern leaders were talking freely of secession, and the more reckless of Northern leaders were expressing themselves in terms of coercion, declaring that eighteen million Northerners with industrial resources would prove more than a match for eight million Southerners lacking the ability to make munitions and to finance a war of rebellion.

Douglas did not fully realize how completely the Southern leaders had rejected him, as the head of their party and their future candidate for the presidency. On the other hand, he did not grasp the truth that his political record had made him unacceptable to the growing sentiment that was spreading its counter-propaganda against the propaganda

THE DOUGLAS STATUE IN SPRINGFIELD

This is a companion memorial to the one of Lincoln reproduced on the opposite page, both erected in the Capitol
grounds upon the occasion of the Illinois centennial in
1918. The Douglas statue is the work of Gilbert P. Ris-
wold of Chicago. Douglas was only 5 feet 4 inches tall,
but so broad and solid that he was called the "Little
Giant." Lincoln was twelve inches taller.

of the slave-holding oligarchy of the South.

In short, he had maneuvered himself into
the position of the leader of a minority faction
of a divided party; and it was too late for him
to seek a commission giving him high command in the Republican camp. He had been
vain enough to think that the Republicans of
Illinois might come to him, or at least meet
him half way; but his hopes were blighted
when the State Convention declared that
Abraham Lincoln was its first and only candidate for the United States Senate.

Lincoln, who had known Douglas throughout his public life, did not for a moment share
the view of certain leaders in the East that
Douglas could be weaned from his devotion
to the Democratic party. Ambition had forced
Douglas into a false attitude when Atchison of
Missouri had taken the initiative with his
Nebraska bill. As chairman of the Senate
Committee on Territories, Douglas was placed
in a position where he must either report the
bill out of committee, or else step aside for the
Missouri Senator. He chose to report the bill
and to make its doctrines his own. He was
further driven to abandon his earlier convictions, and accept as an amendment to the new
bill the explicit repeal of the Missouri Compromise.

He had made such a record in the years
from 1854 to 1858 that there was no alternative for him except to push the Kansas question to a conclusion, in order that the country
might turn to something else and allow slavery
to take its chances in an age that was moving
inevitably toward industrialism and freedom.
He was perfectly ready to admit Kansas as a
free State on the verdict of the settlers; but
this willingness was quite too evident to be
relished by the South.

The South could not forgive its own eminent son, Walker of Mississippi, who had been
appointed Governor of Kansas by President
Buchanan, and who had there enforced law
and order with the aid of United States troops
and had protected actual settlers in their
rights. Neither could it forgive Douglas, who
had opened the door for slavery in the Territories, and had then shown willingness to have
the "squatters" close the door—determined
not to permit slavery in a territory that was
free soil under the old Compromise of 1820.

Lincoln, therefore, was not only entering
the campaign to set forth his own views, but
he was skillfully planning to expose and confirm the dilemma that Douglas was facing.
He succeeded so well that although the Douglas men carried the majority of legislative
districts, Lincoln himself received the popular
majority in the State as a whole. If there had
been an up-to-date re-apportionment of legislative districts, Lincoln would actually have

THE LINCOLN STATUE IN SPRINGFIELD, ILLINOIS

When the people of Illinois were commemorating, in 1918, the one-hundredth anniversary of the admission of their State into the Union, they caused to be erected in the Capitol grounds a statue of Lincoln and one of Douglas. The Lincoln statue is the work of Andrew O'Connor. On the reverse side of the huge granite slab which forms its background is carved Lincoln's farewell address to his fellow-citizens in Springfield as he departed for Washington to become President in 1861, in which occur these words: "Here I have lived a quarter of a century, and have passed from a young to an old man. Here my children have been born and one is buried. I now leave, not knowing when or whether ever I may return, with a task before me greater than that which rested upon Washington. Without the assistance of that Divine Being who ever attended him, I cannot succeed. With that assistance, I cannot fail."

been elected Senator. The northern part of the State had been growing much more rapidly than the southern part, and, with unchanged apportionment, the Democratic part of the State was now greatly over-represented in the Legislature.

The main lines of Lincoln's arguments throughout the summer are found in his address of June 16th. The debates as a whole were published and widely circulated through-out the country, and even today they are well worth reading for the place they occupy in the history of American politics. But while we shall try here to show clearly their character and significance, we shall not review them in detail. The more convenient way, then, to find just what were Lincoln's positions is to study his speech on June 16th; while those of Douglas are to be found in his Chicago speech on July 9th. Lincoln opened his Springfield speech to the Convention with the following paragraph that stands among the best known of his utterances:

> If we could first know where we are, and whither we are tending, we could then better judge what to do, and how to do it. We are now far on into our fifth year, since a policy was initiated, with the avowed object and confident promise of putting an end to slavery agitation. Under the operation of that policy, that agitation has not only not ceased, but has constantly augmented. In my opinion it will not cease until a crisis shall have been reached and passed. "A house divided against itself can not stand." I believe this Government can not endure permanently half slave and half free. I do not expect the Union to be dissolved—I do not expect the house to fall—but I do expect it will cease to be divided. It will become all one thing or all the other. Either the opponents of slavery will arrest the further spread of it, and place it where the public mind shall rest in the belief that it is in course of ultimate extinction, or its advocates will push it forward till it shall become alike lawful in all the States—old as well as new—North as well as South.

These were bold words but were supported by the facts. The Dred Scott decision, carefully analyzed, proves to have been merely a denial of Federal jurisdiction in a particular matter. But the extended opinion of Chief Justice Taney, in which a majority of the Justices concurred, set forth a doctrine the ultimate logic of which would have permitted a slave owner to settle anywhere in the Union with his human property, and would have upheld the re-opening of the African slave trade in our Southern seaports. It was Lincoln's belief that the President, the Chief Justice and the authors of the Nebraska-Kansas legislation were working together to arrest what were natural tendencies toward freedom. "The New Year of 1854," he declared, "found slavery excluded from more than half the States by State Constitutions, and from most of the national territory by Congressional prohibition. Four days later commenced the struggle which ended in repealing that Congressional prohibition. This opened all the national territory to slavery and was the first point gained."

Congress having acted, there must be some form of popular endorsement, and the so-called "sacred right of self-government" had been advanced as a principle that President Buchanan at once seized upon as providing a "happy solution," which no reasonable person could dispute. Hence the so-called "new principle" of the Nebraska Bill, further elaborated into the bill which separated Nebraska and Kansas and provided for the organization of the Kansas Territory, the settlers being authorized to decide for themselves whether they would bring slavery in through Missouri and the southward, or repel slavery under the majority influence of colonists from New England, New York, and the States north of the Ohio River. Connecting the two important topics, Lincoln continued as follows:

> While the Nebraska bill was passing through Congress, a law case, involving the question of a Negro's freedom, by reason of his owner having voluntarily taken him first into a free state and then into a territory covered by the Congressional prohibition, and held him as a slave for a long time in each, was passing through the United States Circuit Court for the District of Missouri; and both Nebraska bill and lawsuit were brought to a decision in the same month of May, 1854. The negro's name was Dred Scott, which name now designates the decision finally made in the case. Before the then next presidential election, the law case came to and was argued in the Supreme Court of the United States; but the decision of it was deferred until after the election.

We are next reminded by Lincoln that Douglas had found opportunity to speak in Illinois in support of the Dred Scott decision early in the previous year, President Buchanan also having expressed himself to the same effect. But with all this outlook for Democratic harmony, so acceptable to the Southern leaders, a practical difference had led to new discord, as Lincoln tells his fellow Republicans of Illinois in the following words:

> At length a squabble springs up between the President and the author of the Nebraska bill on the mere question of fact, whether the Lecompton constitution was or was not in any just sense made by the people of Kansas; and in that squabble the latter declares that all he wants is a fair vote for the people, and that he cares not whether slavery be voted down or voted up.

Lincoln's argument becomes somewhat technical as it discusses the application of the Dred Scott decision in various hypothetical cases. But his real object is not disguised for a moment. He is making the South and its northern sympathizers understand that Douglas

CONQUERING PREJUDICE TO SAVE THE UNION

The Fugitive Slave Law, compelling the return of slaves who had escaped into Free States, had been adopted as part of the Compromise of 1850. It was a source of constant irritation in the North, often flagrantly disregarded and in some cases actually nullified by State legislatures. The slave in the foreground of this drawing is being seized because he has transferred himself to a Free State "without the consent of his kind-hearted owner." One of the men arresting the Negro reminds him that he is only "a piece of property," a phrase borrowed from the decision of Chief Justice Taney in the Dred Scott case.

does not care whether slavery is voted up or voted down. On the other hand, he is making Northern anti-slavery men understand that Douglas has no feeling whatever about the moral aspects of slavery, and is perfectly willing to extend slave territory in all directions, provided the local opposition may prove not too intolerant. To those who might have thought that Douglas was on the road to Damascus, so to speak, and that he might soon see the light of the true Republican gospel, Lincoln gave the following warning:

Now, as ever, I wish not to misrepresent Judge Douglas's position, question his motives, or do aught that can be personally offensive to him. Whenever, if ever, he and we can come together on principle, so that our great cause may have assistance from his great ability, I hope to have interposed no ad-

ventitious obstacle. But clearly he is not now with us, he does not pretend to be, he does not promise ever to be. Our cause, then, must be intrusted to, and conducted by, its own undoubted friends—those whose hands are free, whose hearts are in the work —who do care for the result.

A speech of great intellectual authority, without the slightest taint of unfairness or misrepresentation, was concluded by Mr. Lincoln with the following sentences:

Two years ago the Republicans of the nation mustered over thirteen hundred thousand strong. We did this under the single impulse of resistance to a common danger, with every external circumstance against us. Of strange, discordant, and even hostile elements, we gathered from the four winds, and formed and fought the battle through, under the constant hot fire of a disciplined, proud and pampered enemy. Did we brave all then to falter now

COUNTING HIS EGGS AFTER THEY ARE HATCHED
Douglas: Oh Lord, I'm sorry I broke this egg. If I could only keep the Nigger quiet until after the election I'd be all right.

The first Egg Douglas picked was called the Compromise,
  Out popped a little nigger, with the devil in his eyes;
He raised his hands in horror, when Stephen gave a frown,
  Said he, "Little Nigger, I'm bound to keep you down."

Another Egg was Cuba, but it would not pass muster,
  For out of it had sprung a little Filibuster;
The climate was too hot, and he couldn't stand the test.
  With his shell upon his back, he retreated to his nest.

The Squatter Sovereign Egg was broken with an awful shout,
  There being nothing in it, there was nothing to come out.
'Twas a shame to raise a cackle, a Democratic sell,
  A bid for the Senate—a hollow, windy shell.

Free Kansas was a piece of chalk, or else a polished bone,
  The people asked to have an Egg, but only got a stone;
He said he had no great respect for black, or white, or brown,
  And did not care if Slavery was voted up or down.

The Egg "Dred Scot Decision" lies there unbroken still,
  Subject to the election and the fire-eaters' will;
Pandora's Box was harmless, compared with all *its* evil.,
  For out of it there yet may hatch the *very biggest devil*.

(Cartoon and doggerel from the *Rail-Splitter*, Chicago)

—now, when the same enemy is wavering, dissevered, and belligerent? The result is not doubtful. We shall not fail—if we stand firm, we shall not fail. Wise counsels may accelerate or mistakes delay it, but, sooner or later, the victory is sure to come.

Mr. Beveridge is at pains to show us that a great oration owes its power as much to the occasion as to its words and phrases. Many things in this Springfield speech had been said before. In this case it was like Jefferson's Declaration of Independence, Washington's farewell address or Marshall's greatest opinions. There were phrases from Webster in the speech, and thoughts from other masters at whose feet Lincoln had long been a disciple. "But," says Mr. Beveridge, "like Washington, Jefferson and Marshall, Lincoln stated old truths in a simpler form than anyone else had expressed them; like those masters, he stated them when the public mind was intent upon them and impressive numbers of men and women were ready to receive them; and he stated them as the chosen leader of a young, powerful and growing party in a great Western State at a critical time, and as the opponent selected by that party to do battle with the then strongest political man in the United States."

It is also explained by Beveridge that Lincoln broke the speech, as he wrote it out, into very short paragraphs, with many words italicized throughout. Printed in this way, as it is reproduced in Beveridge's pages, its statements seem doubly impressive, and they gain in cumulative force as they proceed. The speech was at once printed in Republican papers throughout Illinois, and it was circulated in pamphlet form. The New York *Tribune* reproduced it without abridgment, and Mr. Greeley was apparently converted from his earlier view that Illinois Republicans might support Douglas. Mr. Beveridge, whose judgment about the matter may be taken as final, declares that this speech of Lincoln's was "his most important move in the game for the presidency, a game Lincoln meant to win." Dr. Barton describes the method by which Lincoln had written bits of the speech as thoughts occurred to him, afterward arranging them in order. He read the final draft to a group of friends the night before the convention. These advisers disapproved of it, Herndon alone favoring it. The Republican cohorts, also, were less enthusiastic about this thoughtful speech than about the improvised effort of 1856. But the orator stood on ground that his party duly accepted.

CHAPTER XXII

Douglas Wins a Costly Victory

*His home-coming speech at Chicago—The candidates question one
another thoroughly as they tour the State before election—Illinois
sectionalism—Immigrants at the polls*

THE REPLY OF DOUGLAS to Lincoln's written speech of June 16th was made in the home-coming speech at Chicago, on July 9th. Regardless of the fact that this great town had become a Republican stronghold, the personal prestige of the gallant Senator was so great as to insure him a magnificent welcome. He was adroit in complimenting Republicans on having stood with him in his recent fight against the Lecompton Constitution, thus seeming to bring them over to his side in support of the doctrine of local sovereignty. Many Republicans, in fact, were losing sight of principles, and were imagining that perhaps Douglas had found the path to actual freedom in the national domain. In somewhat patronizing fashion he referred to Lincoln's candidacy:

I have observed from the public prints that but a few days ago the Republican party of the State of Illinois assembled in convention at Springfield, and not only laid down their platform, but nominated a candidate for the United States Senate as my successor. I take great pleasure in saying that I have known personally and intimately, for about a quarter of a century, the worthy gentleman who has been nominated for my place, and I will say that I regard him as a kind, amiable and intelligent gentleman, a good citizen and an honorable opponent; and whatever issue I may have with him will be of principle, and not involving personalities.

Mr. Lincoln made a speech before the Republican Convention which unanimously nominated him for the Senate—a speech evidently well prepared and carefully written—in which he states the basis upon which he proposes to carry on the campaign during this summer. In it he lays down two distinct propositions which I shall notice, and upon which I shall take a direct and bold issue with him.

Douglas then addressed himself to Lincoln's arguments regarding the dangers of division. He was of the opinion that we could go on perfectly well without being all slave or all free. Douglas was an expansionist, as were most western and southern people, and he was in accord with the Southern desire to purchase Cuba and divide the island into two additional slave States. But Douglas, unlike Buchanan, was not playing the southern game in a submissive spirit; and he was not playing the northern game with any

AN ILLINOIS CARICATURE OF DOUGLAS

A Republican campaign paper called the *Rail-Splitter*, which was issued at Chicago from June to October in 1860, represented Douglas as "the Illinois thimble-rigger," referring to the parent of the later well-known "shell game," popular at county fairs. Douglas, in the guise of professional gambler, declaims: "Walk up, gentlemen, here's your Popular Sovereignty, Dred Scott and Wickliffe thimbles. Now you see it, and now you don't see it. I'll bet you $25,000 you can't tell under which one the little joker is." This analysis of Douglas was anticipated by Lincoln at the close of the debate, as explained in the concluding paragraph of the chapter. Governor Wickliffe of Louisiana, to whom the *Railsplitter* referred, was a Douglas Democrat who had been a member of the platform committee at the Baltimore convention in 1860. As Governor he had sent a secession message to the Louisiana Legislature. His support was to prove costly to Douglas in the North.

pretense of sympathy with northern motives. The very fact that both sections were discrediting his leadership should have been, to him, the most concrete kind of proof that Lincoln was right in his warning that the country could not go on happily with the two systems, slavery in the South, free labor in the North, and rivalry in the new territories.

Douglas assumed that Lincoln's position meant direct activities against slavery in the old Southern States:

His first and main proposition I will give in his own language, Scripture quotation and all; I give his exact language: " 'A house divided against itself can not stand.' I believe this Government can not endure, permanently, half slave and half free. I do not expect the Union to be dissolved. I do not expect the house to fall; but I do expect it to cease to be divided. It will become all one thing or all the other." In other words Mr. Lincoln asserts, as a fundamental principle of this government, that there must be uniformity in the local laws and domestic institutions of each and all the States of the Union; and he therefore invites all the non-slaveholding States to band together, organize as one body, and make war upon slavery in Kentucky, upon slavery in Virginia, upon slavery in the Carolinas, upon slavery in all the slaveholding States in this Union, and to persevere in that war until it shall be exterminated. . . . Now, my friends, I must say to you frankly that I take bold, unqualified issue with him upon that principle. I assert that it is neither desirable nor possible that there should be uniformity in the local institutions and domestic regulations of the different States of this Union.

ABOLITION RIDICULED IN THE NORTH
As late as February, 1861, when this cartoon was published in *Vanity Fair* (New York), those who advocated the abolition of slavery were often the subject of contemptuous satire.

The framers of our government never contemplated uniformity in its internal concerns.

It was a long speech that Douglas made, and it is not necessary to attempt to digest it here as a whole; but the following sentences, dealing with the Dred Scott decision, and Douglas's views upon the question of the legal rights of Negroes, may well be quoted, as showing the kind of argument that was then current even among leaders of such distinction:

The other proposition discussed by Mr. Lincoln in his speech consists in a crusade against the Supreme Court of the United States on account of the Dred Scott decision. On this question, also, I desire to say to you unequivocally that I take direct and distinct issue with him. I have no warfare to make on account of that or any other decision which they have pronounced from that bench. . . . I have no idea of appealing from the decision of the Supreme Court upon a constitutional question to the decisions of a tumultuous town meeting. I am aware that once an eminent lawyer of this city, now no more, said that the State of Illinois had the most perfect judicial system in the world, subject to but one exception, which could be cured by a slight amendment, and that amendment was to so change the law as to allow an appeal from the decisions of the Supreme Court of Illinois, on all constitutional questions, to Justices of the Peace.

("You were then on the Supreme Bench," said Lincoln quietly.)

My friend, Mr. Lincoln, who sits behind me, reminds me that the proposition was made when I was Judge of the Supreme Court. Be that as it may, I do not think that fact adds any greater weight or authority to the suggestion. . . . I am opposed to this doctrine of Mr. Lincoln, by which he proposes to take an appeal from the decision of the Supreme Court of the United States, upon this high constitutional question, to a Republican caucus sitting in the country. Yes, or any other caucus or town meeting, whether it be Republican, American, or Democratic. I respect the decisions of that august tribunal; I shall always bow in deference to them. . . He objects to the Dred Scott decision because it does not put the negro in the possession of the rights of citizenship on an equality with the white man. I am opposed to negro equality. . . . I am opposed to taking any step that recognizes the negro man or the Indian as the equal of the white man. I am opposed to giving him a voice in the administration of the government. I would extend to the negro and the Indian, and to all dependent races, every right, every privilege, and every immunity consistent with the safety and welfare of the white races; but equality they never should have, either political or social, or in any other respect whatever.

The extreme views of Abolitionists were by no means popular in 1858, even in the ranks of the more radical half of the Republican party. Douglas therefore felt himself on safe and solid ground in asserting his views on the subject of racial equality. He was making a somewhat dangerous appeal to southern prejudice when he raised the alarm that Lincoln's argument on the "house divided against itself" indicated an aggressive Republican program to invade the old slave States, in order to make the country "all free." He could hardly have realized that he was spending long weeks and months of the year 1858, with every politician in the South eagerly following his words, in bold reiteration of the idea that the election of a man like Lincoln to the Presidency would create such peril for the South as clearly to justify secession.

What Douglas said at Chicago early in July was repeated by him, with many variations but with increasing ardor and intensity, during the whole period of the strenuous campaign. The following passages from the Chicago speech show the quality and method of the Douglas argument:

I believe this Government of ours was founded on the white basis. I believe it was established for white men, for the benefit of white men and their posterity in all time to come. I do not believe that it was the design or intention of the signers of the Declaration of Independence or the framers of the Constitution to include negroes as citizens. . . . . The position Lincoln has taken on this question not only presents him as claiming for them the right to vote, but their right under the divine law and the Declaration of Independence to be elected to office, to become members of the legislature, to go to Congress, to become Governors or United States Senators, or Judges of the Supreme Court. . . . He would permit them to marry, would he not? And if he gives them that right I suppose he will let them marry whom they please, provided they marry their equals. If the divine law declares that the white man is the equal of the negro woman, that they are on a perfect equality, I suppose he admits the right of the negro woman to marry the white man. . . . I do not believe that the signers of the Declaration

THE UNITED STATES—A BLACK BUSINESS
From *Punch* (London), November 8, 1856

Looking on from a distance, before the day of the transatlantic cable, *Punch* saw clearly that the disagreement over slavery would tear the Union apart. Note the English conception of the Southerner with gun in hand and the Northerner with high hat.

had any reference to negroes when they used the expression that all men were created equal. . . . They were speaking only of the white race. . . . . Every one of the thirteen colonies was a slave-holding constituency. Did they intend. . . . to declare that their own slaves were on an equality with them? What are the negroes' rights and privileges? That is a question which each State and Territory must decide for itself. We have decided that question. We have said that in this State the negro shall not be a slave but that he shall enjoy no political rights; that negro equality shall not exist. . . . For my own part, I do not consider the negro any kin to me nor to any other white man; but I would still carry my humanity and my philanthropy to the extent of giving him every privilege and every immunity that he could enjoy consistent with our own good.

Maine allows the negro to vote on an equality with the white man. New York permits him to vote, provided he owns $250 worth of property. In Kentucky they deny the negro all political and civil rights. Each is a sovereign State and has a right to do as it pleases. Let us mind our own business and not interfere with them. Lincoln is not going into Kentucky, but will plant his batteries on this side of the Ohio and throw his bomb shells—his Abolition documents—over the River and will carry on the political warfare and get up strife between the North and the South until he elects a sectional President, reduces the South to submit to the condition of dependent colonies, raises the negro to an equality and forces the South to submit to the doctrine that a house divided against itself can not stand; that the Union divided into half slave States and half free cannot endure; that they must be all free or all slave; and that, as we in the North are in the majority, we will not permit them to be all slave, and therefore they in the South must consent to the States being all free.

In his Chicago speech on the following evening, Lincoln showed that Douglas had not correctly stated his position, and that he had not, in his Springfield speech of June 16th, said anything at all in favor of taking steps for the extinction of slavery. He now took the opportunity to say, however, that he did desire that slavery be put in course of ultimate extinction, and he went on as follows: "I have always hated slavery, I think, as much as any Abolitionist. I have been an Old Line Whig. I have always hated it, but I have always been quiet about it until this new era of the introduction of the Nebraska bill began. I always believed that everybody was against it, and that it was in course of ultimate extinction." When further elaborating upon this change of attitude, he protested again that there was no right, and ought to be no inclination, to interfere with slavery in the slave States.

These speeches laid the foundation for the weeks of campaigning that followed. There was, of course, much repetition, especially on the part of Douglas. Points became sharply differentiated, and the candidates put questions to each other that were skilfully drawn and intended to create either the embarrassment of evasion or the confusion of inconsistency. In answering Douglas's questions Lincoln said that he had never been committed, (1) to the unconditional repeal of the Fugitive Slave Law, or (2) against the admission of more

THE CONSTITUTIONAL CONVENTION OF KANSAS TERRITORY

From a sketch published in *Leslie's Weekly* (New York), in December, 1855. It represents the convention of Free State supporters which met at Topeka in September of that year. Pro-slavery advocates, two months earlier had met and drawn up a constitution based upon that of the Slave State of Missouri. The Topeka convention declared the existing territorial government illegal, and framed another constitution prohibiting slavery. President Pierce recognized the pro-slavery government, however, in January, 1856, and civil war ensued in the Territory.

slave States into the Union, or (3) against the admission of a new State into the Union with such a Constitution as the people of that State may see fit to make, or (4) in favor of the abolition of slavery in the District of Columbia, or (5) in favor of prohibiting the slave trade between the different States.

He declared that he was (6) impliedly, if not expressly, pledged to the belief in the right and duty of Congress to prohibit slavery in all the United States territories; and (7) he was not opposed to the extension of American territory, provided further acquisition should be made honestly, though in case of any proposed annexation, he would consider what effect it might have upon the agitation of the slave question.

Having answered the seven questions of Douglas, Lincoln in turn asked four questions. He inquired whether Douglas would vote to admit Kansas as a State "before they have the requisite number of inhabitants according to the 'English bill,' some 93,000." In his second question he asked if there was any lawful way by which the people of a territory "against the wish of any citizen of the United States can exclude slavery from its limits." In the third question Douglas was asked if he would acquiesce in the decision if the Supreme Court should decide that States can not exclude slavery from their limits. Finally, he asked if Douglas was in favor of acquiring additional territory "in disregard of how such acquisition may affect the nation on the slavery question."

The crucial question was, of course, the

DOUGLAS READY TO "BURY" LINCOLN POLITICIALLY AS A PATRIOTIC DUTY

On September 12, 1860, a great mass-meeting and barbecue were held in New York City under Tammany auspices at which August Belmont presided. The crowd in attendance was estimated at from 20,000 to 30,000 persons and the New York *Herald* the next morning said of the occasion that nothing like it in politics had ever occurred there before. Douglas took that opportunity to say: "My friends, there is no patriotic duty on earth more gratifying to my feelings than to make a speech over Mr. Lincoln's political grave. (Loud cheers.) I do not make this remark out of any unkindness to Mr. Lincoln, but I believe that the good of his own country requires it." The *Vanity Fair* cartoonist pictures Senator Douglas as "Aminadab Sleek," a character in a comedy called "The Serious Family," which was popular in New York during the '50's.

second one. Douglas answered it promptly in the affirmative. "It matters not," he declared, "what way the Supreme Court may hereafter decide as to the abstract question as to whether slavery may or may not go into a Territory under the Constitution. The people have the lawful means to introduce it or exclude it, as they please, for the reason that slavery can not exist a day or an hour anywhere unless it is supported by local police regulations." He

A 1929 STATUE OF LINCOLN, AT FREEPORT

To commemorate the second debate in the series of seven, this bronze statue was erected in Freeport, Illinois, the work of Leonard Crunelle of Chicago and the gift of W. T. Raleigh. It was unveiled on August 27, 1929, on the seventy-first anniversary of the debate with Douglas.

had evidently intended to widen the gap between the southern and northern wings of the Democratic party. On the expansion question, Douglas was breezy and eloquent. "Just as fast," he said, "as our interests and our destiny require additional territory in the North, in the South or on the islands of the ocean, I am for it, and when we acquire it we will leave the people, according to the Nebraska bill, free to do as they please on the subject of slavery and every other question."

Ottawa, the point chosen for the first of the seven debates, was in a district represented by Owen Lovejoy in Congress, with anti-slavery sentiment permeating the entire group of counties. Douglas was highly entertaining in his review of Lincoln's personal and political career, and the tone of his speech greatly resembled many of the addresses made by Senator Borah, Senator Robinson and other

THE LINCOLN STATUE AT URBANA, ILLINOIS

Many cities and towns throughout his own State of Illinois have found occasion to commemorate Lincoln in bronze and marble. The statue reproduced above is the work of Lorado Taft, a distinguished sculptor of Chicago. As the capital of Champaign County, Urbana was often visited by Lincoln the lawyer.

elaborated this idea further, and declared that no matter what the decision of the Supreme Court might be, "still the right of the people to make a slave Territory or a free Territory is perfect and complete under the Nebraska bill. I hope Mr. Lincoln deems my answer satisfactory on that point."

This was a sort of nullification doctrine, such as many opponents of national Prohibition have recently advocated. The national policy could not be expected, Douglas held, to prevail in a given State or Territory unless local police authority was acting in harmony with national laws, or with Supreme Court decisions. The Fugitive Slave Law had broken down in New England, because local sentiment was so strongly against it.

There was practical common sense in this reply of Senator Douglas; but the South considered it an unpardonable heresy, and Lincoln

A FAMOUS LINCOLN-DOUGLAS DEBATE SCENE RE-ENACTED AFTER SEVENTY YEARS
Knox College at Galesburg, Illinois, was a Lincoln stronghold in 1858. The debate there was con-
ducted from a platform adjacent to one of the college buildings. It was well attended and aroused
much enthusiasm. In October, 1928, on the same spot, Frank McGlynn and A. B. Pierson represented
Lincoln and Douglas, respectively, in a repetition of the Galesburg speeches. In the picture Mr.
Pierson, impersonating Senator Douglas, is delivering his address.

leaders, including Governor Alfred E. Smith himself, in the Presidential campaign of 1928. There was a tendency throughout all of the Douglas speeches to misuse remarkable gifts as a platform entertainer by indulgence in mild ridicule, in misrepresentation through omissions and false emphasis, and in telling plays upon the regional bias of particular audiences. Since the speeches were everywhere distributed in cold type, it so happened that the cleverness with which Douglas won votes and secured his election to the Senate supplied a fund of quotations that it was easy to turn against him when he became a presidential candidate in 1860.

Having listened to Douglas for a solid hour at Ottawa, Lincoln followed with this opening sentence: "When a man hears himself somewhat misrepresented, it provokes him—at least I find it so with myself; but when misrepresentation becomes very gross and palpable, it is more apt to amuse him." He then proceeded

in a straightforward way to present his positions, wasting no time in trying to imitate Douglas's method of disparaging the statements and arguments of his opponent.

Freeport, where the next debate was held, was also in a district in which the Democrats themselves were on record against the aggressions of the pro-slavery politicians. To have seen Douglas arriving in a carriage drawn by four white horses, while Lincoln appeared on the scene in a farmer's wagon with a canvas cover of the type known as "prairie schooner," would have been something to remember. Indeed, there were thousands who were ready for a long time afterwards to describe the scene to a succession of visiting Lincoln biographers. It was here that Lincoln answered the seven questions of Douglas, and propounded his own four interrogatories.

The next debate took the antagonists further South, and at Jonesboro they were in the part of Illinois known as "Egypt." In this atmos-

phere Douglas, whether consciously or unconsciously, played upon the Southern traditions
of the crowd that came to listen and applaud.
Lincoln here presented a fifth question, as
follows: "If slave-holding citizens of a United
States Territory should need and demand Congressional legislation for the protection of
their slave property in such Territory, would
you as a member of Congress vote for or
against such legislation?" Douglas in reply insisted that, even if Congress enacted Legislation to support slave-holders under the Dred
Scott decision, "you cannot maintain slavery
for a day where there is an unwilling people
and an unfriendly legislature. If the people
want slavery they will have it, and if they do
not want it you cannot force it upon them."

Possibly Lincoln's antagonism to the Dred
Scott decision was slowly assuming a tone that
might be construed as revolutionary; while on
the other hand the Douglas doctrine that localities could lawfully exclude an institution that
had been made lawful by the national government, was nullification pure and simple, besides being an incitement to revolution. Thus
the tendency of the Lincoln-Douglas debates
was to make parties and sections less patient
and less tolerant.

Mr. Gardner comments to the effect that
"there was a marked falling off in the good
temper and mutual courtesy of the combatants

in the later stages of the contest." This writer
further remarks: "The abiding question to
which the argument constantly recurred was
that of negro slavery, as to which Lincoln
was darkly oracular and Douglas was reso-
lutely evasive. Lincoln again and again pressed
Douglas to say whether he regarded slavery
as wrong. Douglas persistently declined the
plea as one wholly foreign to national politics."

"I look forward," said Douglas, "to the
time when each State shall be allowed to do
as it pleases. If it chooses to keep slavery forever, it is not my business, but its own. If it
chooses to abolish slavery, it is its own business, not mine. I care more for the great
principle of self-government, the right of the
people to rule, than for all the negroes in
Christendom. I would not endanger the per-
petuity of this Union; I would not blot out the
great inalienable rights of the white man for
all the negroes that ever existed."

At Galesburg, where Knox College was the
dominant influence, the audience was relatively sympathetic with Lincoln. Douglas
opened the debate very ably, with that instinctive change of tone and attitude that recognized the difference between a Galesburg audience and those to which he had been appealing
"down in Egypt." Lincoln dwelt upon the
significance of the Declaration of Independence, declaring that "the entire records of the
world, from the date of the
Declaration of Independence up
to within three years ago, may be
searched in vain for one single
affirmation from one single man
that the negro was not included
in the Declaration of Independence. We are now far in this canvass," said Mr. Lincoln; "Judge
Douglas and I have made perhaps
forty speeches apiece, and we
have now for the fifth time met
face to face in debate."

It was in the Galesburg speech
that Lincoln made his prophetic
remarks upon the fact that Douglas himself was becoming sectional, even while twitting Lincoln and the Republicans upon

THE KNOX COLLEGE BUILDING AT GALESBURG
Against the end of this building the speakers' stand was built for the fifth
debate in the series between Lincoln and Douglas, on October 7, 1858.

their being exclusively a Northern party. The following sentences are well worth quoting at this point:

I ask his attention to the fact that his speeches would not go as current now, South of the Ohio River, as they have formerly gone there. I ask his attention to the fact that he felicitates himself today that all the Democrats of the free States are agreeing with him, while he omits to tell us that the Democrats of any slave State agree with him. If he has not thought of this, I commend to his consideration the evidence in his own declaration, on this day, of his becoming sectional too. I see it rapidly approaching. Whatever may be the result of this ephemeral contest between Judge Douglas and myself, I see the day rapidly approaching when his pill of sectionalism, which he has been thrusting down the throats of Republicans for years past, will be crowded down his own throat.

© 1903, N. B. Fey

SITE OF THE QUINCY DEBATE

In front of the old Court House on Fourth Street (the building with the columns in the right center of the picture) the stand was erected for the sixth of the debates, on October 13th.

The debate at Quincy on October 13th was followed two days later by the final meeting at Alton. Referring to his "popular sovereignty" principle, and his stand in Congress against Buchanan, Douglas declared: "I will never violate or abandon that doctrine if I have to stand alone. I have resisted the blandishments and threats of power on one side, and seduction on the other, and I have stood immovably for that principle, fighting for it when assaulted by northern mobs or threatened by southern hostility." There was a note of rather desperate defiance in this challenge to his opponents in both sections.

Two weeks after the Alton debate the election was held, on November 2nd. The Republican State ticket was elected; but the Democrats carried the majority of the legislative districts. The aggregate Lincoln vote for members of the Legislature exceeded the Douglas vote by a total of perhaps four thousand. Douglas had won a small victory, at the expense of a greater one. Lincoln's conduct of the campaign had given him national standing, and had contributed greatly to the prospects of the Republican party as a whole. The campaign of Douglas had cost him his place as the most influential statesman of that decade, and had contributed to the discord that was breaking asunder the great Democratic party that Jackson had built upon the foundations laid by Jefferson.

At a meeting in Springfield on Saturday, October 30th, with several speakers on the platform at the final rally of the campaign, Lincoln had made a speech which for some reason of inadvertence was not published. We now have access to it in the excellent Lincoln biography by William E. Barton, who first brought it to light in 1925. As a summing up of his arguments and his platform methods in the long contest with Douglas, and as a revelation of his patriotic spirit, this brief concluding speech should stand as a Lincoln document of rare value. Dr. Barton well characterizes it when he says: "These are not the words of a politician whose ethics are those of opportunism. They are the words of a noble statesman and an honest man. They are words that deserve to become as well known and as immortal as the best known and most cherished of the utterances of Lincoln." The speech in its entirety is as follows:

My friends, today closes the discussions of this canvass. The planting and the culture are over;

and there remains but the preparation, and the harvest.

I stand here surrounded by friends—some *political, all personal* friends, I trust. May I be indulged, in this closing scene, to say a few words of myself. I have borne a laborious, and, in some respects to myself, a painful part in the contest. Through all, I have neither assailed, nor wrestled with any part of the Constitution. The legal right of the southern people to reclaim their fugitives I have constantly admitted. The legal right of Congress to interfere with their institutions in the States, I have constantly denied. In resisting the spread of slavery to new territory, and with that, what appears to me to be a tendency to subvert the first principle of free government itself my whole effort has consisted. To the best of my judgment I have labored *for,* and not *against,* the Union. As I have not felt, so I have not expressed any harsh sentiment towards our southern brethren. I have constantly declared, as I have really believed, the only difference between them and us, is the difference of circumstances.

I have meant to assail the motives of no party, or individual; and if I have, in any instance (of which I am not conscious) departed from my purpose, I regret it.

I have said that in some respects the contest has been painful to me. Myself, and those with whom I act, have been constantly accused of a purpose to destroy the Union; and bespattered with every imaginable odious epithet; and some who were friends, as it were but yesterday, have made themselves most active in this. I have cultivated patience, and made no attempt at a retort.

Ambition has been ascribed to me. God knows how sincerely I prayed from the first that this field of ambition might not be opened. I claim no insensibility to political honors; but today

Last Great Discussion.

Let all take notice, that on Friday next, Hon. S. A. Douglas and Hon. A. Lincoln, will hold the seventh and closing joint debate of the canvass at this place. We hope the country will turn out, to a man, to hear these gentlemen.

The following programme for the discussion has been decided upon by the Joint Committee appointed by the People's Party Club and the Democratic Club for that purpose.

Arrangements for the 15th inst.

The two Committees—one from each party—heretofore appointed to make arrangements for the public speaking on the 15th inst., met in joint Committee, and the following programme of proceedings was adopted, viz:

1st. The place for said speaking shall be on the east side of City Hall.

2d. The time shall be 1½ o'clock, P. M. on said day.

3d. That Messes. C. Stigleman and W. T. Miller be a Committee to erect a platform; also, seats to accommodate ladies.

4th. That Messrs. B. F. Barry and William Post superintend music and salutes.

5th. Messrs. H. G. McPike and W. C. Quigley be a committee having charge of the platform, and reception of ladies, and have power to appoint assistants.

6th. That the reception of Messrs. Douglas and Lincoln shall be a quiet one, and no public display.

7th. That no banner or motto, except national colors, shall be allowed on the speakers' stand.

On motion, a committee, consisting of Messrs. W. C. Quigley and H. G. McPike, be appointed to publish this programme of proceedings.
        W. C. QUIGLEY,
        H. G. McPIKE.
Alton, Oct. 13, 1858.

To the above it should be added that the C. A. & St. Louis Railroad, will, on Friday, carry passengers to and from this city at half its usual rates. Persons can come in on the 10:40 a. m. train, and go out at 6:20 in the evening.

ANNOUNCEMENT OF THE CLOSING DEBATE AT ALTON

This clipping from the Alton *Daily Whig* carries an advertisement of the last of the seven debates, at Alton on October 15th. The attendance, although numbering more than 5000, was smaller than at most of the earlier debates. This was attributed by some of the newspapers to the conservative character of the Madison County voters, many of whom were old-line Whigs. Missourians from across the Mississippi River helped to make up the audience.

could the Missouri restriction be restored, and the whole slavery question replaced on the old ground of "toleration" by *necessity* where it exists, with unyielding hostility to the spread of it, on principle, I would, in consideration, gladly agree, that Judge Douglas, should never be *out,* and I never *in,* an office, so long as we both, or either, live.

After the election was over, Lincoln's junior law partner, energetic campaign manager and devoted friend, William H. Herndon, wrote a letter in which he told of the difficulties of the contest as felt by a party manager. He emphasized the difference of origin and mentality in the State of Illinois among the people of the north and those of the middle and those of the south. All the pro-slavery influences of the nation were, in Herndon's opinion, working for Douglas, while on the other hand there was no corresponding support for Lincoln from the great leaders of the Republican party in the East. The feeling in New York and New England, as among some of Lincoln's oldest friends in the West like Crittenden of Kentucky, was favorable to Douglas merely because Douglas had momentarily joined the Republican Senators against President Buchanan and the South in opposing the acceptance of the Lecompton Constitution.

In the bitterness of the reaction felt by a young campaign manager who had lost an election, Herndon wrote: "Greeley never gave us one single solitary manly lift. On the contrary, his silence was his opposition. This our people felt. We never got a smile or a word of encouragement outside of Illinois from any quarter during all this great canvass. The East was for Douglas *by silence.* This silence was terrible to us. Seward was against us too. Thirdly, Crittenden wrote letters to Illinois urging the Americans and Old Line Whigs to go for Douglas, and so they went "helter skelter." Thousands of Whigs dropped us just on the eve of the election, through the influence of Crittenden."

They were building railroads and canals in Illinois, and they were using the available labor of the newest types of immigrants, as has always been the case at every stage of our industrial progress. There had been a large recent Irish immigration, and for well-known reasons the Irish-Americans had mainly joined the Democratic party. The more anxiously the older Americans—who in several states were acting politically as "Know-Nothings" or "Americans"—were arousing one another against foreign-born naturalized citizens in New York and elsewhere, the easier it had become for the Democratic politicians to gather in to their fold these ignorant and well-meaning recruits from the over-populated and poverty-stricken regions of Europe.

The infusion of this prejudice against the new citizens into political campaigns had been a disfiguring characteristic of politics in the East for two decades. Its recurrence at intervals, under changing conditions of immigration, had continued to be a factor in campaigns for almost a century, when it was revived again in the Hoover-Smith campaign of 1928. Herndon's letter was, of course, not intended for publication, and this fact gives it an engaging candor that adds to its value as throwing light upon the conditions of that time. Thus, after mentioning four causes of Lincoln's defeat, he remarks: "Fifthly, thousands of roving, robbing, bloated, pock-marked Catholic Irish were imported upon us from Philadelphia, New York, St. Louis, and other cities. I myself know of such, by their own confession. Some have been arrested, and are now in jail awaiting trial."

It was to no one of these causes, but to all

Commercial Register

Published Daily, Tri-Weekly & Weekly
BY HENRY D. COOKE AND C. C. BILL.

SANDUSKY, OHIO,
SATURDAY MORNING, NOV. 6, 1858.

Lincoln for President.

We are indebted to a friend at Mansfield for the following special dispatch:

"MANSFIELD, Nov. 5th, 1858.

"EDITOR SANDUSKY REGISTER:—An enthusiastic meeting is in progress here to-night in favor of Lincoln for the next Republican candidate for President. REPORTER."

LINCOLN PROPOSED FOR PRESIDENT IN 1858

An unexpected outcome of Lincoln's defeat in the senatorial contest was the suggestion of his name for the Republican presidential candidacy in 1860. At Mansfield, Ohio, the home of Representative (later Senator) John Sherman, a Republican gathering proclaimed Lincoln as its choice as early as November 5, 1858. This has been thought to be the first public announcement of his candidacy.

of them in combination, that Herndon attributed the Douglas victory. And he summed it up by asking: "Do you not *now* see that there is a conspiracy afloat which threatens the disorganization of the Republican party? Do you not see that Seward, Greeley, Crittenden, etc., are at this moment in a joint common understanding to lower our platform?" Such was the natural petulance and irritation of a tired young campaign manager. Lincoln, on the other hand, calmly explained that Douglas had been so ingenious in the late contest as to be supported by those who thought his victory the best means to break down the slave interest, and by those, on the other hand, who thought it the best means to uphold that interest. "No ingenuity," he declared, "can keep those antagonistic elements in harmony long. Another explosion will soon occur."

The Lincoln-Douglas debates have been described by most historians and biographers from the standpoint of the main arguments of the two speakers, and from that of the political bearings of the campaign for the senatorship. Mr. Carl Sandburg, in his important work entitled, "Abraham Lincoln, The Prairie Years," has succeeded in enlivening this episode with so many descriptive and personal touches, in addition to his analysis of the fundamental issues, that his chapters possess a rare literary value. And they are also of weight in their historical statements and interpretations. Looking at Lincoln the man, as the hard campaign reached its end, Mr. Sandburg remarks: "The open air, the travel and excitement of the sixty speeches Lincoln made through the campaign, threw him back to flatboating days; his voice grew clearer and stronger; in November he was heavier by nearly twenty pounds than he was at the beginning of the canvass."

Mr. Sandburg reminds us that Lincoln, when he spoke at Quincy, was visited by a political writer afterwards famous, namely, David R. Locke of the Toledo, Ohio, *Blade*. He quotes from the report Mr. Locke made at that time. Mr. Sandburg might have reminded his readers that this Mr. Locke was the celebrated "Petroleum Vesuvius Nasby," whose humorous satires on politics came to be quoted throughout the country, and were read by Lincoln constantly in his White House years. Answering Locke's questions, Lincoln predicted that he would not be elected to the United States Senate; he would carry the State and the popular vote, but because of the arrangement of legislative districts (under which the northern part of the State, which had grown rapidly, was not fully represented), Douglas would be elected by the Legislature. Locke quotes Lincoln as saying: "You can't overturn a pyramid, but you can undermine it; that's what I've been trying to do."

How Mr. Lincoln relaxed in his hotel room after a public appearance, Mr. Locke describes as follows: "I found Mr. Lincoln surrounded by admirers, who had made the discovery that one who had previously been considered merely a curious compound of genius and simplicity was really a great man. I obtained an interview after the crowd had departed. He sat in the room with his boots off, to relieve his very large feet from the pain occasioned by continuous standing; or, to put it in his own words: 'I like to give my feet a chance to breathe.' He had removed his coat and vest, dropped one suspender from his shoulder, taken off his necktie and collar, and he sat tilted back in one chair with his feet upon another in perfect ease. He seemed to dislike clothing, and in privacy wore as little of it as he could."

Such sentences might seem like an undue exposure of a public man's informality in his hotel bedroom; but Mr. Locke did not fail to give an excellent description of Lincoln's skill as a debater, or to note the intellectual power of his arguments. Passing from mere details of attire or manner, Mr. Locke made a memorable statement when he said: "I never saw a more thoughtful face. I never saw a more dignified face. I never saw so sad a face."

THE UNDECIDED POLITICAL PRIZE FIGHT

In the debates of 1858, between Lincoln and Douglas, a seat in the United States Senate was at stake. But two years later the same Illinois statesmen were candidates for a higher office, the Presidency of the United States.

CHAPTER XXIII

Buchanan Surveys the World At Large

A mild-mannered Expansionist, highly alarming to Europe and Latin-America—Talk of re-opening the African slave trade—Northern Abolitionists and their activity

THE PERSONAL STANDING of Lincoln was notably enhanced by the ability with which in his own State he had confronted the foremost debater of the age. But it is to be remembered that his political fortunes were bound up not so much with electoral results in Illinois as with the success of the Republican party at large. We may, therefore, note the broad fact that the elections in the summer and autumn of 1858 showed marked Republican gains in many States. In Illinois the nine districts returned to Congress five Democrats and four Republicans, while in most other northern States the results of the Congressional elections were sweepingly favorable to the new party.

Senator Seward of New York had avoided the Republican presidential nomination of 1856 because the party strength was not yet sufficient for victory. This was true of several other leading men, so that it was without disappointment that they had hailed the nomination of John C. Frémont. But the indications in 1858 encouraged party hopes for Republican success in 1860. New England was uniformly and completely Republican by this time, and the State of New York was carried, under Senator Seward's leadership, with the result that Edwin D. Morgan, the Republican candidate, was elected Governor, while three-fourths of the Congressional districts were won by the new party. This situation turned Seward into a confident and willing aspirant for the Presidency.

For two terms Salmon P. Chase had been Governor of Ohio, and in the coming year he was to be followed by the worthy and patriotic William Dennison, and was himself to be successful in his candidacy for a seat in the United States Senate, with a record that entitled him to rank with Seward and Lincoln as a prospective Republican standard bearer in 1860.

A BUSINESS CRISIS IN BUCHANAN'S FIRST YEAR

Just twenty years after the great financial depression of 1837 the spread of "wild-cat" banking brought on a serious panic in the early months of the Buchanan administration. There had been an era of extravagance. John Bull thought it a fitting time to give America a bit of fatherly advice: "The fact is, Jonathan, both you and your wife have been living too fast." It is a cartoon from *Punch* (London), November, 1857.

President Buchanan, whose success in his own state of Pennsylvania in 1856 had turned the scales for his party, was now deeply distressed by the fact that the Republicans had carried their state ticket and had increased their strength in the Congressional districts. Pennsylvania after long decades of unbroken Democratic majorities had now joined with New England in support of a more decided protective tariff policy; and this fact contributed to the further disaffection of the free-trade South. Below Mason and Dixon's line and the Ohio River, the elections showed a

219

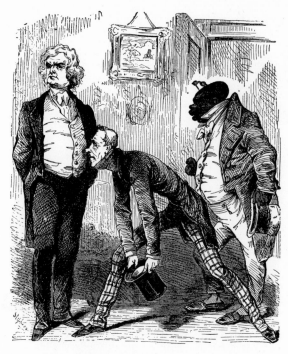

MR. DALLAS RECEIVES AN APOLOGY

This cartoon from *Vanity Fair* (New York), refers not to a formal apology from Palmerston, British Prime Minister, for the searching of American ships by British cruisers seeking to suppress the slave trade; it relates to an incident at an international congress in London, when Mr. Dallas, the American Minister and former Vice-President, was introduced to a Negro by Lord Brougham.

greater degree of sectionalism than ever before. In Missouri, Democrats were elected in every Congressional district.

The Congress in which the Kansas question had been fought over had still its short session remaining, and President Buchanan had his opportunity to address it in his annual message of December 6th. Early in the year he had been dealing with Kansas troubles, with the defiant Mormon colony in Utah, and with filibustering expeditions to Nicaragua. In this message of December, he reported upon the Utah situation, declaring that "the authority of the Constitution and the laws has been fully restored and peace prevails throughout the Territory."

He reported, also, upon a controversy with Great Britain that had come to a fortunate end. Two main subjects were involved, one of them being the right of "visitation and search" at sea in times of peace, and the other being the practical execution of our joint ar-

rangement for the suppression of the African slave trade. Slaves in immense numbers had been persistently landed on the coast of the Spanish island colony of Cuba. The British, apparently with far greater zeal than our government was showing, were patrolling the Atlantic and overhauling slave ships in pursuance of a policy that both countries had entered upon in 1808. A number of small British cruisers, with nothing in particular to do after the end of the Crimean War in 1856, were sent to the West Indies with instructions to board without ceremony any ship of any nation suspected of being engaged in the outlawed slave traffic.

The British cruisers proceeded within a short time to overhaul and search more than forty vessels flying the American flag. This, of course, was contrary to international law as laid down by recognized authorities, including those of Great Britain. Secretary Cass through Mr. Dallas, our Minister at London, succeeded in obtaining apologies from Palmerston, on behalf of the British Government. While we were wholly right on the point of international law, we should have stood better in a court of ethics if we could have shown

THE SPOILED CHILD

England looked on at the increasing turmoil in the United States with a superiority complex easily induced by age. That spirit is reflected in the accompanying cartoon from *Punch*. John Bull, as the parent of the American child, remarks: "I don't like to correct him just now because he's about his teeth, and sickening for his measles—but he certainly deserves a clout on the head." There were numerous exhibitions of a belligerent spirit in international affairs, on the part of young America.

that we had been using our own cruisers effectively in Caribbean waters not only to stop the slave trade from Africa under the American flag, but, what was more pertinent, to stop the smuggling of slaves from the Cuban *entrepot* to their intended destination in our own cotton States.

The Administration was not content to rest with having curbed the activity of the British cruisers. Mr. Buchanan affected a great concern about the slave trade, and made this an excuse for returning to the subject of the desirability of our annexation of Cuba. He declared Cuba to be "a constant source of injury and annoyance to the American people." And he proceeded as follows: "It is the only spot in the civilized world where the African slave trade is tolerated, and we are bound by treaty with Great Britain to maintain a naval force on the coast of Africa at great expense, both in life and treasure, solely for the purpose of arresting slavers bound to that island. As long as this market shall remain open, there can be no hope for the civilization of benighted Africa. Whilst the demand for slaves continues in Cuba, wars will be waged among the petty and barbarous chiefs for the purpose of seizing subjects to supply this trade."

He protested that we would not think of acquiring Cuba from Spain except by honorable negotiations. His advice was followed by the introduction of a bill in Congress to appropriate a large sum of money, as preliminary to taking up the diplomatic question. Spain was, of course, as indignant as on previous like occasions, and the appropriation bill was not passed—partly, indeed, because of bad financial calculations and treasury deficits, following the severe panic and business collapse of 1857.

SETTLING VEXATION BY ANNEXATION

JOHN BULL: "My dear boy, if it comes to the worst, you'll see your Old Dad out of this plaguy French business, won't you?"

JONATHAN: "Well, can't without seeing the boys first. I tell you what, though, 'spose we annex you! That'll settle this business right away!"

(Anti-British propaganda in the French press had caused some worriment in England. This American cartoon reflects the expansionist attitude assumed by President Buchanan, which caused no small measure of irritation abroad.)

The mild-mannered President Buchanan was now in a surprisingly aggressive mood, as he invited the country to forget its internal differences while joining in foreign adventures. He stated grievances against Mexico, and declared that "abundant cause now undoubtedly exists for a resort to hostilities against the government still holding possession of the [Mexican] capital." He intimated that we might take possession of portions of Mexican territory to be held in pledge. He went so far even as to declare, after reciting lawless conditions in the Mexican states of Chihuahua and Sonora, that our Government ought "to assume a temporary protectorate over the northern portions. . . . and to establish military posts within the same."

No President before Buchanan, and none since, is on record as proposing to enter so deliberately upon an expansion policy. With a hope of new slave states in Cuba and northern Mexico, the South might be less chagrined over its failure in Kansas. But the North was

A SERVICEABLE GARMENT__
OR REVERIE OF A BACHELOR.

President-elect Buchanan recalls, in his reverie, that the coat was in
fashionable Federal style when it was new—its owner began his
political life as a Federalist—but that patching and turning have
made it a Democratic model. The "Cuba patch" (referring to
Buchanan's part, as Minister to England, in writing the Ostend
Manifesto) is admittedly unsightly, though quite in line with Southern fashions. But the bachelor President, the only one before Grover
Cleveland occupied the White House, thinks that perhaps he can
afford a new outfit.

in no mood for expansion under those circumstances; and Buchanan's proposals, while extremely irritating to other governments, were
wholly without effect at home. Latin America
was seriously displeased, and the British and
French Governments were preparing to support Spain in holding Cuba, and to defend
Mexico in case of aggression on our part.

Our citizens had been going to California
by the Panama route, and also by way of

Mexico and Nicaragua. Rights previously negotiated over the Nicaragua
route had now been officially revoked.
"Under these circumstances," said Mr.
Buchanan, "I earnestly recommend to
Congress the passage of an act, authorizing the President, under such restrictions as they may deem proper,
to employ the land and naval forces of
the United States in preventing the
transit from being obstructed or closed
by lawless violence. He asked similar authority to protect the Panama
route, and also the Tehuantepec route
across Mexico.

We had some question of difference
with Paraguay over an attack upon
a United States steamer. Mr. Buchanan declared to Congress that if
amicable negotiations failed, "then no
alternative will remain but the employment of force. In view of this con-
tingency, a naval force has been des-
patched to rendezvous near Buenos
Aires." None of these affairs in the
foreign field, however, led the country
into a war that might have diverted attention from domestic politics.

With the 4th of March, 1859, there
expired a Congress that had few
worthy achievements to its credit. Yet
things were happening in the world
that, in the course of decades, were to
contribute towards a finer civilization.
Thus, five days before the first of the
Lincoln-Douglas debates, the completion of the Atlantic cable had permitted the exchange of greetings between Queen Victoria and President
Buchanan. On the 26th of August,
there was cabled the news that a treaty had
closed one of England's periodic wars with
China; and this was a welcome message to lov-
ers of peace. On our own part, we had recently
opened relations with China and Japan in a
friendly and honorable fashion. Contradic-
tory forces were then, as always, making for
war in some directions as in others for peace.
Minnesota had been admitted to the Union in
May, 1858, and later on, in February, 1859,

Oregon's application had been granted, both new States prohibiting slavery in their constitutions, while Oregon also forbade Negroes to settle in the State.

It is to be noted that when this Congress of the first half of Buchanan's Administration had been elected, there were fifteen slave States and sixteen that prohibited slavery. With the two new States admitted, the fifteen slave States were confronted by eighteen which excluded slavery. There was not much reason to think that the economic conditions of the vast unsettled areas, subsequently to be converted into fourteen additional States that are now flourishing members of the Union, would ever invite slave owners to utilize their bondmen in great numbers. Nevertheless, Kansas was in the same latitude as Missouri and several of the older slave States; and the question of slavery in the unorganized country farther west had its practical as well as its theoretical bearings.

The South was principally concerned, however, with the political aspects of the problem. They now saw slavery in a new economic aspect, and they were seeking to protect the institution, at first by a decisive check upon national anti-slavery tendencies and afterwards by a bold reversal of international policies.

There was comparative quiet at Washington in 1859, after the adjournment of Congress on March 4th, with the halls of legislation closed for nine months. But within party circles and in various local centers, there was no adjournment of politics; and everybody was looking forward to the fateful political year 1860. It would be gravely improper to attribute motives or purposes to parties, groups or individuals in either section without evidence. But there are ample facts to show that the anti-slavery movement in the North was becoming Abolitionist in its temper, with more defiance in its leadership and less disposition to explain its acquiescence in the permanent Constitutional status of slavery where it actually existed.

As for the South, it was abandoning the defensive and openly planning for a new type of high civilization in an extended empire, with African slavery as the economic and

JAMES BUCHANAN
Fifteenth President of the United States

A lawyer of Lancaster, Pennsylvania, in his first year at the bar, Buchanan enlisted as a private in the War of 1812. He was then twenty-one years old. After the war he served in the Pennsylvania legislature. In 1820 he was elected to Congress as a Federalist, remaining there for five terms until he went to Russia as Minister, 1831-33, by appointment of President Jackson. There followed a period of twelve years as Senator from Pennsylvania. During President Polk's entire term, 1845-49, Buchanan was Secretary of State, dealing with the Oregon crisis and the War with Mexico. From 1853 to 1856 he was Minister to England under President Pierce. In the Democratic conventions of 1844, 1848, and 1852, Buchanan was a candidate for the presidential nomination, and in 1856 he was the convention's choice. In the election that followed he obtained a decisive majority of the electoral votes, though his popular vote fell considerably short of exceeding that of Frémont and Fillmore combined.

social foundation. Thomas Jefferson in his annual presidential message to Congress on December 2, 1806, had made the following reference to the African slave trade:

"I congratulate you, fellow-citizens, on the approach of the period at which you may interpose your authority constitutionally to withdraw the citizens of the United States from all further participation in those violations of human rights which have been so long continued on the unoffending inhabitants

HENRY WARD BEECHER

Forty years pastor of Plymouth (Congregational) Church, Brooklyn, N. Y., Beecher was the most famous preacher of his generation. He was active in the anti-slavery movement from an early date, co-operating with the Abolitionists while not assenting to their more radical positions. As to the Fugitive Slave Act, he accepted the doctrine that there was a "Higher Law" than the Constitution. He urged the settlement of Kansas by Free State men and condoned the use of force, but regarded John Brown as an irresponsible fanatic. Harriet Beecher Stowe was his sister. It was Beecher who brought Lincoln to New York in 1857, for the Cooper Union address.

of Africa, and which the morality, the reputation, and the best interests of our country have long been eager to proscribe. Although no law you may pass can take prohibitory effect till the first day of the year 1808, yet the intervening period is not too long to prevent by timely notice expeditions which can not be completed before that day."

In the month of May, 1859, the cotton-raising States were represented in a significant convention at Vicksburg, Mississippi. By a vote of more than two to one a resolution was passed in this convention to the effect that "all laws State or Federal prohibiting the

African slave trade ought to be repealed." Regardless of laws, the external slave trade was encouraged and Southern juries would not convict those responsible for the illegal landing of fresh cargoes, whether direct from Africa or from the slave-markets of Cuba. Jefferson Davis, and the other Southern leaders, were making important speeches during the summer in which they demanded national legislation to protect slave owners in the Territories, and elaborated upon the views of the Vicksburg Convention.

The South was not able to obtain a sufficient supply of slaves for its later necessities by natural increase of those already here; and therefore it was demanded that Congress should repeal the law of Jefferson's time which made the African slave trade piracy. It was declared that a slave costing $1500 in Virginia could be bought for $600 in Cuba and for $100 or much less in Africa. It was the proposal of these foremost Southern leaders that control of the slave trade should be relegated to the individual States. With slavery protected in the Territories, and with the African slave trade reopened, it was further demanded by Southern leaders that the United States should proceed by force to acquire Cuba, Mexico and Central America, from which to form a series of new slave States.

Mr. Davis spoke for the maintenance of the Union if Southern policies were not blocked. But he stated plainly that he was for separation if the principles laid down by Senator Seward in his speech at Rochester were to guide the policy of the nation. He thought the annexation of Cuba would be desirable for the entire United States, but especially desirable for the South in case of the forming of a new Southern Confederacy.

It must not be supposed that in the minds of leaders in South Carolina, Georgia, Alabama, and Mississippi, Secession was contemplated merely as a defensive program. They adhered to the view that further annexations were practicable, and that some slight aid to filibustering parties and insurrectionists would create so much difficulty for Spain that Cuba could be purchased on our own terms. Northern Mexico was scantily populated, and could

WENDELL PHILLIPS

It was the mob attack on William Lloyd Garrison, in Boston, which led Phillips when only four years out of Harvard to become interested in the anti-slavery movement. Later, when the courts held that a fugitive slave had no right to a trial by jury, he gave up the practice of law rather than abide by his oath to support the Constitution. He even refused to vote and thus participate in such a government. Phillips was the leading orator of the anti-slavery movement, in great demand as a lyceum speaker. He was later an active worker for the abolition of capital punishment, for women's rights, and for prohibition.

WILLIAM LLOYD GARRISON

From his fourteenth year until he was twenty-one, Garrison was a printer's apprentice at Newburyport, Massachusetts. Soon afterward (1829), as a Baltimore editor, his fulminations against slavery got him into jail for libel. On January 1, 1831, at Boston, he began publishing the *Liberator,* and became the leader in the agitation against slavery, the veritable embodiment of the abolitionist cause. Four years later he was roughly treated by a mob in Boston. Garrison was a moral crusader who disdained moderation. He lived to see slavery abolished, and died in 1879.

GERRIT SMITH

Ten years older than Garrison, and sixteen years older than Phillips, Gerrit Smith was the financial backer of the anti-slavery movement. He inherited a fortune from his father, a fur trader of northern New York. In 1848 and 1852 he was the presidential candidate of the Liberty party, which he had organized. He was a personal friend of John Brown and supplied some of the money required for the raid on Harper's Ferry. It was Gerrit Smith who joined Horace Greeley in signing the bail bond for the release of Jefferson Davis after the Civil War.

be acquired by processes similar to those which had given us Texas and New Mexico.

In less than forty years the number of slaves in the South had doubled, and the demand was so great that average prices had advanced by three or four hundred per cent. At an earlier period Southern churches had been apologetic, and had looked to the ultimate training of Negroes for freedom. But under the pressure of new political and economic motives the Southern churches had been studying the Bible with more diligence and respect, and had brought slavery under the protection of the Christian religion. Convinced of the hopeless inferiority of the Negro race, and of the terrible plight of Negroes remaining in their savage state in the jungles of Africa,

they persuaded themselves that the best thing that could possibly befall these unhappy and degraded Africans was to be brought to America to have their fortunate place in the domestic organization of a refined and Christian South. Moreover, this was not a hard doctrine for people whose convenience it happened to serve.

On the other hand, the churches of the North had become infected with the doctrines of the Abolitionists. Accepting the principle that slavery was morally wrong, they began to universalize exceptional facts as to the cruelties and hardships of slavery in the South. These views were increasingly proclaimed from Northern pulpits, and their dissemination had been promoted by the publication of

Senator Seward's Rochester speech, to which Senator Jefferson Davis had referred, stands as the most famous utterance of the man who was everywhere recognized as the foremost Republican leader of the country. It had been delivered on October 25, 1858. Analyzing the recent progress of the country, Seward developed the argument that with growing populations, railroad systems and domestic trade, the slave system and the northern system of free labor were approaching an inevitable and sharp collision. This led to such conclusions as are set forth in the following paragraph:

Shall I tell you what this collision means? They who think that it is accidental, unnecessary, the work of interested or fanatical agitators, and therefore ephemeral, mistake the case altogether. It is an irrepressible conflict between opposing and enduring forces, and it means that the United States must and will, sooner or later, become either entirely a slave-holding nation or entirely a free-labor nation. Either the cotton and rice-fields of South Carolina and the sugar plantations of Louisiana will ultimately be tilled by free labor, and Charleston and New Orleans become marts for legitimate merchandise alone, or else the rye-fields and wheat-fields of Massachusetts and New York must again be surrendered by their farmers to slave-culture and to the production of slaves, and Boston and New York become once more markets for trade in the bodies and souls of men.

Seward had further proceeded to state the

LIFE IN THE SOUTH

This is an illustration from a book published at Buffalo in 1852, as a reply to "Uncle Tom's Cabin." It shows a Sunday School class conducted for the young people in the slave quarters of a Southern plantation. Not all slave-owners were cruel, and there was widespread effort in the South to uplift the Negro race. In South Carolina, especially, religious instruction of slaves was encouraged.

such books as Uncle Tom's Cabin. Mrs. Harriet Beecher Stowe in this novel had done more to stimulate the anti-slavery movement than all the Garrisons and Phillipses of the Abolition party, and the less anarchical preachers and lecturers, of whom her gifted brother, Henry Ward Beecher, was foremost. Thus while Washington on the Potomac was so calm, with Congress adjourned for nine months in 1859, public opinion was crystallizing dangerously in the North as well as in the South.

THE DEATH OF UNCLE TOM

In the book by Mrs. Stowe, which inflamed the North against slavery, the thoroughly likeable old Negro known as Uncle Tom is beaten to death by his new master. In this drawing for the original illustrated edition, Cassie is ministering to the dying slave.

THE NEGRO IN THE NORTH—AND IN THE SOUTH

One might assume from this contemporary cartoon that it is a product of the South. It was actually published in New York, however, and represents a considerable belief in the North that the plantation life of most Negroes was contented and far from unbearable. The Negro at the right asks: "Say, Massa Jim, is I wun of them unfurtunate Niggers as you was readin' about? Well, it's a great pity about me—I'se berry badly off, I is." In the scene at the left, by contrast, is the artist's conception of a Negro in the North, "a fish out of water."

southern program, in the most positive terms and with somewhat doleful and harsh exaggeration. Where Lincoln was always speaking temperately, in order to make men think and reason, Seward was taking the tone of prophetic warning, and intensifying the spirit of sectionalism. Whether rightly or wrongly, the New York papers now regarded Seward as an agitator more dangerous than Beecher, Garrison or Parker. This phrase "irrepressible conflict," however true or otherwise, was associated throughout the country henceforth with the name and fame of William H. Seward. He had appealed from the Supreme Court to the "higher law" of right and wrong: and for this suggestion by so famous a lawyer he was reprobated in the South.

I have already referred to the Ohio election that was to be held in 1859. Douglas went to the help of the Democrats, and spoke at Columbus and at Cincinnati. Lincoln, whose mission it had been through long years to trail Douglas, soon afterwards appeared at both places to speak for Republicanism, for William Dennison who was running for the governorship, and for Chase who was seeking to secure a Republican majority in the Legislature that would send him to the Senate. A few weeks before going to Ohio, Lincoln had written to a Congressman in that state to convey warning against the Douglas ideas. Because Douglas had become unpopular in the South, there remained some confusion about him among Republicans in the North. Lincoln said that their leaning toward "popular sovereignty" was giving him some uneasiness. "No party," he declared, "can command respect which sustains this year what it opposed last." He was not vindictive, but he was firm in exposing Douglas:

"LIKE MEETS LIKE"

William Lloyd Garrison (at the right), the ultra-Abolitionist of Boston, goes half way to join forces with the South Carolina secessionist, Laurence M. Keitt. "Well, my friend," the cartoonist fancies him as saying, "at last we meet in unity to destroy 'this accursed union.' 'Twas only a misunderstanding this many years. We were always one at heart." Note the garb in which the artist disguises Garrison—a common device in the anti-slavery agitation. It may have been the ancestor of the Anti-Saloon League cartoon employed so freely after the adoption of the Eighteenth Amendment

"Secondly, Douglas (who is the most dangerous enemy of liberty, because the most insidious one) would have but little support in the North, and, by consequence, no capital to trade on in the South, if it were not for our friends thus magnifying him and his humbug. But lastly, and chiefly, Douglas's popular sovereignty, accepted by the public mind as a great principle, nationalizes slavery and revives the African slave trade inevitably. Taking slaves into new Territories and buying slaves in Africa are identical things—identical rights or identical wrongs—and the argument which establishes one will establish the other. Try a thousand years for a sound reason why Con-

gress shall not hinder the people of Kansas from having slaves, and when you have found it, it will be an equally good one why Congress should not hinder the people of Georgia from importing slaves from Africa.

"As for Governor Chase, I have a kind side for him. He was one of the few distinguished men of the nation who gave us their sympathy last year. I never saw him—suppose him to be able and right-minded, but still he may not be the most suitable as a candidate for the Presidency. I must say, I do not think myself fit for the Presidency."

In his speech at Columbus on the 16th of September, Lincoln combated the Douglas doctrines, particularly as Douglas had set them forth in an article that had recently appeared in *Harper's Magazine*. At Cincinnati on the following day, Lincoln looked across the Ohio River to Kentucky and addressed himself in direct terms to the Democrats of that State. He was not trying to proselytize them, for that would have been a vain effort. "I only propose," he said, "to try to show you that you ought to nominate for the next Presidency at Charleston, my distinguished friend, Judge Douglas. In whatever there is a difference between you and him, I understand he is sincerely for you and more wisely for you than you are for yourselves." Looking ahead to the presidential contest, he spoke to the Kentuckians in a neighborly tone that was strikingly in contrast with the eloquent but gloomy forecasts of Seward.

The following sentences are eminently Lincolnian: "We mean to treat you, as nearly as we possibly can, as Washington, Jefferson and Madison treated you. We mean to leave you alone and in no way to interfere with your institutions; to abide by all and every compromise of the Constitution, and, in a word, coming back to the original proposition, to treat you, as far as degenerated men (if we have degenerated) may, according to the example of those noble fathers, Washington, Jefferson and Madison."

NO COMMUNION WITH SLAVEHOLDERS!

"Stand aside, you Old Sinner! We are holier than thou!" Henry Ward Beecher and John Brown
are represented as sponsors of this impious decree, while the ghost of Washington himself, kneeling
at the altar, meets with harsh rebuff because there had been slaves on the Mount Vernon estate. Lincoln and Greeley are to be seen among the communicants.

CHAPTER XXIV

John Brown Attempts Emancipation

*Our statesmen on their travels in the summer of 1859—Brown's record
in Kansas and his invasion of Virginia—Lincoln's views on the Harper's Ferry raid—The martyrdom of John Brown*

Although the prevailing tendencies of
the summer and autumn of 1859 as regards political weather were cloudy and
menacing, with the occasional incident of a resounding thunder storm, there were lulls and
truces of sunshine and calm. Lincoln's campaign had cost him a few hundred dollars, and
he was now taking, modestly and locally, to the
lecture platform, especially with a discourse
on "Discoveries and Inventions," showing
somewhat the quality of mind that Franklin
and Jefferson disclosed in those congenial
times when they were not engaged in politics
and public service. On the last day of September, Lincoln was the orator at the Wisconsin State Fair, having been invited to give
the annual address before the State Agricultural Society at Milwaukee.

The problems of the farmer have been
greatly changed, with our further advancement in the methods of quantity production.
But Lincoln's exposition of the status and the
supreme importance of agriculture is by no
means obsolete. The independent farmer was,
in Lincoln's mind, the typical American citizen. He held that the interest of farmers is
"most worthy of all to be cherished and cultivated," and declared that "if there be inevitable conflict between that interest and any
other, that other should yield." The address

229

was carefully prepared, and is an admirable example of Lincoln's best literary form. It was wholly free from political allusion, unless for a single remark as to land conditions in the South. He had been explaining that our farmers as a class were neither capitalists nor laborers, but did their own work on their own land. "Even in all our slave States except South Carolina," he declared, "a majority of the whole people of all colors are neither slaves nor masters." He was far from thinking that our Southern States were in the condition of the West Indian sugar colonies—too far com-

mitted to the manual labor of a subordinate race to be capable of a prevailing society of white men, working without apology on their own farms, or at trades and handicrafts.

It seems to have been wholly forgotten, until Mr. Dunbar Rowland compiled the writings of Jefferson Davis, that this foremost leader of the South was, in that summer of 1859, enjoying a vacation on the coast of Maine, and that, in response to an invitation of the Agricultural Society of that State, he delivered an address which, in many ways, is as noteworthy as that of Abraham Lincoln at Milwaukee. Mr. Davis eulogized the farmers of New England, and praised them for their qualities of character. He explained the grounds upon which his own State of Mississippi had become so marked an example of specialization in agriculture, and he thought the differences of the sections, leading to an exchange of products, ought to be a uniting bond rather than a cause of separation. He said nothing about slavery; but he argued that the country as a whole would be benefited by further expanding the national territories. It was his view that with the greater variety of products that would result from the addition of Cuba, for example, we would find increased advantages in the freedom of our internal trade, making us "almost independent of other countries for the supply of every object, whether of necessity or of luxury." The tone of Mr. Davis's speech was that of a man whose feeling was broadly national, and whose hope was for the perpetuation of the Union.

Another of the most influential of Southern statesmen, Alexander H. Stephens, of Georgia, had just retired from Congress (in March, 1859), in frail health, altogether weary of public life. He was declining honors and testimonials; and while Mr. Davis was so-journing for his health at New England's coast resorts, Mr. Stephens was traveling in the far Northwest, to see the country and gain physical recuperation. He declared that he had no political ambitions, and that he would exceedingly dislike to be President. "What amazes me in Douglas," he remarked, "is his desire to be President. I have sometimes asked him what he desired the office for. It has never yet added to the fame of a single man. You may look over the list of Presidents; which of them made any reputation after his election? Four years or even eight years is too short a time to enable a man to pursue a policy which will be permanent enough to give him reputation."

Mr. Stephens was devoted to the Union, although he could not detach himself from his association with the people of his own State. No man in the Union, North or South, was further from consciousness of being engaged in plots for the break-up of the country, in that ominous year 1859, than was this man, who was so soon to be serving as Vice-President of the Confederacy.

As for the eastern Republican leaders, they were not spending the summer of 1859 in plotting to destroy the peculiar institution upon which the South was relying for its expanding prosperity, with its cotton gins turning out ever-increasing quantities of the royal crop, for the mills of Europe and New England. Seward, as his biographer tells us, had

already planned to take a long vacation, and to make a trip through Europe and the Holy Land; and we have this quotation from his affectionate farewell note to his wife as his admirers, early in May, escorted him down New York Bay: "The sky is bright and the waters are calm; the ship is strong and safe; the season of storms is past." It was not until late in December that Seward returned from his interesting travels and from his study of the civilizations and social problems of Europe and Asia. The "irrepressible conflict" was not in the forefront of Seward's mental activity, as he toured foreign lands.

As for that famous Republican journalist Horace Greeley, who was in many respects the most pervasively influential man in the new party, he also was off on his travels, visiting the West and particularly occupying himself in seeing the wonders of California. He was full of enthusiasm, talking incessantly about agriculture, mining, and western pioneering, and attracting attention everywhere as he went bumping over western roads in stage coaches. No one was more innocent, in that fateful season, than Horace Greeley of any kind of agitation to provoke discord among brethren in our great Republic.

Among the vacation travelers of 1859 was John Sherman of Ohio. He had been elected to Congress in 1854, again in 1856, and now, for the third time, in the fall of 1858. He had been a rising young Republican while his party

GREELEY'S RIDE

In the summer of 1859 the famous New York editor journeyed overland to California, seeing the new country at first hand and writing letters to the *Tribune* that were later published in book form. Twelve years afterward Mark Twain went over some of the same ground and picked up a Greeley anecdote from a stage-coach driver, which, together with the drawing above, we reproduce from "Roughing It": "When Horace Greeley was leaving Carson City he told the driver, Hank Monk, that he had an engagement to lecture at Placerville and was very anxious to go through quick. Hank Monk cracked his whip and started off at an awful pace. The coach bounced up and down in such a terrible way that it jolted the buttons all off of Horace's coat, and finally shot his head clean through the roof of the stage, and then he yelled at Hank Monk, and begged him to go easier—said he warn't in as much of a hurry as he was awhile ago. But Hank Monk said, 'Keep your seat, Horace, and I'll get you there on time'—and he did, what was left of him!"

was in a hopeless minority. But at last he had taken his part in a vigorous campaign that was to give his party a decided plurality in the next House of Representatives. He was looking forward with some confidence to being chosen as Speaker when the new Congress should meet in December, 1859, which was sufficiently rapid advancement for a serious young statesman at the age of thirty-five. Having done his share as a minority member of the expiring Democratic House in the short session from December, 1858, to March, 1859, he had two-thirds of a year of freedom ahead of him, and planned to use the time in a broadening of his observations and experience. In April he went to Europe, where he studied many situations that were of more than usual historical significance. To his brother William, afterwards the redoubtable general who was Grant's foremost military associate, he sent careful letters on the war in Italy, and later upon the British system of government.

I might easily continue, with the aid of excellent biographers, to trace the summer movements of other American statesmen in the in-

terval between sessions of that year 1859. I have, in this manner, mentioned Seward and Greeley, Jefferson Davis and Alexander H. Stephens, besides this allusion to John Sherman. Douglas's movements also are well recorded, and I shall allude to them in later paragraphs of the present chapter.

Meanwhile, however, the biographers of no other American statesman have been so intent upon completeness and inclusiveness as those who have recorded the public and private life of Abraham Lincoln. Why, then, in the vast literature that includes hundreds of accounts, have we had no definite record regarding the comings and goings, during the summer of 1859, of the man whose qualities had been revealed in the Lincoln-Douglas debates?

How it happens that obvious things of considerable importance fail to appear in most biographies, is a question that belongs to the curiosities of literature, and I shall not try to answer it. Lincoln's biographers do not fail to record the well-known fact that he made a speech at Columbus on September 16th, and one at Cincinnati on September 17th, following Douglas at the request of the Republican authorities in a campaign for the election of a Governor and State officers. Also they are fully aware that in December Lincoln went to Kansas, where he gave five lectures. Mr. Sandburg, who follows Lincoln's movements with greater amplitude of detail than most other biographers, finds him speaking in Chicago on the night of the city election, March 1st. He reports what Lincoln wrote to the Boston committee which had invited him to speak at a Jefferson dinner in April. He quotes various comments of that season on Lincoln as a presidential possibility, and finds his hero invited everywhere to speak as the foremost Republican figure of the West.

Mr. Sandburg, as also Dr. Barton, finds Lincoln on May 30th drawing up a contract under which he became the owner of a small German-language newspaper published at Springfield, called the Illinois *Staats-Anzeiger*. Its editor, Theodore Canisius, was in debt, and Lincoln bought him out for $400. The principal German paper of Chicago was supporting Seward; and Lincoln now had a paper printed in that

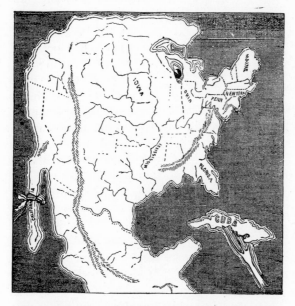

"THE IMPENDING CRISIS" OF A DAINTY MORSEL
Douglas in the summer of 1859 made a journey from New Orleans to Cuba, to obtain first-hand knowledge of the Spanish island that President Buchanan and other leading Democrats were proposing to annex, and that was used as a base by slave smugglers. Douglas was then chairman of the Senate Committee on Territories. Reproduced above is a New York cartoon published early in 1860.

language which could be scattered among influential Germans in order to promote the political fortunes of a certain Illinois gentleman whose ownership of the paper was kept an absolute secret. Mr. Sandburg's delightful narrative now jumps, like all the others, to the Ohio speeches of September.

It happens, however, that Lincoln, too, felt like a vacation trip, and he made no secret of it. It is curious that his temporary ownership of a German - language newspaper (which it is supposed that he never mentioned, even to his partner and political manager, William H. Herndon) should later have become so well known a fact, while his unconcealed August excursion in a steamboat up the Missouri River, his sojourn at Council Bluffs, Iowa, and his study there of railway questions and the future route of the first trans-continental railroad, should have become almost hopelessly lost to students of the career of the one American whose life has been most assiduously investigated.

It merely happens that the later biographers found themselves following Nicolay and Hay, who also, it would seem, had overlooked the trip to which I have alluded. My own first knowledge of it came with the reading, many years ago, of a book on the life and adventures of Joseph La Barge, published in 1903 as a "History of Early Steamboat Navigation on the Missouri River." One of the chapters is entitled "Abraham Lincoln on the Missouri." Gen. H. M. Chittenden, the author of this work, remarks: "It was during the boating season of 1859 that Captain La Barge first saw Abraham Lincoln. Among the more ob-

scure incidents in that great man's career were his visits to the Missouri River in the summer and fall of this year. In August he visited Council Bluffs and in December several towns in Kansas. The purpose of his first visit was not political, although during his stay at the Bluffs he was induced to make a political speech. He had evidently come out to take a look at the great West, and possibly, also, to make some investments in real estate." It is true that Mr. Lincoln did make an investment in one or more lots in Council Bluffs, these transactions being associated with his friend, N. B. Judd, the Rock Island Railroad lawyer, who was a close legal and personal friend of Mr. Lincoln, and among the shrewdest of the political backers who in the following year brought the National Convention to Chicago as a step toward securing Lincoln's nomination.

The Council Bluffs newspapers gave reports, quoted by Mr. Chittenden in foot-notes, of a speech upon political issues, delivered by Mr. Lincoln on Saturday evening, August 13th. Among those who heard the address was Grenville M. Dodge, a young railroad surveyor, who had just arrived from a study of possible routes across Nebraska. Lincoln met Dodge on that occasion, and had a long talk with him on the subject of the proposed transcontinental railroad. Dodge afterwards became a distinguished general in the Civil War, and a railroad builder identified with the transportation history of the West. It fell to the lot of President Lincoln, in 1864, to settle the location of the eastern terminus of the Union Pacific Railway; and the fact that Council Bluffs on the East side of the Missouri River

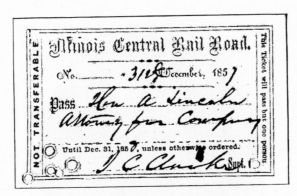

A RAILROAD LAWYER'S PASS

Lincoln's first employment as special counsel for the Illinois Central Railroad was in 1855, nineteen years after his admission to the bar. Then he argued against the attempt of McLean County to upset the Legislature's grant of tax exemption to the new railroad, and won his case. His most important assignment came in September, 1857, in which he argued successfully the right of a railroad to cross the Mississippi so long as its bridge piers did not unnecessarily obstruct traffic. It was Norman B. Judd, the leading railroad attorney of Illinois, who brought the Republican National Convention to Chicago in 1860 (to promote Lincoln's candidacy), and who made the speech nominating Lincoln.

rather than Omaha on the West side was designated, gives a significance that need not be exaggerated to the study Lincoln made on the ground in those August days of 1859.

This Iowa visit of Mr. Lincoln was not forgotten by General Dodge, who attempted in his old age to write a volume of recollections, which was never completed or published. The Dodge manuscript with other material was safely deposited in the archives of the State, and in due time an authorized biography was written by Mr. J. R. Perkins and published in 1929. Mr. Perkins, in his chapter entitled "Lincoln Visits Dodge's Home Town," gives us a more intimate account of the Lincoln trip than is contained in the earlier volume on the experiences of an old Missouri River steamboat captain. Mr. Perkins finds that Lincoln embarked on the stern-wheel steamboat at St. Joseph, Missouri, which took him upstream nearly two hundred miles to Council Bluffs. He tells us that Norman Judd had pecuniary reasons for seeking to interest Lincoln in the river bottom lands, now a network of tracks. Grenville Dodge, as land purchaser for the railroad that was crossing Iowa, had also made Judd an investor.

As for the people of Council Bluffs, it seems that the Lincoln visit had never been lost sight of. Says Mr. Perkins: "Dodge's home town, unto this day, speaks with pride and joy of the visit Lincoln made to it nine months before his nomination; of the reception tendered him at the Pusey home; of his speech in Concert Hall in the dim light of the tallow candles; of his stroll up the ravine to the top of a great hill, Moses-like to view the landscape; of how he

JOHN BROWN AS "SHUBEL MORGAN"
With four of his sons, Brown had so conducted himself in Kansas, in 1856, that there was a reward offered for his arrest; but in Iowa, Ohio, his home State of New York, and elsewhere in the North, he was highly esteemed by anti-slavery leaders. Two years later, when Brown wished to return to Kansas, he found it desirable to shave off his beard and use an assumed name.

sat on the porch of the Pacific House and talked with the citizens; and finally, of his departure, standing at the rail of the steamboat as it swung out into the river, with his hat in his hand and his face toward the yellow cliffs that lifted above the sun-scorched village on that mid-August afternoon."

There seems no record that pictures Senator Douglas, however, as having forgotten politics, or as engaged in mere vacation travels, in 1859. Upon the conclusion of the campaign of '58, with his re-election to the Senate assured, he had, indeed, set forth upon a long trip through the South, speaking in various places in the most conciliatory tone that he could assume. After visiting and speaking at New Orleans, he had satisfied his curiosity about the great island that we were proposing to acquire, by making a trip to Havana. In the earlier months of 1859, he was engaged in Senate debates at Washington that made him a comparatively isolated figure. There was no sharp issue like the Lecompton Constitution that now brought him applause from the Republican side of the Senate; and he was chiefly engaged in controversies with Senator Davis and other leaders of the South.

The session had begun before his return from the trip to Cuba; and he was chagrined to find that in his absence the Southern Democrats, who were still in control of the upper branch of Congress, had deposed him from his position as chairman of the important Committee on Territories. I have already noted that he made speeches in September in the Ohio State campaign, and he was planning carefully for the Democratic National Convention that was to be held at Charleston, South Carolina, early in 1860.

On October 17th came the news of the raid of John Brown at Harper's Ferry; and this tragic event startled the country like a bolt out of a clear sky, inasmuch as the truce in politics had promised to give the leaders a welcome season of devotion to farming, industry, vacation trips and private affairs in general.

John Brown at this time was in his sixtieth year. He was of Connecticut birth, but was taken to Ohio when five or six years of age. He had tried all sorts of business ventures, and had lived in one place after another. For several years he had oscillated between Ohio and a place called North Elba near Lake Placid, New York, where Gerrit Smith in the heart of the Adirondacks maintained a settlement of refugee Negroes. Returning from Ohio to North Elba in 1855, he left his family there. Taking his four oldest sons, he joined a rush of Free State men to Kansas, where he soon became known as the redoubtable "Captain John Brown of Ossawatomie."

He had been active all his life in helping fugitive slaves to escape, and had been for years a principal agent in the running of the so-called "Underground Railroad." He was a man of intense and moody nature; a man of action rather than of words; whose belief in freedom for the slaves was bound to show itself in attempts to bring the thing about, if necessary, by fire and sword and insurrection. His violent and ruthless conduct in Kansas had led to the offer of a reward of $3000 for his arrest by the Governor of Missouri, while President Pierce himself had offered $250.

It was on the night of the twenty-fourth of May, 1856, at the height of the period of guerrilla clashes in Kansas, that John Brown and his little band massacred five pro-slavery men on Pottawatomie Creek. Perhaps these men were not of the most desirable and unoffending type; but there can be no doubt of the criminality as well as the brutality of the conduct of John Brown. His sons had been hypnotized by the homicidal fanaticism of their father. Brown's own defense was that it had become necessary "to strike terror into the hearts of the pro-slavery people."

JOHN BROWN

After participating in the fight to keep slavery out of Kansas, in 1856, Brown returned to his home in northern New York. There he planned the raid on a government arsenal, to obtain rifles for an uprising of Negro slaves. He was captured, found guilty of treason, and hanged at Charlestown, Virginia, on December 2, 1859.

Endeavor was vainly made to fix responsibility for this action upon leaders of the Free Soil cause. Our foremost authority upon the deeds of John Brown and their relation to the anti-slavery movement and the political controversies of that period, is the remarkable biography by Mr. Oswald Garrison Villard, published in 1910, and entitled "John Brown 1800-1859: A Biography Fifty Years After." Mr. Villard makes it clear that Brown had gone to Kansas with arms and munitions, fully intending to fight. The Free Soil settlers in general were of the most peaceable type, whose purpose, apart from obtaining land and tilling the soil, was to help cast a preponderant vote at the polls in favor of making Kansas a free State. This massacre made trouble for many innocent free-state people; for there were wholesale arrests, with attempts to fasten responsibility upon prominent men who had no sympathy with John Brown's methods.

John Brown and his group were now outlaws, and Kansas was in wild turmoil. President Pierce constantly admonished Governor Shannon to maintain the laws, but without much effect. A few weeks later Brown with several sons and other followers escaped from Kansas and crossed the Nebraska line. Before long, however, the indomitable foe of slavery was in Kansas again, a sort of mythical personage, credited by friends and foes alike with various exploits in most of which he had no part. With Governor Geary's advent, and with United States troops under his direction, peace came to Kansas. John Brown, who had gone there to fight but not to settle, had returned to the East. Just how he could have been permitted to travel openly, and to remain at large after his exciting year in Kansas, is not quite clear; but he had given himself a permanent place in the history of that Commonwealth, and it is undoubtedly true that his crimes were condoned, and his methods widely praised and admired, among the anti-slavery people of the North.

Unquestionably John Brown was treated as a hero in the Abolitionist communities of Iowa, notably in the little town of Tabor. From Iowa he set out for Chicago, where he arrived late in October with two sons, and where he was well received at the offices of the National Kansas Committee. At that time Horace White was assistant secretary of that committee, and a note from him to Brown is in evidence to show how highly this man of blood and iron was esteemed by the leaders of the anti-slavery propaganda. After further adventures, John Brown went to Ohio and then returned to northern New York. Early in 1857 he was in Boston, a hero in the group that formed the Massachusetts State Kansas Committee. The Bostonians were helping him in his plans to raise money and equip a company for further exploits.

The great literary lights, philanthropists, preachers, orators and merchant princes of Boston were the enthusiastic supporters of John Brown at this time. It should be understood that they probably knew little of the precise facts regarding the Pottawatomie Creek massacre. They imagined that Brown's operations had been defensive, against the so-called "Border Ruffians" of Missouri. Undoubtedly he received much financial and moral support for his mysterious plans, and was not closely cross-examined about them by any of these New England patrons.

The details of these endeavors are fully recorded by Mr. Villard. In point of fact, John Brown, with the money contributed by his New England backers, was quietly and deliberately preparing for the Harper's Ferry raid. He was having certain weapons forged, particularly a type of spear that he was intending to place in the hands of slaves not accustomed to firearms. There were various causes of delay in Brown's preparations, all of which are set forth in Mr. Villard's fascinating volume. Among other things, he was buying revolvers from the Massachusetts Arms Company. With various supplies, and in disguise under an assumed name, Brown set out again for Kansas, by way of Iowa.

The eminent statesman Robert J. Walker, of Mississippi, was now Governor of Kansas under President Buchanan; and the Territory had become too peaceful and law-abiding to give John Brown any excuse for his proposed invasion. He staid only a few days in Kansas, and his mind was undoubtedly at work upon his ultimate object, the Harper's Ferry attack. It would not serve my purpose to continue with the details of John Brown's movements. He was now thinking of Virginia rather than of Kansas. Again he was visiting in the East, raising money and developing his hidden program. His mind was wholly fixed upon the idea of provoking an insurrection of Negroes that should sweep through the entire domain of slavery. He had gone so far as to draw up a Provisional Constitution for the government of the new, emancipated America, for which he was planning. He was storing arms and preparing for the onslaught. He had sent a man in the summer of 1858 to live at Harper's Ferry as a spy.

Brown next adopted the name of "Shubel

YE ABOLITIONISTS IN COUNCIL—YE ORATOR OF YE DAY DENOUNCING THE UNION
Many radical abolitionists in the North believed in disunion just as strongly as did the most sincere pro-slavery advocates in the South. The Constitution was "a covenant with hell" because it recognized slavery. Wendell Phillips of Boston was the leader of those Northerners who demanded dissolution of the Union; he wanted a nation of nineteen Free States. The wood engraving printed above was published in New York in May, 1859.

Morgan," shaved off his beard, and made another expeditionary visit to the West. In June, 1858, we find him in Kansas experimenting on the Missouri border, with the general idea of carrying alarm into slavery territory. Again, he found himself the object of hero-worship in the Abolitionist communities of Iowa. In March, 1859, he was in Ohio, where he gave a lecture at Cleveland on Kansas, and on his late so-called "invasion of Missouri." He had allowed his beard to grow again, and was described by the Cleveland papers as a man of extraordinary quickness of mind and physical vitality.

Back in Boston Brown was among his admiring friends, but we soon find him again in New York and Ohio, intensely occupied with his plans. Under a non-de-plume, from Chambersburg, Pennsylvania, June 30, 1859, he wrote: "We leave here today for Harper's

Ferry; via Hagerstown. When you get there you had best look on the hotel register for I. Smith and Sons, without making much inquiry. We shall be looking for cheap lands near the railroad in all probability. You can write I. Smith and Sons at Harper's Ferry, should you need to do so."

On the fourth of July, John Brown with three companions was in Maryland, ostensibly looking for land in the vicinity of Harper's Ferry. He found a place that he decided to rent rather than to buy, and hired a small property, about five miles from Harper's Ferry, for $35 until March 1, 1860. His young daughter and a daughter-in-law came to keep house, the better to help support the pretense that he was in the neighborhood as a farmer or cattle-buyer. Cautiously his arms and munitions were transported to this Kennedy Farm.

Brown's associates were not discreet, how-

"HERE! TAKE THIS AND FOLLOW ME!"
"Please God, Mr. Brown, dat is onpossible. We aint done seedin' yit at our house."

The U. S. Arsenal at Harper's Ferry was at the point where the Potomac and Shenandoah rivers enclose an elevated promontory—a spot famous for its scenic beauty and interest. We are concerned rather with the political phase than with the details of the raid itself. It was on Sunday night, October 16th, that, after cutting telegraph wires and guarding the approaches, Brown seized the arsenal. It contained an immense number of military rifles, this fact, of course, being the reason for the project. Brown had intended to distribute the arms to Negroes who were expected to rise against their masters. The arsenal was guarded by two or three men but was without a garrison, and the seizure was easily accomplished. A few slaves were brought in from neighboring plantations; but militia gathered rapidly and United States Marines from Washington were on the scene within a few hours. Col. Robert E. Lee, who headed the

ever, and they fell under suspicion. One of them wrote to his mother, for instance, two weeks before the raid, explaining with boyish enthusiasm that he was engaged in war with slavery in a southern slave State that, before he left, would be free. He added: "In Explanation of my Absence from you for so long a time I would tell you that for three years I have been Engaged in a Secret Association of as gallant fellows as ever pulled a trigger with the sole purpose of the *extermination of slavery*." Too many people already knew about the raid, and even Floyd, the Secretary of War, had been warned in a letter that, though anonymous, was intelligent and explicit. But Secretary Floyd was easy-going, as Mr. Villard says, and he was on vacation at a mountain resort in Virginia, so that he took no precautionary steps.

The plans were not developing well, and what Mr. Villard calls "the officers and men of the tiny provisional government" were only twenty-two in all. As the time for the raid approached, the two Brown girls left for their home in the Adirondacks, and the preparations for the attack became more serious. It was altogether a forlorn and pathetic adventure on the part of men of whom history must say that they had the spirit of heroes, but were utterly devoid of practical sense.

EFFECT OF JOHN BROWN'S RAID
"Much obliged to Possum Wattomie for dese pikes he gin us—dey's turrible handy to dig taters wid."

(Brown had believed that the news of his attack would lead to an immediate and widespread uprising of slaves, whom he planned to arm with pikes of his own design. The pikes were ready, but no slaves came to use them.)

AFTER JOHN BROWN'S RAID: THE TAKING OF THE ENGINE HOUSE

On October 16, 1859, John Brown and a handful of men whom he had gathered about him seized the
United States arsenal at Harper's Ferry, in what is now the State of West Virginia. He intended to
arm Negro slaves with rifles stored there. Government reinforcements under Col. Robert E. Lee
arrived promptly, besieged the raiders in the engine house at the arsenal, and easily captured Brown
and those of his comrades who survived the fighting.

Marines, instantly stopped needless bloodshed and entered the arsenal to find John Brown badly wounded and two of his sons lying dead.

Ten of the nineteen raiders were killed, two escaped, and the remaining seven were sent to jail. It has been the fashion of northern historians to treat with sarcasm the tremendous excitement of Virginia and the South, in view of the pitiable and hopeless nature of John Brown's project. But Brown had for years been receiving pecuniary aid from the most conspicuous anti-slavery men of the North; and it was natural enough that the South should have believed that behind this initial movement lay some larger scheme, worthy of the intelligence and the resources of Brown's eminent friends who were spread across the country from all parts of New England to Iowa and Kansas.

The actual incident was almost ludicrous in its abortive and futile character. Vast schemes indeed were floating in the deluded mind of John Brown; but his actual undertaking was that of a man of exceedingly limited capacity for bringing about a serious insurrection. With his surviving comrades, John Brown was promptly tried, and executed by hanging, under Virginia laws. Brown himself was the first on the scaffold, and his execution occurred on December 2, 1859.

Every public man in the country had his word to say about the raid at Harper's Ferry. Lincoln's conclusive statement took form some weeks later in his Cooper Union speech of February 27, 1860. We may quote his calm and philosophical expression:

John Brown's effort was peculiar. It was not a slave insurrection. It was an attempt by white men to get up a revolt among slaves, in which the slaves refused to participate. In fact, it was so absurd that the slaves, with all their ignorance, saw plainly enough it could not succeed. That affair, in its philosophy, corresponds with the many attempts related in history, at the assassination of kings and emperors. An enthusiast broods over the oppression of the people till he fancies himself commissioned by Heaven to liberate them. He ventures the attempt, which ends in little else than his own execution. Orsini's attempt on Louis Napoleon, and John Brown's attempt at Harper's Ferry were, in their philosophy, precisely the same. The eagerness to cast blame on old England in the one case, and on New England in the other, does not disprove the sameness of the two things.

Many northern men were more sympathetic than Lincoln in their allusions. Mr. Barrett, in his work on Lincoln, prints for the first time a letter that he himself received from Governor Chase of Ohio, who was soon to take his seat in the Senate. Chase was already Seward's rival as a Republican presidential candidate, and he was destined to be serving in Lincoln's cabinet only a year and a half later. In this letter, written by Governor Chase to Mr. Barrett on October 29th, a few days after the Harper's Ferry attack, we find these prophetic words about John Brown:

Poor old man! How sadly misled by his own imagination! How rash, how mad, how criminal,

thus to stir up insurrection, which, if successful, would deluge the land with blood and make void the fairest hopes of mankind! And yet how hard to condemn him, when we remember the provocation, the unselfish desire to set free the oppressed, the bravery, the humanity towards his prisoners, which defeated his purposes! This is a tragedy which will supply themes for novelists and poets for centuries. Men will condemn his act and pity his fate forever. But while pity and condemnation mingle for him, how stern will be the reprobation which must fall upon the guiltiness of forcing slavery upon Kansas, which began it all, and upon slavery itself, which underlies it all!

The verdicts of history have borne out Lincoln's remarks, and the predictions of Chase have already been fulfilled. Mr. Bancroft, the accomplished biographer of Seward, says:

Before the year expired, John Brown had become a hero in the opinion of a large proportion of the best persons in the free states, not on account of any wisdom in his acts, but because of his bold assault upon slavery. The fear shown by the South was not feigned; it was deep and almost hysterical. Warlike preparations were going on in every county of Virginia. Some districts were still under martial law, and the legislature was considering "the full and complete arming of the whole State."

Elsewhere the alarm was not so intense, but throughout the South men believed that the country was on the brink of a terrible crisis. The slaveholders would not have been so much frightened if they had not made the mistake of believing that the slaves would fight for their liberty—a belief that had also been the greatest factor in leading Brown into the wild delusion that he could smite the rock of slavery and call forth from it a continuous fountain of freedom. Fear soon gave place to anger, and the conviction became common in the South that John Brown differed from a majority of Northerners merely in the boldness and desperation of his methods.

President Buchanan in his message to Congress, on December 19th, stated that he would not "refer in detail to the recent and bloody occurrences at Harper's

THE GRAVE OF JOHN BROWN

The boulder lies only a few yards from the door of the farmhouse built by Brown in the Adirondacks. The same headstone had served for the grave of his grandfather, Captain John Brown of the Revolution. The newer carving relates the fact that John Brown, born May 9, 1800, was executed at Charleston, Virginia, December 2, 1859, and that Oliver Brown, born in 1839, was killed at Harper's Ferry.

THE COURTHOUSE AT CHARLESTOWN, VIRGINIA, WHERE JOHN BROWN WAS
TRIED AND SENTENCED TO DEATH

From a drawing made during the trial.

Ferry. Still, it is to be observed that these events, however bad and cruel in themselves, derive their chief importance from the apprehension that they are but symptoms of an incurable disease in the public mind which may break out in still more dangerous outrages and terminate, at last, in an open war by the North to abolish slavery in the South." This was a wholly unjustifiable reflection upon the purposes and plans of the Republican party; but the mere fact that the President could have made such suggestion in a message to Congress, stands as evidence of the profound importance in the political sense of Brown's raid.

Jefferson Davis did not exaggerate southern feeling when he declared that this was "the invasion of a State by a murderous gang of Abolitionists. . . . to incite slaves to murder helpless women and children." Douglas, in turn, sought to recover favor in the South by saying that it was his "firm and deliberate belief that the Harper's Ferry crime was the natural, logical and inevitable result of the doctrines and teachings of the Republican party."

The raid was timed with the object of intensifying antagonism between the sections before the Republicans should have their opportunity in 1860 to carry the elections. Brown believed that they would enter upon a conservative policy intended to save the Union, while they would as a party adhere firmly to Lincoln's views of the constitutional rights of the slave States. It might even be said that John Brown was more bitterly opposed to Lincoln and men of his type than to the Democratic leaders. Extremists on both sides were helping to bring affairs to a crisis, and this was what John Brown was seeking.

There was a certain common ground upon which northern Abolitionists and southern Secessionists could meet. They were alike in detesting compromises, and in wanting to live in a country that was wholly one thing or wholly the other. Republicans of the Lincoln school on the contrary hoped for a gradual extinction of slavery in the future, on moral and economic grounds. With these views the radicals of both sides had no sympathy.

CHAPTER XXV

Congress Meets in Bitter Dissension

*The most turbulent session in our history—An anti-slavery book,
endorsed by John Sherman, causes a deadlock in the election of a
Speaker—Senator Davis formulates Southern views*

I N THE THIRTY-FIFTH CONGRESS, which
had ended its unprofitable career on
March 4, 1859, there were a total of 64
Senators of whom 39 were Democrats, 20 Re-
publicans, and 5 Americans. These five—
Thompson and Crittenden of Kentucky, John
Bell of Tennessee, Sam Houston of Texas, and
Anthony Kennedy of Maryland—were not
anti-slavery men, but were Unionists of con-

JOHN BROWN

*Meeting the Slave mother and her Child on the steps of Charlestown jail on his way to execution.
The Artist has represented Capt Brown regarding with a look of compassion a Slave-mother and Child who obstructed
the passage on his way to the Scaffold ... Capt Brown stooped and kissed the Child ... then met his fate*

FROM THE ORIGINAL PAINTING BY LOUIS RANSOM

A contemporary painting by Louis Ransom depicted John
Brown on his way to the scaffold pausing to give his
blessing to a slave mother and her child. That no such
incident could have happened did not at all lessen the effect
that the picture produced in the North, where it was
engraved and distributed broadcast. Note the Latin
motto of Virginia in the background.

242

servative stamp, with a tendency to look backward rather than forward. In the House of
Representatives there were 237 members, of
whom the Administration Democrats numbered 116, the so-called anti-Lecompton Democrats 11, the Republicans 92, and the Americans or "Know-nothings" 15, with two vacan-
cies. John C. Breckinridge of Kentucky, as
Vice-President of the United States, presided
over the Senate, and James L. Orr of South
Carolina was Speaker of the House.

When the Thirty-sixth Congress convened
on December 5, 1859, an additional State,
Minnesota, had brought the number of Senators up to 66, of whom 38 were Democrats
and 25 Republicans, with two Americans and
one vacancy. Vice-President Breckinridge
continued to preside.

It was in the House of Representatives that
the great change had come about, the Republicans now numbering 113, the Administration
Democrats 93, the anti-Lecompton Democrats
8, and the so-called "South Americans" 23.
These last were Southern Congressmen surviving from Whig days, Unionists who were
out of sympathy with the divisive attitude of
the Southern Democracy. Two of them were
from Georgia, five from Kentucky, one from
Louisiana, three from Maryland, three from
North Carolina, seven from Tennessee (as
against only three Democrats in the delegation
of that State), and one from Virginia (with
twelve Democrats completing the Virginia
delegation).

This session was perhaps the most turbulent
of any in the entire history of our national
legislature. For the first time in many years
the Democrats had lost control of the House,
although the Republicans had not gained a
clear majority. The balance of power lay with
the southern group representing the American
party. John Brown's execution had occurred

SOON TO BE OUT OF A JOB

Mrs. Columbia: "Well, Bridget, I guess we sha'n't want your services after next March."
Biddy Buchanan: "An' shure thin will yezz be afther giving me back me charackther?'

(This cartoon from *Vanity Fair* of April 7, 1860, reflects some of the dissatisfaction with Buchanan that developed in the latter part of his administration. Neither North nor South was pleased, and it was evident that the President would not be renominated. Wheatland, which appears on Buchanan's handbag, was the name of his estate near Lancaster, Pennsylvania).

only three days before Congress convened.

The South was in a state of frenzied alarm over that incident. Governor Wise of Virginia was leading his State in all kinds of local preparations for military defense. The disposition to make a martyr out of John Brown throughout the North was too evident to be successfully denied. Idealists in England were already eulogizing him as a hero, and a panegyric of Victor Hugo in France was prophetic and eloquent. For a number of years the South had been aggressive in its determination to nationalize the institution of slavery, and it had been greatly annoyed by the Abolitionist propaganda. But the exasperation and alarm had been rather in the North than in the South. The Slave States had been so much more successful in political management, and their

leaders so much more confident, that they were not profoundly disturbed until the tide had seemed to turn against them with the failure of their Kansas policy. But in the winter of 1859-'60 they were exasperated beyond all hope that calm attempts at reconciliation could influence them.

The House assembled in the newly completed wing of the Capitol after having used what is the present Statuary Hall for several decades. The seating arrangement brought members into dangerously close contact with one another, benches having been substituted for individual desks and chairs. Gentlemen who would have gone hungry rather than shoot a rabbit or decapitate a chicken, found themselves carrying revolvers to every sitting of Congress; while some of the Southern members carried two guns apiece besides bowie knives. Rancor and recrimination were without restraint.

With only the clerk of the House to act as temporary chairman, long weeks were occupied in a stubborn dispute over the election of the Speaker. Mr. Fuller in his useful work on "The Speakers of the House" remarks that "the Republican party, although in the majority [meaning plurality], was such a loose coalition that it was unable to complete the organization of the House except by assistance from without the party." Referring to Congressional personalities he observes: "Colfax of Indiana, the eloquent Burlingame of Massachusetts, Morrill of Vermont, Grow and Covode of Pennsylvania, all were destined to political fame. Tom Corwin and Thaddeus Stevens were back again amid the unfamiliar scenes of the new legislative chamber. William Pennington, a former Governor of New Jersey, took the oath of office for the first time. Charles Francis Adams, now a national figure of heroic proportions, mingled with such novitiates as Train, of his own State, Windom of Minnesota, and Roscoe Conkling of New York."

Looking across to the Democratic side, Mr. Fuller notes "Sunset" Cox and Pendleton of Ohio, together with Vallandigham from the same State, one of the most partisan slave advocates. "The talented Lucius Lamar answered the roll call for Mississippi, and Sickles of New York, who in defense of his family honor had but recently shot the brother of that Key who wrote the Star Spangled Banner, with Logan and McClernand from Illinois. Among the so-called independent members were Gilmer and Vance of North Carolina, Hickman of Pennsylvania, Henry Winter Davis of Maryland, and Maynard and Etheridge of Tennessee."

On the first ballot for Speaker the Democrats gave Thomas S. Bocock of Virginia 86 votes. The Republicans cast 66 ballots for John Sherman of Ohio and 43 for Galusha A. Grow of Pennsylvania, whereupon Mr. Grow immediately withdrew his name in favor of Sherman.

Representative Clark of Missouri then introduced a resolution that was so important in its consequences that it can never be omitted from the record of significant things in the history of American politics. Fame beyond its merits had suddenly overtaken a book, first published in 1857, entitled "The Impending Crisis of the South" by a previously obscure and unknown citizen of North Carolina named Helper. The apparent object of the book had been to arouse the non-slaveholding Whites of the South, who were in the large majority, against the slaveholders on the one hand and against the Negroes on the other.

The Abolitionists of the North had been making their attack upon slavery from the standpoint of the rights of the Negroes as human beings. Helper's book approached the subject from a totally different angle. Mrs. Stowe's "Uncle Tom's Cabin" was circulating throughout the North in edition after edition. It had carried the sentimental appeal against American slavery to the Liberal elements of Great Britain and continental Europe. It had instantly made its dramatized appearance in the theaters of the Northern cities and towns. John Brown's gesture had aimed at arousing the Negroes themselves to insurrection after the manner of the Blacks in Santo Domingo; and although it was a failure in the immediate and practical sense, it was justly regarded in the South as having a most dangerous bearing upon future conditions.

It was partly because the Helper book came as an added grievance that it provoked so great excitement. But the real complaint lay not so much in the fact that the book was written and published, as in the use that had been made by Northern Republican politicians in the recent congressional campaign of this ill-written and violent attack by a Southerner on Southern institutions. A condensed edition of "The Impending Crisis" had been prepared for free distribution throughout the North, and widely read. Those who were circulating this edition had gained publicity and influence for it by publishing the names of a long list of men giving their endorsement. The list included the names of about seventy Republican Congressmen, two of them being Galusha Grow and John Sherman.

We may now quote the resolution offered by Clark of Missouri, immediately after the initial ballot for Speaker:

Whereas certain members of this House, now in nomination for Speaker, did endorse and recommend the book hereinafter mentioned, Resolved, that the doctrines and sentiments of a certain book called "The Impending Crisis of the South—How to Meet It," purporting to have been written by one Hinton R. Helper, are insurrectionary and hostile to the domestic peace and tranquillity of the country, and that no member of this House who has endorsed and recommended it is fit to be chosen to be Speaker of this House.

It is difficult now to realize the upheaval that was caused by Clark's motion. The Republicans were taken by surprise and met the attack with confused evasions and apologies, but the Democrats were merciless in their furious onslaught. John Sherman could not deny having allowed his name to appear in the list of those endorsing the book, but he explained that he had not actually read Helper, and was not aware of the provocative character of portions of that trouble-making volume. As Mr. Fuller puts it, "to desert Sherman, whom the Republicans had supported on the first ballot, would be a confession of error and an admission that they had been bullied by the fire-eating slaveholders. On the other hand, to persist in their support of this candidate would proclaim their adherence to Helper's doctrines, and for this they were not prepared."

Clark held the advantage and persisted in quoting incendiary passages from Helper's book, and in reading the names of all those who had indorsed it. Mr. Millson, a foremost Southern leader, declared that "one who consciously, deliberately, and of purpose, lent his name and influence to the propagation of such writings, is not only not fit to be Speaker, but is not fit to live." Thaddeus Stevens of Pennsylvania, as masterful and uncompromising as any of the Southern members, contributed to the exchange of invectives.

It was eight weeks before the raging battle of vituperative oratory ended in the election of Mr. Pennington of New Jersey as Speaker, with 117 votes in his favor, this number constituting the smallest possible majority. At one time Sherman had come within three votes

JOHN SHERMAN (1823-1900)

A member of Congress since 1855, John Sherman of Ohio was brought into prominence by the Speakership contest of 1859-60. His long career in the Senate, beginning in 1861, was broken by his service as Secretary of the Treasury in the Hayes administration. In that office he brought about the resumption of specie payments in 1879. Returning to the Senate, he was the author of two important statutes—the Sherman Silver Law and the Sherman Anti-Trust Law. He left the Senate in 1897 to become McKinley's Secretary of State, but resigned soon after the beginning of the war with Spain and died two years later. The portrait reproduced here was published during the Speakership contest. It was seen by John Sherman's elder brother, William T. Sherman—later famous as a General but then Superintendent of the Louisiana State Military Academy—who expressed this opinion: "I see you are suffering some of the penalties of greatness, having an awful likeness paraded in *Harper's*, to decorate the walls of country inns."

of election, while at another time an American named Smith, of North Carolina, had received enough Democratic support to have been elected but for the switching of several Northern votes. Congress had begun balloting on December 5, 1859, and had elected a Speaker on February 1, 1860. Four years earlier, Banks had been elected Speaker after a deadlock that had lasted even three days longer than this one of 1860. But that contest had been marked by courtesy and good humor, when compared with the violence and bitterness of the struggle that defeated Sherman.

We have an interesting light upon John Sherman's position in the volume entitled "The Sherman Letters." For a period of fifty-four years, John Sherman and his brother, Gen. William T. Sherman, maintained a correspondence, a large part of which was devoted to the discussion of current public affairs. The letters were edited by General Sherman's daughter and published in 1894. In 1859 William T. Sherman was the superintendent of the Louisiana Military Academy. On December 12th, he wrote a letter from New Orleans in which the following sentences occur: "I have watched the despatches, which are up to December 10th, and hoped your election would occur without the usual excitement, and believe such would have been the case had it not been for your signing for that Helper's Book. Of it I know nothing; but extracts made copiously in Southern papers show it to be not only abolition, but assailing. Now I hoped you would be theoretical and not practical; for practical abolition is disunion, civil war, and anarchy universal on this continent, and I do not believe you want that. I do hope the discussion in Congress will not be protracted, and that your election, if possible, will occur soon. Write me how you came to sign for that book. Now that you are in, I hope you will conduct yourself manfully. Bear with taunts as far as possible, biding your time to retaliate. An opportunity always occurs."

John Sherman did not reply until December 24th, when he wrote as follows: "You ask

AN UNSATISFACTORY HELPER IN THE HOUSE

John Sherman was to have been Speaker of the House, in the Republican Congress which met in December, 1859. But he had endorsed a book on slavery, by a man named Helper, that was offensive to the South; and the incident actually prevented his election. It is John Sherman who appears in this rôle of "helper in the house."

why I signed the recommendation of the Helper Book. It was a thoughtless, foolish, and unfortunate act. I relied upon the representation that it was a political tract, to be published under the supervision of a committee of which Mr. Blair, a slaveholder, was a member. I was assured that there should be nothing offensive in it, and so, in the hurry of business of the House, I told Morgan, a member of the last Congress, to use my name. I never read the book, knew nothing of it, and now cannot recall that I authorized the use of my name. Everybody knows that the ultra sentiments in the book are as obnoxious to me as they can be to any one; and in proper circumstances I would distinctly say so, but under the threat of Clark's resolution, I could not, with self respect, say more than I have. Whether elected or not, I will at a proper time disclaim all sympathy with agrarianism, insurrection, and other abominations in the book."

This illuminating letter was followed by a most readable and interesting one from Brother William; but I must not yield to the temptation to quote the Sherman letters *ad infinitum*. I may therefore remark that Brother William, writing on January 16th says: "If Pennington succeeds, he will of course give you some conspicuous committee, probably quite as well for you in the long run as Speaker." As a matter of fact, Speaker Pennington did give Brother John the most important appointment possible, the chairmanship of the Ways and Means Committee.

I may make one more brief quotation from this brotherly letter sent from Louisiana: "I was in hopes the crisis would have been deferred till the States of the Northwest became so populous as to hold both extremes in check. Disunion would be civil war, and you politicians would lose all charm. Military men would then step on the tapis, and you would have to retire. Though you think such a thing absurd, it is not so, and there would be vast numbers who would think the change for the better."

President Buchanan's annual message of that session bears the official date of December 19th, but in point of fact he did not send it to Congress until December 27th. It was read in the Senate and printed in the newspapers, but was left unnoticed in the House until some time after. There had been no adjournment for holidays, the House having kept up its wrangling on Christmas Day and continuously thereafter. In defeating Sherman, the South had won in a practical way, although the Clark resolution never came to a vote.

Buchanan in his message moralized in polite and mild phrases, warning against the danger of agitation and declaring that "those who announce abstract doctrines subversive of the Constitution and the Union, must not be surprised should their heated partisans advance one step further and attempt by violence to carry these doctrines into practical effect."

After much disquieting comment, however, he resumed a cheerful tone, declaring: "But I indulge in no such gloomy forebodings." He reviewed with much elaboration the history of the African slave-trade, taking strong grounds against reopening that traffic. He tried to make this discussion agreeable at once to the North and to the South. Undoubtedly his expressions were sincere, but they were too mild and innocuous to suit the temper of either section. The message was very long, and it gave much more extended treatment to our relations with Mexico than to the questions that were agitating Congress. He seriously proposed our intervention and occupation of Mexico, that republic being, as he declared, "in

TOO MUCH CRINOLINE

One way of stating the obvious fact that John Sherman had been sadly hampered by his thoughtless endorsement of "The Impending Crisis." Senator Seward of New York looks on. It is a New York cartoon, which appeared in the eighth week of the deadlock over the speakership.

a state of anarchy and confusion from which she is proved to be wholly unable to extricate herself."

In March, 1860, the House of Representatives adopted a resolution calling for the appointment of a committee of five members by the Speaker, one object of which was to investigate the question whether the President had sought by improper means to influence the actions of Congress in any matter relating "to the rights of any State or Territory." Buchanan on March 28th sent a vigorous protest, and asserted his personal and official integrity throughout a long career of public service. Referring to George Washington's exasperation at false charges made during his Presidency, Buchanan declared: "I may now, however, exclaim in the language of complaint employed by my first and greatest predecessor, that I have been abused 'in such exaggerated and indecent terms as could scarcely be applied to a Nero, to a notorious defaulter, or even to a common pickpocket'." It was, certainly, not appropriate to have investigated President Buchanan's conduct by the precise methods that this first Republican House had chosen to employ. But the situation afforded merely another evidence of the extremes to which sectional antagonism had driven both parties.

This was the long session of the Thirty-sixth Congress, and in so far as oratory in the two chambers of the Capitol was concerned, it brought to a climax all the personal and sectional bitterness and vituperation of the quarrel over slavery that had been gaining in destructive momentum for many years. In the Senate, leaders were shaping arguments for the platforms upon which the presidential contest was soon to be fought out. Party conventions were to be held in April and May, the Democrats meeting at Charleston, South Carolina, and the Republicans at Chicago, with Congress, as it turned out, remaining in session until June 25th.

When this Congress met at the regular date in December for its final session, the November election had been held and the Republicans had been successful. Lincoln was to enter the White House in three months. Most of the Senators and Representatives returned to their seats. But the movement for secession was definitely under way in South Carolina, to be followed rapidly by like activities in other States of the lower South. The Southerners in Washington were preparing to give up their rooms and pack their trunks for home.

It is in the records of the previous long session, therefore, that one finds most of the political history of this last Congress of the Buchanan Administration—the last one also of the ante-bellum period.

In the Senate, Jefferson Davis had in February introduced a series of resolutions affirming the Southern view of the nature of the Federal Government and the rights of the States. He denied that Congress had power to forbid slavery in the Territories, and with equal vigor he opposed the Douglas doctrine that the Territories themselves had any right, whether legal or inherent, to interfere with a slaveholder's possession and use of his prop-

erty. The rights of slaveholders ought, according to Mr. Davis, to be upheld by Federal laws and executive action. Senator Douglas, on his part, adhered firmly to his doctrine of popular sovereignty. The people of the Territories should decide the slavery question for themselves, according to Douglas and the Northern Democrats.

Thus while Lincoln was speaking in New York and New England, Davis and Douglas were debating in the Senate the doctrines upon which they were seeking, as rivals, to shape the platforms of the Democratic convention. Seward in the Senate was discussing slavery from the Republican standpoint, taking a tone more conciliatory than had been his custom, in view of the confident expectation that he was to be the Republican nominee, and would need the votes of moderate as well as extreme opponents of slavery. In those weeks Douglas, Davis, and Seward were the foremost political figures of the country, with Lincoln's star now well above the horizon.

The Republican House had passed various measures that the Democratic Senate had rejected. Thus the Territory of New Mexico, acting upon the Douglas doctrine, and setting at naught the prophecies of Daniel Webster, had actually established slavery and provided a drastic code for the encouragement of that institution. The House at Washington passed a bill sweeping away that New Mexico provision, but the Senate did not concur. The House voted to admit Kansas as a State under a free constitution that had been adopted at Wyandotte, but again the Senate would not agree. The Morrill tariff bill, somewhat increasing duties, was passed in the House but was not acted upon by Senators. The House stood for a liberal land law to settle the western prairies, and it accepted the Senate's less generous amendments; but President Buchanan vetoed the measure. Early in Lincoln's Administration all these measures—the Morrill Tariff, the Homestead bill, the admission of Kansas, and the repudiation of slavery in New Mexico and elsewhere in the Territories —were adopted by Republican votes in both houses, with Southern seats ominously vacant.

MISS COLUMBIA CALLS HER UNRULY SCHOOL TO ORDER

On the Southern side of this national schoolroom we see the writing on the wall, "Let us alone!" On the Northern side of the room Senator Seward of New York, is falling over his "Irrepressible Conflict" slate. It is a New York cartoon, dated January 7, 1860.

CHAPTER XXVI

Lincoln Addresses the East

He visits New York and speaks in Cooper Union—A notable effort that makes him a national figure—His brief speaking tour in New England strengthens the Republican cause

THE LONG DEBATE over the Speakership had made the threats of Secession increasingly frequent and definite. Names were mentioned without hesitation. Senator Seward was by all means the foremost Republican candidate for the Presidency, as he had now returned to Washington in restored health from his extended travels abroad. Southerners who had formerly been careful and moderate in tone were saying freely that the nomination and election of Seward would be followed immediately by secession. Governor Chase of Ohio, now a new member of the Senate, was regarded by the South as even a more pronounced anti-slavery man than

Seward; and he would have been as little acceptable in the presidential rôle.

Lincoln's name was not on men's tongues at Washington, because the Southern leaders had their minds on Douglas as the presidential personality of Illinois and the West. They were thinking of him altogether in terms of the approaching Charleston Democratic convention. Douglas's position was becoming somewhat ambiguous and isolated. He was still the political idol of the Northern Democratic masses, but he had fallen from grace in the South; and his recent partisan speeches in the cotton States, with his visit to Cuba, had not sufficed to restore his lost leadership.

But although the Southern Democrats were not at this time considering Lincoln as a probable leader of the North, that maturing political philosopher and statesman was thinking more clearly, and with more accurate perception of realities, than any other man in the entire list of presidential possibilities. While Congress was still wrangling over the Speakership, Lincoln was following events and corresponding extensively with men in the border States. He was confident that the North would hold together, and he also knew that the lower South would be united under the leadership of men like Jefferson Davis and Senator Toombs. But he was strongly hoping to keep the border States on the side of the Union. We are fortunate in having in Mr. Tracy's collection of letters of Abraham Lincoln, the following, written December 22, 1859, to the famous Unionist Senator of Kentucky, John J. Crittenden:

December 22, 1859.
Address Springfield, Illinois

Hon. J. J. Crittenden,
U. S. Senate.

My dear Sir: I should not care to be a candidate of a party having as its only platform "The Constitution, the Union and the enforcement of the laws." "The Constitution," as we understand it, has been the shibboleth of every party or malcontent from the Hartford Convention that wanted to secede from slave territory and the "Blue Light" burners who were in British sympathy in 1812, to John C. Calhoun and South Carolina Nullification.

The Union, we intend to keep, and loyal states will not let disloyal ones break it. Its constitution and laws made in pursuance thereof must and shall remain, "the supreme law of the land." The enforcement of what laws? If they are those which give the use of jails and domestic police for masters seeking "fugitives from labor," that means war in the North. No law is stronger than is the public sentiment where it is to be enforced. Free speech and discussion and immunity from whip and tar and feathers seem implied by the guarantee to each state of "a republican form of government." Try Henry Clay's "gradual emancipation" scheme now in Kentucky, or to circulate W. L. Garrison's *Liberator* where the most men are salivated by the excessive use of the Charleston *Mercury*. Father told a story of a man in your parts required to give a warrantee bill of sale with a horse. He wrote, "I warrant him sound in skin and skeleton and without faults or faculties." That is more than I can say of an un-

meaning platform. Compromises of principles break of their own weight.
Yours very respectfully,
A. LINCOLN.

Lincoln had been spending part of the month of December in a visit to Kansas, where he gave a series of lectures and addresses. Just as in his Cincinnati speech he had talked across the Ohio to the people of Kentucky, so now he made an appeal to the voters of Missouri in his political address at the Kansas border town of Atchison. This was in pursuance of his effort to keep the northernmost of the slave states from drifting to an alliance with the lower South. His appeal to the Missourians was very explicit. As shown in the letter to Crittenden, Lincoln's analysis of the state of the country was better than that of any other man whose expressions of that season are preserved for our study. The following remarks, from his talk to the Missourians as he looked across at their fine State from the Kansas side of the Missouri River at Atchison, are typical of his extemporaneous manner:

But you Democrats are for the Union; and you greatly fear the success of the Republicans would destroy the Union. Why? Do the Republicans declare against the Union? Nothing like it. Your own statement of it is that if the Black Republicans elect a President, you "won't stand it." You will break up the Union. If we shall constitutionally elect a President, it will be our duty to see that you submit. Old John Brown has been executed for treason against a State. We can not object, even though he agreed with us in thinking slavery wrong. That can not excuse violence, bloodshed and treason. It could avail him nothing that he might think himself right. So, if we constitutionally elect a President, and therefore you undertake to destroy the Union, it will be our duty to deal with you as Old John Brown has been dealt with. We shall try to do our duty. We hope and believe that in no section will a majority so act as to render such extreme measures necessary.

It was now high time that Lincoln should come to the East to stand or fall under the criticism of such New York editors as Horace Greeley of the *Tribune* and Henry J. Raymond of the *Times,* and to let the Republicans of New York and New England take the measure of a western Republican about whom they had heard somewhat, but who was not in their calculations as a rival of Seward for the Presidency. On the 27th of February Lincoln made his Cooper Union speech in New York City and thereupon the East proclaimed the discovery of a new leader of the first rank.

Henry Ward Beecher's far-famed Plymouth Church in Brooklyn had been carrying on a series of general lectures; and Mr. Beecher, who had lived in the West and as a public lecturer was now from time to time speaking in the States beyond the Alleghenies, was well aware of the position Lincoln had gained in the debates with Douglas, and knew him as a picturesque platform character. Accordingly, Mr. Beecher and his lecture committee had invited Lincoln to come to Brooklyn to give one of the weekly lectures in the course they were arranging for that season.

As the time approached, however, it was agreed that Lincoln should be permitted, in view of the excitement of the entire country following the John Brown episode, to make a political address rather than to deliver a lecture on some non-political theme. And, with this change in the plans, the arrangements passed from the hands of Beecher's lecture committee to those of the Young Men's Republican Union of New York. The best available place for the address was the great hall of the new Cooper Institute that had been built by the philanthropist, Peter Cooper, for purposes of popular education.

Lincoln's previous speeches, while reasonable and persuasive rather than bitterly controversial, had almost invariably been made in the heat of electoral campaigns, with a view to influencing voters in an immediate contest. On this occasion the invitation, conveyed in a letter written by Mr. Charles C. Nott (afterwards a distinguished Judge), dated February 9, 1860, was in the following terms: "The Young Men's Central Republican Union of this city, very cordially desire that you should deliver during the ensuing month, what I may term a *political lecture*." The letter further explained that this was to be one of a series, the first having been delivered by Mr. Blair of St. Louis (himself a Republican favorite who afterwards became a member of Lincoln's Cabinet), and the second by Mr. Cassius M.

"A HOUSE DIVIDED AGAINST ITSELF CANNOT STAND"

An expression used by Lincoln in June, 1858, in accepting his nomination for the Illinois senatorship, became familiar throughout the country in the three years that followed. "I do not expect this house to fall," he continued, "but I do expect it will cease to be divided."

Clay of Kentucky, famous as an orator, who afterwards became Lincoln's influential Minister to Russia, having come near success as Hamlin's rival at Chicago for second place on the Lincoln ticket. "These lectures," Mr. Nott explained to Mr. Lincoln, "have been contrived to call out our better but busier citizens who never attend political meetings." Mr. Nott ended his letter by saying: "You are, I believe, an entire stranger to your Republican brethren here; but they have for you the highest esteem, and your celebrated contest with Judge Douglas awoke their warmest sympathy and admiration. Those of us who are in the ranks would regard your presence as of very material aid and as an honor and pleasure which I cannot sufficiently express."

These compliments, while doubtless sincere, were somewhat overdrawn as regards the reputation that had preceded "an entire stranger" who arrived at the old Astor House in New York with much misgiving on the Saturday before Monday's address, and who went on Sunday to hear Beecher preach, as was the fashion for western visitors, for a full quarter-century.

It was not, therefore, to deliver a stump speech that Lincoln came to New York, but with the full understanding that he was to make an address dealing with fundamental principles and intended for an audience of highly intelligent character, rather than for an ordinary partisan mass meeting. William Cullen Bryant, editor of the New York *Evening Post,* famous as a poet and a man of letters, presided and introduced the speaker of the evening, while David Dudley Field, eminent at the bar, and brother of the Cyrus Field who had laid the Atlantic cable, escorted the speaker to the platform. Horace Greeley of the *Tribune,* Henry J. Raymond of the *Times,* and many men prominent in business, in professions, and in politics, were on the platform or in the audience.

We have numerous accounts of the occasion, some of them contemporary and others reminiscent. They are all agreed in regarding the speech itself as a masterly effort. The opinion is general that Lincoln's success advanced him at once to a position second only to that of Seward as a possible nominee of the Republican convention to be held less than three months later in Chicago. Mr. Greeley, as editor of the foremost Republican newspaper, declared in the *Tribune* the following morning: "Since the days of Clay and Webster no one has spoken to a larger assemblage of the intellect and mental culture of our city." And he praised the speech in superlative terms. Most Eastern men who had heard about Lincoln had thought of him as a shrewd, story-telling son of the frontier, who had failed in his campaign for the Senate, but had shown much homespun ingenuity and cleverness in his debates with the most brilliant and eloquent member of the United States Senate.

Precisely what Lincoln needed, therefore, was the opportunity to show himself before a New York audience of the highest intelligence in his real character as a thorough student of our constitutional history, as a master of diction perfectly suited to his theme, and as a man of dignified personality, far removed from the grotesque mountebank about whose uncouthness there had been many rumors afloat. If Seward, whose pre-eminent qualifications as a leader were not in dispute, should prove for certain reasons to be disqualified as a vote-getter, who else could be selected as the best compromise candidate? The answer to that question

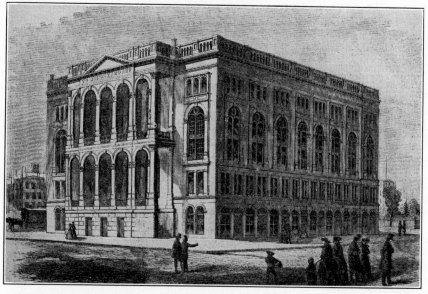

COOPER UNION, IN NEW YORK, WHERE LINCOLN SPOKE IN FEBRUARY, 1860
After Lincoln had accepted an invitation to deliver an address in Dr. Beecher's church in Brooklyn, it seemed to those in charge of the meeting that a larger auditorium should be secured. Cooper Union, across the river in New York City, was selected. It had recently been erected through the generosity of Peter Cooper, designer and builder of the first American steam locomotive, the practical application of his idea for the free instruction of the working classes in science and art. Our picture shows the building as it was in 1860, there having been minor changes in outward appearance made many years afterward.

was found in this successful appearance of Lincoln for the first time on a New York platform.

One of the men most prominent on that occasion was the New York publisher, George P. Putnam. His son, George Haven Putnam, who was then a boy of nearly sixteen, and who was destined not much later to enter the army as a volunteer, attended this meeting with his father. In 1909, on occasion of the centenary of Lincoln's birth, Major Putnam delivered an extended address on Lincoln's life and career, which he soon afterwards expanded and published as an admirable volume. He printed the Cooper Union speech and the correspondence accompanying it as an appendix. The occasion itself and the bearings of the speech are so well described by Major Putnam, that I think it well to quote at some length from his chapter dealing with that episode:

The Committee of Invitation included, in addition to a group of the old Whigs (of whom my father was one), representative Free Soil Democrats like William C. Bryant and John King. Lincoln's methods as a political leader and orator were known to one or two men on the committee, but his name was still unfamiliar to an Eastern audience. It was understood that the new leader from the West was going to talk to New York about the fight against slavery. It is probable that at least the larger part of the audience expected something "wild and woolly."

The West at that time seemed very far off from New York and was still but little understood by the Eastern communities. New Yorkers found it difficult to believe that a man who could influence Western audiences could have anything to say that would count with the cultivated citizens of the East. The more optimistic of the hearers were hoping, however, that perhaps a new Henry Clay had arisen and were looking for utterances of the ornate and grandiloquent kind such as they had heard frequently from Clay and from other statesmen of the South.

The first impression of the man from the West did nothing to contradict the expectation of something weird, rough, and uncultivated. The long, ungainly figure upon which hung clothes that, while

A LINCOLN PORTRAIT OF THE PERIOD 1858-60

This photograph, assigned by Lincoln authorities to the year 1854, was actually taken as late as 1858. In that year the Chicago *Tribune* absorbed the *Democrat Press* and became known as the *Press and Tribune*, a copy of which Lincoln is holding. That name ceased to be used in 1860. Our information regarding the date of the portrait was confirmed by the editors of the Chicago *Tribune*.

new for this trip, were evidently the work of an unskilful tailor; the large feet, and clumsy hands of which, at the outset, at least, the orator seemed to be unduly conscious; the long, gaunt head, capped by a shock of hair that seemed not to have been thoroughly brushed out, made a picture which did not fit in with New York's conception of a finished statesman. The first utterance of the voice was not pleasant to the ear, the tone being harsh and the key too high.

As the speech progressed, however, the speaker seemed to get into control of himself; the voice gained a natural and impressive modulation, the gestures were dignified and appropriate, and the hearers came under the influence of the earnest look from the deeply-set eyes and of the absolute integrity of purpose and of devotion to principle which were behind the thought and the words of the speaker. In place of a "wild and woolly" talk, illuminated by more or less incongruous ancedotes;

THE SPIRIT OF DISUNION

The contrasting illustrations on these facing pages symbolize states of mind in the North in 1860. They are the work of a distinguished artist, J. McNevin. The editors of *Harper's Weekly* believed them to be so notable as to deserve, each of them, a full page in that periodical.

rights of the men whose views he was helping to shape and he insisted that there should be no wavering or weakening in regard to the enforcement of those rights. He made it clear that the continued existence of the nation depended upon having these issues equitably adjusted, and he held that the equitable adjustment meant the restriction of slavery within its present boundaries. He maintained that such restrictions were just and necessary as well for the sake of fairness to the blacks as for the final welfare of the whites.

He insisted that the voters of the present States of the Union had upon them the largest possible measure of responsibility in so controlling the great domain of the Republic that the States in which their children and their grandchildren were to grow up as citizens, must be preserved in full liberty, must be protected against any invasion of an institution which represented barbarity. He maintained that such a contention could interfere in no way with the due recognition of the legitimate property rights of present owners of slaves. He pointed out to the New Englanders of the anti-slavery group that the restriction of slavery meant its early extermination.

He insisted that war for the purpose of exterminating slavery from existing slave territory could not be justified. He was prepared, for the purpose of defending against slavery the national territory that was still free, to take the risk of war which the South threatened, because he believed that only through such defence could the existence of the nation be maintained; and he believed, further, that the maintenance of the great Republic was essential, not only for the interests of its own citizens, but for the interests of free government throughout the world. He spoke with full sympathy of the difficulties and problems resting upon the South, and he insisted that the matters at issue could be adjusted only with a fair recognition of these difficulties. Aggression from either side of Mason and Dixon's Line must be withstood.

in place of a high-strung exhortation of general principles or of a fierce protest against Southern arrogance, the New Yorkers had presented to them a calm but forcible series of well-reasoned considerations upon which their action as citizens was to be based.

It was evident that the man from the West understood thoroughly the constitutional history of the country; he had mastered the issues that had grown up about the slavery question; he knew thoroughly, and was prepared to respect, the rights of his political opponents; he knew with equal thoroughness the

I was but a boy when I first looked upon the gaunt figure of the man who was to become the people's leader, and listened to his calm but forcible arguments in behalf of the principles of the Republican party. It is not likely that at the time I took in, with any adequate appreciation, the weight of the speaker's reasoning. I have read the address more than once since, and it is, of course, impossible to separate my first impressions from my later direct knowledge. I do remember that I was at once impressed with the feeling that here was a political leader whose methods differed from those of any politician to whom I had listened. His contentions were based not upon invective or abuse of "the other fellow," but purely on considerations of justice, on that everlasting principle that what is just, and only what is just, represents the largest and highest interests of the nation as a whole.

When first invited in the previous autumn to appear in the Plymouth Church lecture course, Lincoln had not fully realized the political significance of his Eastern journey. His acceptance had been chiefly influenced by the fact that his young son, Robert Todd Lincoln, was attending a New England school, Phillips Exeter Academy, preparing under much difficulty to pass examinations for the freshman class at Harvard.

THE SPIRIT OF UNION

A sectional difference of opinion over the Negro and his status in a free country had lasted more than forty years, defying all attempts at solution and compromise. The fact that secession was a real possibility gave impetus to the efforts of those who, like Lincoln, sought to preserve the Union.

Lincoln thought of the lecture as an opportunity to come East and visit his son, who had failed in his entrance examinations in the previous summer, and had been sent to the Academy for an additional year of preparation, finally entering college in the fall of 1860. Mr. Barton remarks of Robert Lincoln that he had been accustomed to say, with some touch of humor, that if he had not failed in the summer of 1859 to pass in fifteen out of sixteen subjects his father might have been less solicitous and might not have delivered the Cooper Union speech.

In the campaign of 1848 Lincoln had made a few speeches in New England on behalf of the Whig ticket headed by General Zachary Taylor, the Louisiana slave-owner; and the object of his arguments in Massachusetts at that time had been to keep Whigs from going over to the support of the new Free Soil movement. But on this second trip he was himself a leader of the anti-slavery movement, and he was in demand for important public meetings. First came a speech at Providence, and next several speeches in Connecticut and New Hampshire, all in the same week with the Cooper Union speech. After spending Sunday with Robert, he made speeches at Hartford, New Haven, Bridgeport and elsewhere in Rhode Island and Connecticut. Local elections were pending, and undoubtedly Lincoln's presence turned the scales and elected a Republican Governor of Connecticut. It was reassuring to Eastern Republicans to hear a leader whose calmness and poised judgment contrasted well with the tendencies to hysteria that were prevalent on account of recent occurrences.

The reactions of the Eastern trip were favorable in Illinois, and Lincoln returned to find himself steadily displacing Seward as the favorite candidate of his own State for the nomination. His friend Judd, as Illinois member of the Republican National Committee, had been shrewd enough well in advance to secure the convention for Chicago. Meanwhile, the influential Chicago *Tribune,* edited by Joseph Medill, had come out for Lincoln just before the Cooper Union speech, and it was increasingly earnest in its support when it found itself able to quote the praises of the now enthusiastic Horace Greeley of the New York *Tribune,* and further to report the triumphs of the New England tour.

It was not necessary to report in Illinois that on the night of February 17th, after the Cooper Union speech, one or two very young and unimportant Republicans of New York had given the Illinois orator a bit of supper at a club, and had then allowed him to go all alone, in an otherwise empty horse-drawn street-car, down Broadway to the old Astor House, rather tired and depressed, wondering what sort of an impression he had really made. His next visit to New York was a year later, when he traversed Broadway in an open barouche drawn by four white horses, amidst the applause of multitudes, on his way to be inaugurated at Washington as President of the United States.

WHY NOT HANG THEM ALL?

John Brown had been executed in Virginia for his insurrection at Harper's Ferry. But the Governor of Virginia, Henry A. Wise, believed that punishment should not end there. The cartoon shows him as desirous of dragging into his State, for prosecution, those Abolitionists of the North who were held as partly responsible for John Brown's activities. The Abolitionists are: Joshua R. Giddings, of Ohio, who was at that time a member of the House; William H. Seward, Senator from New York; Horace Greeley, editor of the New York *Tribune;* Frederick Douglass, the famous mulatto orator and editor who had himself been a slave and had purchased his freedom; and Gerrit Smith, of New York, intimate friend and financial supporter of John Brown.

INDEX

INDEX